THE ENDURING LEGACY
Alexander Pope tercentenary essays

THE ENDURING LEGACY

Alexander Pope tercentenary essays

Edited by

G. S. ROUSSEAU AND PAT ROGERS

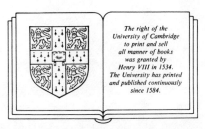

The right of the
University of Cambridge
to print and sell
all manner of books
was granted by
Henry VIII in 1534.
The University has printed
and published continuously
since 1584.

CAMBRIDGE UNIVERSITY PRESS

CAMBRIDGE

NEW YORK   NEW ROCHELLE   MELBOURNE   SYDNEY

Published by the Press Syndicate of the University of Cambridge
The Pitt Building, Trumpington Street, Cambridge CB2 1RP
32 East 57th Street, New York, NY 10022, USA
10 Stamford Road, Oakleigh, Melbourne 3166, Australia

First published 1988

Printed in Great Britain at
the University Press, Cambridge

British Library cataloguing in publication data

The enduring legacy: Alexander Pope
tercentenary essays.
1. Poetry in English. Pope, Alexander –
Critical studies
I. Rousseau, G. S. (George Sebastian)
II. Rogers, Pat
821'.5

Library of Congress cataloguing in publication data

The enduring legacy: Alexander Pope tercentenary essays
edited by G. S. Rousseau and Pat Rogers.
p.   cm.
Includes index.
ISBN 0–521–30581–0
1. Pope, Alexander, 1688–1744 – Criticism and interpretation.
I. Pope, Alexander, 1688–1744.   II. Rousseau, G. S. (George
Sebastian)   III. Rogers, Pat.
PR3634.E53 1988
821'.5 – dc 19   88–1914

ISBN 0 521 30581 0

FP

Contents

Plates

Notes on contributors

Morris Brownell is Professor of English at the University of Nevada at Reno, and the author of *Alexander Pope and the arts of Georgian England* (1984).

Patricia Brückmann is Professor of English at Trinity College, University of Toronto, and the editor of a collection of essays presented to A. E. Barker (1978).

Howard Erskine-Hill is Reader in English at the University of Cambridge, Fellow of Pembroke College and the author of *Pope: The Dunciad* (1972), *The social milieu of Alexander Pope* (1975), and *The Augustan idea in English literature* (1983).

Donald Greene is Leo S. Bing Professor of English Emeritus at the University of Southern California. The doyen of living Johnson scholars, he has also written several articles on Pope, on subjects including Pope and organic form, Pope's couplet verse, and Pope's reputation in the nineteenth and twentieth centuries.

John Dixon Hunt is Professor of English Literature in the School of English and American Studies at the University of East Anglia. He has written *Pope: The Rape of the Lock: a casebook* (1968) and *The figure in the landscape* (1976). With Peter Willis he has edited *The genius of the place* (1975).

Wallace Jackson is Professor of English at Duke University and the author of books about the concept of immediacy in neo-classical criticism and Dryden, and, most recently, he has written *Vision and re-vision: Alexander Pope* (1983).

David B. Morris is a writer who lives in Kalamazoo, Michigan. His *Alexander Pope: the genius of sense* (1984) won the Louis Gottschalk Prize of the American Society for Eighteenth-Century Studies.

A. D. Nuttall is Fellow of New College, Oxford and author of *A common sky* (1974), *Pope's Essay on Man* (1984) and *A new mimesis* (1983).

Pat Rogers is DeBartolo Professor in the Liberal Arts at the University of South Florida, and author of *Grub Street* (1972), and *An introduction to Pope* (1976), as well as editor of *Poems of Jonathan Swift* (1983).

Felicity Rosslyn is Lecturer in English at the University of Lancaster, editor of *Pope's Iliad* (1985) and contributor to *The art of Alexander Pope* (1979).

G. S. Rousseau is Professor of English and Eighteenth-Century Studies at the University of California at Los Angeles, where he has also served as the Clark Library Professor. He is the author, with the late Marjorie Hope Nicolson, of *This long disease, my life: Alexander Pope and the sciences* (1968) and the editor of *Twentieth century interpretations of The Rape of the Lock* (1969).

Howard D. Weinbrot is Professor of English at the University of Wisconsin at Madison and, most recently, the author of *Alexander Pope and the traditions of formal verse satire* (1982). His forthcoming collection of essays on satire will be published by the Cambridge University Press in 1988.

Penelope Wilson is Fellow of New Hall, Cambridge, and is preparing a book on Pindar and has contributed to *Books and their readers in eighteenth-century England* (1982).

Preface

This volume originated in the summer of 1982 in leisured conversations between its two editors who, while rambling through Henry Hoare's magnificent eighteenth-century gardens at Stourhead in Wiltshire, wondered what, if anything, the tercentenary of Pope's birth in 1688 would signify for his reputation at the end of the twentieth century.

One of the editors lamented that Pope's poetry had long ago ceased to communicate any essential humanism to the educated masses and that, more recently, the criticism of Pope's works had been transformed into a rarefied dialogue among an ever-diminishing number of specialists. He inquired if there were some way to retrieve Pope's reputation and bring it, so to speak, before the educated reading public once again. The other editor affirmed, more optimistically, that Pope was still a great poet and would always find some readers, no matter how few in number or how perpetually diminishing; he saw less need for retrieval and wished that more attention could be expended in careful reading and close analysis.

As we wandered past the Temples of Ceres, Apollo and Flora, over Colen Campbell's Palladian bridge, and by the grotto at the springs of the river Stour to which Pope himself contributed an inscription, we also wondered about Pope in the brave new world of the twentieth-century *fin-de-siècle*. We inquired if a new generation of readers would restore Pope the poet to the high position he seems to have occupied after the Second World War, especially now that Professor Maynard Mack's classic biography has appeared. These speculations – in turn sincere, enthusiastic and nostalgic – prompted us to conjecture more soberly about the biographical Pope living the first decade of his own life in the 1690s; about the reversal of his poetic niche (for the worse) as the French Revolution took its toll in the 1790s; about the effect of pejorative Victorian criticism of the entire eighteenth century on his reputation; about the only complete Victorian edition of his works by Elwin and Courthope published on the eve of the 1890s; and now, as the 1990s approach, about Pope's late twentieth-century fate among readers whose interests continue to shift.

Soon we found ourselves planning a volume of tercentenary essays. From the start it was our hope to reach a wide reading audience by including at least a few general essays with broad contemporary interest, rather than cater to a narrow group of Pope specialists and their students. But at the same time we realized the vanity of this all too human wish, and accepted the facts of literary life, which mean that a commemorative volume ultimately relies on the best talent available, no matter how specialized the concerns of those authors. Eventually we compromised, as our table of contents abundantly demonstrates. From the beginning it was imperative that this enterprise be an international venture. We had no concept – and still harbour none – of a commemorative volume written by native English-speaking authors only. It is therefore the work of chance that no Continental critic–scholar is represented in these pages. There are, of course, fine readers as well as fine critics of Pope in Europe, but neither of us was lucky enough to have come upon them at the right moment or in the right place, and we hope that none of our readers will consider our project provincial as a consequence of this all too apparent omission.

Nor should readers expect to find any systematic coverage of Pope's life and works in these very eclectic essays. The contributors were invited to write about any aspect of Pope in which they were interested; indeed, the editors guaranteed them free rein as well as the freedom to duplicate the interests of their fellow contributors. The balance and emphasis found in this book are therefore as random as the absence of contributors from the European Continent, and the fact that *The Rape of the Lock*, for example, captures two essays whereas other major poems by Pope claim none signifies nothing more calculated than the preference of these particular contributors. To what degree these topics and approaches signify 'trends' in contemporary criticism and theoretical filiation, both intrinsic and extrinsic to Pope, we leave it to our readers to judge.

Almost from the first day, the project began to acquire friends who are too numerous to list here by name. Virtually all the contributors helped out in one way or another, either in the early stages of planning or later on when the dedication to detail became everything, and our respective universities also contributed their share by providing us with typists, and then, word processors. Even so, we must single out three staff members of the Cambridge University Press for the assistance they have continuously given us throughout the long course of this enterprise. Dr Andrew Brown, a sensitive literary critic in his own right, recognized the boon for Pope studies a celebratory volume would have, and encouraged us to persist on both sides of the Atlantic Ocean; Kevin Taylor, whose energy has never flagged despite our inevitable delays and crossed wires, has proved how well he understands what Pope meant by being wedded 'to the dull duty of an editor'. And Karin Horowitz prepared our manuscript for the printer with editorial care rarely found these days.

Finally, George Rousseau is particularly grateful to his research assistant, Mrs Leila Brownfield, who checked obscure references in several of the essays and proofread the entire manuscript, and also acknowledges his gratitude to the Academic Senate of the University of California at Los Angeles which provided him with a modest research grant to edit the typescript for publication. Jointly we acknowledge the New York office of the Cambridge University Press, which acted as a clearing house for our transatlantic telecommunications, and whose staff soon began to refer to our pipeline communications as the 'Popeline'.

Abbreviations

Brownell	Morris Brownell, *Alexander Pope and the arts of Georgian England* (Oxford, 1978)
Collected in himself	Maynard Mack, *'Collected in himself': Essays critical, biographical, and bibliographical on Pope and some of his contemporaries* (Newark, Delaware, 1982).
Correspondence	George Sherburn (ed.), *The correspondence of Alexander Pope*, 5 vols (Oxford, 1956)
Dryden, *Poems*	James Kinsley (ed.), *The poems of John Dryden*, 4 vols. (Oxford, 1958)
E-C	Whitwell Elwin and W. J. Courthope (eds.), *The works of Alexander Pope*, 10 vols. (1871–89)
Early career	George Sherburn, *The early career of Alexander Pope* (Oxford, 1934)
Guerinot	J. V. Guerinot, *Pamphlet attacks on Alexander Pope, 1711–1744* (London 1969)
Pope: a life	Maynard Mack, *Alexander Pope: a life* (New Haven and London, 1985)
Spence	J. M. Osborn (ed.), *Observations, anecdotes, and characters of books and men*, 2 vols. (Oxford, 1966)
Swift, *Correspondence*	Harold Williams (ed.), *The correspondence of Jonathan Swift*, 5 vols. (Oxford, 1963)
TE	John Butt *et al.* (eds.), *The Twickenham Edition of poems of Alexander Pope*, 11 vols. (London, 1938–68)

PART ONE
The Rape of the Lock

1

Virgins visited by angel powers: *The Rape of the Lock*, platonick love, sylphs and some mysticks

Although nearly all exclaim over the sylph machinery Pope added to *The Rape of the Lock* in 1714, no one has yet given close attention to the suggestions they offer for a reading of the poem, despite the fact that Tillotson long ago provided an elaborate appendix on *The Count of Gabalis*, the seventeenth-century satire on Rosicrucianism on which his machinery was modelled.

Praise for the sylphs has not always been unqualified. At least two critics in Pope's own century had reservations. In his 'Remarks on Mr. Pope's *Rape of the Lock*', Dennis says, '[W]hat he calls his *Machinery* has no Manner of Influence upon what he calls his *Poem*, not in the least promoting, or preventing, or retarding the Action of it.'[1] The Ancients and the Moderns, he says, took their machinery from contemporary religion, but 'the Author of the *Rape* has not taken his *Machines* from the Religion of his Country, nor from any Religion, nor from Morality' (p. 337). 'They are Beings so *diminutive*, that they bear the same Proportion to the rest of the intellectual, that Eels in Vinegar do to the rest of the material world. The latter are only to be seen thro' *Microscopes*, and the former only thro' the false Optics of a *Rosycrucian* Understanding' (p. 339). It might be easier to dismiss Dennis if Johnson were not, regretfully, on his side:

Pope is said by an objector not to have been the inventor of this petty nation; a charge which might with more justice been brought against the author of the *Iliad*, who doubtless adopted the religious system of his country . . . Has he not assigned them characters and operations never heard of before? Has he not, at least, given them their first poetical existence?[2]

Johnson cannot, however, find defence for Dennis' objection

that the machinery is superfluous; that by all the bustle of preternatural operation the main event is neither hastened nor retarded . . . The sylphs cannot be said to help or to oppose, and it must be allowed to imply some want of art that their power has not been sufficiently intermingled with the action. (p. 235)

[1] John Dennis, *Works*, E. N. Hooker (ed.), 2 vols. (Baltimore, 1939–43), II, p. 328.
[2] Samuel Johnson, *Lives of the English poets*, George Birkbeck Hill (ed.) (New York, 1967), III, p. 233.

Dennis and Johnson argue from their considerable knowledge of those dictates of epic experience which insist that machinery, an essential feature, bear some relation by way of amplification to a larger context within an epically rendered society, and that it act.

Tillotson comments:

> If [Dennis'] . . . pamphlet had been sound in argument and fact its pedantry would have had its importance . . . Pope had his eye on the rules for epic, and since Dennis was arguing from these rules, his attack was potentially serious. But there are two great flaws in his pamphlet. Dennis fails to see that the poem is not an epic but a mock-epic . . . He fails also to see that any new poem must to some extent modify the rules, especially when it is a poem doing several things at the same time – following a given story, satisfying a social occasion, satirizing society as well as epic. Much of his criticism is automatically silenced by reference to these two principles.[3]

Although Tillotson is right about the pedantry, one wonders about the two principles which are said to silence it. A future translator of Homer and an admirer of Virgil would hardly satirize epic, although he might think, with Spenser and Milton, that one looked for proper epic words for a special epic space and time. There is no reason why a mock-epic (Pope's own description was, more accurately, 'heroi-comical') cannot be highly serious. Chaucer's Nun's Priest tells a tale of a fox, a cock and a hen that is a witty reflection on central questions in fourteenth-century theology and on the *Tales* as a whole. Johnson, who understands the moral implications of the poem better than any other critic, might not himself have been persuaded by Tillotson's reply.

For help with the sylphs we can turn first to Pope's Epistle Dedicatory to the 1714 edition:

> The *Machinery*, Madam, is a Term invented by the Criticks, to signify that Part which the Deities, Angels, or Daemons, are made to act in a Poem: For the ancient Poets are in one respect like many modern Ladies; Let an Action be never so trivial in itself, they always make it appear of the utmost Importance. These Machines I determin'd to raise on a very new and odd Foundation, the *Rosicrucian* Doctrine of Spirits . . . The *Rosicrucians* are a People I must bring you acquainted with. The best Account I know of them is in a French Book call'd *Le Comte de Gabalis*, which both in its Title and Size is so like a *Novel*, that many of the Fair Sex have read it for one by Mistake. According to these Gentlemen, the four Elements are inhabited by Spirits, which they call *Sylphs*, *Gnomes*, *Nymphs* and *Salamanders*. The *Gnomes* or Daemons of Earth, delight in Mischief; but the *Sylphs*, whose Habitation is in the Air, are the best-condition'd Creatures imaginable. For they say, any Mortals may enjoy the most intimate Familiarities with the gentle Spirits, upon a Condition very easie to all true *Adepts*, an inviolate Preservation of Chastity.   (pp. 142–3)

The passage is obviously playfully superior; it goes from a witty man to a witless lady, whose quarrel over her lock had created a serious breach in the

---

[3] *TE* ii, third edition, p. 393.

small circle of Roman Catholics to whom unity was so important.[4] But Pope's lecture provides information to which Warburton responds in his note to line 20 of the first canto:

When Mr. Pope had projected to give this Poem its present form, he was obliged to find it with its Machinery, For as the subject of the Epic Poem consists of two parts, the *metaphysical* and the *civil*; so this . . . was to have the same division of the subject. And, as the *civil* part is intentionally debased by the choice of an insignificant action; so should the *metaphysical*, by the use of some very extravagant system . . . There was but one System in all nature which was to his purpose, the *Rosicrusian Philosophy* . . . a kind of Theological–Philosophy, made up of almost equal mixtures of Pagan Platonism, Christian Quietism, and the Jewish Cabbala; a composition enough to fright Reason from human commerce.[5]

Noting Gabalis as the source, Warburton adds:

But as . . . Mr. P. found several whimsies of a very high mysterious kind, told of the nature of these elementary beings, which were very unfit to come into the machinery of such a sort of poem, he has . . . in their stead, made use of the Legendary stories of Guardian Angels, and the Nursery Tales of the Fairies: which he has artfully accommodated to the rest of the *Rosicrucian System*.   (p. 222n)

A brief (and pointed) account of this theological philosophy as de Villars gives it may place the sylphs more clearly in the total action (or inaction) of the poem.

The Count of Gabalis appears (like an epic muse, a courtesy book writer, or a spiritual director of souls) to introduce a new way of life to a prospective initiate. Since the real order of nature is spiritual and all else appearance, those who aspire to perfection must disengage themselves from the sensual distraction that disturbs celestial rhythms. To restore these, to himself and to mankind, the sage must 'his own Importance know', subdue his passions and become a mirror of heavenly order itself. The uninitiate bind their 'narrow Views to Things below'; they have no intuition about what Pope described in a note of 1751 as '*The Language of the Platonists, the writers of the intelligible world of Spirits*' (p. 154n).

The complexities and high mysterious whimsies of the Count's system demand not only a horoscope with Saturn in prime, that is, melancholy, but a life free from carnality. His initiate must be prepared to forgo intercourse, but he is not expected to give up 'marriage'. As his too solid flesh melts, he weds elemental forces, with great wisdom for 'instead of *Women*, whose fading Beauty pass way in a short time, and are followed with horrible Wrinkles and Uglyness, the *Philosophers* enjoy Beauties which never wax old, and whom they

[4] Douglas Brooks-Davies, in his *The mercurian monarch: magical politics from Spenser to Pope* (Manchester, 1983), p. 182, sees the importance of the breach but is too extravagant, I think, to say that 'Catholic union [i.e., political union] is the clue to the poem's larger meaning'. That reading both expands and limits the meaning.
[5] Alexander Pope, *Works*, William Warburton (ed.) (London, 1751), I, p. 221n.

have the glory to make Immortal'.[6] As Gabalis attempts to lend historical dimension to his system, it looks as if all actions of moral and heroic stature can be attributed to such celestial marriages. Oracles announcing these speak from many places, including odd vessels like drinking glasses and looking glasses (p. 95). They can also appear transformed into domestic animals. I have argued elsewhere that Shock is just such a transformed sprite.[7]

The Count's provisions for a ready and easy way to establish new common-wealths of spirits trouble the candidate and as we read we wonder whether mankind could bear very much of this ideality. Ayres, one of the early English translators, comments cynically on the Cabalist, whom he describes as 'a miserable Blind Creature, fit for a Dog and a Bell; yet in his own Conceit, more seeing than all the World, and best qualifyed for the Office of a Guide: much devoted to idle Traditions; by which crooked Line, he measures *Religion* and *Reason*: A great Hater of *Women*; yet much addicted to Venery, in a Philo-sophick Way' (de Villars, p. 1).

A Rosicrucian programme for salvation through the power of positive thinking may seem far removed from what happens to Belinda at home and at Hampton Court, but the attitude of mind de Villars describes has an analogy within Mrs Arabella's own experience, and that of the fair sex who are said to have read his book for a novel by mistake. While Pope's epistle suggests that the ladies err through judging *The Count of Gabalis* by the size of its cover, the inner shape of the volume might strike them as consonant with the doctrine they accepted socially. In the seventy-third number of the *Spectator* (24 May 1711), Addison speaks satirically of the homage a lady might expect, by paralleling her place with the status of an idol:

They are to be accosted in the Language proper to the Deity. Life and Death are at their disposal . . . Raptures, Transports, and Extasies are the Rewards which they confer: Sighs and Tears, Prayers and broken Hearts are the Offerings which are paid to them . . . An *Idol* may be Undeified by many accidental Causes. Marriage in particular is a kind of Counter-*Apotheosis*, or a Deification inverted. When a Man becomes familiar with his Goddess, she quickly sinks into a Woman.[8]

As soon as the union of minds transubstantiates, as it were, into body, the idol loses her power to act as a modernized version of the medieval courtly lady.

The attitude Addison satirizes is related to that seventeenth- and eighteenth-century phenomenon which *is* reminiscent of the conversations in Andreas Capellanus' *Art of Courtly Love*, the discussion of platonic love. George Sensabaugh has written of the influence of seventeenth-century reflections of this kind on *Comus*; Kathleen Lynch describes the part they play in the social mode of Restoration comedy, what a later writer calls the comedy of habit.

[6] Nicolas Montfauçon de Villars, *The Count of Gabalis*, trans. Philip Ayres (Amsterdam, 1715), p. 36.
[7] P. Brückmann, 'Pope's Shock and the Count of Gabalis,' *ELN* 1 (1964), 261–2.
[8] Joseph Addison, *The Spectator*, D. F. Bond (ed.), 5 vols. (Oxford, 1965), 1, pp. 313–15.

Writing of the 'romantic love' in seventeenth-century French romances, Arthur Johnston associates this attitude with platonic love.[9] In *Un paradis désespéré*, Jacques Ehrmann addresses the pastoral quality of romances like the *Astrée*, but his discussion of their rhetoric illuminates the language of platonic love: 'En devenant presque uniquement une rhétorique, la passion amoureuse est dissociée du réel. Ce phénomène est évident, non seulement dans *l'Astrée*, mais dans la plupart des romans contemporains où la description de l'amour équivaut presque à la définition de l'amour.'[10] But before reflecting on these rhetorical implications, some contemporary description will be useful. John Dunton says:

Platonick Love (or a Tender Friendship between Persons of a different Sex) is not only innocent, but commendable, and as advantageous as delightful: A strict Union of Souls (as *Plato* asserts) is the Essence of Friendship: *Souls have no Sexes*, nor while those only are concern'd can any thing that's Criminal intrude. 'Tis a Conversation truly Angelical; and has so many Charms In't, that the Friendships between Man and Man, deserve not to be compared with it . . .'[11]

Leaving marriage and other 'such coarse and homely Drudgeries' to 'Porters and Carmen', he continues:

if we wed no further than *Plato* allows, we may lawfully beget *Reflections* in each others Eyes, and those immaterial Creatures cannot sin or inherit any thing; this Life the Angels lead, and to court thus, is to court like them, for they no Sexes know, but ever live in Meditation, not in Act. (p. 10)

He alludes to 'Màdam Astel' and expands in a note: '*The Lady the Reverend and Learned* Mr. John Norris *corresponded with in his Book entituled,* Letters concerning the Love of God, between the Author of the Proposal to the Ladies; and Mr. *John Norris*, &c.' (p. 8). Certainly the Count of Gabalis or the Ariel who lectures Belinda in Canto I would subscribe to Norris' description of the worldly understanding of love and to his recommendation of a higher kind.

'tis so Common with men thus to *descend*, rather than love *Platonically* or *Abstractedly*, that the name of love is almost wholly appropriated to *this* Affection, and *to be in Love* signifies as much as to be inclined to *Corporal Contact* by the Occasion of Corporeal Beauty . . . And that which increases the wonder is the vileness of that structure which is made the Object of this sensual Love.[12]

In platonic letters to Pylades, Mrs Elizabeth Thomas, the unspeakable Curll's mistress, but here writing as Corinna, in the style of that 'professed Platonne' of which the *Tatler*[13] speaks, defends Norris' doctrine of love, saying:

---

[9] George Sensabaugh, 'The milieu of Comus', *Studies in Philology* 41 (1944), 238–49; Kathleen Lynch, *The social mode of Restoration comedy* (New York, 1926); D. R. M. Wilkinson, *The comedy of habit* (Leiden, 1964); Arthur Johnston, *Enchanted ground* (London, 1964), pp. 201–2.

[10] Jacques Ehrmann, *Un paradis désespéré: l'amour et l'illusion dans l'Astrée* (New Haven, 1963), p. 35.

[11] John Dunton, *Athenianism* (London, 1710), p. 6.

[12] John Norris, *Theory and regulation of love* (Oxford, 1688), pp. 46–7.

[13] *Tatler*, George Aitken (ed.), 4 vols. (London, 1898), i, pp. 262–8.

Ah, Sir! Mistake no more, the divinest *Modification* of the *Soul* for a meer Appetite common to *Brutes*, with *Human Nature*; but far, far beneath the Dignity of a rational and immortal Being.[14]

Another of these letters is '*Sent with the* HISTORY of the Count DE GABA-LIS' (i, p. 82), in Ozell's translation, published by Curll after *The Rape of the Lock*. The writer imagines an interview with the Count himself, and threatens him with

a tremendous Hero in the Company, who would kill him slapdash with a Fuzee, and by Dint of Arms, or an Innate presence of Mind . . . eternally silence his mystic Eloquence.

(i, p. 83)

The hero is 'a *Stoick*, and *so rigid a Stoick*, that he will certainly despise your Arguments, and prefer the Contemplation of his dear self before the delectable Company of the most beautiful *Gnome, Nymph, Sylph*, or *Salamander*' (i, p. 83). The Count replies:

O, how I long to convert a STOICK! *they are the most Difficult to be gained . . . but when they are enlightened by the glorious Mystery of the perpetual* CABALA, *there are none of the Brethren more constant, more zealous, or a greater Honour to our Illustrious Society.*   (i, p. 84)

The Count's companion sees the point; projecting a '*Metaphysical Union*' between the hero and one of the airy ladies, she observes:

Certainly you cannot wish him a more suitable Match, he is a *Philosopher*, he is a *Stoick*, he loves nothing that is *imperfect*, nothing that is *vulgar*, where then can he hope for a more sublime Consort than one of these *etherial Nymphs*, who being formed of the purest, the most subtile Part of the *Elements*, is entirely free from the Defects and Vanities of our *frail Sex*.   (i, p. 84)

A note identifies the hero as a Captain Hemington, 'an Admirer of Corinna, who . . . held a Philosophical Correspondence with her, concerning the true Nature of *Love* and *Friendship*' (i, p. 83n); in a later letter, Pylades calls him the '*Rosycrucian*' (i, p. 108). In the second volume (Lady Mary Chudleigh's letters to Corinna), there is another reference to Hemington's 'designed Match with the Aetherial Nymph mentioned in Count *Gabalis*' (ii, p. 250) and, earlier, a conversation between Lady Chudleigh, Mrs Bridgeman, Corinna and Hemington. This refers back to the Gabalis materials in Volume I and adds:

Mr. Hemington, said my Lady, *has desired me to chuse him a Wife, and I would have your Advice. What think you of* CORINNA? *I think*, said I . . . *the Captain is so refined a Philosopher that my Friend the Count* DE GABALIS *would be the fittest Person . . . to direct his Choice. One of his* SYLPHS, *or* GNOMES *would make an admirable Consort for a Person of such a Metaphysical Constitution.*   (ii, p. 79)

In *The Platonic Lovers* (1720, 1729, and 1732) dedicated to Judith Bond, with, the first edition carrying another pastoral title in 'Clio and Strephon', we find

---

[14] Richard Gwinnett, *Pylades and Corinna* (London, 1732), ii, p. 33.

passages that are reminiscent of the *Eloisa* ('You may admire me, *all the Ways* you can, / Give me the *Lover*, but keep back the Man', p. 79),[15] and a passage rehearsing some of Ariel's themes:

> Oft have I pray'd, and Heav'n has heard my Pray'r,
> To grant a Lover made like thee of Air,
> For I am tir'd with being long pursu'd,
> By low Desires of mortal Flesh and Blood,
> A greater Complement you cou'd not pay,
> Than throwing all the Dross of Love away,
> Then coming to my Bosom thus refin'd,
> And leaving Sex and Interest behind . . .
> What tell-tale *Sylph familiar* to my Heart,
> Cou'd this dear Secret to my Ear impart,
> One Way there was my nicer Taste to move,
> And that alone was Numbers dress'd in Love.   (p. 64)

The resonances of this last couplet in familiar Renaissance imagery of immortality through verse will be clear. The allusion to the sylph evidently needed no expansion; the poem ends with a stellification of the lovers. The author adds that

a Subject more noble and delicate than *that* of Honourable Love, (and it is upon *that* the following Verses were form'd) cannot enter into the Heads or Hearts of Men and Women . . .   (p. 64)

The subtitle of the *Pylades and Corinna* correspondence is in fact *The Honourable Lovers*. Honour is a word for 'platonic love'; it *is* as the familiar lines from *The Rape* suggest the 'Word with Men below' (1, p. 78).' The collation of these contexts indicates, as Ariel says, that 'Tis but their *Sylph*, the wise Celestials know.'

John Norris' attitude toward love physically expressed and the appropriateness of a stoic converted both resemble Ariel's advice in his opening address, when he punningly encourages Belinda to beware of Man and hence of Ombre and Night/Knight, lest she descend from the shady spaces of philosophy and pure love. The passages I have cited from *Pylades and Corinna* suggest that others easily saw the relationship between Pope's machinery and platonic love. Not all (not even, in fact, the author of *Platonic Lovers*, or Dunton himself) are without mortal longings as they expatiate over the scene of pure love. Many before Richardson's Lovelace (who had no liking, as we all know, for Norris) are inclined to think that pure love ends where platonic love always does. In Susannah Centlivre's *The Platonick Lady* (London, 1707), Lucinda asks: 'Is not Friendship the noblest Aim of human Kind?' and Belvill replies: 'Had your Parents thought so, the World had never known your Charms' (p. 18). In his *The Antiplatonick*, Cleveland says:

[15] *The platonic lovers* (London, 1732), pp. 60–5.

> Love, that's in Contemplation plac'd,
> Is *Venus* drawn but to the waste.
> Unless your Flame confess its Gender,
> And your Parly cause surrender,
> Y'are *Salamanders* of a cold Desire,
> That live untouch'd amidst the hottest fire.[16]

The Spectator (1, p. 387) suggests that the platonic stance may be a mask for impotence.

Tatler 32, chiefly about the problems of platonic love (1, pp. 262–8), begins with Norris and starts the satire of no. 63 on Mary Astell, who, as Madonella, 'had long since taken her flight towards the etherial mansions' (11, p. 103) and founded, as noted in 32 and here elaborated, a monastic school for young ladies, where needlework gave way to academic subjects:

Only on holidays the students will, for moderate exercise, be allowed to divert them-selves with the use of some of the lightest and most voluble weapons; and proper care will be taken to give them at least a superficial tincture of the ancient and modern Amazonian tactics.

The Amazons, with Pope's Thalestris leading, are familiar figures. Mary Astell has a long section in her *Essay in defence of the female sex* on '*Amazons, why they rejected the Society of Men*'.[17] Wasserman gives extended meaning for Pope's Amazons through a Virgilian context of thwarted marriage.[18] While the *Tatler*'s concern in the Madonella parody is probably his resentment of a learned lady taking her cause too far, other lines suggest worry about a decline in marriage (p. 261), talk nervously of the marriage laws (p. 223) and dis-course on ways and means for encouraging marriage and repeopling the island.

Even at a time when, as Lawrence Stone tells us, there was an articulate theory of companionate marriage,[19] there was evidently counsel for withdraw-al to a learned life in quasi-retreat, like retreat in the spiritual life, feared lest it cancel marriage altogether. Thomas Salmon's *Critical essay concerning marriage* urges his readers 'not to leave the Road that Nature has trac'd out, and aspiring to be Angels before our Time, render our selves less able to perform the common Offices of Humanity'.[20] In a very real way, the platonic stance, expressed in the anti-marital, Amazonian, battling images of the kind Brigid Brophy renders remarkably in her essay on the 'Rococo seducer' (Pope's Baron is a pale Don Giovanni) was probably associated with the pressures

[16] John Cleveland, *Works* (London, 1687), p. 11.
[17] Mary Astell, *Defence of the female sex* (London, 1696), p. 24.
[18] Earl Wasserman, 'The limits of allusion in *The Rape of the Lock*', *Journal of English and Germanic Philology* 65 (1966), 425–44.
[19] Lawrence Stone, *The family, sex and marriage in England, 1500–1800* (New York, 1977), pp. 325–41.
[20] Thomas Salmon, *Critical essay concerning marriage* (London, 1724), p. 16.

against learning for women.[21] The *Tatler* Amazon practising with her fan is only early assertiveness training.

Pope's early translations of Chaucer are also preoccupied with marriage. He chooses the Wife of Bath and the Merchant. Martinus Scriblerus is at his most comic in the novel of the Double Mistress, when he attempts a set of Siamese twins, most inconveniently joined and sounding in their names (Lindamira and Indamora), as in Martinus' action, like characters out of heroic drama or those vast romances, gilt and French, that are the repositories of the Platonic stance. The talk of Platonics is clearest and most suggestive in *Three Hours after Marriage*. Fossile administers drops to the ladies in a classic replay of the old virginity test. Phoebe Clinket, tireless poetess, type of many female scribblers in and outside Pope's circle, says that she can drink without fear; her 'Love was always Platonick'.[22] To a lady who refuses to drink, 'My Niece professes her self a *Platonick*. You are rather a *Cartesian*. (Clinket) Ah dear Uncle! How do the *Platonicks* and *Cartesians* differ? (Fossile) The *Platonicks* are for *Idea's*, the *Cartesians* for Matter and Motion' (p. 39).

This sly comment is more direct in the *Mechanical Operation of the Spirit*: 'Lovers, for the sake of Celestial Converse, are but another sort of *Platonicks*, who pretend to see Stars and Heaven in Ladies Eyes, and to look or think no lower; but the same *Pit* is provided for both.'[23] Swift underlines the disparity between profession and practice and the parallel between ordinary conduct and a more philosophical stance. An earlier part of this passage goes at the subject in a different way that can, by general allusion to Swift's use of occult imagery in the *Mechanical Operation* and in the *Tale*, move us from the sylphs as proselytizers for Platonic love to the sylphs in a different kind of inspirational role. '[H]ow unaccountably all Females are attracted by Visionary or Enthusiastick Preachers, tho' never so contemptible in their *outward Men* [*sic*] . . . however Spiritual Intrigues begin, they generally conclude like all others . . .' (p. 288).

Queen Henrietta Maria, Catholic and proselytizer for the Platonic, is an apt image of the constellation of notions that I think are operative in Pope. Her entirely chaste Amazonian costume on the occasion of one of the dramas she encouraged is only a minor detail, although it leads us into the reason why: she illuminates Pope's position about platonic love.[24] She performed then in a masque, having earlier shocked the court by appearing in the Sieur de Racan's pastoral drama, *Artenice*.[25] As Sensabaugh and others tell us, she was a

---

[21] Brigid Brophy, 'The rococo seducer', *The London Magazine* 2 (1962), 54–71.
[22] Pope, Gay, Arbuthnot, *Three Hours after Marriage*, in *Burlesque plays of the eighteenth century*, Simon Trussler (ed.) (Oxford, 1969), p. 125.
[23] Jonathan Swift, *A tale of a tub*, Guthkelch and Smith (eds) (Oxford, 1958), pp. 288–9.
[24] Carola Oman, *Henrietta Maria* (London, 1936), p. 109. See also Brooks-Davies, p. 182: 'it is this courtly background of the Caroline masque that Pope revives in *The Rape*'.
[25] John Harris, Stephen Orgel and Roy Strong, *The king's arcadia: Inigo Jones and the Stuart Court* (London, 1973), pp. 159–60.

considerable supporter of the cult and the language of platonic love, a veritable
Caroline, Countess Marie de Champagne, supporting new Andrew Chaplains
and the elaborate masques that furthered the 'King's Arcadia' and annoyed
the Puritans, who echoed Swift on the Platonicks in their criticism, of the
moral conduct of Henrietta's retinue, of the expense and the hieroglyphics of
the highly-wrought decoration. The masques were themselves intricately
Neoplatonic in matter.[26] But Henrietta's critics were most vocal about her
extravagant Catholicism and the Mariolatry that goes so well, here as in
medieval courtly love, with the platonic bias. In the dedication to *The flaming
hart* (1642) we hear that the queen had '*an extraordinary devotion; and not only
devotion to herselfe*, [St Teresa] *but affection also, to the holy Religious Women of her
Angelicall Order; whereof, the English Nation . . . hath a Monastery at Antwerpe*'.[27]

The ladies of St Teresa were not the only sisters located on the edge of the
Continent. I want to return to others, notably those managed by English
recusants, a little later. For the moment I should like to emphasize Norris of
Bemerton, correspondent of Mary Astell and Lady Catherine Jones, as well as
of Damaris Masham and other learned ladies. His *Theory and regulation of love*
(1688) associates him primarily with a theory of mysticism, and certainly with
the Neoplatonic bias and anti-rational element conventionally associated with
the tradition. What I would emphasize is the connection between Norris on
pure love, Norris on mysticism and and Norris on friendship.[28] In Elizabeth
Griffiths' *The Platonick Wife* (1765), we find Lady Fanshaw reading Pope's
Eloisa. While Eloisa is, on one level, perhaps the least platonic of lovers, her
extravagant language is like the sensuous vocabulary of mystical literature.

In a study of the process of *Eloisa*, I have elsewhere underlined that indebted-
ness to the mystical tradition earlier perceived by Ruffhead and Johnson, and
have suggested that Eloisa's process is in some ways a move from romantic
mysticism to realistic irony.[29] Ruffhead says that Pope would have found such
material in his mother's closet and that he himself numbered the best of the
mystic writers in his library.[30] Certainly this kind of literature, and devotional
material like it in orientation, was valued by and present to Pope's community
in the Forest.

[26] See Allardyce Nicoll, *Stuart masques and the Renaissance stage* (New York, 1968), pp. 154–7,
[27] *The flaming hart* (Antwerp, 1642), p. 2v.
[28] John Norris, *A collection of miscellanies* (Oxford, 1687). See especially pp. 295–300, on contemplation; pp. 435–45, on platonic love; and pp. 450–5, on friendship. See also his *Letters concerning
the love of God* (London, 1695), especially the allusions in the preface to St Teresa, Bona and St
Augustine.
[29] P. Brückmann, 'Religious hope and resignation: the process of Eloisa to Abelard', *English
Studies in Canada* 3 (1977), 136–52. See for a different approach, David Morris, *Alexander Pope:
the genius of sense* (Cambridge, Massachusetts, 1984), pp. 131–51. For an extension of this
feeling, see Steven Shankman, *Pope's 'Iliad': Homer in the age of passion* (Princeton, 1983),
especially p. xvi, where Shankman cites Kenneth MacLean's *John Locke* as the source for 'The
age of passion'.
[30] Owen Ruffhead, *The works of Alexander Pope* (London, 1764), v, p. 132.

As Anthony Allison and David Rogers, and, after them, Thomas Clancy have shown,[31] Catholic writers and publishers took their duty to provide books for the faithful very seriously and there was, until the very late seventeenth century, a supply of lively volumes, coming both from the continental presses at places like St Omer and from surreptitious presses in England. The so-called 'Catholic Wing' is still in progress and books continue to turn up, most often, predictably, in private libraries. Some 300 items at Mapledurham House alone are not in any catalogue; there are items at Downside Abbey that are not in Clancy's 1974 catalogue.

As Nicholas Bacon remarks in his *Journal of meditations* (1687), while recommending mental prayer: '*Neither are we in* England *destitute of these helps, having in our own language* Luiz de Puentes, Luiz Granada's, and Vincentio Bruno's *Meditations, and some others whose pious labours have proved singularly beneficial to the Christian world.*'[32] Among those easily available to late seventeenth-century Roman Catholics are important figures like Augustine Baker (in Serenus Cressy's edition), Boutauld, St Bernard, Blosius, Bona, Drexel, Caussin (in a series of Holy fictions), Walter Hilton, Julian of Norwich (Cressy brought her out in 1670 and there are many more copies of the text about than the standard bibliographical works indicate – again including one at Downside Abbey that no one has noted); Francis de Sales (much read, as one might predict), Losa, Lopez, Luis de Puente, Louis of Granada (everywhere), Gertrude More, Molina, Peter of Alcantara, Mary Magdalen dei Pazzi, Rodriguez, Scarisbrick's Lady Warner, St Teresa, Thomas à Kempis, St Catherine of Siena. These have a continuing thread of reference to those earlier standard writers in the mystical tradition: John of the Cross, Harp, Tauler, Suso, Richard of St Victor, Gerson, and the author of the *Cloud of Unknowing*.

Popular devotional works were documents like John Heigham's *Touchstone*, with at least one edition in nearly every year between 1691 and 1774. The prolific Arthur Crowther's *Dayly exercise of the devout christian* (1685), *The manner of performing the novena; or the nine days devotion* (1741), probably by Levinius Brown (present on that famous occasion at the Carylls when Pope rendered English verses into Latin), evidence for devotion to St Joseph, Scarisbrick's *Rules for the sodality of the Blessed Virgin Mary*, a variety of treatises for meditations on the Rosary (with litanies for Our Lady of Loretto). As my Appendix will suggest, Pope was close to a particularly rich collection of books like these. Horton Davies well describes the typical early seventeenth-century text, not essentially different from the later, as

an account of [the Catholic's] duties as a member of the Church, which would spur him to accept its doctrine with firmer faith, provide him with officially approved devotions,

---

[31] A. F. Allison and D. M. Rogers, *A catalogue of Catholic books in English . . . 1558–1640* (London, 1968); Thomas Clancy, *English Catholic books: 1641–1700: a bibliography* (Chicago, 1974).
[32] [Nicholas Bacon], *A journal of meditations for every day in the year* (London, 1687), A₂r.

as well as kindle his love for Christ and the saints. It might even encourage him to see mystical experience.[33]

Although there was a supply of priests for the English mission at every point of the period, the Roman Church was an isolated community, vividly conscious of itself as living under penalty.[34] This isolation from formal structure would make emphasis on private devotion both natural and enthusiastically dangerous. Some of these books were taken over by the opposition, who were careful to edit out some of the higher flights. One comments sharply on St Teresa, 'from whom all the Modern Mysticks and Quietists have taken their copy'[35] and observes, looking back at Catherine and Brigit (p. 8) that these are 'Bedlam Divinity'. Stillingfleet's battles with the Benedictine Serenus Cressy, point up the issues. A convert from the Church of England, Cressy's *Exomologesis* (dedicated to Mary Blount) explains his conversion as in part effected by reflection on mystical theology.[36] He cites, among mystics, 'St Teresa, S. Catherine of Siena . . . silly ignorant woemen [*sic*]' (p. 636), meaning, of course, 'innocent'. Later he cites Saints Augustine, Basil, Francis de Sales and Charles Borromeo, giving their background in Tauler, Harp and Ruysbroeck. The 1653 edition expands the mystical emphasis (pp. 639–40). Chaplain to Catherine of Braganza, he ran the Roman Catholic propaganda machine from Somerset House, before retiring to the Caryll estate, where he died in 1674.

Have we [says Stillingfleet in response to Cressy] any Mother *Juliana's* among us? Or do we publish to the World the *Fanatick Revelations* of *distempered Brains*, as Mr. *Cressy* hath very late . . . *the sixteen Revelations of Divine Love shewed to a devout servant of our Lord* (and Lady too) *called Mother* Juliana? . . . Did ever *H. N. Jacob Behmen*, or the highest *Enthusiasts* talk at a more extravagant rate than this *Juliana* doth?[37]

'I might', he says in another place, 'have expected this Answer from a follower of *Jacob Behmen* . . . I might have expected it from a *Rosycrucian*; for I find, that he who writ the *Epistle Apologetical* for the *Brethren* of that *Order*, produces the very same places of *Scripture* to justifie them, that *O.N.* and Mr. *Cressy* do for *Mystical Divinity*.'[38] Enthusiasm also brings 'obscure, strained, affected, unintelligible phrases' (p. 24). St Teresa has

nothing . . . but what might be a natural effect of an overheated Imagination, in a Person of a very melancholy devout temper, especially being before-hand possessed with the *Notions* of *Mystical Divinity* . . . I do exceedingly admire at those persons, who dare to bring the single *instance* of S. *Pauls Rapture*, to justifie all the pretences to *Visions* and *Raptures*, of the Melancholy and distempered *Women* of their *Church* (p. 51)

---

[33] Horton Davies, *Worship and theology in England* (Princeton, 1970), III, p. 425. See also II (1975), pp. 79–92, 459–89.

[34] See, for example, A. C. F. Beales, *Education under penalty* (London, 1963). See my Appendix.

[35] William Nicholls, 'Of the rise and progress, of spiritual books in the Romish church', prefatory essay for the *Introduction to the devout life* [Francis de Sales] (London, 1701) a₂v.

[36] Serenus Cressy, *Exomologesis* (Paris, 1647), p. 634.

[37] Edward Stillingfleet, *Works*, 6 vols. (London, 1707–10), V, p. 99.

[38] Edward Stillingfleet, *An answer to Mr. Cressy's epistle apologetical* (London, 1675), p. 32.

He might easily describe them as dwellers in a Cave of Spleen. The tone of James Price's earlier epistle dedicatory to Bona's *Guide* (1673), to another female superior, suggests his awareness of problems and a need to issue a warning:

As I doe not love our pretended Illuminees *and* imaginary Saints, *soe I doe not much affect* imaginary Writing *... that will sooner make one* mad *then make one a* Saint. *Certainly, there is more profit in a little* intelligible Piety, *then in whole* volumes of un-intelligible Raptures *and* Chimericall Elevations. *I like those who take more care to live well, then to be esteemed* Devotes: *who take more pains to doe good* Works, *then to fancy high* notions: *who are more diligent to mortify their* Passions, *then to fill their heads with unprofitable* Conceits.[39]

The disturbed wits are often women, pious second Eves.

John Caryll contributed heavily to these addresses.

All [his] ... daughters were educated abroad in ... convents; of these only Catherine ... failed to become a nun. Elizabeth, and Anne were professed ... Liège, while Fanny died there during her noviciate. Mary and Arabella were professed nuns of the Dames Benedictine of Dunkirk, which their great aunt Mary ... founded ... of which she had been abbess forty nine years.[40]

Lady Mary Caryll had the ten *Fridays* volume dedicated to her, because of her special devotion to Francis Xavier.

It was, of course, to John Caryll that Pope dedicated *The Rape of the Lock*, as it was Caryll who had commissioned it, aware of the importance of harmony in that small community reading its devotional books. Howard Erskine-Hill has recently made the Caryll connection closer and sharper: the first line of *The Rape of the Lock* echoes Lord Caryll's rendering of a key-line of Virgil's First Eclogue:

What dire effects from civil Discord flow! The complimentary allusion, which would be recognized by John Caryll, makes the shortly following line: '–This Verse to *Caryll*, Muse! is due' more widely suggestive, and (to the dedicatee and some others) brought the troubled history of the Caryll family during the previous thirty years, through Virgil, into the heroic reference of Pope's poem.   (Erskine-Hill, p. 68)

The Pope–Caryll friendship was warmest in 1715–16. Pope's response to the Catholic ambience of Windsor Forest was ambivalent. His letters to Caryll are carefully orthodox and respectful. He has considerable sympathy for those 'poor distressed Roman Catholics' (p. 65) living under penalty and occasionally reflects ruefully on his own situation. He alleges that he read all the controversies and varied between papist and protestant (I, p. 453, to Atterbury, 1717). He speaks lightly of fasting (I, pp. 114–15) and of mortification in Lent (I, p. 214). In a letter to Cromwell in 1719, he says:

---

[39] James Price, *A guide to heaven*, trans. John de Bona (Roan, 1673), c^v–d^v.
[40] Howard Erskine-Hill, *The social milieu of Alexander Pope* (New Haven, Connecticut, 1975), p. 63.

I had written to you sooner but that I made some Scruple of sending Profane Things to
You in Holy week. Besides our Family would have been Scandalized to see me write,
who take it for granted I write nothing but ungodly Verses; and They say here so many
Pray'rs, that I can make few Poems.   (I, p. 81)

This kind of remark, even if in the context of a letter to Cromwell, may reflect a
response to a Catholic household probably being run as, say, John Gother's
Instruction would suggest, with considerable dedication to prayer and some
sternness.[41] When asked to define his own commitment, Pope allied himself
with 'the Religion of Erasmus' (III, p. 81) and with Pascal and Fénelon, whom
he would, he says, 'most readily imitate, in submitting all my Opinions of the
Decision of the Church' (IV, p. 416, to Louis Racine). The postscript to
Sherburn's *Correspondence* gives some passages from Spence's notes on the
poet's last days (IV, p. 526). If the Mr Hooke who was present in Pope's last
days was the Hooke who translated Ramsay and was much interested (as was
Dr George Cheyne) in quietism and mysticism, then evidence for Pope's
knowledge of this kind of devotion in his own church is even further
strengthened.[42] Pope's allusion to Fénelon's submission reminds us that the
Archbishop of Cambrai's trials were specifically related to his views of mystical theology, to say nothing of his unhappy association with Mme Guyon. It is
surely Fénelon's attractive charity Pope means to commend, as it is the
contentiousness of Erasmus he means to espouse, but the tenor of their piety is
related to the simplicities that are particularly hospitable to the more obvious
kinds of mystical prayer. I am suggesting a temperamental affinity that would
have been fostered by an environment to which Pope was clearly not entirely
hostile, an environment he never renounced. He would also have been imaginatively struck by some of the language used by the devotional writers, as
Ruffhead saw him responding in *Eloisa*. Giving Wednesday over to celebrating
the guardian angel was a relatively recent innovation, one that underlines the
kind of devotional context I suggested earlier. Speaking of the angel's tasks
Gobinet says:

This Remedy . . . is very powerful in all Temptations, and especially in those which
combat Chastity, of which the Angels are Lovers, and particular Protectors, as being a
Vertue which renders Men like unto them, and which makes them imitate upon Earth
their most pure and celestial Life. From whence it happens, says St. *Ambrose*, that it is no
wonder if Angels defend chast Souls, who lead upon Earth a Life of Angels.[43]

The hymn at evensong and matins for the Feast of the Guardian Angel (2
October) as cited in the Primer of 1717 reads:

[41] John Bossy, *The English Catholic community, 1570–1850* (London, 1975), pp. 171–2.
[42] G. D. Henderson, *Mystics of the Northeast* (Aberdeen: University of Aberdeen Press, 1934), p. 67.
[43] Charles Gobinet, *The instruction of youth in Christian piety . . . with a very particular instruction for
      meditation, or mental prayer*, 2 vols. (London, 1687), I, p. 162.

> We sing the Guardian Angels Heaven has sent
> To help and guide us in our Banishment;
> Lest wily Foes surprize our will,
> Too heedless of the ways of Ill.
> For Traytor–Angels justly disposest
> Of their exalted Thrones amongst the Blest,
> Now turn their Spleen on human Race
> Created to supply their Place.
> Haste then you watchful Spirits to suppress
> The tumults of the Province you possess,
> And gently calm our lab'ring Breast
> With sweet Repose in Heavenly Rest.[44]

In Crowther's *Dayly exercise*, the prayer for the morning reads:

Thou summon'st me (O my God!) by thy Angel, my Guardian, to appear before thee, and to praise thy divine Majesty. I seem to hear thee sweetly calling me, inviting me, expecting me . . .[45]

And finally, in Boutauld's *Method of conversing with God*:

Others have Hours of Separation, there is no separation from God, all times are proper to make Holy Love to him *When the Sun retires*, says *Solomon, he retires not*; in the Night he remains by your Pillow, to entertain you in the silence of the Night by his secret Inspirations, and to help you to make a Holy and Sweet Repose amidst the Sweetnesses and Coelestial Pleasures of this Interior Conversation.[46]

The sensuous tone of these passages brings us back to the ironic responders to platonic love and connects the Platonics with the mystics. Writing of *La Mystique chrétienne et l'avenir de l'homme*, Claude Tresmontant places mystics and prophets together[47] precisely because they illustrate, as Steven Ozment says, 'God's sovereign freedom to operate beyond what he himself has established as normative.'[48] Ozment adds:

Even the most traditional, church-supporting form of mystical theology carries a . . . potential anti-intellectualism . . . not only [says Gerson] is mystical theology the 'most perfect knowledge possible' but it is also a knowledge in which even 'young girls and simpletons' can excel. Indeed the latter can be much closer to the ultimate truth of life than those with technical knowledge sufficient to move mountains.   (pp. 8–9)

Guardian angels and young girls bring one to du Guernier's contemporary illustration for *The Rape of the Lock*, Ariel's appearance to Belinda, a virgin being visited most sensuously by an angel power, for what comes to a lecture

[44] *The Primer* (London, 1717), p. 403.
[45] Arthur Crowther, *Dayly exercise* (1688), p. 3.
[46] M. Boutauld, *A method of conversing with God*. Translated out of *French* by J[ohn] W[arner], (London, 1688), pp. 14–15.
[47] Claude Tresmontant, *La Mystique chrétienne et l'avenir de l'homme* (Paris, 1977), pp. 205–17.
[48] Steven Ozment, *Mysticism and dissent* (Yale, 1973), p. 2.

upon the shadow.[49] The most obvious context is Satan at the ear of Eve.
Writing 'Three notes on Eve's dream in *Paradise Lost*', A. B. Chambers speaks
of those 'parallels and contrasts traditionally drawn between Mary and Eve'
and notes that 'according to one standard view, when Gabriel brought the
Annunciation to the Virgin, he quite literally enunciated God's Word: the
Word entered Mary's ear, she conceived and the Word became flesh.'[50] The
Annunciation itself is, of course, a miracle and a mystical experience in
Ozment's terms. Pope's scene is thus rich in implication: Ariel (who also has a
Shakespearean context of a paradisal and pastoral kind) is like Milton's Satan
and Belinda like Eve; both contexts recall a scriptural scene. Placed with
Belinda and the mirror, and the parody of the Mass, the scene lends an
extraordinary dimension to the action or impotent inaction of the machinery of
the poem.

Arthur Hoffman extends the Twickenham annotation and explication of the
Spenserian context, notably towards *Prothalamion* and the *Epithalamion*.[51] Oddly, he misses what seems to me the most Spenserian echo of them all, at the
beginning of Canto II, when the lines about Belinda's cross are so obviously an
echo of Red Crosse at the beginning of the *Faerie Queene*. In addition (perhaps)
to providing a pun, the evocation reinforces the courtly tone of romance and
invites contrast (as does the Milton). In St Jure's *The holy life of M. de Renty* we
find the author recommending exemplary lives with:

> Such nourishment as the reading of vain Romances, or the Lives of Secular Love-Knights . . . supply to
> the earthly principle in us our carnal lusts and ambitions set upon fading glories and beauties; the same
> do the Histories of Saints, and persons enamoured of Heaven, administer to the other celestial principle
> in us, the H. Spirit.[52]

St Jure's prescription is for spiritual romance, but one kind of static simplicity
has been exchanged for another. Ozment's discussion in *Mysticism and dissent*
lends another context:

> The impulse to reform, [he says], competes with a desire to abandon society altogether
> – truly to die to the world. It is not too much to say that in such dissent, the seeds of
> social disintegration are as prominent as those of individual liberation.   (p. 247)

For his dissenters,

> final authority lay in principle with the individual, the invisible, the ethically ideal, the
> perfect community – things no earthly society could ever be.

Translated to another context, the ethics suggested here are those of the

---

[49] See the illustration facing p. 11 in Robert Halsband, *The Rape of the Lock and its illustrations:
    1714–1896* (Oxford, 1980).
[50] A. B. Chambers, 'Three notes on Eve's dream in *Paradise Lost*', *Philological Quarterly*, 46 (1967),
    191.
[51] Arthur Hoffman, 'Spenser and *The Rape of the Lock*', *Philological Quarterly*, 59 (1970), 530–46.
[52] John Baptist St Jure, *The holy life of Monsieur M. De Renty*, trans. E. Scarisbrick (London, 1684),
    Ar$_2$.

platonic dramas of the millenary tones of the mystics or, to shift to another context of which *The Rape* is strongly evocative, the pastoral world of the seventeenth century whose perfections Belinda laments after the rape of the lock, the world Renato Poggioli describes as the pastoral of the self.[53] In his study of this world in *Un Paradis désespéré*, Jacques Ehrmann writes:

Il semble que le monde pastoral joue un rôle comparable à l'autre monde (celui qui se situe souvent par delà les murs d'air) de la littérature chevaleresque du Moyen Age, par rapport au monde réel. Pour le lecteur du XVIIe siècle, le monde pastoral est un prolongement idéal du monde chevaleresque-aristocratique, c'est le monde idyllique, du rêve, de la fantaisie, de la féerie – une féerie, hélas, considérablement rationalisée, déchargée de toute sa poétique surréelle, depuis le Moyen Age.   (p. 18)

The elaborately allusive world of *The Rape of the Lock* gives a new kind of charge to this pastoral, but the feeling about the poem that made Hazlitt ambiguous is explained by what Allen Tate saw long ago as this pastoral quality. The millenarian projections of the sylphs towards Ozment's ideal society, echoed by Belinda's game instincts, are domesticated versions of the world described by Frances Yates in her study of *The Rosicrucian enlightenment*.[54] Her first chapter, on the marriage of the Princess Elizabeth with the Elector Palatine, the Valentine's Day wedding for which Donne wrote an epithalamion: 'Be thou a new starre, that to us portends / Ends of much wonder; and be Thou those ends.' The passage is startlingly predictive of *The Rape of the Lock*, the metamorphosis from lock to comet.

Among the Mysticks [says Chambers] by *Transformation*, is understood a change to the Contemplative Soul, whereby it is in some measure deified or converted into the Substance of God, and wherein it is, as it were, lost and swallow'd up in the Divinity, so as not to perceive its own Distinction from God. The sense of the Word *Transformation* is very liable to be abused; and, in effect, the Quietists and Quakers have abused it.[55]

One factor is clear. There is an obvious emphasis on the place of women in all these traditions, from the Mary Astells and the Mary Chudleighs (or any of the learned ladies in the circles of Norris and Locke) to Donne's 'Shees'. In his *Epistle to a Lady*, Pope insists on the mysteries of women, not just in the vicious, but in the virtuous addressee as well. Like the others, she is 'at best a Contradiction still', capable, like Eve, of wrong and right imaginations and lively projects, sometimes prone to fall. His early interests, from the Wife of Bath to Belinda and then to Eloisa, represent this fascination, one that Johnson understood when he spoke to the importance of *The Rape* because he saw the importance of particular domestic conduct. *The Rape of the Lock*, using its impotent sylphs as cartoons, seems to me to behave more epically precisely because it manages so extensively to catch a variety of matters in the enlightenment and to render their effects (as all epics really do) domestically, with the

---

[53] Renato Poggioli, *The oaten flute* (Cambridge, Mass., 1975), pp. 166–81.
[54] Frances Yates, *The Rosicrucian enlightenment* (London, 1972).
[55] Ephraim Chambers, *Cyclopaedia*, 2 vols. (London, 1728) 11, p. 232.

extremes of Rosicrucian machinery used to light up the pastoral, platonic and mystical particulars of that Windsor Forest that was at once an image of Pope's papist Arcadia and of the faded royal image. *Pace* Dennis and Johnson, Pope has, in the Platonic and mystical reverberations of the materials borrowed from the drama, from *Gabalis* and from the language of his own church, created not just a mock epic, but an epic or, as he said with characteristic precision, 'an heroi-comical' poem, bringing the epic form appropriately into his own time and giving it exactly the right machinery for his own occasion and for the larger occasions worked out around him.

Appendix

In addition to books listed in Maynard Mack's 'A finding list of books surviving from Pope's library', Appendix A in *'Collected in himself': essays critical, biographical and bibliographical on Pope and some of his contemporaries* (London and Toronto, 1982), Pope would have had easy access to the collection of Catholic books owned by the Blount family at Mapledurham House. (See also Mack's commentary on Pope's religious views in his *Alexander Pope: a life* (New Haven and London, 1986), especially pp. 920–1n, and those sections of the biography dealing with Pope's Catholicism and its context). The library includes an extraordinarily large number (as great as the collection was at Ugbrooke, the Clifford seat in South Devon) of credal, devotional and controversial books. The devotional volumes include all the major and some of the minor writers in the mystical tradition. Mack's list includes items like the Erasmus Bible given to Pope by Swift, no. 19, p. 397; Donne's *Pseudo-Martyr* (London, 1710), no. 55, p. 410; Thomas à Kempis, *Sermons of the Incarnation and Passion of Christ*, 1653, no. 159, p. 443; in a translation by Thomas Carre; George Touchet's *Historical Collections, Out of Several Grave Protestant Historians Concerning the Changes of Religion* (London, 1674), no. 164, p. 256.

2

The Rape of the Lock and the contexts of warfare

HOWARD D. WEINBROT

Until recently, all of us knew the essential facts and interpretations regarding *The Rape of the Lock*. It was written as a *jeu d'esprit* to unify two neighbouring Catholic families in hopes that Arabella Fermor and Robert, Lord Petre, would be reconciled. In 1712 it appeared in two cantos; in 1714 in five, with the full machinery of the sylphs and gnomes; and in 1717 in Pope's first collected *Works*, with Clarissa's speech added. The poem, we were told, sets Pope's fragile culture against the superior culture evoked in his parody of epic devices. Pope does not taint Homer's epic, but the modern pseudo-heroes whose moral diminution is well reflected in the sylphs and the trivial act of cutting off a woman's lock of hair. On this hypothesis, even Clarissa, Pope's own spokeswoman, provides good sense because that is all such a world can aspire to. As three shrewd and very different modern commentators have put it, 'in mock-epic a dignified genre is turned to witty use without being cheapened in any way'; 'the essence of Pope's wit in *The Rape of the Lock* lies in . . . the appeal of a better world of noble manners and actions. Cutting the lock is . . . more than absurd'; or in another severe judgment, Pope's lines 'do violence to Homer's passages, adulterate them, because the weak and sordid modern culture adulterates the simple purity of the Homeric life.'[1]

However inadequate, these familiar views served some useful purposes – they directed us to the poem's mock form, epic forebears, and moral norm of Clarissa's speech. All things are subject to decay. In an aberration to which I must in part contribute, the poem's elegant lightness now is darkened by learned allusions; the sylphs are demonic and satanic; Pope's mock epic itself is a capitalist tool and the product of an élitist male poet who ridicules women; and Clarissa's speech is either ironic, or a woeful constraint upon woman's

[1] These are from, respectively, Ian Jack, 'A complex mock-heroic: *The Rape of the Lock*', in his *Augustan satire: intention and idiom in English poetry 1660–1750* (Oxford, 1952), p. 78; Reuben A. Brower, 'Am'rous causes', in his *Alexander Pope: the poetry of allusion* (Oxford, 1959), p. 144; Earl R. Wasserman, 'The limits of allusion in *The Rape of the Lock*', *Journal of English and Germanic Philology*, 65 (1966), 428: They are conveniently gathered in G. S. Rousseau (ed.), *Twentieth century interpretations of The Rape of the Lock*, (New Jersey, 1969), pp. 39, 53, 72. By 1969, indeed, even several of Clarissa's friends had doubts regarding her wisdom. See the remarks by Rousseau (1969) and Brower (1959), *Interpretations*, pp. 9–10, 66, and J. S. Cunningham, *Pope: The Rape of the Lock*, Studies in English Literature no. 2 (New York, 1961), p. 45.

role, or both. She has been called a 'narrow, hypocritical' opportunist, and 'ostrich-like' in preparing one for old age and death; she also is 'an envious prude' who wants to harm Belinda to help herself with the baron; and she is so filled with 'high-minded insincerity' and 'falsity' that in comparison even Thalestris' angry, martial harangue is 'honest, life-engaging'.[2]

Though much of the direction of these enquiries seems to me both wrong and wrongheaded, the search for new light on *The Rape of the Lock* is welcome. We should indeed rethink the poem's epic contexts, the function of its mock-heroic, and Clarissa's and Thalestris' roles in the poem. Discussion of the epic begins with Homer's Anglo-French reputation during the later seventeenth and earlier eighteenth centuries.

A schism among the wits

From at least the early Renaissance, Homer was regarded as the father of poets, the master of all knowledge, and classical antiquity's pre-eminent poet. He also was ideologically pure, since the moral of his *Iliad* was the need for a unified state under Jove's vicegerent. In 1660 John Ogilby thus dedicates his translation of Homer to Charles II and prudently says 'that which may render [Homer] yet more proper for Royal Entertainment is, That he appears a most constant assertor of the Divine Right of Princes and Monarchical Government'. In Hanoverian 1714 that argument was less compelling, but Homer apparently was not. Richard Fiddes speaks of Homer's 'universal Esteem . . . in all Ages', the 'universal Genius' he embodies, and the 'Danger . . . either to revive, or raise Objections against' him. One year later Thomas Parnell

---

[2] Apparently there are two genealogical lines in such criticism. One descends from the Ur text, Rebecca Price Parkin's *The poetic workmanship of Alexander Pope* (Minnesota, 1955), pp. 127, 171 (the first quotation above), and extends to John Trimble, 'Clarissa's role in *The Rape of the Lock*', *Texas Studies in Literature and Language* 15 (1974), 673–91; Ellen Pollak, 'Rereading *The Rape of the Lock*: Pope and the paradox of female power', *Studies in Eighteenth-Century Culture* 10 (1981), 442 (the second quotation above), and her amplification in *The poetics of sexual myth: gender and ideology in the verse of Swift and Pope* (Chicago, 1985), pp. 80–2, 85–6; and C. N. Manlove, 'Change in *The Rape of the Lock*', *Durham University Journal*, n.s. 45 (1983), 48–9. In this critical branch the old new criticism and its perceptions of irony and ambiguity abounding is transmogrified into the new ideological criticism and the politically incorrect abounding. The other branch is self-generating in the manner of unmoved movers. It includes John P. Hardy, *Reinterpretations. Essays on poems by Milton, Pope and Johnson* (London, 1971), pp. 56–8; James Reeves, *The Reputation and writings of Alexander Pope* (London, 1976), pp. 148–9; Sheila Delaney, 'Sexual politics in Pope's *Rape of the Lock*', in Norman Rudich (ed.), *Weapons of criticism: Marxism in America and the literary tradition*, (Palo Alto, California, 1976), pp. 188–9; Robin Grove, 'Uniting airy substance: *The Rape of the Lock*', in Howard Erskine-Hill and Anne Smith (eds.), *The art of Alexander Pope* (London, 1979), pp. 52–88, especially p. 83 (the third quotation above); and Kelly Reynolds, *The Rape of the Lock: love match. The "earthly lover" vs. the 'birth-night beau'* ', *Schola Satyrica* 6 (1980), 3–11. Leaves from either branch share common markings. Clarissa is a prude, tactless, hypocritical, haughty, inferior to Thalestris, unctuous, exploitive, devious, self-interested, insidious, a moral imperialist and opportunist, Belinda's enemy and sexual rival who wishes to destroy her, mischievous, a huntress of the baron, and 'chauvinized'. The change in vision is perhaps a function of Ovid redivivus or some other theology.

concludes his 'Essay on . . . Homer' prefatory to Pope's *Iliad* by reminding us that Homer was the comprehensive 'Father of Learning', and left behind him 'A Work which shall always stand at the top of the sublime Character, to be gaz'd at by Readers with an Admiration of its Perfection, and by Writers with a Despair that it should ever be emulated with Success'.[3]

Nonetheless, all was not placid in the world of letters, and Fiddes and Parnell write as if cloistered from the preceding half century's bitter literary debates. Hostility to Homer had been growing throughout the seventeenth century, especially in France. Desmarets de Saint-Sorlin, for example, wrote several impassioned works urging the virtues of his modern Christian century, and the vices of ancient, pagan, Greece and Rome. By 1671 Gabriel Gueret had written his *Parnasse reformé* and reported that all was changed in the republic of letters. War has broken out among authors, the academy is divided, and there is a schism among the wits. The French academy itself became an anti-Homeric command post, first under the leadership of Charles Perrault in 1687, and then of Houtar de la Motte in 1714.[4] The polite label for this impolite confrontation was the *querelle des anciens et des modernes*, in which Homer figured prominently for two generations in England as in France. By 1707, for example, Samuel Cobb complained that Homer was 'so much the Ridicule of our *Beaux Esprits*'.[5]

This effort was helped by successful attacks on Aristotle's science, which gave aid and comfort to attacks on his literary criticism. As St Evremond put

---

[3] Ogilby, *Homer his Iliads translated* (London, 1669), sig. A1ᵛ; the original is italicized; Fiddes, *A prefatory epistle concerning some remarks to be published on Homer's Iliad; occasion'd by the proposals of Mr. Pope towards a new English version of that poem. To the Reverend Dr. Swift* (London, 1714), pp. 18, 112 (Danger); Parnell, 'An essay on the life, writings, and learning of Homer', in *TE* VII–VIII; Maynard Mack *et al.* (eds.), *The Iliad*, (London, 1967), VII, p. 80.

[4] Desmarets, *Clovis ou la France chrestienne. Poëme hëroique* (Paris, 1657); 'Discours pour prouver que les sujets Chrestiens sont les seuls propres à la poësie hëroique', in *Clovis*, 3rd ed. (Paris, 1673). For some specific remarks, see *La Defense du poëme hëroique* (Paris, 1674), pp. 4, 9, 12–19, among others; Gueret, *Le Parnasse reformé. Nouvelle edition* (1671; Paris, 1674), p. 5; Perrault, *Parallèle des anciens et des modernes* (Paris, 1688–97); Houtar, *A critical discourse upon Homer's Iliad*, trans. Lewis Theobald (London, 1714). Houtar says, for example, that 'the whole *Iliad* is but a piece embroider'd with Pride, Anger and Revenge' (p. 10). These disagreeable arguments in France were of the highest importance both within their own country and for the moderns in England with whom, we shall see, Pope shared several assumptions. The best introductions to the 'querelle' are by H. Rigault, *Histoire de la querelle des anciens et des modernes* (Paris, 1856); A. Lombard, *La Querelle des anciens et des modernes. L'Abbé du Bos* (Neufchâtel, 1908); Noémi Hepp, *Homère en France au XVIIᵉ siècle* (Paris, 1968); A. Owen Aldridge, 'Ancients and Moderns in the eighteenth century', in *Dictionary of the history of ideas* (New York, 1968), I, pp. 76–87: and Kirsti Simonsuuri, *Homer's original genius: eighteenth-century notions of the early Greek epic (1688–1798)* (Cambridge, 1979). Joseph M. Levine attempts to offer some new perspectives in 'Ancients and moderns reconsidered', *Eighteenth-Century Studies* 15 (1981), 72–89, and 'Edward Gibbon and the quarrel between the Ancients and the Moderns', *The Eighteenth Century* 26 (1985), 47–62. In spite of its severity, the debate in France was conducted at a higher level than in England, Bentley's and Wotton's contributions only excepted.

[5] 'A discourse on criticism and the liberty of writing', in *Poems on several occasions* (London, 1707), sigs. A4ʳ⁻ᵛ.

it, natural philosophers observed errors in Aristotle's physics, and poets 'spy'd out faults in his *Poeticks*, at least with respect to us'. Consequently, Pierre Bayle observes, by the later seventeenth century faith in Aristotle 'has been violently shaken'. The abbés Jean Terrasson and Jean-François de Pons recognized, respectively, the roles of Perrault and Houtar in what they regarded as the moderns' victory over the ancients. Accordingly, Terrasson said that 'the fall of *Aristotle* had already . . . prepared men's minds' to reject the ancients and this victory 'carried its light into Homer'.[6] Homer and Aristotle thus were the chief dragons guarding the ancients' gates to Parnassus; slay them and all the other dragonettes – Bossu, the Daciers, Rymer, Dennis – would die as well. That is what the Anglo-French moderns, many of whom also admired classical, especially Latin, literature, set out to do. The many opponents of Homer found four basic areas of weakness: plot, language and decorum, the nastiness of the gods, and the brutality of the heroes.

'Absolutely sunk and Ruin'd': Anti-Homeric paradigms

As René Rapin reported, the *Iliad* has two incoherent actions. That of the Trojan War is imperfect since within the poem it lacks both a beginning and an end; that of Achilles' anger against Agamemnon lacks an end and a middle, for rage against Hector soon replaces it. The defective plot has neither the regularity nor proportion 'in which alone consist the Perfection of a Great Work'.[7] Even after the death of Hector, which ought to have concluded the poem, we find two more books 'which are Foreign to the Purpose, the Principal Action being perfect without them' (p. 178). Homer's plot also includes too many improbable miracles, requires that everything be 'done by Machines' (p. 147), and that the most commonplace of wisdom be ferried to the world by peripatetic gods. Digressions are equally troubling, for Homer rarely keeps to his subject, piles episode upon episode, and is hurried along by his uncontrolled imagination. Every encounter encourages him 'to tell Stories, and derive Genealogies' (p. 153).

Homer's linguistic and moral decorums were no better than his fable. Rapin

---

6 St Evremond, 'Of antient and modern tragedy', in *The Works of Monsieur de St Evremond*, trans. Pierre des Maizeaux (London, 1728), 2, p. 102; Bayle, *A general dictionary, historical and critical* (1697, French), trans. Thomas Birch *et al.* (eds.), (London, 1735), 2, p. 266; Terrasson, *A discourse of ancient and modern learning* (1715, French), trans. Francis Brerewood (London, 1716), p. lxv (Perrault and Aristotle), p. lxviij (Homer). This work later appeared as *A critical dissertation upon Homer's Iliad*, (London, 1722). Homer as a bad model for battles, below, appears there in 2, p. 306. Jean-François de Pons, *Oeuvres [1738] suivies de Lettre à Madame Dacier sur son livre des causes de la corruption du goust* [1715] (Geneva: Slatkin Reprints, 1971), 'Dissertation sur le poème epique', pp. 95–145; 'Lettre à monsieur * * * sur l'Iliade de Monsieur de la Motte', pp. 288–314; 'Observations sur divers points, concernant la traduction d'Homère', pp. 333–54; and 'Lettre à Madame Dacier' (two letters, with new pagination), pp. 1–48.
7 'A comparison of Homer and Virgil' (1666, French), in *The whole critical works of Monsieur Rapin*, trans. Basil Kennet, 2nd ed. (London, 1716), 1, p. 144. Subsequent citations are given in the text.

was outraged that 'Kings and Princes in *Homer* talk to one another with all the Scurrility imaginable'. Agamemnon treats the father and priest Chryses insolently, and that priest himself then behaves without dignity, charity, or patriotism by calling down Apollo's curse on the Greeks, when his office required that he pray for them 'and for the Preservation of the Government'. Homer violates several other social and literary conventions: 'Fathers are harsh and cruel, the Heroes weak and passionate, the Gods expos'd to Miseries, uneasie and quarrelsome, and incens'd against one another' (pp. 152–5). Shortly thereafter, the Abbé d'Aubignac filled his own *Dissertation sur l'Iliade* with specific and general complaints concerning the gods' and heroes' language and conduct towards one another: 'Mars appelle Minerve mouche de chien, Dianne appelle son frère Apollon un fou, et Junon appelle Dianne une chienne. Achille nom Apollon le plus méchant de tous les Dieux, et Hector l'appelle un chien et un fou'. Indeed, when the gods and men were not fighting, they debased themselves by eating. D'Aubignac also laments that 'ils sont toujours à table, ils ont toujours le verre à la main; et toute la félicité de leur vie céleste et glorieuse, n'est qu'une goinfrerie perpétuelle.' Homer wrongly leaves before us 'une image de gens attachés à la crapule'.[8] As the appearance of Mars and Venus trapped in Vulcan's net shows, the unmajestic gods also lack the 'Air of Gravity . . . Essential to an Heroick Poem'. Nor are the human beings more reverent to the gods; the story of Venus being wounded by Diomedes borders on burlesque (p. 160).

Thus harried, Homer's gods found themselves fleeing for their celestial lives through much of Europe. Even René le Bossu, who convinced himself and others that the gods were allegorical, admitted that 'some' think Homer gave those gods 'such *Manners* as turn them into mere Swine'. This judgment was shared by many, including Giambattista Vico, who regarded the gods as villainous, by Houtar who called them despicable, by Saint-Hyacinthe who labelled them vicious, powerless, and often worse than the fools who asked their help, and by Andrew-Michael Ramsay, who thought them debased.[9]

Homer's heroes, especially Achilles, are as unattractively criminal as the gods they resemble. According to Rapin, Homer blundered in making Achilles

---

[8] François Hédelin, Abbé d'Aubignac, *Conjectures académiques ou dissertation sur l'Iliade*, Victor Magnien (ed.), (Paris, 1925), p. 108 (chien et un fou), p. 118. The work was written during the 1670s and published posthumously in 1715.

[9] Le Bossu, *Monsieur Bossu's treatise of the epick poem* (London, 1695), p. 218; Vico, *Principi di una scienza nuova* (Naples, 1725), 'Search for the true Homer', in *The new science*, trans. Thomas G. Bergin and Max H. Fisch (New York, 1984), from the 3rd ed. of 1744, p. 302; Houtar, *A critical discourse upon Homer's Iliad* (note 4 above); Saint-Hyacinthe, Hyacinth Cordonnier, known as Chevalier de Themiseul de, 'Une dissertation sur Homère et sur Chapelain', as in *Le chef d'oeuvre d'un inconu. . . . par M. . . . Chrisostome Matanasius* [pseud.], new pagination for the dissertation (The Hague, 1714), pp. 9–10; Ramsay, 'A discourse upon epick poetry, and the excellency of the poem of Telemachus', in François Salignac de la Motte Fénelon, Archbishop of Cambray, *The adventures of Telemachus . . . with a discourse upon epick poetry*, trans. Isaac Littlebury and Abel Boyer (London, 1719), i, p. 13.

'not so much as Rational' but brutal, a vice Aristotle knew to be 'directly
opposite to Heroick Vertue' and one that disgraced Achilles by causing the
needless death of so many men 'whom he sacrific'd to his Grief and Discontent'
(pp. 124–5). This barbarous and cruel hero, Rapin concludes, epitomizes
'Imperfections and Vices' (p. 131). D'Aubignac both berates the princes who
argue like thieves over their booty and seem to make war for gain not for
honour (p. 84), and rejects the horror of their incessant bloody combat and
vaunting insults to the dead and dying. In 1693 Samuel Wesley labels Achilles
'a perfect Almanzor, with not one spark of Vertue, and only remarkable for his
extraordinary Strength and little Brains'. The widely read Pierre Bayle exemplifies such resentment. He wonders how anyone still can admire the *Iliad*, or
how Horace could boast of memorizing all of that poem in which Achilles
behaves with such inexcusable venality. His acts 'are so repugnant, not only to
heroic virtue, but even to the most common generosity; that we must conclude,
either that Homer had no idea of heroism, or that he designed to draw the
character of a brutal wretch. He represents Achilles, wishing himself brute
enough, to devour Hector's raw flesh.'[10] No wonder that in 1715 Jean Terrasson says that as for battles, one should 'imitate all the Poets in the World
except Homer' (2:306).[11]

His imperfections were enhanced by the many well-known burlesques
which Pope knew and, as the *Dunciad* makes plain, provided congenial devices
for him. In addition, the burlesques also put in rude form what more solemn
commentators had put in polished form. For all the burlesques' vulgarity, they
reflect and enlarge an important body of literary, social and cultural criticism.

Homer à la Mode

The motives of these often obscene poems include exposing Homer for what he
is to make plain that he is not a superior of the moderns. Charles Cornwall
admits that the *Iliad* may be pleasing, but insists that it is no more 'Than a
Parcel of wild, imaginary undertakings' in which an absurd hero does absurd
things beyond the reach of man in some never-never land – 'and this, forsooth,
must be call'd *An Hero*. And . . . must have the exalted Title of *An Heroick Poem*'.
Actually, it is uninformed and 'very inferiour, and paultry' when contrasted
with Christian dispensation.[12]

One reason for this slovenly inadequate mind and its poem was offered in a

[10] Wesley, 'Essay on heroic poetry', prefatory to *The life of our blessed lord & saviour Jesus Christ. An
heroic poem*, 2nd ed. (London, 1697), The Augustan Reprint Society Series Two, Publication no.
5 (Los Angeles, 1947), p. 17; Bayle, *A general dictionary, historical and critical* (London, 1734), 1, p.
178.

[11] *A critical dissertation upon Homer's Iliad*, trans. F. Brerewood (London, 1722).

[12] *Homeros, Homoros. The third book of Homer's Ilias burlesqu'd* (London, 1722), unsigned sigs. A2^{r-v},
with the title page as A1; sig. B1^r (paultry). Cornwall also believes that Homer does 'an
unconceivable deal of Harm; *viz.* by corrupting the Innocence, and Purity of our most Holy
Discipline: and tainting the Minds of Men, with Heathenish, and Anti-christian Trumpery'
(B1^v).

commonplace regarding Homer's genealogy. He was not an exalted man of letters, but a beggarly poet rambling about Aegean Smithfield fairs, singing for his supper, and patching together various incoherent rhapsodies concerning Troy or Ulysses. Alternatively, he never existed at all, and was simply the name given to a rag-tag assortment of ballads which, 500 years later, Pisistratus of Athens organized into loose medleys called the *Iliad* and the *Odyssey*.[13] Nothing could be expected from such a poet who, Burnet and Duckett rationalize, may as well be translated into burlesque verse that a Yorkshire milk-maid could understand.[14] Such language also was appropriate, Abbé Terrasson probably would agree, because as 'the Original, Source, and Principle of all Burlesque Morality' Homer 'presents the most open Vice and Obscenities and formally recommends the most shameful Actions' (2:204). Consequently, the Homer of the parodists supplies a full menu of luscious sins. Many of these writers assumed that Homer's plot was absurd, and so they mingled burlesques of barbarous language and decorum, the heroes, and the gods. No one fared well.

Neither crudity of rhetoric nor of table manners escaped the parodists' notice. A literal translation of Achilles' harangue to Agamemnon in Book 1, Burnet and Duckett claim, will seem more like 'a Dialogue between two *Watermen*' than 'the Speech of one great King to another about a Parson's Daughter, whom they had made a whore of' (pp. 11–12). James Scudamore and the pseudonymous Nickydemus Ninnyhammer characterize the Greeks' disgusting culinary adventures in which, for example, a newly butchered heifer is so mangled, cut, torn, and hashed it was 'enough to make / One spew; it would so turn one's Stomach.'[15] *Deuteripideuteron* of 1681 is even more

---

[13] For some of these views see the second-century AD. Claudius Aelian, *Varia historia*, XIII, 14, which also appeared in Rome, Basle, Leiden, Leipzig, and London. The latter is in Thomas Stanley, trans., as *Claudius Aelianus his various history* (London, 1665). Charles Perrault alludes to Aelian and others who shared his notion: *Parallèle des anciens et des modernes* (Paris, 1692; n. 4 above), 3, pp. 32–6: 'beaucoup d'excellens Critiques soutiennent qu'il n'y a jamais eu au monde un homme nommé Homère, qui ait composé' the *Iliad* and the *Odyssey*. These poems 'ne sont autre chose qu'un amas, qu'une collection de plusieurs petits Poëmes de divers Auteurs qu'on a joints ensemble' (pp. 32–3). See also Samuel Wesley, *The life of our blessed lord and saviour Jesus Christ. An heroic poem*, 2nd ed. (London, 1697), sig. a 3ᵛ (partial refutation), and in the poem itself, p. 201 (partial acceptance); the Abbé d'Aubignac, *Conjectures académique . . . sur l'Iliade* (note 8 above), pp. 51–3, 56, 58, 60, 62, 74, 118; Richard Bentley, *Remarks upon a late discourse of free-thinking* (London, 1713), p. 18; John Oldmixon (ed.), *Poems and translations by several hands* (London, 1714), p. 245; Vico, *The new science* (n. 9 above), pp. 318–28; Charles Cornwall, *Homeros, Homoros*, (n. 12 above), sigs. A2ʳ⁻ᵛ. Some aspects of the controversy have been discussed in the introductory and bibliographic essays in the valuable F. A. Wolf, *Prolegomena to Homer, 1795*, trans. Anthony Grafton *et al.* (Princeton, 1985).

[14] Thomas Burnet and George Duckett, *Homerides: or, a letter to Mr. Pope occasion'd by his intended translation of Homer. By Sir Iliad Doggrel* (London, 1715), p. 10.

[15] Scudamore, *Homer a la mode. A mock poem upon the first and second books of Homer's Iliads* (Oxford, 1664) pp. 53–6; Ninnyhammer, *Homer in a nut shell: or, the Iliad of Homer in immortal doggrel* (London, 1715). p. 44. An early reader of the British Library's copy of Scudamore has placed asterisks next to some characterizations of gross Greek manners, including drunken vomits (p. 55), and farting Jove (p. 60): shelf mark 11315 b. 12.

graphic as it reverses roles. In its epic feast the Cyclops is the hero who turns
two of Ulysses' men into his own rough meal:

> He dasht their brains against the Bed-post;
> Brains (though but few) fell on the ground,
> Comixt with blood, and there this Hound
> Tearing them piece-meal with gub-teeth
> Sat down and eat them just like Beef.
> First he their thighs devour'd gladly,
> Then on their yellow Buttocks fed he,
> Nay guts and garbage, which look nastily;
> One would not eat a turd so hastily;
> As he their flesh and bones did swallow;
> Nay made the very Pr——s to follow;
> And sav'd the Piss, that ran down heels,
> In a huge Bowl, to drink at meals.[16]

The heroes embodied another form of criticized epic barbarism, sexual
vulgarity and indifference to everything but self-gratification. The putative
Henry Fitzcotton's Achilles thus tells us how he and his men satisfy their
tender longings:

> When convents happen in our way,
> Each takes his nun, that very day:
> We make an honest dividend;
> And when that's done – why there's an end.

Such amusements and deposits were meagre in comparison with the many
other references to pudenda, sexual functions and ancillary acts. In *Homer a la
mode. The second part* (1681) Agamemnon promises to give Achilles anything,
including all of his daughters, if he will return to the war. He swears

> By *Gargantua*'s monstrous ware,
> And by *Pantagruel*'s huge Tarse,
> And by the foistings of mine Ar——
> Nay, and I'le swear by that same Odpiece
> Of flesh hangs dangling in *Jove*'s Codpiece.[17]

Lest Homer's women should demand equal treatment, Nickydemus Ninnyhammer parodies Book III of the *Iliad*, in which a reluctant Paris and an eager
Menelaus box in order to end the war and, as Hector puts it, determine who
'May take fair *Nelly* and go f——k her' (p. 52). She watches the unequal battle,
observes her husband's 'swinging B———ks' (p. 57), and retires as her lover is
saved by Venus' intervention. The pimping goddess insists that Helen go to

---

[16] *Deuteripideuteron: the second part of the second part of Homer alamode: or, a mock-poem on the ninth book of
       the Odysses* (London, 1681), p. 33.
[17] Fitzcotton, *A new and accurate translation of the first book of Homer's Iliad* (Dublin and London,
       1749), p. 21; *Homer ala mode. The second part in English burlesque: or, a mock-poem upon the ninth book of
       Iliads* (London, 1681), p. 16.

bed with Paris, searches her out, and finds that so inventive and communal a spirit hardly needs a man:

> in a Garret
> She found her f––gg––g with a Carrot;
> With many a Finger F–k–g Neighbour,
> All groping, just as at a Labour.   (p. 63)

In so iconoclastic a tradition the ancient warriors and wise men received no quarter. For many writers even the courage of those exemplary killing machines was suspect. At different times, both the frightened Greek and Trojan sides beshit themselves, cut their own throats, abandon their men, require the help of the gods to conquer a lone hero, and scarcely deserve that exalted name. As Nickydemus says, Achilles also is a cry-baby, for when he surrenders Briseis he 'cry'd and roar'd like any Noddy' and 'for that Oyster-whore his Mother / He bawl'd, and made an heavy pother' (p. 13). Similarly, the Nestor of *Homer a la mode* in 1681 makes plain that most of the Greeks are witless, that Agamemnon has 'few' brains (pp. 8, 12), and that the other Greek leaders are a filching knave, a fool, and a clown (p. 20).

The parodists also knew that the gods were as scurrilous as those who prayed to them. Their sexual vulgarity could take the form of a goddess seducing a god in order to get brutal wishes granted for a mortal. Achilles thus asks his mother Thetis for a small favour – convincing Jove to permit the Trojans to slaughter all the Greeks as their punishment for angering him. 'Draw your stool nigher' to Jove, James Scudamore's Achilles urges 'And stroke his knees, or something higher' (p. 48). Nickydemus' Vulcan gives the gods the giggles and Juno incontinence when he explains that after being thrown out of heaven and falling for three days, 'I sprain'd Two Legs – but not my middle' (p. 18). Charles Cornwall is especially rich in divine dalliance of varied sorts. To hide the battered Paris, Venus 'Piss't full in *Menelaus*' Eyes' (p. 49); she then becomes 'The pimping *Cytharaean* Queen: With naked Breasts, and brazen Face' (p. 53) who coerces Helen into bed with Paris, and hears that matron lament – 'aren't we cunning Prigs, / To dance to all your bawdy Jigs?' Thanks to Venus, any booby now can have 'A Lick at *Helen*'s Gallipot' (p. 54). This crassness is present as well in Thomas Bridges' long, later-eighteenth-century culmination of the burlesque tradition. Diomedes' wounding of Venus after she protects the vulnerable Aeneas is a comic rendering of sex and violence. Diomedes

> with his tool the goddess enter'd;
> With such a force he drove it in,
> It made the light heel'd gipsy grin:
> Strait from the place where he did stick her
> There came a bright transparent liquor.

Apollo then explains the incident to Mars:

> The whelp at *Venus* push'd and hit her
> With such a tool, I thought he'd split her;
> But she in dangers ever calm,
> Receiv'd it in her sweaty palm,
> There held it fast, and made it stand,
> And *spend* its venom in her hand.[18]

Neither milk-maid nor maid-of-honour could misunderstand such sexual play in the burlesques of Homer: whether in the natural or supernatural, male or female worlds, sex was casual, illicit, violent, self-propelled, prostituted, any or all of the above, and provocation for bloody and lengthy warfare about an irresponsible adulterous woman and her cowardly lover.

Pope's *Rape of the Lock*, then, does not emerge from a perceived grand past that dwarfs an inadequate present. For many commentators, the opposite was true. They might agree that *The Rape* and its contrasting Homeric backgrounds do show the triumph of heroic grandeur, but with more than compensating modern manners and achievements. As Pope's contemporaries recognized, the eras of great epic ventures in Greece and Rome were disjointed and savage times that one would not wish to relive; a great poem is little recompense for great slaughter. In 1735 Thomas Blackwell thus observes that 'tho' the Pleasure arising from a Taste of the sublimer kinds of Writings, may make' readers 'regret the Silence of the [epic] Muses' today, nonetheless we must wish '*That we may never be a proper Subject of an* Heroic Poem'.[19]

Indeed, the more characters in *The Rape of the Lock* embrace epic values and conventions, the less pleasant they are. The baron's prayer to the goddess Love, for example, includes a mischievous combination of Achilles' and Ulysses' traits – he hopes 'by Force to ravish, or by Fraud betray';[20] the gods

---

[18] *A burlesque translation of Homer* (London, 1772), pp. 188, 196. Bridges began to publish his efforts in 1762. His translation also includes anger regarding the Greek 'thick scull'd sons of bitches' who 'In mighty wrath kept boxing on, / And knock'd the foremost Trojans down' (p. 530). A comparable degree of deflation of the gods and discontent with epic values seems to me present as well in Samuel Wesley's *The Iliad in a nutshell: or, Homer's battle of the frogs and mice. Illustrated with notes* (London, 1726).

[19] *An enquiry into the life and writings of Homer* (London, 1735), p. 28. Blackwell also observes that 'Peace, Harmony and good Order which make the happiness of a people, are the *Bane* of a Poem that subsists by Wonder and Surprise' (p. 27). William Melmoth makes a similar argument regarding oratory, which flourishes during turbulence and signals national and personal loss: 'the superior eloquence of Cicero' could not 'make him any amends for his sad catastrophe'. *Letters on several subjects. By the late Sir Thomas Fitzosborne, Bart.* (London, 1748), 2, p. 333.

As Pope knew from Virgil's *Georgics* and Homer's relevant similes, a miniature world need not denote diminished human values. Small things, Pope says of Homer, 'give Lustre to his greatest Heroes'. Pope quotes Eustathius' confirming wisdom: by comparing soldiers to flies Homer does not diminish 'his Heroes by the Size of these small Animals, but . . . [raises] his Comparisons from certain Properties inherent in them, which deserve our Observation' (*TE* VIII, pp. 254–5n; *Iliad* XVI, l. 314).

[20] *TE* II, *The Rape of the Lock* Canto II, l. 32. Subsequent citations to this edition are given in the text by canto and line. The baron's offerings include trophies of his former loves and reflect further modern adaptations of epic behaviour. In *Iliad* XIV, ll. 359–72, Jupiter proves his lust for Juno 'by the Instances of its Warmth to other Women'. Though this seems strange, 'Perhaps a

themselves are characteristically unreliable and later grant only half his prayer so that he acquires but cannot keep the lock (II, l. 45). Both Belinda's triumphant vaunting after her victory in the card-game (II, ll. 99–100) and the baron's refusal to return the raped object (III, ll. 161–70; IV, ll. 131–40) are adaptations of epic heroes' ungenerous self-absorption, like Achilles' refusal to return Hector's body until his suppliant father ransoms it.[21] Sir Plume's drivelling speech (IV, ll. 127–30) is consistent with several commentators' notions of heroic wisdom. The final scenes' collapse of social values and rise of universal violence that pleases the interested gods also is drawn from the Homeric epic.

On the other hand, when the poem is most modern and least disagreeable, it negates epic values. Unlike the apparently rambling *Iliad*, *The Rape of the Lock* is meticulously coherent.[22] It also begins with an allusion to the 'dire Offence [that] from am'rous causes springs' (I, l. 1) – as with the genocide of the Trojan War because of Helen, and the eternal enmity between Rome and Carthage, and its consequent sacking because of Aeneas' abandonment of Dido. In Pope's poem, sexual rapaciousness is sublimated into a courtship ritual. The card-game also is a mating dance and a ritualized expression of potentially violent sexual energy. That world's violence also is restrained through ceremony, so that 'with Sword-knots Sword-knots strive' (I, l. 101). The sword is sheathed, ornamented with ribbons, and serves more like a male peacock's feathers than an instrument of death.[23] Unlike the characteristic exhortation

Man's Love to the Sex in general may be no ill Recommendation of him to a Particular. And to be known, or thought, to have been successful with a good many, is what some Moderns have found no unfortunate Qualification in gaining a lady, even a most virtuous one like *Juno*' (*TE* VIII, p. 180n). On this hypothesis, the baron's reputation attracts Belinda; the hypothesis gains support if one assumes, rightly I believe, that her morning billet-doux was from him, and that her response was in part the suggestive card game.

---

[21] See, for example, Pope's note to *Iliad* XI, l. 565: 'I must confess I am not altogether pleas'd with the Railleries [Homer] sometimes uses to a vanquish'd Warrior, which Inhumanities if spoken to the dying, would I think be yet Worse than after they were dead' (*TE* VIII, p. 59n). See also *TE* VIII, p. 475n to *Iliad* XXII, l. 467.

[22] One commentator has even found a five-act dramatic structure. See James L. Jackson, 'Pope's *Rape of the Lock* considered as a five-act epic', *Publications of the Modern Language Association of America* 65 (1950), 1283–7.

[23] As a gloss upon the ribbon and Belinda's danger, see the 'Dialogue between Surly and Beau. By a person of quality', in [John Oldmixon, ed.] *Poems and translations. By several hands* (London, 1714):

> Under his Left Arm a Bamboo,
> Ribbon dangling at his Sword;
> Tells you all he has, or can do,
> And whom last he laid on Board.

> Well he knows th' Intrigues of *London*,
> Which he whispers round the Room;
> What believing Maids are undone;
> Where they Lay in, and by whom.   (p. 39)

For further sense of the woman's social and sexual danger, see note 28, below.

to kill, Clarissa's speech is an exhortation to engage life. The epic feast is not the Homeric culinary debauch, but an elaborately civilized coffee and tea service that also is an emblem of the pacific interdependence of modern trading nations thought to be God's will.[24] Moreover, this poem also is presented by a protective, encouraging narrator, who begins and ends in his own benevolent voice, and, unlike Homer, refuses to allow the creatures he has made to come to bad ends. He has memorialized Belinda in art, and Belinda has ennobled him by the folly that evoked his poem: 'It will be in vain to deny that I have some Regard for this Piece, since I Dedicate it to You,' he says in his prefatory letter's first line (p. 142). '*This Lock*, the Muse shall consecrate to Fame, / And mid'st the Stars inscribe *Belinda*'s Name' (v, ll. 149–50), he says in the final couplet. For Homer, there is harmony within Achilles, among the Greek leaders, and between men and gods only after the venting of vast amounts of blood. For Pope, such harmony returns after affectionate scolding and a brief allusion to the difference between the permanence of art and the transience of the life we had best live while we can.

Such a view is not inconsistent with Pope's willingness to spend some twenty years translating the deservedly esteemed *poet* Homer. But he was as eclectic and often judicious in his affection for Homer as for Virgil and Horace, each of whom he and many others faulted on moral and political grounds. Pope says, for example, that Homer's plot is 'a confused Heap of Beauties', his love of slaughter is offensive, and his use of some metaphors is indecent. Pope will not even translate the animal's name to which Ajax is likened in Book XI[25]; he assumes that Agamemnon's hold on Chryses' daughter is motivated by lust not by kingly prerogative; and he regards Thetis' advice that Achilles stop mourning Patroclus and take Briseis to bed as an outrage to decency and in its 'Expression ... almost obscene' (*TE* VIII, p. 543n; *Iliad* XXIV, l. 168). In several places he thus makes plain that he has absorbed the ancients' and, especially,

---

[24] For some aspects of trade and *The Rape of the Lock*, see Louis A. Landa, 'Pope's Belinda, the general emporie of the world, and the wondrous worm', and 'Of silkworms and farthingales and the will of God', in *Essays in eighteenth-century English literature* (Princeton, 1980), pp. 178–217. See also Madam du Boccage's letter of 14 April 1750 from London, which includes these 'Verses upon Ranelagh':

> Trade, which connects each distant shore,
> Which makes men various climes explore,
> To all the gifts this land affords,
> Adds *Chinese* Tea to crown their boards;
> Coffee of Moca, which bestows
> Tranquillity and calm repose;
> And the black *Indian* bev'ridge fam'd,
> *Ambrosia* by the *Spaniard* nam'd.

Letters concerning England, Holland, and Italy.... translated from the French (London, 1750), I, p. 20.

[25] *TE* VIII, pp. 65–6; *Iliad* XI, l. 668, translated in XI, l. 681 as 'the slow Beast with heavy strength indu'd'. Though Pope admires the simile, he records several objections to it and omits 'the mention of the word Ass in the Translation' out of respect for 'the Taste of the Age in which he lives' (VIII, p. 64n).

the moderns' objections to Homer. As he says at the end of a long attack on Homer's combats of the gods in *Iliad* xxi, 566, '*Homer* never better deserv'd than in this place the Censure past upon him by the Ancients, that as he rais'd the Characters of his Men up to Gods, so he sunk those of Gods down to Men' (*TE* viii, p. 445n).

These deviations were heresies to a true Homerophile like Madame Dacier, whose second edition of her own translated *Iliad* (1719) includes a gratuitously insulting addendum on Pope's ignorance for even suggesting that Homer's divine robes had moth holes. Perhaps one reason for her rage was that she sensed Pope's mediating role among Homer's detractors. The serious commentators establish a large body of hostile critical discourse; the parodists employ that discourse to reduce Homer to absurdity; Pope then plays a variation on both themes. He accepts each group's criticism of Homer, but unlike his prose ancestors does so in a pleasing way; unlike the parodists he does so in a polite way. The reader drugged by an academic treatise or scandalized by a frigging Helen would find *The Rape of the Lock* a perfect mine for sapping Homeric walls. No wonder Madame Dacier groused that 'The most inveterate Enemies to *Homer* never said any thing more injurious, or more unjust against that Poet' than Pope did in the preface to his *Iliad*.[26] As I hope to show, Pope's rejection of Homer's deification is as present in the body of his mock poem as in the preface and notes to his real translation.

In light of these reclaimed, indeed subversive, contexts and contrasts we may wish to reconsider some of the older critical dogmas with which I began – that Pope's poem shows how 'weak and sordid modern culture adulterates the simple purity of the Homeric life' and that his mock epic does not cheapen the distant 'dignified genre'. We may also wish to reconsider two newer critical dogmas – for several commentators Thalestris is to be applauded, and for many others Clarissa is to be excoriated.

Belinda and Thalestris

The fragility of Belinda's world has long been recognized in images of broken china vessels[27]; but it also is a dangerous world which kills those who make

---

[26] *Madame Dacier's remarks upon Mr. Pope's account of Homer, prefixed to his translation of the Iliad. Made English from the French, by Mr. Parnell* (London, 1724), p. 4. Curll mischievously published this translation. The Parnell who wrote the 'Essay on . . . Homer' prefatory to Pope's *Iliad* died in 1718. For Pope's response to Madame Dacier's *Remarks*, see *Correspondence*, ii, pp. 157–8. Pope's notes to Homer include several disagreements with Madame Dacier's comparable interpretations. On 1 September 1718 he thus tells the Duke of Buckingham: her efforts are too often borrowed from Eustathius without acknowledgment; she is inferior to her husband as a classicist; in general he respects her learning without sharing his grace's high opinion of her; and on rhetorical and poetic grounds Houtar de la Motte has much the better of the argument with Madame Dacier, (*Correspondence*, i, pp. 492–3; see also i, pp. 485–7).

[27] See especially Aubrey Williams, 'The "fall" of China and *The Rape of the Lock*', *Philological Quarterly* 41 (1962), 412–25.

improper moves on its battle field. Britain's statesmen at Hampton Court 'doom' women there; even the ordinary heroes and nymphs so interpret behaviour that 'At ev'ry Word a Reputation dies' (III, ll. 5, 15–16). The famous couplet, 'The hungry Judges soon the Sentence sign, / And Wretches hang that Jury-men may Dine' (III, ll. 21–2), suggests that Belinda is in danger of a parallel social death, degradation and dishonour (IV, ll. 107–12).[28] Like other martial or sexual warriors, however, she courts the death she hopes to avoid. The sylphs' advice in Canto I that she beware of man, for example, vanishes once she awakes and reads a love letter (I, ll. 114–20); she also uses traditional female war-paint for a sexual skirmish at Hampton Court.[29]

The game of ombre there tells us much about Belinda's values. She declares herself the challenger, the ombre or man who hopes to defeat her opponent the baron.[30] As the challenger, she has the right to declare the trumps, and does so in a radically biblical way: '*Let Spades be Trumps!* she said, and Trumps they were' (III, l. 46). Pope gives her both God's creative mantle and a version of the words Longinus cited as the archetype of divine sublimity, in which thought and deed are simultaneous.[31] Since she seems as confidently in control of her world as any god, she 'swells her Breast with Conquests yet to come' (III, l. 28) and makes herself even more attractive to her hopeful lover.

The card-game takes the form of a miniature epic battle, in which each side

[28] Compare Pope's note to *Iliad* XVI, 468–9, '(When guilty Mortals break th' eternal Laws, / And Judges brib'd, betray the righteous Cause).' Pope adapts '*Homer*'s indirect and oblique manner of introducing moral Sentences and Instructions.... We have Virtue put upon us by Surprize, and are pleas'd to find a thing where we should never have look'd to meet with it' (*TE* VIII, 261n). Giles Jacob also saw the potential seriousness and danger in Pope's poem. His unsigned *Rape of the Smock* (1717) shows a suitor, Ambrosio, seriously wounded in a duel, and the woman, Celia, trading her virtue to Philemon in order to reclaim the appearance of virtue – her own stolen smock. The seriousness of a mock epic appears as well in another poem indebted to Pope but far kinder to women than Jacobs's: *Modern fashions. A poem address'd to the ladies* (London, 1745), especially pp. 2, 5, 10, 13–15. The final pages contrast the benevolent female victor in the battle of the sexes, 'whose kindness banishes *Despair*', with the malevolent female tyrant who 'calmly sees the Conquer'd die' (p. 14). The contrast recalls that between Thalestris and Clarissa, as does the consequence of 'mutual Good' (p. 15) for man and woman if the proper advice is taken.

[29] For Pope's contrast of the ancient and modern Beauty at her toilette, see *TE* VIII, p. 169n; *Iliad* XIV, l. 203n; and for one view of why Belinda is so well armed, see *TE* VIII, p. 184n; *Iliad* XIV, l. 442n from the beginning of Plutarch's *Life of Pelopidas*: 'the bravest and stoutest of [Homer's] Warriors march to Battel in the best Arms'.

[30] For the epic challenger's normative mixed tone of challenge, see *TE* VII, p. 367n; *Iliad* VII, l. 79, regarding Hector's boast to the Greek champions: 'If he seems to speak too vainly, we should consider him under the Character of a Challenger, whose Business it is to defy the Enemy. Yet at the same time we find a decent Modesty in his manner of expressing the Conditions of the Combate.' Robert Williams points out that confident Belinda 'plays a military game with "Let Spades be trumps" (from Italian *spada*, a sword)'. 'Fate and the narrative of *The Rape of the Lock*', *Sydney Studies in English* 11 (1985–6), 34.

[31] *Oeuvres diverses du sieur D * * *, avec le traité du sublime* (1674) (Amsterdam, 1674), 2: 39. See also Nicholas Rowe et al. (eds.), *The works of Mons' Boileau Despreaux*, (London, 1711–12), 2, pp. 7–8, 37–8; new title page and pagination for *A treatise of the sublime*.

advances, retreats and takes prisoners on 'the Velvet Plain' (III, l. 44). The battle also cleanses human hostility and becomes a surrogate sexual confrontation, in which the '*Queens* . . . hands sustain a Flow'r, / Th' expressive Emblem of their softer Pow'r' (III, ll. 39–40), knaves hold phallic 'Halberds in their hand' (III, l. 42), and the King of Spades puts forth a sexual 'manly Leg' (III, l. 57). When Belinda seems to be winning, the baron rallies, pours forth his diamonds, routs her cards, 'And wins (oh shameful Chance!) the *Queen of Hearts*. / At this, the Blood the Virgin's Cheek forsook', and she sees herself 'in the Jaws of Ruin' (III, ll. 88–9, 92). With the score tied at four tricks apiece, Belinda in turn rallies and uses her King of Hearts to win the game, which she celebrates with shouts of victory. Belinda, then, shows herself sexually enticing, socially aggressive, apparently dominant, and willing to confront the baron in a game whose rules announce and sublimate cruder passions. At the subsequent coffee-table-cum-epic feast, ceremony and rules begin to collapse.

The baron indecorously clips Belinda's lock, refuses to return it, and shows that he now is master of their world. Belinda must regain authority or suffer a predictable social death, one, Pope's additions and notes make plain, she herself encourages. In new lines added in 1714 Belinda ignores the sylphs' three warnings of the baron's approach, forces Ariel's withdrawal when he sees 'An Earthly Lover lurking at her Heart' (III, l. 144), and implicitly permits the lock to be taken by the man to whom she has just puffed her breasts, and by whom her heart had been put in 'wild Disorder' (III, l. 79). Belinda nonetheless can turn the 'rape' into the purest chastity if she abandons childish games and fantasies of omnipotence and makes a prudent choice. Pope clarified the nature of that choice in his portrait of the fashionable upper-class malady, the spleen.

Ariel's surrender means Umbriel's assumption of power, which he improves by taking an epic journey to the underworld. Traditionally, this served at least two relevant purposes – to bring the tools of the gods to man, and to bring the future to the hero. Umbriel thus acquires a bag which holds 'the Force of Female Lungs, / Sighs, Sobs, and Passions, and the War of Tongues', and a vial with 'fainting Fears, / Soft Sorrows, melting Griefs, and flowing Tears' (IV, ll. 83–6). Aeneas' subterranean adventure shows him Rome's imperial expansion and fulfilment; Umbriel's shows him Belinda's potential world of migraine headaches, ill-nature, painted, wrinkled, ancient maidens, religious hypocrites, lampoons, affectation, languishing pride and horrible visions. Perhaps above all, we see the consequences for maids – a word repeated four times – who accept such sexual and other frustrations: with spleen, 'Maids turn'd Bottels, call aloud for Corks' (IV, l. 54).

Upon returning to the world, Umbriel finds Belinda sunk in Thalestris' arms, releases spleen's bag of Furies over their heads, and evokes Thalestris' furious, consuming speech, as '*Belinda* burns with more than mortal Ire, / And fierce *Thalestris* fans the rising Fire' (IV, ll. 93–4). After some heated jeremiad,

she defines honour as appearance rather than virtue, and characterizes herself
and the danger she believes Belinda is now in:

> Methinks already I your Tears survey,
> Already hear the horrid things they say,
> Already see you a degraded Toast,
> And all your Honour in a Whisper lost!
> How shall I, then, your helpless Fame defend?
> 'Twill then be Infamy to seem your Friend.   (IV, ll. 107–12)

When Sir Plume's foolish speech fails to regain the lock from the baron,
Umbriel breaks the Vial of Sorrows over Belinda's head; she then worsens a
bad situation, and remains trapped by her own self-pity. She curses the day
and wishes that she had abjured the seductive court for 'some lone Isle, or
distant *Northern* Land' (IV, l. 154). Her beauty should have been hidden 'from
mortal Eye, / Like Roses that in Desarts bloom and die' (IV, ll. 157–8). If only,
she moans in lines immediately thought indecent, the baron had 'been content
to seize / Hairs less in sight, or any Hairs but these!' (IV, ll. 175–6).[32] Belinda
thus accepts two sets of threatening values – sexual withdrawal that leads to
the sexual anorexia in the Cave of Spleen, and moral withdrawal that leads to
virtue as a public pose and beauty as an object of sterile adoration rather than
productive attraction. On the poem's own terms, Thalestris as a guide leads
Belinda down dangerous roads.

Thalestris and the Amazons

Pope colours our response to Thalestris in other contextual ways. As an
Amazon she came trailing malevolent associations. If Amazons existed, commentators agreed, they either cut off, burned off, or stunted by binding the
right breast in order to strengthen the right arm and clear an obstruction in
pulling a bow string or throwing a spear. This form of body sculpture was
joined by worse for the male children who were returned to their fathers by an
occasional dovish mother, or if less fortunate were killed, castrated, crippled,
to which Pope must have been especially sensitive, or enslaved as the case may
be.[33] Since children of either sex emerge from traditional copulation, the
Amazons insured that such acts were unblemished by affection. As Samuel
Johnson translates the Abbé Guyon's commonplace *Histoire des Amazones* in
1741, 'lest any Lady might give Reason for Suspicion that she had any tender

---

[32] See 'Remarks on Mr. Pope's *Rape of the Lock*' (written 1714, published 1728) in Edward Niles
Hooker (ed.), *The critical works of John Dennis*, (Baltimore, 1967), 2, p. 342, and [Charles Gildon]
New rehearsal, or Bays the younger. . . . Also a word or two upon Mr. Pope's Rape of the Lock (London,
1714), pp. 43–4. Geoffrey Tillotson records some other responses to the poem's bawdy in *TE* II,
pp. 87–93, especially p. 90, n. 1. See also n. 51 below.

[33] See *TE* VII, p. 124n; *Iliad* I, l. 771, regarding the gods' laughter at Vulcan: yet Homer 'takes care
not to mention a word of his Lameness. It would have been cruel in him and Wit out of Season,
to have enlarg'd with Derision upon an Imperfection which is out of one's power to remedy.'

Passion for the other Sex, no Virgin was allowed to pay this annual Visit [to men of the neighbouring nation], 'till she had, by killing three Men, shewn how much she detested them, and how much her Race deserved to be propagated'.[34]

Such a tale contributed to the image of Amazons in general and Thalestris in particular as types both of the aggressive and sexually hungry woman. In 1679 the amorous author of *The Enjoyment* praises his Silvia for rousing his phallic heroism: 'She like some Amazon' delights in the sexual combat that can 'gently raise his head' when he is briefly conquered and at rest (p. 2). As what John Biddle called 'shameless lewd Viragoes', however, Amazons often were vilified rather than exalted for their sexual prowess. By 1693 Dryden's Juvenal refers to a 'strutting Amazonian Whore'.[35] Thereafter, Pierre Danet, Père Gautruche, and Claude Marie Guyon agree that, in Danet's words, the Amazons 'prostituted their Bodies to Strangers' whom they took, according to Guyon, 'without Distinction of Affection'. By mid century Lord Chesterfield used Amazons to characterize Dutch ponderousness. Dutch women at home, he writes, 'are mere *Amazons*, and their husbands are the wretched captives,

---

[34] 'A dissertation on the Amazons. From the history of the Amazons, written in French by the Abbé de Guyon', in *The Gentleman's Magazine* 11 (1741), 203. For further information regarding this version see John Lawrence Abbott, 'Dr. Johnson and the Amazons', *Philological Quarterly* 44 (1965), 484–95. See also item 53 of J. D. Fleeman, *Preliminary handlist of copies of books associated with Dr. Samuel Johnson*, Oxford Bibliographical Society Occasional Publication no. 17 (Oxford, 1984). This shows Johnson's reading of the entry under 'Amazons' in Pierre Danet, *Complete dictionary of Greek and Roman antiquities* (London, 1700).

As this and other references make plain, the Amazon was not unattractive merely because she was a woman warrior. Boadicea in England and La Pucelle in France were martial heroines who received the nation's well-earned applause. In most instances the difference between the attractive female warrior and the repellent Amazon is acceptance of the conventional mediating power of God, the state, or the male to whom she is or hopes to be attached. Once this female warrior has done her job, she surrenders the arms of war for the arms of man. Spenser's Britomart, for example, so behaves towards Artegall when she defeats the martially and sexually aggressive and unmanning Radegund in Book v, cantos 4–7 of the *Faerie Queene*. Spenser there carefully distinguishes between Radegund as warlike and cruel Amazon, and Britomart as championesse, warrioresse, Britonesse, and conqueresse who nonetheless re-establishes Artegall's authority. For further discussion of this issue, see Susanne Woods, 'Spenser and the problem of women's rule', *Huntington Library Quarterly* 48 (1985), 141–58. In a note to *Iliad* xiv, l. 216, Pope makes plain how, in his judgment, women are most likely to prevail, 'by pure cunning, and the Artful Management of their Persons; For there is but one way for the weak to subdue the mighty, and that is by Pleasure' (*TE* viii, p. 170n). For a benevolent playing out of such a victory and an Amazonian transformation from hostile to amiable sexual relations, see Samuel Wesley, *Battle of the sexes* (1723), 2nd ed. (London, 1724), pp. 11–27. In this well-resolved combat 'the jarring Kinds agree, / With Reconcilement dear, and cordial Amity' (p. 27). Simon Shepherd studies the less accommodating combats in *Amazons and warrior women. Varieties of feminism in seventeenth-century drama* (New York, 1981); see especially pp. 5–17. Shepherd actually deals only with the earlier seventeenth century, and thinks that 'the Amazons of classical authors tend to be glorious Figures' (p. 13).

[35] Biddle, *Virgil's bucolicks Englished. Whereunto is added the translation of the two first satyrs of Iuvenal* (London, 1634), sig. C5ʳ; Dryden, *The works of John Dryden*, vol. 4, A. B. Chambers *et al.* (ed.), *Poems 1693–1696* (California, 1974), p. 171, line 365. The Amazon is not in Juvenal's sixth satire.

destined to perpetuate the *gynarchy*. Accordingly, they people at a great rate, and with all the gravity imaginable'.[36]

Moreover, by choosing the name Thalestris, Pope evoked an Amazon whom Plutarch, Diodorus Siculus, and especially Quintus Curtius described as cupidinous in her meeting with Pope's partial namesake.[37]

The story of Thalestris' visit to Alexander the Great was often doubted and often told. When Alexander was camped in Hyrcania, Thalestris sent word that 'there was a Queen come to visit him, and desiring to be something more intimate'. She arrived with 300 women, saw Alexander, 'alighted, bearing two Lances in her hand', and commenced to examine his frame, bearing and excessively ornamented costume. Her disappointment in these baubles to the contrary, 'she was not asham'd to tell him, she came to be got with Child, and that she was not unworthy to be gratified after that manner; that if it was a Son, she would restore it to the Father, if a Girl, she'd keep it her self'. She then 'desir'd him not to frustrate her expectation; her desire to be satisfied was more vehement than the King's, so that thirteen days being consum'd in those Enjoyments, she return'd to her Kingdom'.[38]

---

[36] Danet, *A complete dictionary of the Greek and Roman antiquities*, 'Amazones'; Gautruche, *Nouvelle histoire poétique* (1671; Paris, 1725), p. 141 ('elles se livroient à de certains Hommes qu'elles prenoient au hazard'); Claude Marie Guyon, *Histoire des amazones anciennes et modernes* (1698; Paris, 1740), as translated in Johnson, n. 34 above, *The Gentleman's Magazine* 11 (1741), 203; Chesterfield, letter of 14 June (old style) 1750 to Madame du Boccage, as in his *Miscellaneous works*, Matthew Maty (ed.) (London, 1777), vol. 2, p. 242, letter 85; number 1710 in *The Letters of . . . Chesterfield*, Bonamy Dobrée (ed.) (London, 1932), vol. 4, 1555–8; p. 1556 quoted, in French. As these and other references suggest, Amazons were popular topics of discourse. For some others of the scholarly sort, see Joannes Columbus, *Disputatio de imperio amazonum* (Stockholm, 1678); Pierre Petit, *De Amazonibus dissertatio* (Paris, 1685), and Andreas Sundius, *De Patria amazonum* (Uppsala, 1716). These enjoyed other editions as well. Less learned, or patient, readers were aided by earlier works cited and by other translations and summaries like those of Pierre Petit's *Traité historique sur les amazones* (Paris, 1718), and [Joseph Towers'] useful *Dialogues concerning the ladies. To which is added an essay on the antient Amazons* (London, 1785). Literary performances include those by Antoine Houtar de la Motte, *Marthesie, premiere reine des amazones* (1699), Louis le Maingre de Bouciqualt, *Les Amazones revoltées* (Paris, 1730), and Madame Marie Anne le Page Fiquet du Boccage, *Les Amazones* (Paris, 1749).

[37] [Nahum Tate *et al.*] *The life of Alexander the Great. Written in Latin by Quintus Curtius Rufus, and translated into English by several gentlemen in the University of Cambridge* (London, 1690), pp. 193–4. This version includes the traditional Amazonian display of the left breast with a draped right breast 'burnt off, that they may with the greater facility, shoot Arrows or throw Darts' (p. 193). Such an image long was preserved, as in D. M., *Ancient Rome and Modern Britain compared. A dialogue, in Westminster Abbey, between Horace and Mr. Pope. A poem* (London, 1793), which may also explain Alexander's cool response to Thalestris. 'Pope' here says:

> Our fair to be victorious are subdued,
> But flying kill, and conquer when pursued.
> With Amazonian terror nods no crest,
> No dart is pointed from the mangled breast:
> That breast preserved, a readier death supplies,
> And all their darts are pointed from their eyes.   (p. 22)

[38] See Plutarch, *Alexander*, 46; Diodorus Siculus, *Bibliotheca historicae*, VIII, 17.77, 1–3; Quintus Curtius Rufus, *Historiarum Alexandri magni Macedonis*, VI, 5. 24–36. See also Marcus Junianus Justinus, epitome of Pompeius Trogus, *Historiae Phillipicae*, XII, 3. 5–7, and Strabo, *Geographia*, XI, 5. 3–4.

She also returned to the Restoration stage. In 1667 John Weston made her tale a bedroom, or camp tent, farce in *The Amazon Queen. Or, The Amours of Thalestris to Alexander the Great*. Thalestris, like any sensible Restoration wit, rejects Alexander's offer of marriage, and wants only one year's sexual companionship to get herself a girl-child; a useless boy will be delivered to his father. When she also stipulates that they be faithful to one another for that year, Alexander rejects such harsh terms, and they part, much to Thalestris' shame. As she says to Hippolyta, 'with my people great will be the stain, / That with this *Macedon* I have not lain' (p. 17). After she and sexually attracted Ptolemy later stab one another, they decide on more amiable combat, and she tells him – Alexander now out of sight out of mind – 'you shall do what you to me propound' (p. 48).

Thereafter, the Reverend Edward Young was of course looking for ammunition when he wrote his satire against women in 1725, but he would have struck responsive chords when he presented a crude, blunt and heretical Thalestris who 'justly gives the jealous husband pain' and proves that 'A Shameless woman is the worst of *Men*.'[39] Whatever the consequences for Restoration rakes or Dutch demographics, Amazonian relations between consenting adults were not thought likely steps to connubial bliss in the eighteenth century.

Nor is that bliss possible among the dead. In spite of formidable martial skills, in most representations of Amazon battles they lose. Visual evidence often shows women defeated by one source of their beauty. As Pope says of Belinda, 'Fair Tresses Man's Imperial Race insnare, / And Beauty draws us with a single Hair' (II, ll. 27–8). Numerous classical pots and friezes show a naked well-muscled male warrior drawn to an Amazon's long hair which he pulls in order to unhorse her, drag her to the ground, and more easily cut her extended throat, spear her elongated torso or club her taut body. This is the dreaded Amazonomachia, the literal war between the sexes that destroys the bodies designed to reproduce the beautiful men and women killing one another.[40]

[39] *Love of fame, the universal passion. In six characteristical satires*, 2nd ed. (London, 1728), p. 111.

[40] See William Blake Tyrell, *Amazons. A study in Athenian mythmaking* (Baltimore, 1984), pp. 56, 113, 128. For example, 'in classical Athens [Amazons] existed expressly to die each time they were seen in paintings or their name was spoken' (p. 113). Tyrell's is only one among the several recent studies of Amazons. The most extensive plates of classical Amazons are in Dietrich von Bothmer, *Amazons in Greek art*, Oxford Monographs on Classical Archaeology (Oxford, 1957), and especially *Lexicon iconographicum mythologia classicae* (Zurich and Munich, 1941), plates, I, ii, 440–532, and commentary by Pierre Devambe, I, i, 586–653, 653–662, especially 639–41. I count 33 plates in which Greek warriors fatally pull Amazons by the hair; there are several others in which they hold Amazons by the helmet or neck. In most cases, it is difficult to determine whether the woman's right breast has been removed or deaccentuated; but there are few such candidates, perhaps for Greek aesthetic purposes. For other Amazonian encounters in the visual arts, see illustrations for the *Histoire universelle* (c. 1223–30), in Hugo Buchtal, *Miniature paintings in the Latin kingdom of Jerusalem* (Oxford, 1957), pp. 68, 81–2, 86, 91–2, and plates 107 a, b, c, 108 a, b, c, 109 a, b, c, 113 a, c, 114 a, b, c (the last especially graphic), 116 a, b, c, and 121 c, 'Alexander the Great and the Queen of the Amazons'. See also two chronologically distant but brutally similar images: Pietro Buonaccorsi, called Perino del

There are, then, important implications in Pope's choice both of an Amazon and of this one among others. I hypothesize that she embodies and enlarges in one character both of Belinda's dangerous traits: her subdued aggression as seen in the card-game, where she is the challenging ombre who wishes to make a world in which she is superior; and her concomitant and conflicting sexual desires manifest in that game's suggestive skirmishes, her swelling breasts, the earthly lover lurking at her heart, and her ever-offered lock, about whose rape she is thrice warned. As a projection of much that is wrong but is attractive to Belinda, Thalestris is a powerful motivating voice which must have an equally powerful foil. That is one main reason why in 1717 Pope added Clarissa's speech, so that Belinda could have an authoritative, clear, and attractive guide away from the hostility of the epic and the ultimate defeat of the Amazon, and towards the sort of victory appropriate for her – if only she would listen. As we shall see, the problem becomes not one of sexual desire, but how to manage it in an acceptable way. Belinda is poised between virginity and marriage, and within this poem's values and Catholic context, she must choose adult marriage or choose wrongly.

Clarissa: 'to open more clearly the moral of the poem'

So optimistic a view of Clarissa's speech, however, is foreign to what has been called the recent 'open season against her'.[41] If she is a norm, the argument goes, why does she become the baron's instrument and arm him for the fight as a lady does her knight in romance (III, ll. 125–30)? Either she is out of touch with Belinda's real needs, or wishes to have the baron for herself and is trying to hurt Belinda. I do not find these objections persuasive. For one thing, a woman arming a knight need not denote romantic exchange. As Spenser's 'Letter of the Authors' makes plain, in the *Faerie Queene* Una arms the 'clownish' Red Crosse when she still thinks him a country bumpkin unfit for the task, and at first accepts him 'much gaine-saying'. Moreover, whether Clarissa, the scissors, or both are the instruments of ill (III, l. 126) does not mean that Clarissa's rather than the baron's motivation was bad; bad action can have a good end if properly controlled. In addition, since the ploy is called one of the 'New Stratagems' (III, l. 120) that rise in the baron's nominal mind as the steam rises from his coffee, he and Clarissa could hardly have had time to

Vaga (1501–47), *The battle of the Amazons*, in *Roman drawings of the sixteenth century from the Musée du Louvre Paris* (Chicago, 1979), pp. 98–9; and Max Beckmann's *Amazonenschlacht* (1911), as reproduced in *Max Beckmann. Katalog der Gemälde*, Erhard and Barbara Göpel (eds.) (Bern, 1976), I, pp. 108–9, catalogue number 146, and II: plate 57.

Amazons in Roman history have recently been studied by Giampiera Arrigoni, 'Amazzoni alla Romana', *Rivista Storica Italiana* 96 (1984), 871–919. T. Sturge Moore's fine *The rout of the Amazons* (London, 1903) treats the Amazon with elegiac respect. It is a poem worth reclaiming.

[41] The term is from *The Scriblerian* 17 (1985), 134, describing recent critical attitudes in general and the approach of C. N. Manlove (n. 2 above) in particular.

hatch a plot – though there is time to get caught up in an adolescent flirtation. Nor is it likely that Clarissa would help herself with the baron by urging Belinda to marry him. Such contradictions either are illogical or too complex for the simple characterization in *The Rape of the Lock*. Finally, Pope, Warburton, or both forgot that Clarissa had given the baron a scissors, for in the 1751 edition she is called '*A new Character introduced in the subsequent Editions to open more clearly the MORAL of the Poem*' (*TE* II, p. 199n). I thus suspect, on the one hand, that the earlier action need not bear too heavy a burden, and, on the other, that Clarissa's name was too apt not to be used for demonstrable wisdom.

If that earlier action is a magnet for interpretation, it probably should be seen not as a rival's mischief, but as a friend's kindness. Solid Clarissa knows what the airy sylphs must learn – that the baron and Belinda are appropriate suitors; as an ally she hopes to bring them together by joining an apparently harmless trick. As Ralph Cohen put it before Clarissa's eclipse, 'her sophisticated approach to adaptation is apparent when she assists the Baron in the rape though she has clearly not anticipated the consequences that follow this action. She sought to satisfy the wish in Belinda's heart, but did not calculate upon the gulf between form and frankness.'[42] Since the lock nonetheless must be regained, though, how better to do so than by such sane adaptation, by, say, inviting its wicked ravisher to return it at tea, then at supper, then at a ball, and then at the nuptials consequent upon so many visits to so good-humoured a belle? Clarissa's error is not in providing the scissors, but in overestimating her rhetorical powers and Belinda's ability to accept her guidance. Instead, she too is carried away in Thalestris' call to arms and is trapped in the modern Amazonomachia, one nonetheless dramatically softened from the horrors of ancient warfare. Whatever Pope's achievement with Clarissa's speech, however, he made clear his often overlooked intention. John Dennis' severe 'Remarks on Mr Pope's *Rape of the Lock*' (1728) observe that in the *Lutrin* Boileau, unlike Pope, 'seems to have given broad Hints at what was his real Meaning'. Pope writes this refutation in the margin – 'Clarissa's Speach'.[43]

As the bearer of that meaning, she receives praise, is graceful, given the honorific 'Dame' (v, l. 35), and has the presence immediately to silence the noisy reproaches around her with the simple wave of her fan (v, ll. 7–8). She also enjoys the narrator's implicit support. Like him, she wishes for a peaceful marriage contract between the combatants; her 'trust me, Dear' (v, l. 31) is echoed in the narrator's own 'trust the Muse' (v, l. 123) as he relates the

---

[42] 'Transformation in *The Rape of the Lock*', *Eighteenth-Century Studies*, 2 (1969), 216. This essay is among the most valuable discussions of the poem.

[43] Geoffrey Tillotson transcribes this and other comments in *TE*, II, p. 395. The analogy with Clarissa's speech is the more telling if, as seems likely, Pope was thinking of Boileau's Canto VI, in which Piété offers a long address that re-establishes theological and clerical order. For a useful discussion of *Le Lutrin* and its moral seriousness, see J. Douglas Canfield, 'The unity of Boileau's *Le Lutrin*: the counter-effect of the mock-heroic', *Philological Quarterly* 53 (1974), 42–58.

apotheosis of the lock; her advice to accept the human situation and the transience of female beauty is reiterated in the narrator's knowledge that Belinda's own 'fair Suns' must set, and that 'all those Tresses shall be laid in Dust' (v, ll. 147–8); her consequent awareness that Belinda must check pride in her beauty (v, ll. 33–4) reinforces the narrator's hope that the beautiful woman will have 'Sweetness void of Pride' (ii, l. 15); and her recommendation of the healing, enticing value of good humour (v, ll. 31–4) and the plea to have 'good Sense preserve what Beauty gains' (v, l. 16) draw on Pope's own introductory letter to Arabella Fermor. He tells her that this poem 'was intended only to divert a few young Ladies, who have good Sense and good humour enough to laugh' both at their own and their sex's follies (p. 142).[44] Clarissa's muted retort also is the final address, is the same length as Thalestris', and is a counter to it. If Belinda is to become an adult, she must have demonstrable options on which to exercise her freedom of choice.

Belinda thus hears an alternative to Amazonian values, and we thus see Pope sharing his moral authority with the clarifying woman who enriches his poem and his narrator's judgment. That narrator regards Belinda as an adored object whose beautiful face makes him forget her flaws (ii, ll. 16–18). Sisterly Clarissa speaks of mature prudence, subtly alerts Belinda to the consequences of attracting and rejecting men, and characterizes the enlarging world still available 'what'er we lose' (v, l. 30). She also adds a hitherto absent didactic tone in her nine probing questions and their spoken or unspoken answers within twenty-six lines. By so doing, she briefly changes the poem's focus from potentially destructive male worship of beauty, to the more important potentially constructive female use of beauty. Thereafter her verbal presence gives the narrator's post-battle peroration the united force of male and female human wisdom, so that both sylph and gnome are excluded from the poem's final paragraph infused with Clarissa's power. The narrator gains as much authority from Clarissa as she gains from the narrator.

That authority begins with Sarpedon's speech to Glaucus in the *Iliad*, xii, ll. 371–96. This speech was one of Pope's favourites, long was regarded as a paradigm of aristocratic responsibility, and was singled out by Madame Dacier and Pope as wisdom worthy of the gods.[45] Sarpedon is introduced with

---

[44] The shared values of the narrator and Clarissa have been noted by William F. Cunningham, Jr., in 'The narrator of *The Rape of the Lock*', in John H. Dorenkamp (ed.), *Literary studies: essays in memory of Francis A. Drumm* (Boston, 1973), pp. 139–40, and Sheila Delaney, 'Sexual politics in Pope's *Rape of the Lock*', in *Weapons of criticism*, p. 188 (n. 2 above).

[45] For Madame Dacier, see *L'Iliade d'Homère traduite en François, avec des remarques* (Paris, 1711), 2, pp. 241–3 for her translation, and 2, pp. 538–9 for her 'Remarques', which observe that Homer has given this extraordinary wisdom 'au fils de Jupiter'. For Pope, see *TE* viii, p. 263n; *Iliad* xii, l. 387n. George Chapman long ago had glossed this speech as '*never equalled by any (in this kind) of all that have written*' (*The whole works of Homer, prince of poets* [London, 1614], 1, p. 165. For objections to Clarissa's speech as a positive adaptation of Sarpedon, see Robert W. Williams (n. 30 above), 'Fate and . . . narrative', pp. 36–9. He also objects that Clarissa cannot be a norm because her counsel relates only to the values of this world of men rather than of God. My discussion of 'use' below may help to remove her from the index.

pomp, so that we will expect greatness from him (*TE* VIII, p. 94n; *Iliad*, XII); by birth he is the superior of all combatants on either side, and thus unlike them has 'the Manners of' a perfect hero and deserves 'universal Esteem' because of his superior merit (*TE* VIII, p. 263n; *Iliad*, XVI, 512n. See also *TE* VIII, p. 268n; *Iliad*, XVI, l. 605n). Before going into battle against the Greeks, Sarpedon tells his cousin that they are honoured as gods in Lycia, given land, privilege, 'foaming Bowls' and feasts enhanced by music. They must deserve such dignities through princely conduct – here, by embracing an ethic in which they either give or take martial glory. Everyone must die, and princes should 'give to Fame what we to Nature owe' (*TE* VIII, p. 96; *Iliad*, XII, l. 394) before age diminishes the nobility of their sacrifice. On this scheme, the leader repays the debt of national homage with his own or his enemy's life in battle. The advice indeed is godlike, for when this son of Zeus and Laodemia was finally slain by Patroclus, Zeus commanded Apollo to preserve his body from Greek desecration and cleanse, anoint, and transport it to an honoured place in Lycia. Glaucus, on the other hand, though also noble, is not so well connected or clever as his relation. When opposed to his family's former guest Diomedes, they refuse to fight and instead exchange compliments and gifts of armour. Since Glaucus' was gold and Diomedes' bronze, the Greek outsmarted the Lycian who, as in *Iliad*, VI, ll. 288–95 (*TE* VII, pp. 340–1), evoked the expression 'gold for bronze' as an emblem of an uneven trade.[46] With these two names as announced backdrop, Pope can suggest that Clarissa's advice both has epic and divine roots, and is offered to someone of lesser wit.

Such divinity, however, was not untarnished, and as with several matters Homeric was subject to reconsideration. In Book II of *Paradise Lost* Milton uses Sarpedon's speech on Satan's behalf. Like Sarpedon, he must reciprocate the splendour and power which adorn and arm his throne (II, ll. 446–73) and repay 'These Royalties' by accepting 'Of hazard more' – that is, take upon himself the fight against humankind (II, ll. 445–6). This successful ploy, Milton's narrator tells us, is but a 'god-like imitated State' and part of the vain wisdom and false philosophy endemic to Hell (II, ll. 511, 565). Shortly thereafter, the Père d'Aubignac deflates Sarpedon's speech by insisting that its emphasis on plentiful food and drink 'n'est pas capable d'émouvoir des goinfres et des pauvres misérables' (p. 117). Sarpedon's speech, then, was noble but potentially flawed and irrelevant for non-Amazonian women.

---

[46] Burnet and Duckett offer a nasty, and familiar, version of the exchange between Diomedes and Glaucus:

> . . . *Saturn*'s Son in the mean Season,
> From *Glaucus* stole away his Reason,
> Who changed with *Diomede* (O Ass!)
> His Arms of Gold for his of Brass;
> And Armour worth a Hundred Cows,
> For one not worth a Hundred Sows.
>
> (p. 29, italics and roman type reversed)

Clarissa meets the challenge of respecting and transcending her source, of avoiding duplicity and sensuality while insisting upon the obligations of those in power, and of turning noble death into useful life.

Unlike both Belinda and Thalestris, Clarissa rejects vanity and suffering presumed pain merely to be worshipped from without while being hollow within. Instead, since she alone of the three women speakers is not tainted by the Cave of Spleen, she can introduce two essential terms foreign to her colleagues – internal good sense and virtue to balance external appearance:

> How vain are all these Glories, all our Pains,
> Unless good Sense preserve what Beauty gains:
> That Men may say, when we the Front-box grace,
> Behold the first in Virtue, as in Face![47]   (v, ll. 15–18)

She also introduces concepts that answer the social bankruptcy of Belinda and Thalestris. Woman is not to be degraded by Belinda's own image of herself as a vegetating flower dignified only by its beauty. Instead, she must learn and accept the extensive housewife's cares, for if mere dancing and dressing kept away defacing illness and the wrinkles of age, 'who would learn one earthly thing of Use?' (v, l. 22). *Use* is more than utilitarian; it is both related to the parable of the talents and to the medieval *usufructus* that Pope advocates in later satires on the use of riches, where land and wealth are God's temporary gifts to one in service to many. ''Tis Use alone that sanctifies expense' (l. 179), Pope tells Burlington in 1731 in the *Epistle to Burlington*. As Swift also told his congregation, God made 'all the Works of Nature to be useful, and in some Manner a Support to each other' in order to solidify 'the whole Frame of the World'. One's advantages thus are not personal property but 'only a Trust . . . lent him for the Service of others'.[48] As such a steward, the girl whom both Belinda and Thalestris characterize as acted upon can become a vigorous woman who in winning her battle of the sexes improves herself and her presumed combatant. She cannot negotiate this enlarging pre-nuptial rite of passage if she becomes an Amazon literally or figuratively destructive of life

---

[47] In rejecting Clarissa's wisdom regarding the transience of beauty, Belinda shows herself unrepresentative of the beautiful woman's psychology as exemplified in Helen. '*Should* Venus *leave thee, ev'ry Charm must fly*' shows the expected result: 'This was the most dreadful of all Threats, Loss of Beauty and of Reputation. *Helen* who had been Proof to the personal Appearance of the Goddess, and durst even reproach her with Bitterness just before, yields to this, and obeys all the Dictates of Love' (*TE* vii, p. 216n; *Iliad* iii, l. 515). Clarissa, on the other hand, offers human alternatives to the loss of beauty.

[48] The line is quoted from *Epistles to Several Persons*, *TE* iii, i, p. 154. Bishop William Warburton commented on the sacred contexts of *use* in this line. See his edition of *The works of Alexander Pope Esq.* (London, 1751), vol. 3, p. 291n. For Swift's undated sermon 'On mutual subjection', see Herbert Davis and Louis Landa (eds.), *Jonathan Swift. Irish tracts 1720–1723 and sermons* (Oxford, 1963), pp. 142, 144. Earl R. Wasserman comments on such stewardship in Pope's *Epistle to Bathurst. A critical reading with an edition of the manuscripts* (Baltimore, 1960), p. 27.

or of heterosexual community. As Clarissa bluntly states, 'she who scorns a Man, must die a Maid' (v, l. 28). Therefore,

> What then remains, but well our Pow'r to use,
> And keep good Humour still whate'er we lose?
> And trust me, Dear! good Humour can prevail,
> When Airs, and Flights, and Screams, and Scolding fail.
> Beauties in vain their pretty Eyes may roll;
> Charms strike the Sight, but Merit wins the Soul.　　　(v, ll. 29–34)

With such an ethic, Belinda need not be a bottle calling for a cork, nor the baron a dim-witted peer whose chief attraction is his title; she becomes a woman of merit, and he a man of soul. If Belinda accepts this counsel of metamorphosis, she can regain her lock and earn an equal share in the consequent human family unavailable to unseen and untouched roses.

That floral image, in fact, suggests one further function of Clarissa's potential prothalamion. We recall that the card-queens in Belinda's hand held a 'Flow'r, / Th' expressive Emblem of their Softer Pow'r' (iii, l. 40) – that is, the flower as traditional symbol of virginity. 'If thou beest yet a fresh uncropped flower, / Choose thou thy husband, and I'll pay thy dower', the King of France says to Diane in *All's Well that Ends Well* (v, iii, ll. 327–8). If Belinda is an unseen, unplucked rose, often thought the 'Flower of Love',[49] and dies in the desert, she abandons her ultimate weapon in the battle of the sexes, whose peace conference is the marriage bed. Pope's poem is profoundly 'traditional' in its insistence on courtship and marriage; it is profoundly, perhaps cynically, 'realistic' in its knowledge of the modern sexual barter that replaces ancient sexual rape.

Addison's *Spectator*, no. 128, 27 July 1711, offers an appropriate gloss for 'good humour', and its meaning in *The Rape of the Lock*. He observes that 'Men and Women were made as Counterparts to one another, that the Pains and Anxieties of the Husband might be relieved by the Sprightliness and good Humour of the Wife. When these are rightly tempered, Care and Chearfulness go Hand in Hand; and the Family, like a Ship that is duly trimmed, wants neither Sail nor Ballast,' each being equally important for smooth sailing. Accordingly, the sexes are fulfilled by one another, and 'Their Virtues are blended in their Children, and diffuse through the whole Family a perpetual Spirit of Benevolence, Complacency, and Satisfaction.' 'A Man must be a

---

[49] See Samuel Wesley, *Poems on several occasions* (London, 1736), p. 113, 'On the Rose; from Anacreon'. That flower is 'Dear to *Venus* and her Boy' (p. 112). See also *Midsummer Night's Dream* i, i, 69–78, where Theseus tells Hermia that those who master their blood as nuns are 'Thrice blessed', though 'earthlier happy is the rose distill'd / Than that which, withering on the virgin thorn, / Grows, lives, and dies in single blessedness' (ll. 76–8). Arthur W. Hoffman has found several of Pope's allusions to Spenser's *Epithalamion* and, especially, *Prothalamion*. See Hoffman's 'Spenser and *The Rape of the Lock*', *Philological Quarterly* 49 (1970), 530–46.

Savage', John Hughes adds on 15 February 1712 (no. 302), not to be improved
and humanized by the good humour of such a woman.[50]

Clarissa's speech, then, is indeed the moral centre of *The Rape of the Lock*. It
rejects spleen, girlhood, hostility, isolation, powerlessness, inutility, folly and
frustration in favour of good humour, womanliness, affection, community,
power, use and virtue. More's the pity that when Belinda now has her own
choice of Hercules the sign on her cross-road points towards Thalestris and the
Amazonomachia this poem was designed to avoid. Belinda rejects Clarissa as
'To Arms, to Arms! the fierce Virago cries, / And swift as Lightning to the
Combate flies' (v, ll. 37–8). The lightning of attraction in Belinda's eyes in
Canto I has become the lightning of destruction in Canto v. Hence once
Clarissa's wisdom is rejected, the repressed sexual and physical combat of the
card-table is acted out in appropriately diminished but serious form – as
wounds, looks, snuff and bodkins harm the combatant while the delighted
gnomes, mimicking the Homeric gods, watch or join the battle. The un-
leashing of sexual tensions is as clear:

> See fierce *Belinda* on the *Baron* flies,
> With more than usual Lightning in her Eyes;
> Nor fear'd the Chief th' unequal Fight to try,
> Who sought no more than on his Foe to die.   (v, ll. 75–8)

From 1714 on several critics, and perhaps Arabella Fermor herself, complained of the poem's indecencies. In 1728 William Bond berated 'this *Chaste
Performance*' and angrily said – 'Every Body knows what, *Dying upon a fair Lady*
means.'[51] Pope's narrator, though, was not angry, for unlike Belinda he shares

---

[50] Donald F. Bond (ed.), *The Spectator* (Oxford, 1965), 2, pp. 9, 11 (No. 128), and 3, pp. 80, 82.
Pope's 'Epistle to Miss Blount; with the Works of Voiture' (1712) also praises good humour in
the woman. Somewhat later, Samuel Wesley also used a comparable image to suggest a
well-balanced woman. He says in 'To Kitty, a Poetical Young Lady' that

> What tho' her Wit should never fail?
> How few will long endure her?
> The Ship that Ballast wants by Sail
> Is overset the surer.

> *Poems on several occasions*, p. 297 (see note 49).

As Mary Astell long had made plain, good humour also was a desirable male trait in the
perennial mating dance. Women are more constant in love than men, she says, 'For not usually
fixing our Affection on so mutable a thing as the *Beauty* of a *Face*, which a Thousand accidents
may destroy, but on *Wit, Good Humour*, and other *Graces* of the *Mind*, as well as of the *Body*, our
Love is more durable, and constant in proportion to the longer continuance of those Qualities
in the Object' (*An essay in defence of the female sex* [London, 1696], pp. 129–30). Like eighteenth-
century commentators, Astell is concerned with not violating '*Modesty* and *Decorum* at the price
of our Fame and Reputation' (p. 130). Astell discusses Amazons, and a possible reason for their
growth as a nation, on p. 24.

[51] H. Stanhope [William Bond], *The progress of dulness. By an eminent hand. Which will serve for an
explanation of the Dunciad* (London, 1728), p. 29. For comparable observations, see John Dennis,
'Remarks on Mr. Pope's *Rape of the Lock*', *Critical works*, 2, p. 347; James Ralph, *Sawney. An heroic
poem. Occasion'd by the Dunciad. Together with a critique of that poem address'd to Mr. T---d, Mr.*

and augments Clarissa's advice regarding the pacification of sexual death. Commentators on the narrator's role have wisely emphasized his direct but affectionate correction of Belinda, and shown how he urges her not to seek untouched permanence in life, but in mythology or art – namely, his own poem. They have not, however, fully appreciated the implications of his allusion to Catullus, known both as an erotic poet and as the celebrant of sexuality in marriage. When Belinda's lock is metamorphosed to a comet, 'Not *Berenice*'s Locks first rose so bright, / The Heav'ns bespangling with dishevell'd Light' (v, ll. 129–30). In the 'Coma Berenices' Berenice promises Aphrodite to sacrifice her abundant hair if her husband Ptolemy returns safely from the wars. When he does, she places her luxuriance upon an altar in Aphrodite's temple, and later is told that the vanished hair became a constellation as a sign of divine approval for such wifely behaviour. Berenice is a helpful *deus ex machina*, a forerunner of Clarissa's wisdom, and another anti-Amazonian model of generosity for Belinda.[52]

That allusion is indeed a fit way to end a discussion of *The Rape of the Lock*, composed during the period when Pope in his young manhood was writing his own 'marriage group' or courtship poems. Catullus reminds us of Pope's inheritance of retreat from pleasure in epic warfare and its butchering heroes and unreliable malevolent gods, and both the gods' and heroes' insufficiently controlled sexuality. It also recalls two other major points – Pope's fidelity to the essence of the poem's superceded occasion, his desire to join two neighbouring aristocratic Catholic families in marriage, and his insistence that for

M.---*r, Mr. Eu*---*n, & c.* (London, 1728), p. 19. The line also has two other possible contexts. Rape was associated with the Amazon myth, especially with Theseus, who raped either an unnamed Amazon, or Antiope, Hippolyte, Melanippe, or Glance. See Tyrell, *Amazons*, pp. 3–6, 91–2, (n. 40 above). Moreover, as Pope, following Eustathius, says about the *Iliad*, VIII, p. 343n, 'nothing was more common than for Heroes of old to take their Female Captives to their Beds; . . . such Captives were then given for a Reward of Valour, and as a Matter of Glory' (*TE* VII, p. 413n).

---

[52] For another point of view regarding Berenice, see Eric Rothstein, *The Routledge history of English poetry*, vol. 3, *Restoration and eighteenth-century poetry 1660–1780* (London, 1981), p: 26. Claudius Aelian records another wifely, civilizing, function of Berenice, who refused to allow Ptolemy to play dice when he was deciding which men should be condemned to death. See *Claudius Aelianus his various history*, trans. Thomas Stanley (n. 13 above), xiv, p. 43. Pope himself mentions Berenice's hair and some symbolic values of cut hair in *Iliad* xviii, p. 566n (*TE*, viii, p. 349n) and *Iliad* xxiii, 166n (*TE*, viii, pp. 495–6n). For a fuller English version of the Berenice story, see the translation of Jean de la Chapelle's *The adventures of Catullus, and history of his amours with Lesbia. Intermixt with translations of his choicest poems. By several hands* (London, 1707), especially pp. 256–64; there are several verbal parallels with Pope's *Rape of the Lock*. The first French edition appeared in 1680–1, the fifth in 1725. For other erotic Catullan suggestions see the unsigned *Basia: or the charms of kissing. Translated from the Latin of Catullus and Secundus, and the Greek of Menage*, 2nd ed. (London, 1719). James A. S. McPeek observes that 'nearly all the significant French and English epithalamies . . . conform unexceptionally to the Catullan tradition': *Catullus in strange and distant Britain*, Harvard Studies in Comparative Literature, vol. 15 (Cambridge, Massachusetts, 1939), p. 236. See pp. 103–43, especially 140–3, for Pope, and pp. 144–236 for relevant texts. The 'Coma Berenices' is well edited as number 66 in D. F. S. Thomson, *Catullus. A critical edition* (North Carolina, 1978).

all the comedy in their diminished world, their little events have serious implications, and can improve upon Homeric values. We find such improvement most notably in Clarissa and her friend the narrator – and not in the Amazon who maims infants, women, men, and the blending of virtues Addison saw as the consequence of the good-humoured wife and the balanced marriage. Clarissa surpasses the ethics of Sarpedon who probably would have shown even less interest in Thalestris than the reluctant Alexander the Great. If Sarpedon so reacted, he again would have endeared himself to the other great Alexander whose comment upon Paris' and Helen's reconciliation in Book III of the *Iliad* epitomizes his attitude in *The Rape of the Lock*: 'since both the Sexes have their Frailties, it would be well for each to forgive the other' (*TE* VII, p. 218n; *Iliad*, III, l. 551).

PART TWO
Pope and Women

3

'Dipt in the rainbow'
Pope on women

FELICITY ROSSLYN

Satire is, notoriously, the most double of genres. The poet's conscious mind is so fully taken up with his moral purpose that his subconscious seems free to ramble off to what ambiguous regions it will. And usually the regions it chooses are those where moral distinctions are bereft of meaning, where the enemy extends the satirist a hearty welcome as '*Mon semblable, mon frère*', and nothing is, but what is not. Thus we have learned to read the subtext of *The Dunciad*, for instance, with as much attention as the text itself, and to feel the deep seduction of Dulness while deploring her power. Pope, we acknowledge, is too rich in meanings to confine himself to one at a time.

Perhaps we should approach the *Epistle to a Lady* ('Of the Characters of Women') with the same alertness, for there is no subject on which either sex is so prone to double meanings as on the other half of the species. As often as not, the allegations women make against men illustrate their own anxieties, and turn on the uncomfortable paradox that men are impossible, but – necessary; and men's charges against women tell us chiefly about the difficulty of being male, and how much easier this would have been, had the creator seen fit to make women more like – well, men. Neither sex can get away from the importunate fact that it takes one of each to perpetuate the species, and neither can be wholly reconciled to it; it is the last subject in the world on which testimony can be disinterested.

All this makes it likely that Pope's satire on women is very double indeed, with the doubleness of male testimony in addition to the natural doubleness of satire. And the suspicion is surely well placed, for the *Epistle to a Lady* is the only one of the four 'Moral Essays' which reverberates in the mind long after reading, and gives the impression of meaning more than it says. Its reputation among critics continues to rise, and few readers finish it without feeling at the end a glow of triumph on the author's part, and a resolution of his creative energies, that has little to do with the ostensible subject. If the vagaries of society ladies are a richly ambiguous subject for Pope, where has his subconscious mind rambled in the course of the poem? What double meanings are supporting its delightful poise?

If we cast around for a new mode of entry to this satire, we may find a suggestive starting place in this fact: that it was in the guise of wayward, fugitive beauties that the young Pope first glimpsed his Muses. He represents himself in a letter to Cromwell as their frustrated admirer:

Those Aeriall Ladies just discover to me enough of their Beauties to urge my Pursuit, and draw me on in a wandring Maze of Thought, still in hopes (and only in hopes) of attaining those favors from 'em, which they confer on their more happy admirers elsewhere.

These 'Aeriall Ladies' are never to be won and held because they are the free play of the artist's own imagination:

We grasp some more beautifull Idea in our Brain, than our Endeavors to express it can set to the view of others; and still do but labour to fall short of our first Imagination. The gay Colouring which Fancy gave to our Design at the first transient glance we had of it, goes off in the Execution; like those various Figures in the gilded Clouds, which while we gaze long upon, to seperate [sic] the parts of each imaginary Image, the whole faints before the Eye, and decays into Confusion.[1]

Pope brings together a knot of ideas here about women, fancy, art, colours and clouds that we can trace in his poetry throughout his career;[2] and if we probe beneath the conscious gallantry, perhaps we can uncover why. To write poetry, for Pope, is to wander forever in pursuit of erotic but coy beauties, whose elusiveness is not affectation, but a law of the mind itself. Setting 'a beautifull Idea . . . to the view of others' requires the use of colour and line, his labour as an artist; but the true perfection of the idea is only to be glimpsed in the 'first transient glance', when the 'gay Colouring which Fancy gave' is yet unspoiled. It inevitably 'goes off in the Execution', just as 'each imaginary Image' we make out in the 'gilded Clouds' disappears at the very moment we distinguish it: there is a perverse law at work by which effort avails nothing, and the ephemeral subject the artist pursues is most itself when it escapes him. It is really the eternal quarrel between Apollo and Dionysus Pope is uncovering here, which he cannot hope to resolve any more than his forebears. The Apollonian art of the artist is perpetually striving to fix what cannot be fixed: the Dionysiac flux of life, never to be repeated or called back, and exquisitely beautiful in proportion to its transience.

   This association of ideas by which Pope sees the essential difficulty of art in terms of pursuing evanescent, airy ladies, sheds interesting new light on all the other 'Aeriall Ladies' that animate his poetry. It reminds us how often he takes femininity for his subject, seeking out the very quality that most rebuffs his art; and it makes it highly unlikely that in the *Epistle to a Lady*, the vagaries of women are a subject for mere satire. Although he pretends to deplore lightness and ephemerality, we can see from the quality of art they draw out of him how thoroughly he responds to their challenge. His portrait of Belinda's guardian

---

[1] *Correspondence* I, p. 135.
[2] For a full account, see T. R. Edwards, 'The colors of Fancy: an image cluster in Pope', *Modern Language Notes*, 53 (1958), 485–9.

sylphs hovering and playing over the Thames is a tribute to airiness that could not be improved upon:

> Some to the Sun their Insect-Wings unfold,
> Waft on the Breeze, or sink in Clouds of Gold.
> Transparent Forms. too fine for mortal Sight,
> Their fluid Bodies half dissolv'd in Light.
> Loose to the Wind their airy Garments flew,
> Thin glitt'ring Textures of the filmy Dew;
> Dipt in the richest Tincture of the Skies,
> Where Light disports in ever-mingling Dies,
> While ev'ry Beam new transient Colours flings,
> Colours that change whene'er they wave their Wings.[3]

These evanescent sylphs are ostensibly, of course, an embodiment of the classic adage, *varium et mutabile semper femina*. But they cannot be only that, for a sense of wonder and something very like love are eliciting the quality of this art. Like the sylphs themselves, the poetry waves, plays, coruscates, comes and goes; it is tangible and transparent, sense and nonsense, altogether 'too fine for mortal Sight' to perceive. Its peculiar triumph is the way it resolves the dilemma Pope described in his letter, by which the Fancy gives a 'gay Colouring' that fades the moment the artist tries to reproduce it, and the figures in the gilded clouds 'decay into Confusion' before his gaze. The Apollonian, ordered couplet accords these sylphs their full nature, which is pure ephemerality. It catches them in their Dionysiac passage, not as dead lepidoptera, but in the very act of unfolding their insect-wings and sinking in clouds of gold. They are still rainbow-hued with life; indeed, 'Dipt in the richest Tincture of the Skies, / Where Light disports in ever-mingling Dies', they become an animated rainbow, which lives only in the moment, has no discoverable location, and is essentially an optical illusion. But just as a rainbow is the effect of light intersecting with raindrops, so these sylphs are the effect of art and fancy encountering in a very pure form. In themselves they are the extremest reach of fancy; and the capturing of them, coruscating and unharmed, is the extremest reach of Pope's art.

This train of thought makes unexpected sense of what might otherwise seem a merely conventional device in the *Epistle to a Lady*: the pretended tour of a portrait gallery with which it opens, and the consequent remarks on the difficulties of painting women. As Pope marvels at their easy transitions from a Countess to Pastora, or Magdalen to St Cecilia, his mind seems to be at least as much on his own art as on the women themselves; and his mock despair as he prepares himself for the test derives from the same knot of feelings he once

---

[3] *The Rape of the Lock* II, ll. 59–68. For a different view of the relation of the sylphs to fancy, see D. Fairer, 'Imagination in *The Rape of the Lock*', *Essays in Criticism*, 29 (1979), 53–74. A revised version appears in Fairer's book, *Pope's imagination* (Manchester, 1984), pp. 53–81. Both Fairer and Edwards (note 2) read 'fancy' in the sense of 'delusion'; which (if the truest poetry is the most feigning) seems unnecessarily narrow.

described to Cromwell. Several decades later, the same images of air and clouds and colours and rainbows recur as when he drew his Muses and the sylphs:

> Come then, the colours and the ground prepare!
> Dip in the Rainbow, trick her off in Air,
> Chuse a firm Cloud, before it fall, and in it
> Catch, ere she change, the Cynthia of this minute.
>
> (*Epistle to a Lady*, ll. 17–20)

Cynthia, goddess of the changeable moon, is only to be caught in passing, 'this minute', and only nature's evanescent colours and textures suffice for the portrait. The artist is forced to 'Dip' her 'in the Rainbow', sketch her in air, and catch her on 'a firm Cloud, before it fall': she is a perfect rebuff to his Apollonian art, with its reliance on line and definition – as he meditates himself, after attempting a few portraits in this mode:

> Pictures like these, dear Madam, to design,
> Asks no firm hand, and no unerring line;
> Some wand'ring touch, or some reflected light,
> Some flying stroke alone can hit 'em right:
> For how should equal Colours do the knack?
> Chameleons who can paint in white and black?   (ll. 151–6)

His moral and aesthetic convictions, of course, are strongly on the side of the 'firm hand', 'unerring line', and 'equal [i.e. unmixed] Colours'. But the poetry itself speaks for the Turneresque charm of the evanescence it deplores, and allows us to see how little the artist would really wish to be confined to 'white and black'. 'Chameleons' teach him to mingle his colours as they are mingled in nature, and when he is robbed of his firm 'line', there is nothing for it but to 'snatch a Grace beyond the reach of Art' – since 'Some flying stroke alone can hit 'em right.' We see that the poet, by way of counter-testimony, is doing the very thing the artist is deprecating: he is catching his subject by the lightest and most indirect means, borrowing the tone of the chatty society painter, and asking amused, rhetorical questions. He does not even exclude vulgarity where it can add life: 'do the knack' was a startling expression in its day; and here, as often in the rest of the satire, we are forced to say that the message of the poem is sabotaged by the style itself. While the artist pretends to despair of his assignment, the poet tosses his caesuras about with fine abandon, and effectually pillows, on a feminine rhyme, his elusive subject:

> Chuse a firm Cloud, before it fall, and in it
> Catch, ere she change, the Cynthia of this minute.

If Pope's mind is indeed on the challenge to his art as well as on women, we can understand why he gives the impression of cherishing what his satire dismisses, and being unwilling to quit the subject in haste. He is not the man to avoid the hardest challenge: his genius, 'in its widest searches still longing to go forward, in its highest flights still wishing to be higher', as Johnson says, is attracted precisely by the difficulties that women, as a subject, present him. Not only do they require to be 'dipt in the rainbow' for their colouring; more radically yet, they throw off the single most consistent tendency of his couplet, which is to convey a meaning. Who would dare deduce a meaning from the butterfly Papillia?

> Papillia, wedded to her doating spark,
> Sighs for the shades – 'How charming is a Park!'
> A Park is purchas'd, but the Fair he sees
> All bath'd in tears – 'Oh odious, odious Trees!'   (ll. 37–40)

When silliness reaches flood-level, the 'nice admirer' knows better than to protest. He gives in, and is as 'taken' by her folly as he would be by the equally meaningless variegations on a prize bloom:

> Ladies, like variegated Tulips, show,
> 'Tis to their Changes that their charms they owe;
> Their happy Spots the nice admirer take,
> Fine by defect, and delicately weak.   (ll. 41–4)

The humour seems light enough; but the real depth of irony in a phrase like 'happy Spots' can only be gauged if we also remember how, at its first drafting, this satire was intended to find its place in that highest flight of Pope's restless intelligence, his project 'to reform the mind' through poetry.[4] The *magnum opus* he planned in the 1730s marked the distinct kinship of part of Pope's genius with Jeremy Bentham's; it set out to describe mankind in its intellectual, social, political, religious and ethical relations, with 'all the great Principles of true and false Governments and Religions' displayed, and a 'Satyr against the misapplication of Wit and Learning' for good measure;[5] and the vaulting ambition it reveals to educate humanity once and for all, cries out for the kind of corrective that Papillia the butterfly administers. It reminds us how there would be something very like tyranny in the comprehensive structures Pope aimed to build for his civilization, if they were not constantly undermined by something else: an instinctive reverence for what those structures could get no hold on; and Papillia's helpless tears here dissolve that coercive meaning to a saving meaninglessness, such as the author of *In Praise of Folly* (if not Bentham) might have smiled to see. Among all the layers of irony in Pope's admiration of Papillia's 'happy Spots' are some that apply to the poet himself; and his gay mimicry of her 'odious, odious Trees!' is one of the reasons why his *magnum opus* never did get written.

In this context, Pope's own explanation for lingering so long on female follies has a suggestive new meaning:

[4] See Spence, I, p. 130.
[5] See the description given by Warburton, in *TE* III, ii, pp. xvii–xix.

> Woman and Fool are two hard things to hit,
> For true No-meaning puzzles more than Wit.   (ll. 113–14)

The satirical point is neatly damning; but in a purely philosophical light, this is also a neat summary of the challenge that folly poses to the couplet. Because the couplet is so habituated to meaning, it is not surprising that it is more puzzled to express 'true No-meaning' than intelligible 'Wit'. But this does not mean that we believe the artist when he tells us he resents his difficulty, and is only examining the 'Tulips' from a sense of duty. He is clearly fascinated by what escapes his categories; flowers, women and fools are puzzling to 'hit' because of their one great virtue, of being haplessly natural. Like Nature herself, they are their own meaning; indeed, 'true No-meaning' could be a synonym for Nature, who has no meaning smaller than herself, and is all the questions and answers embodied. Thus flowers, women and fools bring Pope's couplet up against the extreme limits of its capacities: doing justice to Dionysiac Nature in Apollonian form, and celebrating the play of life without insisting on its meaning.

There is some confirmation of the idea that these subjects lie on the outer limits of Pope's art in the direction taken by his greatest successor, at the end of the century. Wordsworth applied himself to eliciting the meaning of 'true No-meaning' in the *Lyrical Ballads* as if this was precisely the task that Pope had fallen short of; and he located his subject, as often as not, where Pope does – in flowers, women and fools. But in his own ironic mode, Pope anticipates Wordsworth's discoveries, and freely acknowledges the supreme claims of nature in his portraits of women in the satire; even Nature although at odds with everything else he values. The bewitching Calypso, for instance, affronts morality, intelligence and taste. But she is nonetheless naturally erotic, and as able to captivate an unwilling Odysseus as her namesake:

> 'Twas thus Calypso once each heart alarm'd,
> Aw'd without Virtue, without Beauty charm'd;
> Her Tongue bewitch'd as odly as her Eyes,
> Less Wit than Mimic, more a Wit than wise:
> Strange graces still, and stranger flights she had,
> Was just not ugly, and was just not mad;
> Yet ne'er so sure our passion to create,
> As when she touch'd the brink of all we hate.   (ll. 45–52)

Perhaps this analysis deserves to be called more audacious than anything Wordsworth attempted, for while he celebrates a Lucy for being natural, we cannot imagine him admiring a woman for being so very natural that loving and hating her lay very close together. But Pope makes no excuses, only testifying to the bewildering fact that moral disorientation *is* erotic – perhaps because what eludes our categories will always allure us more than what lies contentedly inside them, and in spite of disclaimers, we prefer the play of life to our mental security. 'Strange graces still, and stranger flights she had': Calypso is a kind of sylph, and a man with imagination will catch the play of light on her wings.

These two ambiguous charges against women we have been considering – that they require to be dipt in the Rainbow, and yield no satisfactory meaning – are related to a third Pope makes, more richly ambiguous than either. This is the one he opens the poem with and steadily recurs to throughout: the charge that women are essentially lacking in form. As he phrases it, using a witticism of Martha Blount's:

> Nothing so true as what you once let fall,
> 'Most Women have no Characters at all'.
> Matter too soft a lasting mark to bear,
> And best distinguish'd by black, brown, or fair.   (ll. 1–4)

It is women's peculiar characteristic to take no stamp, to offer no resistance to the engraver. Perhaps Pope is remembering the metaphor that underlies the word 'character', deriving as it does from the Greek for coining, *charassein*: the 'metal' of femininity is 'too soft a lasting mark to bear', and distinguishable, not by form, but colour: 'black, brown, or fair'. We see from this how inevitable it is that women should embody 'No-meaning', for form is the pre-condition of meaning. It is the 'wiry bounding line' that produces shapely significance from soft matter; and the charge that women cannot sustain it is the severest Pope can make. Coming from a poet, as well as a man, it is loaded to a degree – for what does a poet live by, if not form? It is by virtue of forms that he is a poet, and forms are what he makes. Yet worse than this, though women are incapable of bearing a 'lasting mark', they take a temporary one very well:

> How many pictures of one Nymph we view,
> All how unlike each other, all how true!
> Arcadia's Countess, here, in ermin'd pride.
> Is there, Pastora by a fountain side:
> Here Fannia, leering on her own good man,
> Is there, a naked Leda with a Swan.
> Let then the Fair one beautifully cry,
> In Magdalen's loose hair and lifted eye,
> Or drest in smiles of sweet Cecilia shine,
> With simp'ring Angels, Palms, and Harps divine . . .   (ll. 5–14)

Woman, the poet satirically implies, makes play with the forms that are life and death to him. But the essential ambiguity of the charge begins to show through in a catalogue like this: for if we change the metaphor from painting to poetry, we can see that the lady's imaginative range is hardly to be distinguished from the poet's own. She moves from Magdalen to Cecilia, as he might turn from *Eloisa to Abelard* to an *Ode* for the musical saint; and perhaps part of his irritation stems from the suspicion that he and the lady are not unrelated. 'All how unlike each other, all how true!' would be a pertinent comment on Pope's *Collected works*, and in that context Pope would vigorously deny that the genres were inconsistent with one another, greatly as they differed in morality, language and tone: for each possesses its own decorum, and keeps to the rules of the game. The great difference between him and the lady, however, is that he creates poems external to himself, while she is actually abandoning herself to the genres, in the hope of finding who she is. She is, so to speak, the stuff of a poem in search of its form, a Dionysiac creature in search of Apollonian bounds; and his satirical portraits are strung between two opposed choices, both equally offensive to his taste as an artist. The one is perfect formlessness, which as we have seen, makes meaning impossible; and the other, of trusting wholly to external form, which is too weakly related to the inner content to yield a meaning either. Pope's discontent with women is the kind of aesthetic discontent he would have in the midst of an anthology of bad poetry.

On the formless side, for instance, we might find Narcissa, for whom life is a rapid sequence of postures performed with one eye on the mirror:

> Narcissa's nature, tolerably mild,
> To make a wash, would hardly stew a child,
> Has ev'n been prov'd to grant a Lover's pray'r,
> And paid a Tradesman once to make him stare,
> Gave alms at Easter, in a Christian trim,
> And made a Widow happy, for a whim.
> Why then declare Good-nature is her scorn,
> When 'tis by that alone she can be born?
> Why pique all mortals, yet affect a name?
> A fool to Pleasure, and a slave to Fame:
> Now deep in Taylor and the Book of Martyrs,
> Now drinking citron with his Grace and Chartres.
> Now Conscience chills her, and now Passion burns;
> And Atheism and Religion take their turns;
> A very Heathen in the carnal part,
> Yet still a sad, good Christian at her heart.   (ll. 53–68)

'Atheism' and 'Religion' take their turns with Narcissa, because her need for form is so thoroughgoing that all forms serve her equally well; and if we take the Aristotelian view, that character is kinetic and formed in action, we can see how it is that she has no character at all: for no two actions shape her in the same direction. Her body and heart have come to no understanding: one practises pagan freedoms, the other Christian repentance; yet if we look to the finished uniformity of a 'good' character for the alternative, the results are scarcely more encouraging. What is the value of form without content? Cloe can offer nothing more, in spite of Martha Blount's protestations:

> 'Yet Cloe sure was form'd without a spot –'
> Nature in her then err'd not, but forgot.
> 'With ev'ry pleasing, ev'ry prudent part,
> Say, what can Cloe want?' – she wants a Heart.
> She speaks, behaves, and acts just as she ought,
> But never, never, reach'd one gen'rous Thought.

> Virtue she finds too painful an endeavour,
> Content to dwell in Decencies for ever.
> So very reasonable, so unmov'd,
> As never yet to love, or to be lov'd.
> She, while her Lover pants upon her breast,
> Can mark the figures on an Indian chest;
> And when she sees her Friend in deep despair,
> Observes how much a Chintz exceeds Mohair.   (ll. 157–70)

Cloe has put together a consistent character from external forms, and 'speaks, behaves, and acts just as she ought'; but the sole effect is to drive the poet into distinguishing Decency from Virtue. Virtue is too athletic for Cloe, too closely allied to generosity, and its frequent companion, error; thus her formal perfection is a mere parody, more deeply offensive in its similarity to virtue than vice itself. Far from being the content of a poem in search of its form, she is a finished, formal exercise with no content. From such nothingness as Cloe's, nothing can be expected.

The idea that one element in Pope's complex response to women is an artist's frustration at so many poems *manqués*, adds an interesting new dimension to his praise of the one woman he can admire, Martha Blount. Between the two extremes of Narcissa and Cloe lies a character of beautifully mingled qualities, that reconciles form and content to charming effect:

> And yet, believe me, good as well as ill,
> Woman's at best a Contradiction still.
> Heav'n, when it strives to polish all it can
> Its last best work, but forms a softer Man;
> Picks from each sex, to make its Fav'rite blest,
> Your love of Pleasure, our desire of Rest,
> Blends, in exception to all gen'ral rules,
> Your Taste of Follies, with our Scorn of Fools,
> Reserve with Frankness, Art with Truth ally'd,
> Courage with Softness, Modesty with Pride,
> Fix'd Principles, with Fancy ever new;
> Shakes all together, and produces – You.   (ll. 269–80)

Martha, we see, is another kind of sylph, and *varium et mutabile* still. But hers are 'the best kinds of contrarieties', as Pope says in his note (l. 269n): she has the Apollonian, masculine virtues, as well as the Dionysiac, feminine ones, and 'Scorn', 'Frankness', 'Truth', 'Courage', 'Pride' and 'Fix'd Principles' give her character a firmness her sisters lack. She has a natural tendency towards form, and does not need to seek it in conventions like Cloe; but at the same time, a 'Taste of Follies', 'Reserve', 'Art' (presumably 'artifice'), 'Softness', 'Modesty' and a 'Fancy ever new', pull that character back towards the formless spontaneity from which it emerged: a nature as 'ondoyant et divers' as Montaigne's, ready for every folly and fancy, and brilliantly devious in its response to the experience that would shape it.

The vibrant tension held between opposed extremes that Pope finds here in Martha, could equally well be called the mark of a fine poem; indeed, to look no farther, could be called the mark of this epistle, which constantly adapts its form to the challenging vagaries of its subject. There is the vestige of an ambitious overview in the poet's introduction of his cherished notion of the Ruling Passion (ll. 207–10) – this was presumably meant to link it to the *Essay on Man* and the design of the *magnum opus* as a whole – but the poem rapidly sweeps this away, and in its shifts of tone and topic it acknowledges no principles of construction but surprise and delight. Its striking air of spontaneity derives from its blending of rapid composition with polished fragments Pope had long kept in his drawers, or used in other poems (*TE*, III, ii, p. xxxvi). The fluidity of its logic is more than skin-deep, as we see from the fact that it exists in three distinct forms, omitting some of the portraits and conflating others; the 'death-bed' version itself may have only a provisional completeness.[6]

But general considerations of structure aside, we can find quite pertinent applications of Pope's language about Martha to his poem's own mingled qualities. A paradox like 'Your Taste of Follies, with our Scorn of Fools', for instance, nicely hits off its blending of sympathy and satire. Firm as is Pope's 'Scorn of Fools', it is a 'Taste of Follies' that gives the poem its elasticity and fellow-feeling. Pope does not withhold his imagination from Papillia's mortified discovery that a park is only a collection of trees, or from Silia's temper on the day she wakes with a pimple on her nose; as a 'nice admirer' he finds them, in their own way, beyond improvement. 'Reserve with Frankness, Art with Truth ally'd' is another line that carries a double charge; for it was 'Reserve' jostling with 'Frankness' that produced the various suppressions in the first edition, when Pope's originals were still alive. 'Art with Truth ally'd' is a good description of his entire procedure: for Pope stopped short of no art or artifice to promote his 'Truth', as his editors are constantly uncovering, and eternalizing his living friends into types (as Mrs Howard, for instance, became Cloe) took a remarkable combination of warm heart and cold eye, which some readers have found hard to forgive.

Above all, however, it is in the combination of 'Fix'd Principles' with 'Fancy ever new' that we best recognize Pope's art; for although the poem's firmness of principle justifies Warburton's pompous appellation 'Moral Essay', it is only because in another sense, Pope has no principles at all, that the poem survives. 'Fix'd Principles' are what no true artist can allow himself, for they would imply that the reality he is to explore is already known; and worse, that there are areas of it where a gentleman may not go. It is 'Fancy ever new' that impels him down into the black mud of the Thames in *The Dunciad*, or, in another mood, floats him in the air above it with the sylphs. It is not to

[6] See F. Brady, 'The history and structure of Pope's *To a Lady*', *Studies in English Literature* 9 (1969), 439–62.

Principle but Fancy that we owe the insects that sparkle in Pope's lines, and the bugs that crawl and suck their way across his pages; and in this epistle, it is Fancy that causes his infinitely varied portraits of women to wave and coruscate like living rainbows, and to shed new light on so many associated themes. Temporality, Dionysiac life, and the erotic nature of creativity can all be glimpsed beneath the ostensible satire; and Fancy brings Pope to the central perception that he embodies in Martha, that true creativity depends on the union of male and female, in art as in life.

If it is true that Pope's subconscious mind has been on poetry for much of the poem, then the culminating stroke of wit that bestows Apollo on Martha as her guardian god has wider implications than we might have thought:

> This Phoebus promis'd (I forget the year)
> When those blue eyes first open'd on the sphere;
> Ascendant Phoebus watch'd that hour with care,
> Averted half your Parents simple Pray'r,
> And gave you Beauty, but deny'd the Pelf
> Which buys your sex a Tyrant o'er itself.
> The gen'rous God, who Wit and Gold refines,
> And ripens Spirits as he ripens Mines,
> Kept Dross for Duchesses, the world shall know it,
> To you gave Sense, Good-humour, and a Poet.   (ll. 283–92)

The primary meaning is clear enough: Apollo distinguishes between true and false wealth, and his gifts to Martha are the ones that count: ripened 'Sense' and 'Good-humour', which give her the perspective and inner poise that save her from giddy formlessness. It is thanks to Apollo she can make the cool remark that sets the satire in motion, and Apollo supplied the general firmness of outline that enables Pope to talk about her in the terms we might use of a finely-achieved poem. But most important of all, Apollo gave her his last best gift, 'a Poet': and the word perceptibly quivers with its charge of meanings, for by implication he thus gave her a poem, the very poem we are reading, without which her beautifully mingled qualities must have remained unknown. 'Sense' and 'Good-humour' notwithstanding, Martha Blount would have vanished anonymously into the Dionysiac stream of life if Apollo and a poet had not converted her, by form, into eternal meaning. In these two climactic syllables, Pope seems to unite at a stroke his love for Martha, his respect for his own poem, and his reverence for the deity who makes the miracle possible – his guardian god as well as Martha's, Apollo:

> Kept Dross for Duchesses, the world shall know it,
> To you gave Sense, Good-humour, and a Poet.

Though the assertion is made in the lightest conversational tone, and with a feminine rhyme that seals the conclusion with a smile, we recognize the proud boast of the sonneteers:

> So long as men can breathe, or eyes can see,
> So long lives this, and this gives life to thee.

In a poem about painting rainbows and catching butterflies, however, Apollo has learned perfect Dionysiac manners, and he would no more approach his artistic climax with a solemn face than he would put a pin through a butterfly for his collection.

4

Engendering the reader: 'Wit and Poetry and Pope' once more

PENELOPE WILSON

Then the little gentleman said.
He said next,
He said finally,
Here, it cannot be denied, was true wit, true wisdom, true profundity. The company was thrown into complete dismay. One such saying was bad enough; but three, one after another, on the same evening! No society could survive it.
   'Mr Pope,' said old Lady R. in a voice trembling with sarcastic fury, 'you are pleased to be witty.' Mr Pope flushed red. Nobody spoke a word. They sat in dead silence some twenty minutes. Then, one by one, they rose and slunk from the room.

(Virginia Woolf, *Orlando*)

I

This essay is an attempt to explore the sexual politics of Pope's wit: it is, as the *lacunae* in the epigraph suggest, less about attitudes than about rhetoric. As anyone reading early eighteenth-century literature with today's undergraduates – female or male – will recognize, a modern feminist consciousness is likely to want to take issue with many of the attitudes towards women expressed or encoded in the works of Pope and other Augustan writers. But that observation, necessary and salutary as it is in the face of the accommodating nature of most of the available commentaries and criticism, offers in itself limited possibilities for critical development, leading all too easily down a predominantly anachronistic and recriminatory cul de sac. Feminism has only very recently taken up the challenge.[1] My concern here is not so much with female monsters in Augustan satire as with the ways in which opposition is pre-empted, response constrained, the company left without a voice.

   The question of gender functions both as a uniquely problematic area, and as one specific example of the more general power of Pope's satire to marginalize opposing ideologies and to reduce them, effectively, to silence. Pope is the most persuasive of writers partly because his readers are encouraged to see

---

[1] For an exploration of this subject which touches on some of the same issues, see my essay 'Feminism and the Augustans: some readings and problems', *Critical Quarterly*, XXVIII (1986), 80–92. See also Susan Gubar, 'The female monster in Augustan satire', *Signs*, 3 (1977), 380–94; and for a sophisticated full-length feminist study see Ellen Pollak, *The poetics of sexual myth: gender and ideology in the verse of Swift and Pope* (London, 1985).

themselves as rising (intellectually, artistically, morally) to the level of satiric assent, to slot themselves in beside that select coterie of addressees about whom Johnson sardonically remarks that 'it might be inferred that they . . . had engrossed all the understanding and virtue of mankind.'[2] There is a sense in which we all become fifth-columnists with Martha Blount in reading the *Epistle to a Lady*, with its ready-made role of the exceptional woman whose adequacy is measured against the inadequacy of others. The process is wryly recognized in an anecdote in which Laetitia Pilkington recounts her own experience of a characteristically aggressive Swiftian version of the exaction of submission, 'a compliment . . . to some ladies, who supped with him, of whom she had the honour to be one':

The Dean was giving us an account of some woman, who, he told us, was the nastiest, filthiest, most stinking old B——ch that ever was yet seen, except the Company, Ladies! except the Company! for that you know is but civil. We all bowed: could we do less?[3]

From the Dean's supper party to Virginia Woolf's imaginary *soirée* – and beyond – Augustan wit has left its victims with little recourse but silence. The tercentenary of his birth may be an appropriate time to observe that we know more about man's response to Pope than about woman's. It seems to have been an early assumption that Pope's poetry had a particular appeal for women: a satirical drama of 1714 introduces 'Sawney' (that is, Pope) as 'a young Poet of the modern Stamp' who has 'a very pretty Genius, is very Harmonious, and writes a great many fine things, ask the Ladies else'.[4] Maynard Mack's unidentified 'Amica' now offers a convenient illustration of the groupie mentality.[5] Yet a history of Pope and the female reader would be a meagre thing. The most readily available collection of contemporary responses to Pope, in the *Critical heritage* series, includes an extract from the French scholar Anne Dacier's criticism of Pope's Homer, and several passages, predictably, from Lady Mary Wortley Montagu, but otherwise out of 500 pages gives not more than one or two to the response of women to Pope's poetry. All of these express dislike of Pope's invective, the strongest being Elizabeth Rowe's reaction to the 'Atticus' portrait: 'the whole seems writ with a Mallice more than human it has something infernal in it 'tis surprising that a man can divest himself of the tender sentiments of nature so far as deliberately to give Anguish and Confusion to Beings of his own kind'. The Countess of Hertford regrets the devotion of Pope's talents to satire rather than 'divine and good-natured subjects', and Catherine Talbot, writing to Elizabeth Carter, finds herself similarly torn between admiration and 'indignation'. 'At some uncharitable moments one can scarcely help looking upon all those eloquent expressions of benevolence and affection as too much parade, while one sees

---

[2] G. Birkbeck Hill (ed.), *Lives of the English poets* (Oxford, 1905), III, p. 61.
[3] Laetitia Pilkington, *Memoirs* (Dublin, 1748), II, pp. 144–5.
[4] Charles Gildon, *A new rehearsal:* see Guerinot, p. 55.
[5] See *Pope: a life*, pp. 796–801.

them overbalanced by such bitterness and cutting severity . . . While every reading makes me more admire his genius, every one makes me more doubt his heart'.[6] Such comments are not, of course, confined to women, but the emphasis is predictable enough: apart from the particular cases of the woman scholar and the bitter personal enemy, woman's response is characterized by a vocabulary overtly antipathetic to satire, that of sensibility – of tenderness, good nature and the heart.

However chary we may be today of allowing questions of gender into the theory of reader-response, the eighteenth century in general was not an age to eschew the 'fair-sexing' of either writer or reader. Attitudes – overwhelmingly hostile in most cases – towards female writers and 'learned ladies' have been well explored, and literary sociology has long recognized, especially in connection with the novel, the importance of the growth of a new female reading public. There is still room, however, for a more general study of the explicit construction in many of the literary productions of the period of an image of the 'woman reader' as an essentially different and specialized category – both as one for which an appropriate and improving 'Lady's Library' might be devised, and as one from which a certain kind of literary sensibility might be expected, in compensation, often, for the inevitable limitations of female education.

While it is easy to accept that the judgments voiced by the women quoted above draw on a common notion of what is appropriate to 'femininity' in reading, one can only feel sceptical about the likelihood of establishing on any broader grounds a profoundly 'different voice' in women readers of Pope. Carol Gilligan's gender-oriented study of different ways of speaking about questions of identity and about moral problems might offer a suggestive model,[7] but although it is interesting to speculate about the possible results in relation to literary 'reader-response' of this association of male and female voices with distinctive modes of thought, there are a number of forces to sabotage one's findings. In the first place, those who read eighteenth-century literature today are likely to have achieved a high level of competence in controlling response along institutional rather than individual or 'alternative' lines; and if scholarship in general aspires to the unisex, so in particular does Augustanism itself.

There is, anachronistically, a place already marked out in Duncedom for feminist criticism. 'Augustanism', if more than a conventional label, is more usefully seen as a strategy, a range of rhetoric and tactics, than as a set of absolute beliefs.[8] Its strategy is one which, like Roland Barthes' 'myth'[9], takes its strength from the representation of history as nature, of its own values as timeless and universal rather than contingent and partisan. The last book of

[6] John Barnard (ed.), *Pope: the critical heritage* (London, 1973), pp. 247, 329, 366.
[7] Carol Gilligan, *In a different voice: psychological theory and women's development* (London, 1982).
[8] Compare Donald Greene's remarks, pp. 245–6 below.
[9] See *Mythologies* (Paris: Editions du Seuil, 1970.)

The Dunciad makes it clear that misreading is a moral as well as an intellectual heresy: the readers as well as the collectors approved by Dulness might be said to 'see Nature in some partial narrow shape, and let the Author of the whole escape' (*Dunciad*, IV, ll. 455–6). The charge calls attention to two Augustan tenets of characteristic circularity, both of them implicitly threatening to a critique which highlights the issue of gender: that the proper concern of literature is with human nature in general rather than with the particular and the partisan, and that works are to be read not against but following the grain of the author's thought: 'In every Work regard the *Writer's End* / Since none can compass more than they *Intend*' (*Essay on Criticism*, ll. 255–6). The reader's role as laid down by Pope is in this sense at least a decidedly acquiescent one. In conversation in 1730 Pope does substantially qualify the baldly 'intentional' precept ('a writer is not to be blamed if he hits his aim') with what might be taken as *carte blanche* to the ideological opposition by accepting Spence's proviso 'unless he has made a bad choice of an end'.[10] If we return to Pope's instructions to a reader in the *Essay on Criticism*, however, a feminist perspective, even if it can dodge the charge of savouring for its own sake the 'malignant dull Delight' (l. 237) of irrelevant fault-finding, seems most seriously threatened by distinctions like those set up in the language of the following passages:

> Most Criticks, fond of some subservient Art,
> Still make the *Whole* depend upon a *Part*,
> They talk of *Principles*, but Notions prize,
> And All to one lov'd Folly sacrifice . . .
> Thus Criticks, of less *Judgment* than *Caprice*,
> *Curious*, not *Knowing*, not *exact*, but *nice*,
> Form *short Ideas*, and offend in *Arts*,
> (As most in Manners) by a love to *Parts*.   (ll. 263–6, 285–8)

Though Pope could hardly have envisaged such a role for them, it is hard to imagine how the traditional case against feminist readings could be more cogently put than it is in these lines, blending their intimidatingly precise verbal distinctions – or pseudo-distinctions – with the evocation of a social world of folly and the *faux pas*. It is correspondingly hard, given the pressures exerted by the rhetoric of the lines, to maintain what must be the adversarial response: to insist that the distinctions between 'judgment' and 'caprice', 'principles' and 'notions', the 'curious' and the 'knowing', the 'exact' and the 'nice', are themselves as subjective as the verse suggests they are scientific. Capricious notions may not properly be ends in themselves, but they may help to make necessary inroads into the apparent certainties embedded in such confident representations of 'judgment', the 'exact', and 'the whole'. One of the prime uses of feminism, after all, is its ability to perceive that truths 'universally' acknowledged have their own local constituency, that one per-

---

[10] Spence, I, p. 168.

son's whole is another person's part, that what are presented as the structures of a universal, all-embracing humanism tend to be coloured by an unspoken andro-centrism.

Where the question of the 'gendering' of the reader is concerned, there is a further difficulty in the nature of the poetry itself and the codes on which it depends for its intelligibility. The level of sophistication demanded in the reading of Pope's poetry – an awareness of irony, of allusion, of poetic artifice – means that in the process certain traditions, assumptions, or acquired positions are being constantly drawn into play. It is important not to overstate the degree of acquiescence imposed upon the reader by Pope: there are two sides, after all, to his demand that the 'perfect Judge' should read each work of wit *with* (not 'in') 'the same Spirit that its Author writ' (*Essay on Criticism*, ll. 233–4). Despite what I have been describing as the general thrust of Pope's recommendations for reading, in which personal idiosyncrasies and interests should be sunk into a sense of the author's intention and of 'the whole', we find in Pope (as in Swift) that the imaginary recreation of the fascinations of misreading, applying the microscope of wit, often achieves an immediacy which is missing from the general precepts. There is, however, no real or abiding space for the naive, or the ideologically committed, reader: an 'adequate' reader must be to a considerable degree created by the demands of the text. This is the question which I now want to address more closely, in taking another look at the role of the 'reader' in *The Rape of the Lock*, following on to some extent from a classic essay by Earl Wasserman which pre-dated the era either of reader-response or of feminist criticism. In this detailed study of the operation of allusion in the poem Wasserman concludes that 'the mode of existence of Pope's poetry . . . ought to be defined broadly enough to include a creative act by the reader', and that the reader is invited, enticed, or (another revealing choice of verb) 'incited' to exercise almost as much of his own invention and wit in reconstructing the allusive context as did the poet in embedding it in the text.[11] The allusive resonances, he argues, 'are not peripheral but functional to the meaning of the artistic product'; and it is a contention of this essay that such substantive functionality extends beyond the realm of allusion itself to the more general strategies of Pope's wit.

II

''Tis so much the Concern of a Poet to have his Works understood, and particularly by your Sex . . .'   ('To Mrs Arabella Fermor', *TE* ii, p. 142)

The figure of Thalestris – the virago, named for a Queen of the Amazons 'greatly honour'd in her own Country for [her] Brave and Manly Spirit'[12] – provides an obvious starting-point for a reading of *The Rape of the Lock* which

[11] Earl Wasserman, 'The limits of allusion in *The Rape of the Lock*', *Journal of English and Germanic Philology* 55 (1966), 425–44.
[12] See note in *TE* ii, p. 187.

gives any degree of priority to feminist issues. The speech in which she urges
Belinda to action after the 'rape' brings to the forefront one immediately
problematic aspect of the question of gender and rhetoric in the poem.

> Was it for this you took such constant Care
> The Bodkin, Comb, and Essence to prepare;
> For this your Locks in Paper-Durance bound,
> For this with tort'ring Irons wreath'd around?
> For this with Fillets strain'd your tender Head,
> And bravely bore the double Loads of Lead?   (IV, ll. 97–102)

With this resonant formula of wasted effort Thalestris urges her friend
Belinda to join battle with the Baron over her lost curl. In her use of the
formula Thalestris takes her place in a line which stretches back at least to
Cicero and Virgil; she has perhaps her most immediate source in Ariosto's
good sorceress Melissa in *Orlando Furioso*, who, disguised as his guardian Atlas,
rebukes Ruggiero for sinking into the barren sensual enchantment of Alcina's
pavilion of love instead of fulfilling his more glorious destiny as the father of a
race of heroes..

> What was't for this, that I in youth thee fed,
> With marrow of the Beares and Lyons fell?
> That I through caves and deserts have thee led . . .[13]

It has long been noted, however, that the question which is for Thalestris as for
her predecessors merely an emphatic device carrying with it both reproach
and exhortation opens up in a rather special way under the pressure of the
ironies of the speech and of the poem, to become a real question rather than
simply a rhetorical flourish. If Belinda's preparations were not for 'this', for
the arousing of male desire, then for what? The sexual pragmatism of the
knowing reader's reversal of the negative demanded by the rhetoric – and
assumed by Thalestris – is of course more explicitly drawn out in the final
canto in Clarissa's speech, added as Pope tells us 'to open more clearly the
moral of the poem'.

> How vain are all these Glories, all our *Pains*,
> Unless good Sense preserve what Beauty gains . . .   (V, ll. 15–16)

The reader works through the fissures of irony and association in Thalestris'
question towards a perception of the shallowness of the virago's position, a
shallowness rendered more threatening, of course, by the famous giveaways
about 'honour' ('at whose unrival'd Shrine / Ease, Pleasure, Virtue, All, our
Sex resign') and friendship ('''Twill then be Infamy to seem your Friend'), and
also by the sick rewriting of the already narcissistic sacred rituals of the toilet
scene as one of perverse self-mutilation, reminding us of the potentially

---

[13] *Orlando Furioso*, trans. Harington (VII, 49, ll. 1–3). On the formula, see the correspondence in
The Times Literary Supplement, April to September 1975.

demonic aspect of the exquisite world of the sylphs and the coquettes (see Wasserman, p. 433).

But *was* it for this? Was Belinda 'asking for it', rendering herself liable, in the judicial parlance which so naturally attaches to the topic today, to arraignment for contributory negligence (or contributory artifice)? In the case of Miss Arabella Fermor the pleasures of criticism undoubtedly entice the reader towards the verdict of the most unregenerate old codgers of the bench on the singleness of the end of female adornment, with the rider that this end is indeed a great deal more healthful than women's own obsessions allow them to recognize.

There is another dimension. The question 'was it for this?' opens out still further if we follow through the association of the 'rape' and the poet's art, the way in which the poem itself instead of the Baron becomes the medium through which the lock is 'exposed through crystal to the gazing eyes', stellarized as it is in the parallel passage at the end:

> Not all the Tresses that fair Head can boast
> Shall draw such Envy as the Lock you lost.   (v, ll. 143–4)

A disconcertingly direct implication of this association is drawn out in the lines 'To Belinda on the Rape of the Lock', lines which otherwise include one of Pope's most characteristically sensitive expressions of women's predicament:

> Nature to your undoing arms mankind
> With strength of body, artifice of mind;
> But gives your feeble sex, made up of fears,
> No guard but virtue, no redress but tears.
> Yet custom (seldom to your favour gain'd)
> Absolves the virgin when by force constrain'd . . .
> (*TE* vi, p. 108, ll. 15–20)

Lines like these, as so often in Pope, tend to disarm ideological opposition. The poem is essentially a compliment founded, like the coda to *The Rape* itself, on the consolations offered to the victim by literary fame; but the *felix culpa* motif undergoes a notably unpleasant twist in the final lines:

> But would your charms to distant times extend,
> Let *Jervas* paint them, and let *Pope* commend.
> Who censure most, more precious hairs would lose,
> To have the *Rape* recorded by his Muse.   (ll. 27–30)

Thalestris' speech may serve, then, as a general illustration of the way in which textual strategy draws the reader not merely into subscribing to but into an active re-creation of certain positions towards the proper relations of the sexes. The delicacy of the strategy, of course, contrasts strongly with the crudeness, the clumsiness, of the exposure – the rather primitive level of feminist dissent I am inviting by this example can only be a means to an end. Earl Wasserman's essay affords what is in its own way a magnificent practical

illustration of the very similar operation of allusion in the poem. As do Pope's
other poems, he argues, *The Rape of the Lock* asks for 'a reader who is equally
native to the whole classical-Scriptural world, a Christian Greco-Roman
scrutinizing eighteenth-century English culture' (Wasserman, p. 427). In this
sense, the poem perhaps never encountered its 'ideal reader' until Wasserman;
and what we witness in his essay is the way in which the burden of that reader's
variegated Greco-Roman lore consistently deploys itself to underline one
message. Belinda's flaw is not her coquetry itself, but 'her refusal to accept as
its proper consequence the Baron's compulsion . . .' (p. 438); 'the oversense
vividly comments on the unnatural and antisocial character of Belinda's
wishes to avoid wedlock' (p. 440). What the sum of awareness of the context of
allusions in Ovid, Virgil, Livy, Homer, Apollonius, Juvenal, Martial,
Apuleius, Statius, Augustine, and Catullus tells the ideal reader is that
Belinda 'as Pope paints her, . . . is at that age when she thinks she hates the
boys and cannot understand what is really troubling her' (p. 441).

   Conclusions so hard-earned are unlikely to be lightly thrown away: their
validity becomes a function of the degree of expertise involved in working
towards them. The point at issue here is not simply that the central premise of
the *Rape* – what Ellen Pollak calls Pope's 'model of female health'[14] – is from a
feminist point of view an irritant, and an obstacle to appreciation: it is rather
that through the very sophistication of its textual strategies the poem creates
its readers in its own image. There is however a particular piquancy here, in
that at the same time the poem is at work to construct a very different kind of
reader, one characterized by hermeneutic innocence rather than sophistication. The 'ideal readership' extrapolated from the demands imposed by the
text in fact positively excludes, or inhibits, the audience to which the poem is
ostensibly 'dedicated' or addressed. 'You may bear me Witness, it was intended only to divert a few young Ladies, who have good Sense and good
Humour enough, to laugh not only at their Sex's little unguarded Follies, but
at their own' (the dedication 'To Mrs Arabella Fermor'). Wherever the ideal
reader is to be found, it is clearly not within such a group. Good sense and good
humour can take one only so far into the poem: the structure of eighteenth-
century education would ensure that even if Pope's female readers could attain
a general recognition of the mock-epic features of the poem they would
certainly have been prohibited from picking up the more detailed allusive
context of Latinism and Greco-Roman literature and myth. 'I know', apolo-
gizes Pope prettily in the Dedication, 'how disagreeable it is to make use of
hard Words before a Lady . . .'

   This dual standard of readership which operates around the poem finds an
interesting reflection in a similar kind of sexual differentiation within it. The
world of *The Rape* is a supremely unliterary one: the only written materials
which intrude into the frame of reference of the characters themselves are

---

[14] Pollak, *Poetics of sexual myth*, p. 97.

Atalantis, French romances, and billets-doux. Instead of Wassermanic learning we have the expertise of the card table, and the lore 'Of all the Nurse and all
the Priest have taught' (I, 30). The beaux are of course as ignorant as the
belles. Yet even so there is a sense that they may stand in a different relation to
the heroic tradition invoked by the poem. In speeches which bear a variously
close relationship to particular Homeric events (Achilles' lament to Thetis on
the death of Patroclus, and Sarpedon's exhortation to Glaucus), Belinda and
Clarissa are quite unconscious of the heroic dimension which they unwittingly
call into play. It is indeed this innocence, the ironic gap between the perspective of the speaker and that of the poet and his alert (or alerted) reader, which
makes these speeches the perfectly balanced mock-heroic achievements that
they are. The Baron is notably more self-conscious (and consequently from
many points of view a good deal less successfully presented) in his 'heroic'
postures – in his building of the altar to Love, in his version of Achilles' oath
('But by this Lock, this sacred Lock I swear', IV, ll. 133ff.), and in his victory
boast:

> Let Wreaths of Triumph now my Temples twine
> (The Victor cry'd) the glorious Prize is mine!
> While Fish in Streams, or Birds delight in Air,
> Or in a Coach and Six the *British* Fair,
> As long as *Atalantis* shall be read . . .   (III, ll. 161ff.)

In this last example the Baron, with his itemization of eternity in terms of the
trivia of a female day, appears almost as much in control of the mock-heroic as
the poet himself; significantly, although the Baron's speech may be assumed to
end with the verse paragraph and not to include the following reflections on
the power of steel, it is much less easy than usual to tell where the character
ends and the mock-heroic voice begins. Certainly there is none of the sense of
discrepancy of vision so neatly captured in Belinda's case, for example, by the
subtle revision of Achilles' 'Curs'd be that Day, when . . .' into the society
lady's plaintive 'For ever curs'd be this detested Day.'

   This distinction is even more notable in the control of innuendo. The Baron
may not be the sort who could formally adduce Ovid's *Ars Amatoria* as the
model for his 'dying' words in the fifth canto, but there is no doubt that he is
consciously playing on their sexual meaning as a verbal *coup de grâce* delivered
to Belinda:

> Boast not my Fall (he cry'd) insulting Foe!
> Thou by some other shalt be laid as low.
> Nor think, to die dejects my lofty Mind;
> All that I dread, is leaving you behind![15]   (v, ll. 97–100)

Against this has to be set Belinda's innocence of her own notorious slip into
double entendre, or at least of her own unconscious motivation:

---

[15] See W. Rudat, 'Belinda's "painted vessel": allusive technique in *The Rape of the Lock*', *Tennessee
Studies in Literature* 19 (1974), 49–55.

> O hadst thou, Cruel! been content to seize
> Hairs less in sight, or any Hairs but these!   (IV, ll. 175–6)

The significance of this aspect of *The Rape* was not lost on Pope's earliest readers. John Dennis, predictably, complained that Pope was 'putting Bawdy into the Mouth of his own Patroness'[16], while Sawney Dapper himself in Gildon's *A new rehearsal* is made to advocate this 'new manner of Address' at some length:

> You must make the Ladies speak Bawdy, no matter whether they are Women of Honour or not; and then you must dedicate your Poem to the Ladies themselves . . . The *Machinary* of this Poem is admirably contriv'd to convey a luscious Hint to the Ladies, by letting them know, that their Nocturnal Pollutions are a Reward of their Chastity . . .'[17]   (Barnard ed.), pp. 95–6)

The language of this passage suggests the double bind in which the female recipient, or reader, is caught, constructed as both innocence and instigation, as both foolish and salacious; and I want in the final section of this essay to explore some of the further implications of consciousness of 'the Ladies' in the setting of Pope's hermeneutic traps.

III

'I scarce meet with anybody that understands delicacy'

Pope's complaint to Spence (6–10 April 1742) about the absence of 'delicacy' in his readers follows on from a comment on two lines from the *Dunciad* (IV, ll. 223–4) – 'Let Freind affect to speak as Terence spoke, / And Alsop never but like Horace joke.

> Those two lines on Alsop and Freind have more of satire than of compliment in them, though I find they are generally mistaken for the latter only. It goes on Horace's old method ['Ridenti Flaccus amico'] of telling a friend some less fault while you are commending him, and which, indeed, is the best time of doing so.[17]

The illustration makes it clear that what Pope means by 'delicacy' here is a version of what has become known, critically, as ambivalence, and his sense of the lack of appreciation of this especially New Critical virtue among his contemporaries comes as no surprise to anyone who has worked through the evidence of early eighteenth-century response to his works. Nowadays, one rather apprehensively recognizes, even Pope might be more prone to criticize his readers for the over-ingenuity outlined in his first note to Book One of the *Iliad*, which stands with its poetic parallel in the speech of 'Aristarchus' in *Dunciad* IV as one of the most telling of all his critical dicta:

---

[16] *Remarks upon Mr Pope's Translation of Homer* (1717), Guerinot, p. 55.
[17] Spence, I, 150. For a confirmatory example, see Pope's first biographer, William Ayre (*Pope: the critical heritage*, pp. 354–5).

The prevailing Passion of [other scholars] is to discover *New Meanings* in an Author, whom they will cause to appear mysterious purely for the Vanity of being thought to unravel him. If they can but find a Word that has once been strain'd by some dark Writer to signify anything different from its usual Acceptation, it is frequent with them to apply it constantly to that uncommon Meaning, whenever they meet it in a clear Writer: for Reading is so much dearer to them than Sense, that they will discard it at any time to make way for a Criticism. In other Places where they cannot contest the Truth of the common Interpretation, they get themselves room for Dissertation by imaginary *Amphibologies*, which they will have to be design'd by the Author. This Disposition of finding out different Significations in one thing, may be the Effect of either too much, or too little Wit: For Men of a right Understanding generally see at once all that an Author can reasonably mean, but others are apt to fancy Two Meanings for want of knowing One.[18]

Whether or not Pope would have classified himself either in 1715 or in 1742 as a 'clear Writer', his first readers could hardly be taken to task for over-subtlety. It must still be a source of some amazement that Pope's double-edged art could grow out of this background of reader-response. As his comment on the Freind and Alsop lines in *The Dunciad* points out, the tendency was to assume a party spirit in all he wrote, to see 'satire' and 'compliment' in simple black and white – to find Pope over-kind to his friends, merciless to his enemies, and, as Richardson put it, 'having . . . no Opinion of the Lesson, that teaches us *to give the Devil his Due*'.[19]

It is now so generally felt that the image of woman functions in Pope's poetry as a primary site of ambivalence that it may be salutary to recall that in this area too critical sophistication has smoothed over the relative rough and tumble of contemporary perceptions of his stance. The *Epistle to a Lady*, for example, could be treated as straightforwardly misogynistic, the 'loss of their Characters' in line two apparently being enough to precipitate

> that wordy War
> 'Gainst Pope the crooked Poet wag'd,
> By Shoals of Women much enrag'd.[20]

But whatever the force of simple knee-jerk antagonism, the traditions of the verbal commerce of the sexes provide some ready-made structures of 'delicacy' with which even the least sophisticated reader would be able to engage. Compliment itself, the commonest currency in such interchange, is one of them, carrying with it its own critique: in Dr Johnson's dictionary definition, 'an act, or an expression of civility, usually understood to include some hypocrisy, and to mean less than it declares: this is properly *complement*, something superfluous, or more than enough'. A compliment between men

---

[18] Pope, *The Iliad of Homer*, *TE* VII, p. 82.
[19] Quoted in *Pope: The critical heritage*, pp. 340–1. Our assessment of the critical climate of the age is inevitably slanted by the predominance in the remaining evidence of hostile reaction.
[20] *Swift's Vision; or, the Women's Hue and Cry against Alexander Pope, for the loss of their Characters. A Poem, lately found in the Cabinet of a Very Curious Person* (Dublin, 1757), p. 14.

may be, as Pope's own opposition of the word to 'satire' suggests, a more
neutral term. The expectation of the compliment as a mode of addressing a
woman tends to produce, however, a spiral of non-communication, or distrust.
The kind of anxiety induced – in this case on both sides – is recognized in an
early exchange between Pope and Lady Mary Wortley Montagu. ''Tis certain', writes Lady Mary, 'that I may, if I please, take the fine things you say to
me for wit and raillery, and, it may be, would be taking them right. But I never,
in my life, was half so well disposed to take you in earnest, as I am at present . .
.', while Pope responds: 'It would be the most vexatious of all Tyranny, if you
should pretend to take for Raillery, what is the meer disguise of a discontented
heart that is unwilling to make you as melancholy as itself; and for Wit, what is
really only the natural Overflowing and Warmth of the same Heart, as it is
improved & awakened by an Esteem for you.'[21] It is in the nature of such
exchange that the most strenuous efforts of the writer to dissociate himself
from an indulgence in mere forms or in 'raillery' can do nothing to lessen the
suspicion of the recipient that the offering carries with it its own measure of
aggression, an implicit satire on the woman whose vanity allows her to be thus
taken in.

Woman's relation to sexual innuendo is a similarly uneasy one. Pope's own
letters, as well as the recurrent *topoi* of contemporary response to works like *The
Rape of the Lock* or *Three Hours After Marriage*, furnish ample evidence of the kind
of titillation available from the 'engendering' of the reader – a sexual charge
later exploited by Sterne in his recurrent directions to the reader as 'Madam'
in *Tristram Shandy*. The letter in which Pope, anonymously, in the guise of a
'brother', describes a visit to the latest curiosity of the town, a hermaphrodite,
is perhaps the most notorious example, but among others one might note that
Pope considered Teresa Blount a suitable recipient of the alternative version of
his heroic epitaph on the Stanton Harcourt lovers struck by lightning:

> Here lye two poor Lovers, who had the mishap,
> Tho very chaste people, to die of a clap.[22]

There is a corollary joke about Martha Blount's 'hatred' of puns and double
meanings – 'You who are truly virtuous, I know detest all manner of Vices,
whereof Punning is not the least . . .' (*Correspondence*, I, p. 376). In the case of
'bawdy', as Gildon and Dennis clumsily recognize, enjoyment of the text and
of its acts of implication entails complicity, a dereliction of the simplicity and
innocence enjoined upon the ideal woman, as woman and as reader.

I am suggesting, then, not that there is or ever has been any way of simply
pointing to an identifiably 'female' response to Pope, but that the fact of
address to a woman opens up for Pope a special range of 'delicacy' of tactic,
one in which the reader herself is constructed in opposition to the demands –

[21] *Correspondence*, I, pp. 361, 383.
[22] *Correspondence*, I, p. 349. On this topic in general see also Jean Hagstrum, *Sex and sensibility: ideal
and erotic love from Milton to Mozart* (London, 1980) pp. 137–45.

and the pleasures – of the text, and one which has the considerable strategic advantage that the 'delicacy' or double edge is much less likely to be over-looked. Seen from this point of view, the reading experience is not simply a matter of rising to the challenge of unpacking the buried implications of Pope's texts: it becomes a much more uneasy process, in itself embodying part of the satiric thrust. In the *Epistle to a Lady*, where the addressee is constantly edged, even through her apparent demurrals ('"Yet Chloe sure was form'd without a spot–"'), into collusion with the witty defamation of the characters of her own kind, the unease has its grammatical reflection in the play of pronouns, in the slippage of collective reference to 'women' between 'you' and 'they', before we are finally presented with the singular 'You' of the coda. Even for the excep-tional Martha Blount there is no wholly comfortable stance from which to savour the proffered tribute.

As Felicity Rosslyn argues elsewhere in this volume (p. 51ff.) in relation to the *Epistle to a Lady*, the image of woman acts for Pope as a special kind of imaginative release; and in the end the question of the representation of woman as reader takes us beyond matters of 'strategy' and tactics, into what might best be characterized in apparent oxymoron as Pope's rhetorical im-agination. In this paper I have set the topic of gender in the context of what I would see as Pope's abiding concern with matters of reading and misreading. It opens out also, however, on to the question of his own poetic voice. One might note, for example, the fusion in many of his comments on his art of the motifs of writing and sexuality. Ladies and literature could seem poles apart, as when, in a letter to the Blounts, Pope contrasts the 'good figure' he makes 'seated with dignity on the most conspicuous Shelves of a Library' with 'this wretched person in the abject condition of lying at a Lady's feet in Bolton street' (*Correspondence*, I, p. 430); but there is a painful and ambiguous inter-twining of the two motifs in the bitterest of his letters to them. 'I have heard indeed of Women that have had a Kindness for Men of my Make; but it has been after Enjoyment, never before; and I know to my Cost you have had no Taste of that Talent in me, which most Ladies would not only Like better, but Understand better, than any other I have.'[23] As the early *Eloisa* suggests, as well as the tensions of characterization in *To a Lady*, there is often a hint of the androgynous in Pope's sense of his own creativity, reminding us of his charac-terization of himself to the Earl of Peterborough as 'abhominably Epicoene'. He can slip from one convention of poetic creativity, describing his Muse as a wife (rather than a loved mistress), to another, presenting himself as the one who is 'to lye in of a Poetical Child' (*Correspondence*, II, p. 189; I, p. 293). As a final sidelight on the connection for which I have been arguing between poetic indirection and the intricacies of sexual exchange one might turn, however, to

---

[23] *Correspondence*, I, p. 456. For Maynard Mack (*Pope: a life*, p. 310) the 'Talent' is 'the divine gift of poetry'. The ambiguity is reflected in Hagstrum's misquotation 'I know to my Cost that you *have* no Taste of that Talent in me . . .' (*Sex and sensibility*, p. 139); the tense of the original strongly implies a sexual meaning.

a poem not addressed to a woman, to the most famous of Pope's images of confused gender in the Sporus portrait of the *Epistle to Dr Arbuthnot*. There is a striking modulation from this image of epicene evil to the compensatory virility of the poetic apologia which immediately follows it:

> Not Fortune's Worshipper, nor Fashion's Fool,
> Not Lucre's Madman, nor Ambition's Tool,
> Not proud, nor servile, be one Poet's praise
> That if he pleas'd, he pleas'd by manly ways;
> That Flatt'ry, ev'n to Kings, he held a shame,
> And thought a Lye in Verse or Prose the same . . .

The recoil from femininity entails a quite different voice, a mode of epitaphic clarity which eschews the 'lye' at the cost of imaginative complexity, the vile antithesis at the cost of all 'delicacy' and indirection. Few critics, one notes without surprise, have taken up Pope's hint in relation to this particular 'poet's praise'.[24]

[24] This essay is based partly on work done at the Humanities Research Centre, Australian National University, where the author held a Visiting Fellowship from April to July 1985.

PART THREE
An Essay on Man

5

Pope on the origins of society

HOWARD ERSKINE-HILL

I

Most readers agree that Pope's poetry is comprehensively social, and few deny that, implicitly or explicitly, in a variety of ways, it is often political. It is then surprising that in the wave of critical and biographical discussion which has pursued the earlier volumes of the Twickenham Edition relatively little attention has been paid to Epistle III of *An Essay on Man* (May 1733), the one poem in Pope's canon in which he offers an account of the origin of society and the origin of government.[1] For we may safely say of the eighteenth century, more than of our own time, that the quest for the origin of any given phenomenon was thought essential to the understanding of it. In the earlier eighteenth century, debate still continued concerning the origin of the English constitution, whether to be found among the Danes, Saxons, or even the British first encountered by the Romans in their conquest; while proponents of a contractual basis of government were still pressed to show when, historically, that Original Contract had been established.

From these examples alone it can be seen that *An Essay on Man*, Epistle III, 'Of the Nature and State of Man, with respect to Society', ventures upon some of the most fought-over ground in the Renaissance, namely the original state of mankind, the nature of man's fall, and the relation to these of the earliest government. Here, for example, is Henry Parker, most important of the early parliamentary pamphleteers, writing at the outbreak of the Civil War:

[1] Before Maynard Mack's Twickenham Edition of the poem John Laird, in *Philosophical incursions into English literature* (Cambridge, 1946), considered that Pope's third epistle must be allowed to be enormously better argued than its two predecessors, and indeed to be structurally quite well argued (p. 47). But R. A. Brower, that fine critic of Pope, calls Epistle III 'certainly the dullest of the four': *Alexander Pope: the poetry of allusion* (Oxford, 1959), p. 226; Miriam Leranbaum considered Pope's account of the change from a state of nature to civil society 'unsatisfying' (*Alexander Pope's 'opus magnum' 1729–1744* (Oxford, 1977), p. 60; while Brean S. Hammond is concerned with it mainly as an opportunity to reinstate the case for Bolingbroke's influence on Pope (*Pope and Bolingbroke: a study of friendship and influence* (Missouri, 1984), pp. 87–91. Douglas H. White, *Pope and the context of controversy: the manipulation of ideas in An Essay on Man* (Chicago and London, 1970), pays little attention to Epistle III though it lends itself to his valuable approach. More recently, A. D. Nuttall's monograph, *Pope's Essay on Man* (London, 1984), has offered a full, welcome, critical discussion of the whole poem, which touches on the Lockeian features of Epistle III (pp. 101–28). Neither David B. Morris' *Alexander Pope: the genius of sense* (London, 1984) nor, most recently, Maynard Mack's classic biography, *Alexander Pope: a life* (New Haven, New York and London, 1985), had the opportunity to discuss *An Essay on Man* III, very fully.

Man being depraved by the fall of *Adam* grew so untame and uncivil a creature, that the Law of God written in his breast was not sufficient to restrain him from mischief, or to make him sociable, and therefore without some magistracy to provide new orders, and to judge of old, and to execute according to justice, no society could be upheld. Without society men could not live, and without laws men could not be sociable, and without authority somewhere invested, to judge according to Law, and execute according to judgement, Law was a vain and void thing. It was soon therefore provided that laws agreeable to the dictates of reason should be ratified by common consent, and that the execution and interpretation of those Laws should be entrusted to some magistrate, for the prevention of common injuries betwixt Subject and Subject. . . .[2]

and here is Milton within a week of the execution of King Charles I, defending the regicides:

No man who knows ought, can be so stupid to deny that all men naturally were borne free, being the image and resemblance of God himselfe, and were by privilege above all the creatures, borne to command and not to obey: and that they lived so, till from the root of *Adams* transgression, falling among themselves to do wrong and violence, and foreseeing that such courses must needs tend to the destruction of them all, they agreed by common league to bind each other from mutual injury, and joyntly to defend themselves against any that gave disturbance or opposition to such agreement. Hence came Cities, Townes and Common-wealths. And because no faith in all was found sufficiently binding, they saw it needful to ordaine some authoritie, that might restraine by force and punishment what was violated against peace and common right: This authoritie and power of self-defence and preservation being originally and naturally in every one of them, and unitedly in them all, for ease, for order, and least each man should be his owne partial judge, they communicated and deriv'd either to one, whom for the eminence of his wisdom and integritie they chose above the rest, or to more than one whom they thought of equal deserving: the first was calld a King; the other Magistrates.[3]

The concept of a pre-contractual, pre-political, condition of human life could take many forms and be used to support different ends. The savage individualism which Hobbes saw as having been the primitive state of mankind was adduced, not to justify resistance to rulers, as in the arguments of Parker and Milton, but to enjoin the necessity of obedience to the powers that be: whatever government was in a position to give protection to the subject.[4] And against all these Sir Robert Filmer, in a series of topical replies to Parker, Milton, Hobbes and others published during the Civil War, and in his major work *Patriarcha*, composed during the 1630s but not published until 1680, urged that government was ordained of God from the beginning of the world in the patriarchy of Adam, from whom all later government derived and mon-

---

[2] Henry Parker, *Observations upon some of His Majesties late answers and expresses* (1642), in Howard Erskine-Hill and Graham Storey (eds), *Revolutionary prose of the English Civil War* (Cambridge, 1983), p. 45.

[3] John Milton, *The tenure of kings and magistrates* (1649), *Prose . . .*, p. 121.

[4] See Quentin Skinner, 'Conquest and consent: Thomas Hobbes and the engagement controversy' in G. E. Aylmer (ed.), *The interregnum: the quest for settlement, 1646–1660* (London, 1972), pp. 79–98.

archy descended. 'And indeed not only Adam, but the succeeding Patriarchs had, by right of fatherhood, royal authority over their children. . . . . This lordship which Adam by creation had over the whole world, and by right descending from him the Patriarchs did enjoy, was as large and ample as the absolutest dominion of any monarch which hath been since the creation.'[5] Filmer's position seemed stronger than it does today in an age when it was orthodox to go to the Holy Scriptures for the origins of history. Further, his argument challenged the contractualists to show a time when all men gave up their individual sovereignty, equality and freedom in return for the protection of magistracy; but it was vulnerable in its claims concerning true hereditary succession in modern times. Monarchy might have been ordained of God, and Adam the first king, but how was it possible to demonstrate the unbroken hereditary descent of modern monarchs from him?

The 1670s saw the composition of two works on the origin of government known to Pope.[6] The first of these was *An Essay on the original and nature of government* (1672) by the diplomat who was to be Jonathan Swift's patron, Sir William Temple. The second was John Locke's *Two treatises of civil government* (1690) originally composed as theoretical support for the first Earl of Shaftesbury's effort to bar the heir to the throne, the Catholic Duke of York, from the royal succession, thus effectively establishing parliamentary control over the appointment of the monarch. Temple, discussing the origin of government in the light of reason and not professing to speak 'of those Changes and Revolutions of State, of Institutions of Government that are made by the more immediate and evident Operation of Divine Will and Providence, being . . . the Subjects of our Faith, not of Reason', sees authority deriving from virtue, 'from the Opinion of Wisdom, Goodness, and Valour in the Persons who possess it' and from this 'natural Authority, may perhaps be deduced a truer Original of all Governments among Men, than from any Contracts: Tho' these be given us by the great Writers concerning Politicks and Laws.'[7] Temple agrees with Filmer that there is no evidence of 'great Numbers of Men' meeting 'in that natural state of War' to settle the first government by contract, and argues that the 'Principle of Contract as the Original of Government' is like a poet's account of the creation of man, raised out of the ground in great numbers and in perfect stature and strength. Following Aristotle, Temple argues for a

[5] Sir Robert Filmer, *Patriarcha, or, the natural powers of the kings of England asserted*, in *Patriarcha and other political works of Sir Robert Filmer* (Oxford, 1949), pp. 57–8; quoted by Locke in Peter Laslett (ed.), *Two treatises of civil government, The first treatise*, ii, 8; (Cambridge, 1960); Mentor Reprint, pp. 180–1.

[6] It is interesting that Pope, when hard-pressed in his own defence, over *Essay on Man*, iii, ll. 303–04 ('For Forms of Government let fools contest . . .') reached back in his memory, accurately, to Temple: 'There is a passage in Sir W. Temple's Essay on Government, very much of ye same nature' (*TE* iii, i, p. 170). Pope's detailed knowledge of Locke's *Two treatises* is clear from Mack's edition for *TE*: see, for example, iii, p. 114, 214n. In *The Dunciad*, of course, Pope makes general reference to Locke in the eyes of Oxford orthodoxy (iv, l. 196); *TE* v, p. 361.

[7] *The Works of Sir William Temple, Bart. in two volumes* (London, 1731), i, pp. 95–9.

gradual development of monarchy from natural 'paternal Authority', the
origin of government (p. 100). Aristocracy and democracy might indeed have
succeeded monarchy so founded, however, and 'Government founded upon
Contract, may have succeeded those founded upon Authority'; but Temple
sees such contracts as more likely to have taken place between princes and
subjects in the aftermath of a conquest, 'than between Men of equal Rank and
Power' (p. 103).

By contrast with Temple's cautious and flexible patriarchalism Locke,
writing what we now know as *The second treatise of government* towards the end of
the same decade seeks to distinguish 'the Power of the *Magistrate* over a Subject
. . . from that of a *Father* over his Children'. For him 'a State of perfect Freedom
. . . within the bounds of the Law of Nature' precedes the advent of any
government.[8] Locke's account of the origin of government takes us back
(though not, probably, in any conscious echo) to Henry Parker.

Man being born, as has been proved, with a Title to perfect Freedom, and an
uncontrolled enjoyment of all the Rights and Privileges of the Law of Nature, equally
with any other Man, or Number of Men in the World, hath by Nature a Power, not only
to preserve his Property, that is, his Life, Liberty and Estate, against the Injuries and
Attempts of other Men; but to judge of, and punish the breaches of that Law in others,
as he is persuaded the offence deserves. . . . But because no *Political Society* can be, nor
subsist without having within it self the Power to preserve the Property, and in order
thereunto punish the Offences of all those of that Society; there, and there only is
Political Society, where every one of the members hath quitted this natural Power,
resign'd it up into the hands of the Community in all cases that exclude him not from
appealing for Protection to the Law established by it. And thus all private judgement of
every particular Member being excluded, the Community comes to be Umpire, by
settled standing Rules, indifferent, and the same to all Parties; and by Men having
Authority from the Community, for the execution of those Rules, decides all the
differences that may happen between any Members of that Society, concerning any
matter of right; and punishes those Offences, which any Member hath committed
against the Society, with such Penalties as the Law has established (*The Second Treatise*,
VII, 86–7, pp. 366–7).

An account such as this, unlike that of Temple and still more unlike Filmer,
emphasizes a clean break between man's original condition and the beginning
of civil society. He has acknowledged in the previous chapter, 'Of Paternal
Power', how fathers might seem to develop naturally into princes, but he
insists that behind that apparent continuity there was absolute discontinuity
(*The Second Treatise*, VI, 55–9, pp. 346–9). What leads Locke so to insist on this
clean break is the urgent and categorical requirement of his preferred model of
society, the underlying assumptions of which he throws into the form of an
historical narrative. It is notable that he makes no attempt to meet Filmer's
challenge to the contractualists: when historically did this total delegation of
sovereignty occur? It may be thought beside the point to criticize Locke for
writing incredible history: his account, it might be argued, is to be valued as

---

[8] *Two treatises of civil government*, *The second treatise*, I–II, 3–4; II, 6; pp. 308–9, 311.

logical deduction rather than historical narration. It is, however, logical deduction not from society in general but from a particular model. Convincing historical derivation should not then be irrelevant to Locke's persuasive purpose. Nonetheless his case, though argued in prose and in philosophical and legal terms, is really no more than an affirmation of his desired hypothesis. What he offers is a myth, though it does not at first sight look like one. Temple's remark that the 'argument' of contractualists was fittest for poets had been a shrewd hit.

II

'You poets', wrote Bolingbroke in what sounds more like a comment on *An Essay on Man*, III, than the record of one of its sources, 'have given beautiful descriptions of a golden age, with which you suppose that the world began. I do not believe that men were as good, any more than I believe that other animals were as tame, by nature, as you represent them to have been in the primordial world.'[9] It is a fair point that poets have often substituted the pleasant for the probable; but it also suggests an opportunity of which Pope was likely to have been aware. Where a philosopher like Locke purveys a myth *de facto*, a poet can supply one *de jure* and openly. In the present case, if the poet builds his myth of origins upon what appears the most probable the myth will be doubly compelling. What Pope considered the most probable, well-versed as he doubtless was in both the patriarchal and contractual traditions from the talk of Bolingbroke if not from earlier reading, cannot be certainly known. But as he wrote *An Essay on Man*, the design of which was to preclude expression of the revealed truths of Christianity, he may have recalled Temple, in an essay written on the same plan, stating that 'All Nations' appear, 'upon the first Records that are left to us, under the Authority of Kings, or Princes, or some other Magistrates.'[10]

Before discussing Pope's poetic rendering of the origins of government it is worth considering his precedents from earlier poets. For if the myth of an original golden age in Hesiod, Virgil and Ovid leaps first to our mind as it did to Bolingbroke, it was not in fact the only possibility. In 'The Ancient Concept of Progress' E. R. Dodds observes that the idea of progress emerged late from Greek literature to find the field already occupied by two great anti-progressive myths, 'the myth of the Lost Paradise – called by the Greeks "the life under Kronos", by the Romans the *Saturnia regna* or Golden Age – and the myth of Eternal Recurrence'.[11] Still, the very early poet–philosopher Xenophanes could write: 'Not from the first did the gods reveal everything to mankind, / But in course of time by research men discover improvements'

---

[9] 'Fragments or minutes of essays', x; *The works of the late Right Honorable Henry St. John, Lord Viscount Bolingbroke* (London, 1754), V, p. 107.

[10] William Temple, *An essay on the original and nature of government*, in *The works . . .*, I, p. 99.

[11] E. R. Dodds, *The ancient concept of progress and other essays on Greek literature and belief* (Oxford, 1973), p. 3.

(Dodds, p. 4). Posidonius and Lucretius, in the first century B C, saw man emerging from primitivism through the invention of useful arts, and since *De Rerum Natura* was a major model for *An Essay on Man*,[12] it is interesting to consider Lucretius' account. For Lucretius, primitive man, the product like the rest of nature of a random collision of atoms, was, as his seventeenth-century translator Creech put it, 'as hard as *Parent*-stones'.[13] Like other beasts man slept in woods and caves; he lived off acorns, apples and water; went naked; and knew nothing of fire.

> No fixt *Society*, no steddy Laws,
> No *publick* Good was sought, no *common* Cause,
> But all at War, each rang'd, each sought his food,
> By Nature taught to seek his *private* Good.   (p. 169)

Without much explanation, Lucretius recounts the invention of huts and clothes, of the use of fire, and marital fidelity. Then the temper of man's mind grew more gentle: and

> Then *Neighbours*, by degrees *familiar* grown,
> Made Leagues, and Bonds, and each secur'd his *own*:
> And then by *signs* and broken Words agreed,
> That they would keep, preserve, defend, and feed
> Defenceless *Infants*, and the *Women* too,
> As *Natural Pity* prompted them to do.   (p. 171)

In this account of the progress of primitive man is, in loose form, a statement of an original contract as the basis of society.

Analogues to this view of the progress of man were to be found in Cicero and in the Augustan Vitruvius. Cicero, in his early work *De Inventione*, also postulated a primitive stage at which man wandered like the animals living off wild food, relying only on his strength, and enjoying no ordered religion, social duties, legitimate marriage, or equitable law. In Cicero's hypothesis it was then that the gift of eloquence of some great and wise man called together the rest and changed them, not without resistance, from savages into civilized people.[14] Thus Cicero introduced what was to have been a full-scale treatise on eloquence and oratory, and it is to this public and legal ability that, in effect, he ascribes the origins of society. It is not surprising that the sixteenth-century humanist Buchanan had turned to *De Inventione* to help him evolve his own theory of original contract.

[12] On Lucretius and *An Essay on Man* see: Pope to Swift, 15 Sept. 1734, *Correspondence*, III, p. 433; Spence, I, p. 135 (item 305); Miriam Leranbaum, *Alexander Pope's 'opus magnum' 1729–1744* (Oxford, 1977), pp. 40–63; and Bernard Fabian, 'Pope and Lucretius: observations on *An Essay on Man*', *Modern Language Review* LXXIV (1979), 524–37. Brean S. Hammond, *Pope and Bolingbroke: a study of friendship and influence*, pp. 80–5, opposes Fabian's case, in order to make more room for the influence of Bolingbroke.

[13] *Titus Lucretius Carus, his Six books De natura rerum. Done into English verse*, with notes by Thomas Creech (London, 1682), p. 168.

[14] Cicero, *De Inventione*, I, ii, 2.

Vitruvius also saw man as having lived, *more vetero*, in caves, woods and forests like beasts. For him not the advent of an orator but the accidental discovery of fire led to language and a life in common. For Vitruvius, man learned to build by the imitation of nature and, progressing by degrees to other arts and disciplines, pioneered a way from savage life to civilization.[15]

These examples extend our awareness of the choice open to Pope in *An Essay on Man*. The poetic tradition from the ancient world did not point in one direction only; if Pope wished to propound the contractual myth Lucretius afforded him an excellent base on which to build. There was a less close affinity, perhaps, between patriarchalism and the myth of the Golden Age. If in Parker and Milton the contractual myth shows man seeking to make good something lost at his fall, the patriarchal myth proposes an institution which has survived the Fall (in classical terms the loss of the *Saturnia Regna*).[16]

III

Pope's account of the origin of society is based on his particular understanding of the Law of Nature. That is to say that the poet, before he speaks like a political theorist, must speak like a natural philosopher. Hence, writing of the unity of Nature, Pope urges:

> See plastic Nature working to this end,
> The single atoms each to other tend,
> Attract, attracted to, the next in place
> Form'd and impell'd its neighbour to embrace.
> See Matter next, with various life endu'd,
> Press to one centre still, the gen'ral Good.
> See dying vegetables life sustain,
> See life dissolving vegetate again:
> All forms that perish other forms supply,
> (By turns we catch the vital breath, and die)
> Like bubbles on the sea of Matter born,
> They rise, they break, and to that sea return.   (III, ll. 9–20)

Lucretius, who is partly Pope's model here (Leranbaum, p. 54), serves the later poet well with the powerful sense of an objective and impersonal nature which he so often imparts. Pope's optimism in this poem (if optimism it be) depends for conviction on his initial resistance to any obvious, anthropocentric vision. Rather he needed something of the austerity of Rochester's Lucretian imitation of the Chorus from Seneca's *Troades*.[17] This is the great importance in Pope's passage of 'the sea of Matter'. At the same time the passage displays another debt, not this time pagan, early Roman and materialist, but Christian,

---

[15] Vitruvius, *De Architectura*, II, 1.
[16] See Filmer, *Patriarcha*, III, p. 57.
[17] David M. Vieth (ed.), *The complete poems of John Wilmot, Earl of Rochester* (London, 1968), pp. 150–1.

late Roman and Platonic. The chain of love with which this paragraph opens ('behold the chain of Love . . .') is in debt to Boethius' *De Consolatione Philosophiae*, and to Chaucer's echo of a passage from it in Dryden's version.[18] Thus the doctrine of the interdependence of nature, formally announced at the beginning of the paragraph, seems to have emerged from the observation of physical phenomena by the end:

> All serv'd, all serving! nothing stands alone;
> The chain holds on, and where it ends, unknown.   (ll. 25–6)

It carries overtones of divine love despite the austere alienness of vision disclosed by some of the lines. The 'all-preserving Soul' (l. 22) is seen to move on the face of the terrifying 'sea of Matter'.

Passages such as this are important in order that later sequences of the Epistle should not appear anthropocentrically fanciful. In these sequences religious doctrine is meant to have some natural–philosophical force, the implied argument for God's existence from design brought to life:

> Who taught the nations of the field and wood
> To shun their poison, and to chuse their food?
> Prescient, the tides or tempests to withstand,
> Build on the wave, or arch beneath the sand?
> Who made the spider parallels design,
> Sure as De-moivre, without rule or line?
> Who bid the stork, Columbus-like, explore
> Heav'ns not his own, and worlds unknown before?
> Who calls the council, states the certain day,
> Who forms the phalanx, and who points the way?
>   God, in the nature of each being, founds
> Its proper bliss, and sets its proper bounds.   (ll. 99–110)

Is it quite clear that the human world is being *imposed* on the natural in this passage? Did not (Pope thought) the halcyon really nest on the wave and the kingfisher beneath the sand? Was there not a natural geometry in the spider's web? Did not and do not migratory birds find by instinct worlds to them unknown?[19] Interesting, too, is the political language used at the beginning and end: 'the nations of the field and wood' have their own councils and communal appointments.

The Epistle, like some others by Pope at this period, may be seen to have an alternating procedure. An 'objective', Lucretian account alternates with more evidently human and religious terms. Thus the role of the natural passions is

---

[18] See *An Essay on Man, TE*, III, p. 92 (ll. 7–26n). These references, pointing back to Dryden's *Fables*, and to Boethius, parts of whom Pope translated in his youth, seem to indicate early and important influences.

[19] Note the discussion of a modern naturalist, W. H. Thorpe, *Animal nature and human nature* (New York, 1974), pp. 191–203.

next allowed to pick up the interdependence of Nature, once again showing
man to resemble the animal, though not in any merely brutal way:

> Not Man alone, but all that roam the wood,
> Or wing the sky, or roll along the flood,
> Each loves itself, but not itself alone,
> Each sex desires alike, 'till two are one.
> Nor ends the pleasure with the fierce embrace;
> They love themselves, a third time, in their race.
> Thus beast and bird their common charge attend . . .   (ll. 119–25)

This meditation on natural ties immediately precedes that formal poetic
portrait of 'The state of Nature' which Bolingbroke seems to have been
complaining about in his Fragment X.

> Nor think, in NATURE'S STATE they blindly trod;
> The state of Nature was the reign of God:
> Self-love and Social at her birth began,
> Union the bond of all things, and of Man.
> Pride then was not; nor Arts, that Pride to aid;
> Man walk'd with beast, joint tenant of the shade;
> The same his table, and the same his bed . . .   (ll. 147–53)

The paradox of Pope's presentation of 'a golden age' – if that indeed is what
Pope thought he was offering – is that, while not without a proleptic view of
future fall ('Ah! how unlike the man of times to come', l. 161), it is succeeded
not by an account of degeneration but of gradual progress:

> See him from Nature rising slow to Art!
> To copy Instinct then was Reason's part;
> Thus then to Man the voice of Nature spake –
> 'Go, from the Creatures thy instructions take:
> 'Learn from the birds what food the thickets yield;
> 'Learn from the beasts the physic of the field;
> 'Thy arts of building from the bee receive;
> 'Learn of the mole to plow, the worm to weave;
> 'Learn of the little Nautilus to sail,
> 'Spread the thin oar, and catch the driving gale.
> 'Here too all forms of social union find,
> 'And hence let Reason, late, instruct Mankind:
> 'Here subterranean works and cities see;
> 'There towns aerial on the waving tree.
> 'Learn each small People's genius, policies,
> 'The Ant's republic, and the realm of Bees;
> 'How those in common all their wealth bestow,
> 'And Anarchy without confusion know;
> 'And these for ever, tho' a Monarch reign,
> 'Their sep'rate cells and properties maintain.
> 'Mark what unvary'd laws preserve each state,
> 'Laws wise as Nature, and as fix'd as Fate.'   (ll. 169–90)

Perhaps, then, Bolingbroke was wide of the mark, if he referred to this passage? Perhaps Pope aimed at the presentation of a 'state of Nature' precisely, rather than a Golden Age, with the possibility of progress thereafter, as envisaged by Lucretius, Cicero and Vitruvius. Of the three Cicero is closest to Pope here, for he does not, as it happens, compare the life of primitive man to that of the wild beast, *more ferarum*. Pope has retained the bond between primitive man and beast, not by conceding that man was once savage, but by supposing that beasts were gentle.

Pope seems generally closer to these Latin authors than to the English authors of the contractual tradition. Unlike Parker and Milton Pope lays no stress on man's Fall. He rejects Milton's insistence on man's superiority to and 'command' over animals; and he does not, like Hobbes, see primitive human life as 'brutish'. Unlike Locke, to whom the Law of Nature endorsed in principle but could not enforce in practice man's original freedoms and rights, Pope paints a picture of primitive man happy in what he had in common with the beasts. However, a Lockeian moment occurs within the passage quoted when 'the realm of Bees' exemplifies a combination of monarchy with individual rights: ''tho a Monarch reign, / Their sep'rate cells and properties maintain.'[20] In another respect too man's rise to art recalls Locke, or rather what Locke has in common with the contractual tradition:

> Here too all forms of social union find   (l. 179)

Something like society is to be observed among the beasts (the argument is as valid today as it was in the eighteenth century) but man has not yet reached formal political community. That point is described in a later passage:

> Great Nature spoke; observant Men obey'd;
> Cities were built, Societies were made:
> Here rose one little state; another near
> Grew by like means, and join'd, thro' love or fear.
> Did here the trees with ruddier burdens bend,
> And there the streams in purer rills descend?
> What war could ravish, Commerce could bestow,
> And he return'd a friend, who came a foe.
> Converse and Love mankind might strongly draw,
> When Love was Liberty, and Nature Law.
> Thus States were form'd; the name of King unknown,
> 'Till common int'rest plac'd the sway in one.
> 'Twas VIRTUE ONLY (or in arts or arms,
> Diffusing blessings, or averting harms)
> The same which in a Sire the Sons obey'd,
> A Prince the Father of a People made.   (ll. 199–214)

This paragraph is worth close attention. 'Cities', 'Societies' and states (l. 200) show that Pope now treats the origin of government ('Origine of POLITICAL

---

[20] A. D. Nuttall calls it 'a very British defence of small-scale private property' in his monograph, p. 114.

SOCIETIES' as Pope's note had once stated; *TE* iii, i, p. 113). It is clear that government as such evolves before contract. When, on the other hand, Pope comes to those lines by which he once placed the gloss: 'The Origine of MONARCHY' (ll. 210ff.) we find the one clearly contractual moment – it is hardly given great prominence – in the whole Epistle. Pope strikes a careful and intelligent balance. In lines 209–10 Pope affirms that states evolved before the formal institution of monarchy, thus repudiating the strong form of Filmer's argument for patriarchal monarchy; and declares that monarchy was based on consent, though he does not thereby affirm the strong form of Locke's argument, according to which every sovereign individual willingly, though not irrevocably, entrusted magistracy with his own rights. Pope's moment of original contract is presented less as a public legal transaction than as a recognition of appropriate merit, and the context of the Epistle as a whole, with its emphasis upon evolution through imitation of nature, induces us to interpret the contract as a stage in a process rather than a start on a totally new foundation. The conclusion of the paragraph fully adopts the idiom of patriarchalism and, taken out of context, would suggest that Pope's account of the origin of government was Filmerian.[21] In fact Pope has, in six lines, registered his awareness of both Filmerian and Lockeian positions, recognizing a measure of validity in each. What mediates between the Lockeian and Filmerian moments, interestingly enough, is the notion of natural authority (ll. 211–12) derived from Temple's *Essay upon the original and nature of government* with Lucretius, among others, behind him (v, ll. 1105–9), in which both patriarchal and contractual argument found a place.

In the next paragraph the patriarchal idiom continues strongly, so strongly in fact that a retrospective emphasis is thrown on a word in an earlier line: 'the *name* of King unknown' (my italics). The implication is that kings had existed earlier in fact though not in name:

> 'Till then, by Nature crown'd, each Patriarch sate,
> King, priest, and parent of his growing state;
> On him, their second Providence, they hung,
> Their law his eye, their oracle his tongue.

---

[21] It is taken as such by J. C. D. Clark in his powerful and challenging study, *English society 1688–1832: ideology, social structure and political practice during the ancien régime* (Cambridge, 1985), p. 80. The couplet is indeed an instance of what Clark terms 'The Survival of Patriarchalism' and so is much else in this Epistle, but it is a qualified survival. Nuttall errs more obviously in the opposite direction: perceiving that 'Pope found what he wanted' in a patriarchal sentence at the end of Locke's chapter 'Of Paternal Power' in *The second treatise*, he concludes that 'Pope's scheme obviously resembles Locke's in that the rise of human institutions is seen, not as an extrinsic curbing of anarchic appetite, but as the gradual codification of impulses already present and "naturally governed" by the law of human nature' (p. 116). He ignores the point that the sentence which 'Pope wanted' is in the same paragraph repudiated by Locke as a basis for any kingly title; and that Locke's general argument in this and the following chapter does not 'obviously resemble' Pope's 'scheme'. (Nuttall is also wrong to give the date of Locke's *Second treatise* as 1714.)

He from the wond'ring furrow call'd the food,
Taught to command the fire, controul the flood,
Draw forth the monsters of th'abyss profound,
Or fetch th'aerial eagle to the ground.
'Till drooping, sick'ning, dying, they began
Whom they rever'd as God to mourn as Man:
Then, looking up from sire to sire, explor'd
One great first father, and that first ador'd.
Or plain tradition that this All begun,
Convey'd unbroken faith from sire to son,
The worker from the work distinct was known,
And simple Reason never sought but one:
Ere Wit oblique had broke that steddy light,
Man, like his Maker, saw that all was right,
To Virtue, in the paths of Pleasure, trod,
And own'd a Father when he own'd a God.
LOVE all the faith, and all th'allegiance then;
For Nature knew no right divine in Men,
No ill could fear in God; and understood
A sov'reign being but a sov'reign good.   (ll. 215–238)

The concept of patriarchy could hardly be more pervasive than it is here, the natural fount of families, of kingship, of priesthood, of monotheism. It is patriarchal monarchy in all but name, the name only denied because the patriarch is a monarch and more. Pope wishes to show the root of rule in Nature. The more divided and sophisticated state in which, for example, kingship and priesthood were distinguished had not yet arisen. The godlike creativeness which for the first time cultivated the earth, exploited fire and controlled water was that of natural authority. Being natural, however, it was mortal; decay was as natural as command. This feature of Nature thus gave rise to a further natural principle which transcended decay and death, that of succession and inheritance, which was the temporal chain leading backward and upward to God, downward and onward to the rulers which the future would need.

It is in the context of this picture of natural society that Pope sets forth the grounds of political allegiance, and here, in this affirmation of a myth of natural patriarchy, that he repudiates the formal patriarchalism we associate with Filmer ('Nature knew no right divine in Men'). If in his earlier repudiation of Filmer (ll. 209–10) Pope conceded contract, here it is love of the 'sov'reign good' of natural authority that is proposed in place of obedience to the lineal successors of Adam. Pope thus denies original equality and individual freedom but finds happiness in natural subordination to the sway of the patriarchs. And from this it can be seen that when, for Pope, 'common interest plac'd the sway in one', this social contract was not, as for Parker, Milton and Locke, a radical discontinuity in life but rather the recognition through monarchy of the natural structure of patriarchalism. This brings Pope closer to Temple than to Locke. Though Pope is sometimes close to specific passages in Locke his poem does not centrally affirm the Lockeian myth of contract.

IV

The resemblance of Pope's position to that of Bolingbroke in his posthumous *Fragments or minutes of essays* (1754) raises the question of Bolingbroke's influence on *An Essay on Man*, urged afresh by Brean Hammond in his *Pope and Bolingbroke: a study of friendship and influence*. Hammond rightly says that Pope and Bolingbroke share the Aristotelian 'view of monarchy as a development from paternal authority' and 'consider familial bonds precedent to civil obligations' (p. 89). That in *An Essay on Man* and elsewhere Pope acknowledged a major general debt to Bolingbroke is a matter of record; that some written materials were communicated by Bolingbroke to Pope for the poem was stated by several contemporaries and is entirely probable. That the *Fragments or minutes of essays* as we have them were written as well as published after *An Essay on Man* is also clear, however, and unless new evidence comes to light it must remain a matter of speculation as to how faithfully they preserve any materials supplied to Pope when the poem was being composed. The Bolingbroke who had turned against the memory of the dead poet was not above wanting to claim credit for Pope's most internationally famous poem (to win it back, as it were, from Warburton), and Maynard Mack's argument that the *Essay* may have influenced the *Fragments* remains intrinsically cogent, and on present evidence virtually impossible to refute.[22] A common tradition of political thought deriving from Aristotle and critical of Hobbes and Locke on contract and the state of nature flows through both Pope and Bolingbroke, and Pope could find all his leading ideas from earlier sources. There was, possibly, an intricate relationship of mutual influence between Pope and Bolingbroke; but whichever side the balance of debt came down on hardly affects the political character of Epistle III, which it has been the aim of the present essay to delineate.

It may however be worth noting the very different manner and tone of the relevant *Fragments*, x–xvi, from Pope's Epistle. Addressed to Pope when, or as if, he was alive, the *Fragments* is an overtly controversial work, full of citation, quotation and refutation. It is filled with learned names, and Bolingbroke disposes grandly and usually very intelligently with them all. Pope, in his Epistle, might have chosen to evoke a genealogy of famous names as Thomson had six years earlier in his 'Summer' (and in amplified form in first publication of the whole *Seasons* as recently as 1730). Thomson's list of classical and English worthies, which included Plato, Aristotle, and Cicero; Bacon, Boyle and Locke, would have afforded Pope a poetic idiom capable of assimilating the author-laden paragraphs of the *Fragments*.[23] But Pope aimed at a totally

[22] See *An Essay on Man*, *TE* III, i, pp. xxvi–xxxi; and Hammond, pp. 69–79, 84–91.
[23] 'Summer', ll. 1535–59; James Sambrook (ed.), *The Seasons* (Oxford, 1981), pp. 128–31.

different effect. If possible he wished to dispel the tang of controversy, to melt down opinion into myth, and draw close imaginatively to his picture of primitive society.

It may also be noted that Bolingbroke, in his specific management of a controversial idiom, is at pains to strike a modern and indeed 'enlightened' attitude. This leads him into open mockery of 'that ridiculous writer FILMER', with whom he has in fact much in common, and makes him ostentatiously respectful to Locke (with Hooker one of 'our best writers')[24] whose leading political argument he explicitly rejects. Bolingbroke's tone, though not his content, is distinctly Whiggish. This is hardly the case with Pope, who manages his own attempt at the reconciliation of opposing principles in a very different way.

V

In 'steering betwixt the extremes of doctrines seemingly opposite', Pope succeeds in the reconciliation of opposites to a considerable degree. He has something for the contractualists, and something more for the patriarchalists. Yet, despite ubiquitous local borrowing and echoing, his poem is not equally hospitable to all traditions of political thought. Nobody who subscribed to the full argument of Locke's *Two treatises*, or to Hobbes, Milton and Parker before him, could be satisfied with Pope's narrative. The Original Contract by which each free, equal and sovereign individual was supposed to have entrusted his rights to magistracy of some kind has a very diminished role here. On the other hand, though Pope denies formal political monarchy in primitive society, and emphatically denies the patriarchs that unique mark of the magistrate the 'right divine' to be judged by God alone, the whole spirit and tone of his story is patriarchalist. Godhead is found through fatherhood; kingship is bequeathed by it. As in Temple's *Essay*, however, the patriarchal principle has been disentangled from the specific historical difficulties of tracing true royal successions from Adam. Patriarchalism is not proffered, as in Filmer, in the form of sacred history, but in the easier and more flexible form of a poetic 'natural philosophy'.

This permits Pope to combine with it those progressive accounts of the early life of man to be found in Vitruvius, Cicero and above all Lucretius. It is not the case that in Epistle III Pope offers a myth of the origin of society the implicit effect of which is to ratify a social *status quo*: to borrow the original title of *Caleb Williams*, *things as they are*. Furthermore it is the case that, immediately after the passages in Epistle III we have been considering, Pope added a usurpation myth:

> Force first made Conquest, and that conquest, Law;
> 'Till Superstition taught the tyrant awe,
> Then shar'd the Tyranny . . .   (ll. 245–7)

---

[24] Bolingbroke, *Works* v, 114, 125.

Not only are such myths of immense importance in theodicy, whether narrative or discursive in form, but they are, like the myth of the Norman Yoke, available to justify fundamental change. This can be seen from Pope's use of more or less the same myth of usurpation in *An Essay on Criticism* (ll. 681–92) and *Windsor Forest* (ll. 43–92). All this is worth emphasis since readers of *An Essay on Man*, and especially those whose idea of the poem is based on Epistle I, so often interpret it as an apologia for Things as they Were or Things as They Had Been: 'Cosmic Toryism' or 'the Politics of Nostalgia'.[25] The larger design of Pope's poem, however, would seem to have been to commend humility and resignation where man's relation with God was concerned, but to allow for and even applaud man's capacity for social and political evolution in obedience to Nature. This does not, of course, mean that Pope foresaw and approved the ways by which his own society was to change. It means merely that he found no conflict between the idea of patriarchalism and the idea of progress.

[25] The phrase, apparently first used by Basil Willey as a chapter-title in *The eighteenth-century background: studies on the idea of nature in the thought of the period* (London, 1940) is also found in J. M. Cameron, 'Doctrinal to an age: notes towards a revaluation of Pope's *Essay on Man*', originally published in the *Dublin Review* (1951), reprinted in revised form in Maynard Mack (ed.), *Essential articles for the study of Alexander Pope*, (Connecticut, 1968), p. 358. It involves a misconstruction of eighteenth-century Toryism as well as of Pope's poem. For the influential half-truths involved in the terms 'The politics of nostalgia' and 'The nostalgia of the Augustan poets', see Isaac Kramnick, *Bolingbroke and his circle: the politics of nostalgia in the age of Walpole* (London, 1968): an important book which needs to be re-assessed. I am grateful for the advice of Mr A. S. A. Rushdy in this note.

6

Pope and the arts of pleasure

DAVID B. MORRIS

We are always being told about Desire, never about Pleasure.
(Roland Barthes, *The Pleasure of the Text*)

I never saw him laugh very heartily in all my life.
(Magdalen Rackett, Pope's half-sister)[1]

Lionel Trilling expressed surprise that one of Wordsworth's boldest claims in the Preface to *Lyrical Ballads* ('bold to the point of being shocking') had gone completely unnoticed. 'I refer,' Trilling wrote, 'to the sentence in which Wordsworth speaks of what he calls "the grand elementary principle of pleasure," and says of it that it constitutes "the naked and native dignity of man," that it is the principle by which man "knows, and feels, and lives, and moves." '[2] What proves shocking is not simply Wordsworth's unambiguous, sweeping assertion that human dignity and knowledge take their origin in something so mundane as pleasure. As Trilling points out, Wordsworth's diction echoes and controverts St Paul's declaration that 'we live, and move, and have our being' in God (Acts 17:28). This provocative aggrandizement of pleasure is not uncommon among Romantic writers, for whom it points ultimately towards an enraptured delight in which the boundaries of ego and of world temporarily dissolve. (Dejection, of course, is the linked but opposite state, characterized not so much by the absence of pleasure as by its failures.) For Trilling, the boldly diverse Romantic engagements with pleasure create a stark contrast to modern thought. The devaluations of pleasure which he observes in writers from Nietzsche to Kafka reflect how far we have relocated significance in activities devoted to pleasurelessness, to unpleasure, and (as I would add) to pain. We stand at least twice removed from the attitudes and values which help to define the world of Alexander Pope, where familiar words such as 'pleasure' sometimes conceal a strangeness we mistake for our own ordinary speech.

Augustan pleasure achieves a distinctive (but never completely unique) character which separates it unmistakably from modern and from Romantic versions. Major cultural differences thus prevent us from understanding pleasure solely through a universal physiology of nerve impulses or brain states.

---

[1] Roland Barthes, *The pleasure of the text* (1973), trans. Richard Miller (New York, 1975), p. 57. Magdalen Rackett is quoted by Spence, 1, p. 6.

[2] 'The fate of pleasure', in *Beyond culture: essays on literature and learning* (New York, 1965), p. 58.

Even identical sensations (if they could be measured and proved identical) will in different cultures and periods evoke quite different values, perceptions, emotions, and meanings. We may therefore leave unresolved the presently unanswerable question 'what is pleasure?' For Locke – as for most readers of Pope, no doubt – pleasure ranks among the elemental 'clear and distinct' ideas which cannot be effectively defined but only known 'by experience'.[3] Instead of labouring vainly to define pleasure or to order its varying shades and intensities, we might better ask what particular issues and conflicts accrued to the experience of pleasure during Pope's lifetime and in his writing. Because Pope's work participates in a distinctively Augustan view of pleasure, his poetry reflects more than wholly personal, idiosyncratic choices, and yet his treatment of pleasure also remains at times thoroughly individual: not only in opposition to contemporary thought but also divided against itself. Pleasure for Pope grows increasingly complex as new poems engage new aspects of a subject which is (after all) immense and which elicits his characteristic preference (often expressed as irony) for multiple points of view. In exploring these Popean and Augustan versions of pleasure, we may find that Pope, like Wordsworth, has some surprises in reserve.

My inquiry takes as its point of departure a single statement from *An Essay on Man*. The statement would sound quite alien if paraphrased (or quoted as prose) in most accounts of Pope's thought. Tillotson, Sherburn, Brower, and Mack, for example, simply do not discuss it. Pope, indeed, is somewhat easier to understand if we ignore the couplet or dismiss it as a meaningless slip of the pen. Here are the verses – to which, for clarity, I have added the implied but unwritten verb:

> Pleasure, or wrong or rightly understood, [is]
> Our greatest evil, or our greatest good.
>
> (*TE* III, pp. 65–6, ll. 91–2)

This is an extraordinary claim. Pleasure, Pope says, is both the best thing and the worst thing that could befall us. It is perhaps plausible (although misguided) to imagine Pope-the-moralist asserting that pleasure is an evil. But our *greatest* evil? (Elsewhere, *An Essay on Man* follows the main tendency of Pope's work in describing the greatest danger to our moral life not as pleasure but as pride.) Even if we invent persuasive arguments to explain why Pope unexpectedly elevates pleasure to the position of supreme evil, there is nothing

---

[3] Alexander Campbell Fraser (ed.), *An essay concerning human understanding* (1690), 2 vols. (1894; rpt. New York, 1959), I, p. 302 (II.xx.1). Gilbert Ryle, for example, while accepting a distinction between localized and non-localized pain, refuses to accept a similar distinction regarding pleasure. For Ryle, pleasure is not a sensation and cannot, like headaches, be localized in a specific bodily part (see 'Pleasure', in *Dilemmas* (Cambridge, 1954), pp. 54–67). For other modern discussions of pleasure – from philosophical, psychological and physiological perspectives – see J. L. Cowan, *Pleasure and pain: a study in philosophical psychology* (London, 1968); Rem B. Edwards, *Pleasures and pains: a theory of qualitative hedonism* (New York, 1979); and Thomas S. Szasz, M.D., *Pain and pleasure: a study of bodily feelings*, 2nd edn. (New York, 1975).

plausible in the claim that Pope views pleasure as man's greatest *good*. An exploration of Pope's ideas about pleasure will not only enrich our understanding of specific lines or poems but also clarify in his work a mode of thought so fundamental that, when exposed, as in his unadorned couplet from *An Essay on Man*, it seems almost shockingly crude – as if it could bear the weight of subtler poetic elaboration only when discreetly hidden from sight.

Pope's couplet about pleasure escapes from meaningless self-contradiction by a loophole. Despite its narrowness, the escape is deft and certain. Pope assures us that the paradox will unravel its mystery in plain sense as soon as we know the differences between pleasure when it is 'wrong or rightly understood'. This assurance, however, cannot resolve or entirely dissolve the questions which arise. Is pleasure wrongly understood still pleasure? What *is* a right understanding of pleasure and how do we recognize it? Behind such perplexities lies the larger question of why Pope should employ pleasure to define the boundaries which organize his moral vision. His couplet typically withholds more meaning than it supplies, even as its implications extend far beyond *An Essay on Man*. In fact, from the stylized, amorous play of his pastoral lovers in 'Spring' to the obscene epic games of *The Dunciad*, Pope depicts a multi-levelled social milieu in which seeking pleasure is among the few unvarying features. Pleasure-seeking takes so many different forms that it seems one of the basic human activities – like waking and sleeping – which tend to pass without notice, although Pope endows pleasure with the same unexpected prominence he attributes to sleep and wakefulness. Still, it is easy to nod off when general truths appear so general as to resemble truisms. 'Each Mortal has his Pleasure,' Pope writes, but much the same could be said for noses and ears.[4]

The first thing to notice about Augustan pleasure is that it carries a rich cultural and intellectual history. Pope's age, if it did not exactly rediscover pleasure after the austerities of the Puritan interregnum, effectively redefined and redistributed it. The redefinition implicitly criticized not only puritanical rigour but also the excess of Restoration antidotes to rigour. The court of Charles II and the obliging muse of Dryden both suffer rebuke in Pope's description of their era as 'the fat Age of Pleasure, Wealth, and Ease' (*An Essay on Criticism*, *TE* I, p. 297, l. 534). Augustan enjoyments sometimes retain or extend Restoration licentiousness, as in John Cleland's famous narrative of Fanny Hill, entitled *Memoirs of a woman of pleasure*. More often, however, they are chastened with politeness and evade the monopoly of aristocratic and of masculine privilege. Such privileges were still asserted. Chesterfield wrote to his son in a witty play on words, 'Pleasure is now, and ought to be, your business.'[5] As his maxim suggests, traditional divisions of age, gender and

---

[4] *The First Satire of the Second Book of Horace Imitated*, *TE* IV, p. 9, l. 45. Pope's line has no specific source in Horace.

[5] Charles Strachey (ed.), *The letters of the Earl of Chesterfield to his son*, 2 vols., 3rd edn. (London, 1932), II, p. 133.

social class still separated the workaday world of common labour from the glittering sphere of aristocratic self-indulgence, but these barriers, although they did not vanish, were rapidly breaking down. The redefinition of polite enjoyments released pleasure from the confinements of Restoration hedonism and of élite taste. Pleasure had become, with a few obvious exceptions, almost everybody's business.

The redistribution of pleasure helped to create a changed social landscape, much as social changes created both a wider access to enjoyment and new pleasures to enjoy. Unrestricted to the appointed times of popular holidays or to the circumscribed spaces of tavern, brothel, fairground and ballroom, pleasure-seeking spread from the re-opened theatres and proliferating coffee-houses to race-tracks, country villas, opera, spas, masquerades, prize-fights, fashion, novels and gardens, including such lavish new centres of public amusement as Vauxhall and Ranelagh.[6] What J. H. Plumb has called the 'commercialization of leisure' meant, above all, that pleasure had achieved unprecedented status as a commodity. Pope's loving catalogues of trinkets reflect more than (an often ironic) pride in England's recent mercantile achievements. His satiric portraits frequently show human beings (through their passion as consumers) in effect dispossessed by the objects they consume. Separated from his marbled cane and silver snuffbox, Sir Plume would possess no more weight of identity than an expensive feather, while Timon ('A puny insect, shiv'ring at a breeze') wholly depends upon the objects purchased for his gargantuan estate to give him whatever visibility he attains.[7] Pope intro-duces us to the historical moment when to the timeless amusements of eating, drinking, singing, dancing and loving – all of which receive distinctive eighteenth-century refinements – we must add the peculiarly modern passion for shopping. The Augustan encounter with pleasure moves us from Hercules' allegorical crossroad, where (alluring) vice and (stern) virtue point in opposite directions, to the ever-expanding and deeply ambiguous network of the mar-ketplace.

The changing social history of pleasure did not erase but abruptly superim-posed itself upon an intellectual history which is equally important to recover. Pleasure, that is, constitutes a traditional topic in philosophy: if you are a philosopher (at least before modernism changed the agenda of philosophy)

---

[6] For excellent surveys of social pleasures, see Warwick Wroth, *The London pleasure gardens of the eighteenth century* (1896; rpt. Connecticut, 1979) and Roy Porter, *English society in the eighteenth century* (Harmondsworth, 1982) – especially chapters 5 and 6 ('Getting and spending', 'Having and enjoying').

[7] *To Burlington*, *TE* III, ii, p. 148, l. 108. Plumb's essay 'The commercialization of leisure in eighteenth-century England' appears in the collection of essays he wrote with co-authors Neil McKendrick and John Brewer, *The birth of a consumer society: the commercialization of eighteenth century England* (London, 1982), pp. 265–85. (The essay revisits ground covered in Plumb's 1972 Stenton Lecture, *The commercialisation of leisure in eighteenth-century England* (Reading, 1973).) Pope's attention to the world of commodities and of commerce is part of Laura Brown's subject in *Alexander Pope* (New York, 1985).

pleasure is one of the things you are expected to think about. As an age of classicists perfectly understood, pleasure belongs among the central preoccupations of Greek and Roman thought, and a major question facing ancient philosophers from the pre-Socratics to Seneca and Cicero was how far pleasure coincided with various conceptions of the good life. For example, Aristippus (the favourite philosopher of Pope's friend Bolingbroke) regarded physical, sensual pleasure as the *summum bonum* and urged a life filled to the maximum with agreeable sensation. The opposite extreme of pleasure-hating is well represented by Antisthenes, a pupil of Socrates, who insisted that he would rather go mad than feel pleasure.[8] While rejecting the extreme ('sybaritic') hedonism of Aristippus, Greek philosophy tends to follow Socrates in weighing carefully – as specific questions alter points of emphasis – the just claims of pleasure within a life lived according to reason. This Socratic analysis (carried forward in the *Protagoras*, in the *Gorgias*, and above all in the *Philebus*) provides the basis for Aristotle's revisionary discussion of pleasure in books seven and ten of the *Nicomachean ethics*. Is pleasure an action or a state of being? Do pleasures of the mind differ from sensual pleasure? Is pleasure consistent with the good? identical? incompatible? These basic questions, especially as interpreted by Stoic and by Epicurean thought, Pope could find conveniently discussed in such Roman abridgements as Cicero's *De Finibus Bonorum et Malorum*. As his educated eighteenth-century readers understood, pleasure is a concept which reverberates with the wisdom of ancient philosophical thought.

So far, in what is doubtless an artificial division, I have emphasized two main ways of thinking about pleasure: as a philosophical topic and as a social practice. These two approaches sometimes utterly diverge, as they do in our Disneyland era of mass-produced entertainment, where ancient pleasure has dwindled into *fun* ('A low cant word' as defined in Johnson's *Dictionary*). Pope and his contemporaries, by contrast, understood an intimate kinship between social practice and philosophical thought. Pleasure mattered to philosophy, we might say, because philosophers recognized its importance to such basic social practices as friendship or the experience of beauty. Pleasure, after all, is what beauty produces, and (although solitary enjoyment is not unknown to eighteenth-century poets) the pleasures of Augustan solitude always imply a return to the circle of family and neighbours and friends. Indeed, pleasure experienced in total isolation – divorced from its natural setting of social life – quickly generates a contrary, desolate feeling, as if enjoyment withers without friends to nourish it. Pleasure, especially in its characteristic Augustan form known as good humour, is among the bonds which hold society together, and numerous eighteenth-century tombstones praise now-forgotten individuals

---

[8] See J. C. B. Gosling and C. C. W. Taylor, *The Greeks on pleasure* (Oxford, 1982). Also helpful are Julia Annas, 'Aristotle on pleasure and goodness', in Amélie Oksenberg Rorty (ed.), *Essays on Aristotle's Ethics* (Berkeley, 1980), pp. 285–99; and J. O. Urmson, 'Aristotle on pleasure', in J. M. E. Moravcsik (ed.), *Aristotle: a collection of critical essays* (New York, 1967), pp. 323–33.

whose chief merit (according to their survivors) was pre-eminence in the
'convivial arts'. As Hume wrote: 'A perfect solitude is, perhaps, the greatest
punishment we can suffer. Every pleasure languishes when enjoy'd a-part
from company.'[9]

The eighteenth-century convergence of social practice and of philosophical
thought imparts to pleasure a unity and importance it has now lost. Hume, in
addition to describing the way in which enjoyment tends to create 'company',
also found it natural as a philosopher to extend the ancient dialogues which
understood pleasure as an unavoidable topic for philosophy. He also openly
repeats and passes on the widespread belief among eighteenth-century philosophers that pleasure is what regulates all thought and behaviour. 'The chief
spring or actuating principle of the human mind,' he asserts broadly, 'is
pleasure or pain.'[10] For Pope as for Hume, pleasure remains so fundamental to
thought and to action that it cannot be ignored as a trivial fact of social practice
or dismissed as a remote philosophical abstraction. Their outlook perceived a
unity and significance where we now tend to see merely pointless division.
What I wish to argue is that Pope – while embracing a relatively unified
tradition which reconciled or interfused practice with philosophy – nevertheless responded to pleasure with a completely characteristic doubleness.

The doubleness in Pope's response to pleasure might be described as an
alternating (and sometimes simultaneous) affirmation and rejection. Paradox
and irony, as we might expect, are the poetic figures which most often express
this ambivalence in Pope's thought. Even affirmation possesses an intrinsic
doubleness, in the sense of extending to opposites which we would normally
consider incompatible. An indirect illustration of this affirmative doubleness
appears in the passage where – imitating Horace – Pope explains that he is
sworn to no master or sect. As an example of his eclectic independence and
attraction to variety, he cites his taste for two very different literary styles: one
public and intensely partisan, the other personal and agreeably flexible. Here
is his description:

> As drives the storm, at any door I knock,
> And house with Montagne now, or now with Lock.
> Sometimes a Patriot, active in debate,

---

[9] L. A. Selby-Bigge (ed.), *A treatise of human nature* (1739–40), 2nd edn., revised by P. H. Nidditch
(Oxford, 1978), p. 363. Addison remarks in *Spectator* no. 411: 'A Man of a Polite Imagination, is
let into a great many Pleasures that the Vulgar are not capable of receiving. He can converse
with a Picture, and find an agreeable Companion in a Statue' (Donald F. Bond (ed.), *The
Spectator*, 5 vols. (Oxford, 1965)). Split along rough lines of class, Augustan pleasure even in
solitude is essentially social, full of companionship and conversation.

[10] *A treatise of human nature*, p. 574. The importance and persistence of the tradition which Hume
extends in this passage can be judged from the first sentence of Jeremy Bentham's *An introduction
to the principles of morals and legislation* (1789): 'Nature has placed mankind under the governance
of two sovereign masters, *pain* and *pleasure*. It is for them alone to point out what we ought to do,
as well as to determine what we shall do.'

> Mix with the World, and battle for the State . . .
> Sometimes with Aristippus, or St Paul,
> Indulge my Candor, and grow all to all . . .[11]

The ironic mischief implicit in yoking together Aristippus and St Paul might be best conveyed by analogy. Saying that you practise the candour of Aristippus and Saint Paul is a little like saying you admire the strength of character in Mae West and Mother Teresa. There is nothing innocent about the combination of names. Aristippus, whatever his virtues as a stylist, is far better known as the ancient exemplar of sybaritic hedonism, who (as we have seen) defined the greatest good as sensual pleasure. St Paul initiates the long tradition of Christian contempt for pleasures of the senses. 'Who are in the flesh,' he writes bluntly to the Romans, 'cannot please God' (Acts 8:8).

The attraction to opposed points of view – like the doubleness expressed in his paradoxical affirmation and rejection of pleasure – never takes Pope so far as endorsing either a philosophical commitment to sensuality or a theological contempt for the flesh. Yet this brush with contradiction finds a close parallel in his personal life, where biographers can produce colourful episodes of ascetic self-denial and of sensual self-indulgence. For example, the poet who asserts that pleasure is our greatest good passed his days, so we are told, insensible to the music of laughter. Smiles, acknowledging wry amusement or dry approval, seem to be the limit which Pope imposed upon polite expressions of enjoyment. Of course, the Augustan death of laughter cannot be restricted or attributed to Pope. Hobbes, Swift, and Chesterfield all attest that open laughter was considered a sign of low intelligence and bad manners: *not*-laughing signified a truly superior nature.[12] More is at stake here, however, than conventions of politeness or marks of class difference. Deep, visceral, explosive Rabelaisian laughter is antithetical to Pope's whole outlook and normal modes of humour. The irony which is Pope's favoured instrument almost always implies an increase – not a jubilant release – of tension. Pleasure, in Pope's art as in his life, invariably requires conscious and habitual renunciations.

The extreme positions on pleasure represented by Aristippus and St Paul provide the boundaries which help us to locate Pope's more moderate, Aris-

---

[11] *The First Epistle of The First Book of Horace Imitated*, *TE* IV, p. 281, ll. 25–32. Horace, of course, says nothing of St Paul, although Pope adopts (and adapts) the Horatian reference to Aristippus. Bolingbroke's preference for Aristippus is observed by John Butt in his note to this passage in the Twickenham Edition.
[12] Chesterfield wrote to his son: 'I am neither of a melancholy nor a cynical disposition, and am as willing and as apt to be pleased as anybody; but I am sure that since I have had the full use of my reason, nobody has ever heard me laugh' (*Letters to his son*, I, p. 213). Like Pope and Chesterfield, Swift too had a reputation for not laughing. Although Hobbes' claim that laughter represents a 'sudden glory' of superiority is well known, we usually ignore his statement that persons most given to laughter are conscious of the fewest abilities in themselves (*Leviathan* (1651), I.vi). On the general subject of Augustan laughter, see Virgil B. Heltzel' 'Chesterfield and the anti-laughter tradition', *Modern Philology*, 26 (1928), 73–90.

totelian standpoint. Popean moderation – when the storm drives and occasion
calls – does not absolutely *exclude* such extremes as asceticism or sensuality. On
the contrary, it recognizes that even self-denial (if temporary) can serve as a
source of pleasure, while excusing an occasional feast or fling. Wisdom for
Pope *employs* the conflict of opposing forces and conditions in order to assure
vitality, and therefore he does not regard pleasure as a uniformly placid middle
state stuck somewhere in between sublime rapture and the unruffled satisfactions of gardening. Our difficulties as readers arise precisely because Pope
understands pleasure as a dynamic, often unstable energy belonging to widely
diverse actions and occasions, from Homeric sublimity to theatrical farce.
Indeed, there are really two types of doubleness which we must distinguish,
although in practice they are not always distinct. First, Pope expresses a
doubleness *toward* pleasure, which means that he will sometimes affirm and
sometimes reject the possibilities of enjoyment. Second, he recognizes a
doubleness *within* pleasure, which means that enjoyment (like so much else in
his binary field of vision) tends to divide into dualisms of false and true, of
mental and physical, of male and female, of lavish and spare. These intersecting types of doubleness make it impossible to extract from Pope's work a
single, summarizing couplet which adequately reflects his thinking about
pleasure. His work, by design, leads us beyond the nutshells of doctrine such as
a couplet might contain.

Within the ambiguous terrain where pleasure for Pope entangles mankind
in doubleness and contradiction, he nonetheless situates something like an
ideal vision. This ideal – no matter what space it grants, selectively, to the vast,
exaggerated and superhuman – centres upon a conception of life in which
pleasure flows, with healing and consoling steadiness, from small and
measured things. The quiet regularity of common events (an afternoon walk, a
dinner with simple fare and cherished companions, an evening of books or
conversation) underlies a characteristically Popean vision of pleasure. This
vision – truly incompatible with the erotic bliss or spiritual transcendence of
Romantic traditions – easily degenerates into the self-satisfied celebrations of
tedium and riskless seclusion which minor Augustan poets called imitating
Horace. Pope, however, did not confuse dullness with a life of bounded and
therefore abundant pleasure. The enjoyment provided by small, measured,
everyday, domestic events is crucial for Pope and includes the composition of
occasional verse so nugatory that from Homeric heights it would be invisible.
Such pleasures are crucial to Pope for many reasons but not least because we
consistently overlook and undervalue them. In recovering the small pleasures
of daily life, we not only increase our sum of possible enjoyment but also save
ourselves from the folly of persons who imagine that genuine satisfaction must
lie elsewhere.

Pope perfectly recognizes the strains and troubles which disfigure his picture of ideal pleasure as it encounters the unideal world of history and
misfortune. The disturbances which pierce his thickets and grotto, however,

do not call into question the ideal which they violate. The classical – Socratic and Horatian – concept of measure survives the inevitable assaults upon it by a chaotic world which simply demonstrates the need for an ordering ideal. *An Essay on Man* thus replies to its own riddling couplet about pleasure by specifying – some six hundred lines later – exactly what constitutes human enjoyment:

> Reason's whole pleasure, all the joys of Sense,
> Lie in three words, Health, Peace, and Competence.
> (*TE* III, i, p. 136, ll. 79–80)

The measured life – impossible without the guidance of reason and perhaps best symbolized in recurring allusions to Pope's small estate at Twickenham – offers us an ideal of pleasure which is itself appropriately chastened and restrained. Competence, health and peace of mind cannot compete for customers with the pleasure domes of magic, sex and technology, but their absence (as Pope knew firsthand) is likely to make sublimer enjoyments seem suddenly meaningless.

The complicated doublings and redoublings of pleasure outside the measured garden at Twickenham lead in many directions. Poetics and ethics constitute two of Pope's major preoccupations, and they provide an ample field in which assertions about Pope's treatment of pleasure must be tested. Surprisingly, the relation linking pleasure to poetics and to ethics has been consistently ignored, both in Pope's work and in wider eighteenth-century contexts. Few truisms, for example, have slumbered more peacefully than the founding principle of Augustan poetics that literature must always please and instruct. Perhaps because the Horatian formula *dulce et utile* reappears with the banality of a cliché, we fail to ask whether pleasure and instruction are more than dissociated pieties of critical discourse. Yet the influential Socratic theory of pleasure as a *plerosis* – an almost literal 'filling up' in response to a hunger-like lack or void or absence – closely agrees with Samuel Johnson's conviction that 'knowledge is certainly one of the means of pleasure, as is confessed by the natural desire which every mind feels of increasing its ideas'.[13] In describing his own studies, Pope emphasized that delight both guided and interpenetrated learning, as he claims he never 'followed anything that I could not follow with pleasure'.[14] In *The Dunciad*, it is the sons of Dulness who padlock the young mind with burdensome precepts and arid learning (*TE* v, pp. 356–7, ll. 15–16). The Augustan taste for didactic poetry – however abhorrent to Romantic and to post-Romantic sensibilities – is best understood not as the

[13] Geoffrey Tillotson and Brian Jenkins (eds), *The history of Rasselas, prince of Abissinia* (1759) (London, 1971), p. 32. As Imlac concludes: 'Without knowing why, we always rejoice when we learn, and grieve when we forget.'

[14] In Spence, I, p. 10. Of his move to Binfield and his tireless reading there, Pope observes: 'I was between twelve and thirteen when I first went thither, and continued in this close pursuit of pleasure and languages till nineteen or twenty' (I, p. 11).

victory of instruction over pleasure but as unfolding the pleasures inherent in knowledge.

The poetics of pleasure involved Pope in complicated struggles with its apparently straightforward requirements. Indeed, many of the difficulties and dangers he recognized in poetry depend upon the central role which Pope grants to pleasure. This centrality is evident in the half-serious description he provided of his motives for writing: 'I writ because it amused me; I corrected because it was as pleasant to me to correct as to write; and I publish'd because I was told I might please such as it was a credit to please.'[15] This is not the whole story, but even here we can recognize Pope's effort to outflank hostile critics by seizing the issue of pleasure. It is no credit, he implies, to please a certain class of reader, while the pleasure of a far wiser readership is a wholly sufficient argument for publishing his work. Much of *An Essay on Criticism* necessarily addresses the delicate role of pleasure in literary experience, and predictably Pope urges the judicious critic to avoid the extremes of readers who 'still are pleas'd *too little*, or *too much*' (*TE* I, p. 284, l. 385). Measure remains the ideal. In practice, however, even Pope's ideal readers – who, unlike the typical hard-to-please critic, still retain the *'gen'rous Pleasure* to be charm'd with Wit' (*TE* I, p. 267, l. 238) – attest to the dilemma which poets face and for which measure is no sure solution. The act of giving pleasure is thoroughly mysterious: more precisely, pleasure cannot be given but only received. Who can force us to feel pleased? As Pope puts it metaphorically: 'The pleasure lies in *you*, and not the meat' (*The Second Satire of the Second Book of Horace Paraphrased, TE* IV, p. 55, l. 16).

Two brief passages will help illustrate the practical difficulties concealed in the bland requirement that poetry must please the reader. As recent theories of reader-response criticism have revealed, the concept of reader is controversial rather than self-evident, and Pope regarded some readers as not worth pleasing. Yet even worthy readers frequently disagree about what they like in a text. The mathematics of taste guarantees to frustrate the truly gifted poet who takes pleasure seriously:

> But after all, what wou'd you have me do?
> When out of twenty I can please not two;
> When this Heroicks only deigns to praise,
> Sharp Satire that, and that Pindaric lays?[16]

---

[15] Preface to *The works of Alexander Pope* (1717), in Norman Ault (ed.), *The prose works of Alexander Pope* (Oxford, 1936), p. 292. On post-classical theories of literary pleasure, see Phillips Salman, 'Instruction and delight in medieval and Renaissance literary criticism', *Renaissance Quarterly*, 32 (1979), 303–32; and Glending Olson, *Literature as recreation in the later Middle Ages* (New York, 1982).

[16] *The Second Epistle of the Second Book of Horace, TE* IV, p. 171, ll. 80–3. The resistance to pleasure among literary critics was regarded by Pope and his age as an article of faith. As he wrote: 'Criticks in Wit, or Life, are hard to please' ('Epistle to Miss Blount, With the Works of VOITURE', *TE* VI, p. 63, l. 29).

The poet's difficulties are multiplied again by the normal failings and foibles of ordinary people, so that the powerful are pleased only by flattery, the fashionable by novelty, and the dull by dullness. The means for pleasing readers, like the readers to be pleased, belong to a continuum ranging from the worthiest to the most contemptible. Thus in *An Epistle to Dr. Arbuthnot* Pope takes pains to separate himself from the versifying courtier Sporus by emphasizing their opposite relations to pleasure:

> Not proud, nor servile, be one Poet's praise
> That, if he pleas'd, he pleas'd by manly ways.
> (*TE* IV, p. 120, ll. 336–7)

Together these two passages suggest the potent contradictions and unacceptable compromises which Pope associated with a poetics of pleasure and also suggest why he could imagine wholly rejecting it. The world which took pleasure in the verse of sycophantic androgynes such as Sporus soon inspired Pope with Swiftian thoughts of reprisal. 'I'll sooner write something to anger it, than to please it,' he wrote to his friend John Caryll.[17] Satire, indeed, thoroughly complicates whatever claims it makes to pleasure by linking itself (as Pope understood) with an aesthetics of pain and punishment.

No doubt the gravest difficulties implicit in a poetics of pleasure derive for Augustan writers from the interlocking relation which binds pleasure to imagination. This bond provides the subject for Addison's famous series of *Spectator* papers called 'The Pleasures of the Imagination' (nos. 411–21) and underlies later well-known treatises, in prose and verse, by Mark Akenside and by David Hartley. It is also what permits Johnson's famous definition of poetry as 'the art of uniting pleasure with truth, by calling imagination to the help of reason'.[18] Just as reason (in Johnson's account) is the faculty of mind directly concerned with truth, imagination holds special responsibility for pleasure. With such responsibilities, however, come dangers, and it was Johnson who described most eloquently the perils of a domineering imagination. Pleasure indeed is the seldom-noticed, crucial term in Imlac's speech from *Rasselas*. 'He who has nothing external that can divert him,' Imlac begins, 'must find pleasure in his own thoughts, and must conceive himself what he is not; for who is pleased with what he is? He then expatiates in boundless futurity, and culls from all imaginable conditions that which for the present moment he should most desire, [and] amuses his desires with impossible enjoyments. . . . The mind dances from scene to scene, unites all pleasures in all combinations, and riots in delights which nature and fortune, with all their

---

[17] *Correspondence*, II, p. 341. On relations between pain and satire, see my chapter 'The muse of pain' in *Alexander Pope: the genius of sense* (Cambridge, Massachusetts, 1984). Margaret Anne Doody discusses how traditions of Ovidian transformation – by mingling the beautiful with the grotesque – encouraged an awareness of the mingling of aesthetic pleasure and pain (*The daring muse: Augustan poetry reconsidered* (Cambridge, 1985), pp. 159–98).

[18] 'Milton', George Birkbeck Hill (ed.), in *Lives of the English poets* (1779–81), 3 vols. (Oxford, 1905), I, p. 170.

bounty, cannot bestow.'[19] The chief danger of the imagination reposes in the paradox that – no matter how empty or irrational the imaginative visions are – the pleasure we experience is absolutely real.

Pope certainly shared with Johnson the belief that the intense and undeniable reality of imaginative pleasure held the power to seduce us away from an engagement with the external world. Here is the point where poetics for Pope passes invisibly but ineluctably into ethics. Improving upon the spareness or even Johnsonian bitterness of the external world, Pope's satiric characters often turn for solace to an internal world of their own imagining, where they re-fashion reality after the image of their own desires. In *The Dunciad*, the children of Dulness mostly inhabit a somnambulistic realm halfway in between a debased reality and baseless fantasy, where pleasing phantoms and phantasmagoria have replaced the solid stuff of everyday life. (Pope gives the screws of satire yet another turn by enlisting many of his 'phantoms' from actual persons and productions of the Grub Street literary world.) Such pleasures, in estranging Pope's duncies from the social world outside the self, also tend to endow meaningless or trivial fragments of matter with magical charm. It is the collector who thus emerges in Pope's urban mythology as an archetypal figure of mankind beguiled by shards, forever obsessed with the missing item. The satiric sketch of Curio, who neglects his bride and bedmate in yearning for an absent Roman coin, might serve as Pope's metaphor for what Johnson in *Rasselas* called 'that hunger of imagination which preys incessantly upon life' (p. 85). Pope's duncies, we might recall, spend much of their time wrapped in the idle pleasures of sleep: a state of such pure, dreamlike satisfaction that there is nothing left to desire.

The quest for pleasure not only threatens to immerse us in an imaginary, irrational world of the dreaming mind. By a reflex typical in Pope's work, it also threatens to overwhelm us in a world which is all body. Like the duncies who give themselves wholly to the primitive, bodily pleasures of shouting, jumping, pissing and tickling, many of Pope's satiric characters inhabit a world which is built upon a failure to credit anything they do not experience immediately through the five senses. Sir Balaam perhaps best represents this zero degree of the imagination. As his fortune multiplies almost supernaturally, his highest conception of increased pleasure is to double his weekly allotment of pudding (*To Bathurst*, *TE* III, ii, pp. 122–3, ll. 346, 360). Like the duncies who prefer 'solid pudding' to 'empty praise' (*TE* v, p. 66, l. 52), Sir Balaam is satirized not so much for his unimaginative taste in food as for his

---

[19] *Rasselas*, p. 114. A major difference between Pope and Johnson involves the pleasures of self-love. For Johnson it is axiomatic that man is always displeased with himself: 'To make a man pleased with himself, let me tell you, is doing a very great thing' (in James Boswell, *Life of Johnson* (1791), R. W. Chapman (ed.), corrected by J. D. Fleeman, 3rd edn. (1953; rpt. London, 1970), p. 975). By contrast, *An Essay on Man* devotes a long verse paragraph to describing our ineradicable self-satisfaction: 'See the blind beggar dance, the cripple sing, / The sot a hero, lunatic a king', *TE* III, i, p. 87, ll. 267–8.

inability to find pleasure in anything which cannot be eaten. They reflect the point of view which understands pleasure as nothing more than the satisfaction of an appetite.

Rightly understood, pleasure for Pope must not be falsely divided into dissociated categories of mind and body, one praised as good, the other damned as evil. There is doubtless a rough hierarchy discernible in Pope's work which places the pleasures of eating potted eel somewhat lower than the pleasures of reading Milton. Good sense would dictate as much. Yet no law requires the person who enjoys reading Milton to forswear potted eel. The pleasures of mind and of body, even if separable, are for Pope frequently mixed, as when stimulating conversation accompanies good food or drink. Moreover, even the predominance of body or of mind in a specific activity will call forth its opposite and balancing enjoyment in a life lived according to Popean measure. It is the fools – not the wise – who in Pope's work unnaturally split minds from bodies, as if pleasure were the exclusive property of passion or of reason. Reason is not antithetical to pleasure, its enemy or reluctant, jealous, schoolmasterly chaperon. Pope resembles the philosophers who see human nature drawn towards pleasure not simply by passion but by reason too. An Essay on Man states this idea – however much it contradicts popular misreadings of Pope – unequivocally: 'Self-love and Reason to one end aspire, / Pain their aversion, Pleasure their desire' (TE iii, i, p. 65, ll. 87–8).

Pope in the Essay on Man leaves no doubt that pleasure is the energy (rational as well as passionate) which drives us irresistibly towards virtue or towards vice. In this specific sense, pleasure (when it drives us towards virtue) might well be called our 'greatest good'. By contrast, the pleasure which estranges us from the world or forces us into divided and dissociated realms split between minds and bodies in effect drives us away from virtue – thereby constituting, in Pope's view, our 'greatest evil'. We should notice that good and evil are subtly redefined or transvalued here, in keeping with Pope's reinterpretation of such founding Christian doctrines as the Fall.[20] What authorizes this reinterpretation of good and evil (making it more than arbitrary) is Pope's argument that pleasure supplies the energy for human action and his assumption that pleasure must be understood (much in the way Socrates and Aristotle understood it) as a moral state. Pope might have found his own view summarized in the Nicomachean ethics when Aristotle wrote that 'there is no more important element in the formation of a virtuous character than a rightly directed sense of pleasure and dislike'.[21]

The conception of pleasure as a moral state underlies Pope's development of

[20] See Douglas Canfield, 'The fate of the Fall in Pope's Essay on Man', in The Eighteenth Century: Theory and Interpretation, 23 (1982), 134–50. Pope rarely employs the noun 'evil' – with its weight of theological implications – but normally chooses the plural form 'evils' or 'ills' (a choice which tends to skirt theological controversies).

[21] Trans. J. E. C. Weldon (London, 1927), p. 315 (X.i). Pope shares the Aristotelian idea that virtue is a mean between opposing extremes.

a poetry which seeks to engage the reader in discriminating carefully between harmful and virtuous (or harmless) pleasures. Popean satire seeks to direct our sense of pleasure and dislike in ways which ultimately endow virtue with attractions which vice cannot sustain. In fact, Pope seeks to make literary pleasure an instrument of ethics by turning poetry itself from idle or destructive illusion ('Wit's false mirror') to rational delight (*An Essay on Man*, *TE* III, i, p. 166, l. 393). Unfortunately, this high-minded account of Pope's practice fails to acknowledge the slipperiness of literary pleasure, which as Pope knew often takes leave of virtue and sometimes depends upon our taste for whatever promises to scandalize morality. Like his indecent parody of the first psalm, which he disowned as soon as Curll (in revenge) made it public, Pope's work includes pleasures too shifty and too impure for moral edification. We must not assume that by identifying pleasure (rightly understood) with virtue Pope has fully resolved its paradoxical doubleness. Beyond this edifying but simplified solution to the problem of how to domesticate pleasure, there are twists and turns in Pope's thinking which still need to be explored.

The apparent contradictions and sinuosity of Pope's thinking on pleasure require the hypothesis that there are really two explanatory systems at work. What I will call the primary system centres on the belief that pleasure (as we have seen) may be considered a moral state, where right action depends upon mastering a typical Popean opposition between false and true: true pleasures directing us towards virtue, false (or harmful) pleasures impelling us towards vice. This system – primary in the sense that it remains usually in the foreground – embraces even innocent holidays from moral action, such as the playful occasional poems which derive their significance for Pope in temporarily suspending (not denying or permanently abrogating) the seriousness of ethical choice. The primary system thus holds ample room for trifling literary entertainments entirely consumed, for example, by a recipe for soup or by an invitation to dinner, and it easily accommodates the delightful, innocent flashes of wit that simply float free from everything grave and heavy. Nonetheless, there seems also to be a secondary system generating a very different relation to pleasure in Pope's thought, even though it remains most often in the background, invisible and unacknowledged. Socrates in his influential theory of *plerosis* had proposed that pleasure operates by filling a lack or void. Pope, like Johnson, while in general accepting the theory of *plerosis*, also seems to recognize a sense in which all pleasures – the true as well as the false – contain an intrinsic emptiness.

The emptiness of pleasure – of all pleasures – will grow clearer if we consider the relationship linking pleasure to desire. Desire of course is an unavoidable (if overworked) topic in modern studies of the novel, where the authorities invoked by literary critics range from Freud to William Gass and Jacques Lacan. We must respect major differences separating contemporary theories of desire from the practice and assumptions of eighteenth-century writers such as Pope.[22] Nonetheless, it is particularly helpful in thinking about Pope to consider the theoretical distinction between pleasure and desire. Simplified, the contrast identifies pleasure with the satisfaction of specific physical or emotional needs, expressed most directly as the possession of an object: the mother's breast, a pot of gold. One ignoble illustration must suffice. A good sandwich when we are hungry is a widely-recognized source of pleasure, almost literally (in the classical theory of *plerosis*) filling a lack or void. A twelve-course formal dinner, however, supplies something beyond the pleasures of good food. Its excess, we might say, reflects the mysterious workings of desire, whose source is usually located deep within the unconscious mind, perhaps irrecoverably lost, so that specific objects or longed-for luxuries offer no more than ineffectual, melancholy substitutes for something ultimately unnameable, ungraspable. If the pleasures of good food effectively satisfy our appetite, the hunger of desire is unappeasable. Desire, in effect, exposes a blankness at the very heart of pleasure, such that pleasure is never enough.

The contrast between pleasure and desire that flows from nameless sources lost to conscious reflection may sound quite alien to the robust, wenching hedonism of eighteenth-century literature. It is hard to imagine Squire Western moved by anything more mysterious than old-fashioned lust or greed. Yet while we may safely leave Squire Western to his pleasures, the contrasting concept of desire provides useful insights about the period which transformed Miltonic pensiveness into epidemic melancholy. In fact, a blankness at the heart of pleasure – which is what desire reveals – might be considered the half-understood perception or intuition which expels the Augustan hero from whatever temporary Eden he inhabits, from Twickenham to the Happy Valley. Johnson at the opening of *Rasselas* portrays his young prince as mysteriously restless amid an environment which denies him almost nothing. Desire is silently at work undermining pleasure, exposing its insufficiency, its paradoxical self-contradiction: 'I fly from pleasure, said the prince, because pleasure has ceased to please' (p. 8). In *Rasselas*, the failure of any specific, determinate object or choice to satisfy desire is symbolized directly for the Johnsonian philosopher Imlac in the figure of the pyramid. 'I consider this mighty structure,' Imlac explains, 'as a monument of the insufficiency of human enjoyments.'[23] We should notice that Imlac is not discriminating carefully here – in typical Popean style – between true enjoyment and false. The insufficiency which he describes is an emptiness inherent in every human pleasure.

---

[22] One major difference between modern and eighteenth-century theories of desire would focus on the ego. Lacan, for example, views the absence or lack intrinsic to desire as referring ultimately to the subject's lack of being: a splintering or dispersion of the fixed ego of classical psychology. For Pope, virtue prevents exactly this splintering of the ego.

[23] *Rasselas*, p. 85. 'Those who have already all that they can enjoy,' Imlac contends, 'must enlarge their desires.' It is the nature of desire thus always to leave man unsatisfied, always to create a space which pleasure cannot fill.

I wish to claim that both Pope and Johnson (despite their differences) understand pleasure as implicated in a process by which desire tends to drain pleasure of its satisfactions, emptying it of its power to answer or to fulfil human needs. The process or mechanism by which desire empties pleasure of its satisfactions is suggested for eighteenth-century writers by the elastic noun 'imagination'. The imagination not only serves as a source of pleasure, as Pope and Addison insist, but also holds the power to undermine or to destroy the pleasure it provides. Imagination, not only in its excess, becomes the instrument of desire; it tantalizes man with something always out of reach, so that pleasure and desire never attain a full equipoise. This gap between what we can imagine and what we can attain Pope understood quite well. 'We grasp some more beautifull Idea in our Brain,' he wrote of himself as poet, 'than our Endeavors to express it can set to the view of others; & still do but labour to fall short of our first Imagination. The gay Colouring which Fancy gave to our Design at the first transient glance we had of it, goes off in the Execution; like those various Figures in the gilded Clouds, which while we gaze long upon, to seperate [*sic*] the Parts of each imaginary Image, the whole faints before the Eye, & decays into Confusion.'[24] The poet's desire transforms every poem into a disappointment.

The elegiac tone with which Pope contemplates the gap between poetic imagination and poetic performance carries over to his meditations on pleasure. Images and diction associated with the *vanitas* tradition add a sombre note to more general reflections on the inevitable temporality of human enjoyments. From this perspective, all pleasures are fleeting, inscribed within the sublunary realm of Belinda's lock, where nothing gold can last. Time thus aids imagination and desire in relentlessly undermining pleasure and in strengthening the melancholy which Pope understood as intrinsic to his character as a poet. Not all pleasures issue in mirth, but it is significant – reflecting his distance from festive comedy – that Pope in an early letter could describe mirth as 'but a fluttering unquiet Motion, that beats about the breast for a few moments, and after leaves it void and empty'.[25] The delight which Sterne later represents as life-giving and restorative Pope here regards as merely distracting and hollow. Such pleasures for Pope deplete rather than

---

[24] *Correspondence*, I, p. 135. Unlike poems, gardens always seem to improve in the passage from conception to execution – to bloom and to exfoliate with time far beyond our first imagining – which might help to explain Pope's statement that of all his works he was most proud of his garden (Joseph Warton, *An essay on the genius and writings of Pope*, 2 vols. (London, 1756–82), II, p. 180).

[25] *Correspondence*, I, p. 330. Freud, like Pope, emphasizes both the importance of pleasure and its futility: 'What decides the purpose of life is simply the programme of the pleasure principle. This principle dominates the operation of the mental apparatus from the start. There can be no doubt about its efficacy, and yet its programme is at loggerheads with the whole world, with the macrocosm as much as with the microcosm. There is no possibility at all of its being carried through' (James Strachey (ed.), *Civilization and its discontents* (1929), trans. Joan Riviere (1930; rpt. London, 1972), p. 13).

replenish us, much like the self-consuming blankness Socrates envisaged when he described the intemperate man as condemned to carry water in sieves to fill a leaky jar.

Pope's secondary system – exposing a blankness or emptiness inherent in pleasure, undermining every enjoyment – seems thoroughly inconsistent with his primary system, in which careful discriminations between false and true pleasure constitute a basic requirement of the ethical life. The secondary system, in recognizing every pleasure as ultimately divided against itself, appears to deny the possibility of a delight which is truly substantial. Yet these two systems of thought may co-exist within the same poem. Although *An Essay on Man* explicitly identifies rational or true pleasure with the trio of health, competence and peace of mind, it also portrays a vision of human life in which reasonable pleasure seems simply unavailable. Shakespeare's seven-ages-of-man becomes for Pope not a progress-and-return but a fixed circle in which nothing really changes. Life is the pursuit of pleasure, and pleasure is deceiving:

> Behold the child, by Nature's kindly law,
> Pleas'd with a rattle, tickled with a straw:
> Some livelier play-thing gives his youth delight,
> A little louder, but as empty quite:
> Scarfs, garters, gold, amuse his riper stage;
> And beads and pray'r-books are the toys of age:
> Pleas'd with this bauble still, as that before;
> 'Till tir'd he sleeps, and Life's poor play is o'er!
>
> (*TE* III, i, p. 88, ll. 275–82)

It is easy to protect ourselves with the self-serving argument that Pope here describes only fools and knaves, as if the wise will select substantial pleasures which do not deceive. Pope, however, did not allow himself such a comfortable evasion. 'I should be sorry and ashamed,' he wrote at twenty-six concerning his vocation as poet, 'to go on gingling to the last step, like a waggoner's horse in the same road, to leave my bells to the next silly animal that will be proud of them. That man makes a mean figure in eyes of reason who is measuring of syllables and coupling rhimes [sic], when he should be mending his own soul and securing his own immortality' (*Correspondence*, I, p. 236). This is not an isolated comment but a recurring refrain in Pope's thought. Reason may drive us towards pleasure, but it also exposes the emptiness of our quest.

The discrepancies between Pope's two systems seem best explained not as logical contradictions but as the sign of contrary visions. Logic, at any rate, is not the measure of all things for Pope, who shared Montaigne's belief that we are consistent mainly in our capacity for self-contradiction. More important, his perspective encompasses both maze and plan, both the disarray of man's feeble schemes and the luminous order of God's cosmic design. This double perspective suggests that for Pope both systems of pleasure are necessary, somehow impinging upon each other, not simply adjacent and complementary. The primary system, with its requirement of careful discriminations between true pleasure and false, remains dominant, faintly shadowed nonetheless by the knowledge that all pleasure is ultimately empty. Yet occasionally their relation is reversed, and then the emptiness of pleasure becomes oppressively clear, redeemed only by the faint confidence that we will go on choosing among competing pleasures regardless. Pleasure for Pope simply cannot be adequately understood from a single, fixed, unmodified perspective, from which it appears entirely and always either empty or solid. Thus it made perfect sense that he should describe friendship as the 'Toppleasure' of his existence, while also observing how each passing year seemed to rob him of a friend.[26] Even his purest pleasure cannot be disentangled from the accompanying melancholy of loss.

Pleasure achieves its centrality for Pope by serving as the point where numerous lines of inquiry converge. Indeed, with its several types of doubleness, pleasure seldom presents itself pure and unmixed, in such a way that we could know it apart from its modifying circumstances or occasions. A full discussion of Popean pleasure consequently will grow enmeshed in a multitude of intersecting and overlapping inquiries, without hope of finding an end. My more pragmatic (if less interminable) approach in exploring the importance Pope attached to pleasure is to conclude by focusing on two specific issues which illustrate the complex convergences at play: happiness and women.

   Common usage might seem to indicate that happiness and pleasure are identical – or loose synonyms – but Johnson would not tolerate such lazy thinking in his friend Boswell. 'Philosophers tell you,' he explained impatiently, 'that pleasure is *contrary* to happiness' (Boswell, *Life of Johnson*, p. 912). The long-standing philosophical distinction between pleasure (as a sensation) and happiness (as a state of mind) certainly held for Johnson, who launched devastating replies to Boswell's persistent questions about whether man might not occasionally find happiness. (Johnson: 'Never, but when he is drunk.'[27]) The differences between happiness and pleasure reduce for Johnson to a moral opposition between illusion and fact. Thus in *Rasselas* Johnson portrays the search for happiness as a doomed, impossible quest, like hunting for unicorns, and his narrative gathers great force by contrasting illusions of happiness with the absolute reality of pain and pleasure. In his writing and conversation, Johnson varies the same basic argument in numerous, sometimes subtle ways:

[26] *Correspondence*, II, p. 185; *The Second Epistle of the Second Book of Horace*, TE IV, p. 171, ll. 72–5.
[27] Boswell, *Life of Johnson*, p. 618. Boswell also reports: 'Mr. Johnson observed that it seemed certain that happiness could not be found in this life, because so many had tried to find it in such a variety of ways, and had not found it' (Frederick A. Pottle and Charles H. Bennett (eds.), *The journal of a tour to the Hebrides with Samuel Johnson, LL.D.* (1785), revised edn. (New Haven, Connecticut, 1961), p. 155). Although sometimes, in talking for victory, Johnson temporarily accepted an opponent's premise that happiness was not an illusion, his only consistent modification was to recognize a very limited happiness produced by hope (*Idler* no. 58). Hope, nonetheless, still projects happiness forward and thus denies it any solid footing in the present.

while we waste our lives searching for an impossible, illusory happiness, we may fail to engage the difficult ethical problems associated with pleasure and fail to grasp the few flawed but authentic pleasures which temporarily disburden an otherwise pain-filled existence. Pleasure may not be enough, but it is something, whereas happiness disappears in fume and vapour. His extravagant praise of Garrick (which mystified Boswell) shows how far Johnson was willing to approve of pleasures he nonetheless recognized as fleeting and as unable to fill the ever-expanding void of desire. 'To furnish pleasure that is harmless,' he concluded, 'pleasure pure and unalloyed, is as great a power as man can possess' (Boswell, *Life of Johnson*, p. 1021).

The sharp, extreme distinction which Johnson drew between happiness and pleasure helps to illuminate Pope's very different outlook. Instead of opposing the reality of pleasure to the unreality of happiness, Pope emphasizes the emptiness of pleasure in order to affirm the contrasting reality of happiness. True happiness (here too he distinguishes false from true) is for Pope real, attainable and steadfast. As opposed to the inherent transience of pleasure, it provides a satisfaction and contentment which time cannot damage. *An Essay on Man* thus devotes its entire last epistle to persuading us that happiness lies within our grasp and that we can grasp it by devoting ourselves to virtue. It is virtue – and virtue alone – which for Pope allows man to create (not simply find) a genuine, lasting happiness:

> The only point where human bliss stands still,
> And tastes the good without the fall to ill.
>
> (*TE* III, i, p. 157, ll. 311–12)

Virtue in effect reconstitutes a paradise within, where falling (with its theological connotations of temporality and of moral disorder) yields to an imagery of uprightness, stillness and permanence.

Pope's ethical theory allows for the possibility that happiness and pleasure might, in part, overlap. When rightly understood and providing the energy which drives us towards virtue, pleasure becomes a vehicle for attaining the happiness which perfects and supersedes it. Yet Pope warns that no pleasure – however innocent – stands secure from change and misfortune. The virtuous individual may one day awake stripped of every rational pleasure: broken in health, tormented by enemies, powerless to exercise or to regain former talents. The poet who concludes Dialogue I of Pope's *Epilogue to the Satires* has nearly reached the state in which pleasure becomes impossible. *An Essay on Man* nonetheless insists that even the most embattled and unfortunate person (if secure in virtue) is never cut off from happiness. The confident and resourceful poet who concludes Dialogue II of *Epilogue to the Satires* embodies Pope's conviction that virtue will create an imperishable happiness amid the worst of times. Such happiness is consolation not only for inescapable misfortunes but also for the emptiness and transience of every pleasure.

Pope's commitment to a contrast opposing the transience of pleasure to the fixity of happiness underlies his (frequently one-dimensional) portraits of women. The opposition which contrasts pleasure with happiness does not replicate itself exactly in a dualism of male and female. Like vice and virtue, folly and wisdom freely cross lines of gender in Pope's work, so that happiness proves as accessible to virtuous women (such as Martha Blount or Mrs Corbet) as to virtuous men. Men, it remains true, are more prominent for their virtue (and prominent men are more numerous) than women are in Pope's work. In addition, his work creates extra difficulties for modern readers by proposing and by portraying a special link between women and pleasure. The opening lines of Pope's *Sober Advice from Horace* – in describing responses to the death of the actress Anne Oldfield – provide a good introduction to these difficulties:

> The Tribe of Templars, Play'rs, Apothecaries,
> Pimps, Poets, Wits, Lord *Fanny*'s, Lady *Mary*'s
> And all the Court in Tears, and half the Town,
> Lament dear charming *Oldfield*, dead and gone!
> Engaging *Oldfield*! who, with Grace and Ease,
> Could joyn the Arts, to ruin, and to please.
>
> (TE iv, p. 75, ll. 1–6)

The ironies of this passage are sufficiently multi-layered to require a brief unfolding.

The flood of tears which opens *Sober Advice From Horace* introduces us to the controlling idea of falseness. Indeed, Pope's opening implicitly compares the exaggerated (and doubtless insincere, evanescent) grief of a court/town pastoral with the Arcadian myth in which the death of an innocent maid plunges all nature into disconsolate sorrow ('Now *Daphne*'s dead, and Pleasure is no more!' in 'Winter', *TE* i, p. 92, l. 44). Nothing can stop the town's quest for pleasure, and if the court were capable of genuine mourning (which is impossible) it surely would not mourn Mrs Oldfield but the interruption of its accustomed entertainment. She is of course no Daphne. Mrs Oldfield's disreputable profession guarantees, in fact, something like the opposite of innocence. Further, in joining pleasure with ruin, she receives credit for uniting two categories which are normally inseparable. For Pope, true art involves *separating* pleasure from its familiar ally, vice. These ironies, unfortunately, cannot fully explain why Pope selected Mrs Oldfield for this important, introductory role, and scholars cannot tell us how she might have offended him. In a poem which devotes its entire length to an excoriation of female lust, Mrs Oldfield's prominence may depend more upon her gender and profession than upon unknown, personal quarrels with Pope. Almost any dead actress might epitomize the bond in Pope's work which links women and pleasure with illusion, emptiness and death.

The theory explaining Pope's special link between women and pleasure is developed in *To a Lady*. There (and in its companion-poem, *To Cobham*) Pope seeks to identify the differences in character distinguishing women from men and argues that men embody a greater number of 'ruling passions', from the love of money to the fear of ridicule. Women, by contrast, reveal only a single, uniform ruling passion: the love of pleasure. As he summarized in a notorious couplet:

> Men, some to Bus'ness, some to Pleasure take;
> But ev'ry Woman is at heart a Rake.[28]

The metaphor of woman as rake encourages the inference that female pleasure-seeking – regardless of how secretive or how intricately sublimated – is always ultimately ('at heart') sexual. Moreover, Pope consistently portrays female sexuality as ominous or threatening in ways that normal male sexuality is not. The rich widow who chooses a plebeian lover for his power to give her sexual pleasure becomes, automatically, an object of satire, while the aristocrat Bathurst demonstrates his modesty and good hygiene in rejecting duchesses for 'a tight, neat Girl' to 'serve the Turn'.[29] Eighteenth-century social practices have clearly influenced Pope's literary values here. When female sexuality grows most ominous or threatening in his work, the cause does not lie simply in the violation of moral law. What distinguishes female sexuality for Pope is the disposition among women – so different from the reciprocal and multiplied interests he attributes to Lord Bathurst ('Philosopher and Rake')[30] – to pursue pleasure with an all-consuming single-mindedness.

Pope's portraits of women do not so much substantiate his general theory of the ruling passions as provide emblems for the doubleness which divides and undermines pleasure. Pleasure-seeking among Popean women reflects quite different styles and intensities, from the impassioned Eloisa (who even in memory retraces 'the paths of pleasing sense') to the coolly self-absorbed Chloe (who pleases herself by tracing decorative patterns while a lover 'pants

[28] *To a Lady, TE* III, ii, pp. 67–8, ll. 215–16. Pope explicitly states that the love of power (the second ruling passion he attributes to women) serves only for gaining and securing pleasure (l. 214). On Pope's treatment of women, see Ellen Pollak, *The poetics of sexual myth: gender and ideology in the verse of Swift and Pope* (Chicago, 1985); and Felicity A. Nussbaum, 'Pope's "To a Lady" and the eighteenth-century woman', *Philological Quarterly*, 54 (1975), 444–56. For more general social and literary contexts, see Nussbaum's *The brink of all we hate: English satires on women, 1660–1750* (Kentucky, 1984); Paul-Gabriel Boucé (ed.), *Sexuality in eighteenth-century Britain* (Manchester, 1982); Olivier Bernier, *The eighteenth-century woman* (New York, 1981); and Patricia Meyer Spacks, '"Ev'ry Woman is at heart a rake"', *E-CS*, 8 (1974–5), 27–46.

[29] *The First Epistle of The First Book of Horace Imitated, TE* IV, p. 289, l. 131; *Sober Advice From Horace, TE* IV, p. 87, l. 151.

[30] *Sober Advice From Horace, TE* IV, p. 89, l. 158. In 'A Farewell to London', Pope had represented himself similarly as the 'Most thinking Rake alive', *TE* VI, p. 129, l. 40. For such male figures with a passion for thought, sensual pleasure serves to maintain balance and health. There is a mixture of ironic self-congratulation and self-reproach when the poet in 'Farewell' claims to spend seven hours out of eight following 'Girls' whom, he says hygienically, 'I need but once a Week', *TE* VI, p. 129, ll. 35–6.

upon her breast').[31] Despite major differences, however, women in Pope's
work are preoccupied with the social requirement that they give pleasure and
with the psychological necessity that they receive it. Pope is sometimes sympathetic to the conflicts which arise in giving pleasure (as poets too face this
dilemma) but the pursuit of pleasure inspires some of his most chilling satire,
in which women form a class apart:

> Pleasures the sex, as children Birds, pursue,
> Still out of reach, yet never out of view,
> Sure, if they catch, to spoil the Toy at most,
> To covet flying, and regret when lost:
> At last, to follies Youth could scarce defend,
> 'Tis half their Age's prudence to pretend;
> Asham'd to own they gave delight before,
> Reduc'd to feign it, when they give no more:
> As Hags hold Sabbaths, less for joy than spight,
> So these their merry, miserable Night;
> Still round and round the Ghosts of Beauty glide,
> And haunt the places where their Honour dy'd.

In this famous passage, metaphors for the life of pleasure carry an increasingly
grim subtextual argument: women, children, hags, ghosts, death. Women, in
fact, have become almost allegories of desire. They are less emblems of sexual
appetite than figures doomed to live out the contradiction between our unend-
ing quest for pleasure and the emptiness we experience each time a specific
object or event – savoured in imagination like a rich wine – proves again
radically unstable, incapable of satisfying the permanent, objectless hunger of
desire.

Allegory is a mode which Pope generally avoided or else exploited for its
archaic, Spenserian charm. No reading of Pope will stand if it reduces to an
allegorical figure every female character mentioned or described throughout
his more than three decades of writing. The contradictions embodied in Pope's
women likewise cannot be explained solely through a study of pleasure but
involve as well far-reaching and unacknowledged social contradictions which
Pope in part shared. Yet there is a sense in which women in Pope's work carry
the burden of pleasure which, strictly speaking, belongs also to men, because
men no less than women obey the primal law of Popean psychology that we
seek pleasure and avoid pain. Only in *Sober Advice from Horace* – with its heritage
of classical and medieval satiric misogyny – does Pope openly represent the
female quest for pleasure as obsessively, grotesquely, sexual. Elsewhere, to the
degree that Pope's women are representative, they show us the impossibility of

---

[31] 'Eloisa to Abelard', *TE* II, p. 304, l. 69; *To a Lady*, *TE* III, ii, p. 64, l. 167. The relation to pleasure
darkens in such female figures as Rufa ('at either end a Common Shoar'), Philomedé ('Chaste
to her Husband, frank to all beside'), and, pre-eminently, Atossa ('The Pleasure miss'd her,
and the Scandal hit').

finding satisfaction in *any* appetite. Their characters and histories, in tracing the consequences of a desire which finds no bounds and no fulfilment, argue indirectly for the consolations of measure, whereby rightly understood (understood in its rational and domestic limitations as well as in its fundamental emptiness) pleasure seems somehow less appealing than it once did.

PART FOUR
Landscape gardening and the villa at Twickenham

7

Pope, Kent and 'Palladian' gardening

JOHN DIXON HUNT

'Kent is much your servant': thus Burlington to Pope in November 1729[1]. It was a decade since Burlington's protégé had returned from his ten years in Italy[2] and had taken up his residence in the Burlington household. Kent's anticipated career as a history painter was not prospering as had been hoped, but under Burlington's management and encouragement he was clearly enjoying the diversification of his activities into stage design, book illustration, architecture, and garden and furniture design. Inevitably he had become an acquaintance and friend of Pope: the phrase 'your servant' in 1729 suggests a closeness as well as a typically facetious gesture on Kent's part to signal both his independence and his reliance upon patronage. But the exact relationship between Kent and Pope has never been satisfactorily examined: recent biographies of both men either remain silent or admit to the impossibility of adjudicating the contribution of each to their most important joint concern, landscape gardening.[3] And a recent study devoted wholly to Pope's 'gardening world' also ducks the issue.[4] Yet it is vital. William Kent is slowly but steadily emerging from under the shadow of Burlington, a creative artist in his own right; his garden designs clearly constitute the most innovative strand of his career;[5] so what exactly his part was in the early landscape movement and how much Pope was involved in directing Kent's garden tastes and ideas (or *vice versa*) are questions which deserve as thorough an airing as the available evidence will allow.

Pope moved to Twickenham in the year of Kent's return from Italy, 1719. Although his involvement in garden design, therefore, necessarily began at an

---

[1] *Correspondence*, III, p. 67.

[2] Kent had been sent to study in Italy by a group of Yorkshire patrons in 1709; he returned in 1719 and joined the household of Lord Burlington, whom he had encountered in Italy; he remained a favourite intimate until his death in 1748.

[3] *Pope: a life*; Michael I. Wilson, *William Kent. architect, designer, painter, gardener, 1685–1748* (London, 1984).

[4] Peter Martin, *Pursuing innocent pleasures: The gardening world of Alexander Pope* (Connecticut, 1984). But see note 31 below.

[5] Kent's importance has been firmly established both by the recent exhibition at the University of Hull (catalogue by John Wilton-Ely *et al.*, 1985) and by many new perspectives upon him contributed by speakers at the recent symposium in Washington D.C., 'The fashioning and functioning of the British country house', the papers of which will be published in *Studies in the history of art*.

earlier stage than Kent's (as far as we can tell), their activities as gardenists are intricately linked. What we know of the two men suggests that Pope would provide the ideas, Kent their realization in sketches and on the ground. The ideas that Pope would contribute would have to do with the intellectual justifications of gardening, its place in the modern cultural declensions of classicism; yet where Kent must have been supremely privileged in Pope's eyes was in having firsthand experience of classical and modern Italian gardens. Kent was also a painter and a theatre designer, two modes which Pope would invoke frequently in his justifications of garden design; though Pope's own interest in both painting and theatre was independent of Kent's, their application to gardening may well have been Kent's contribution. But Pope was the literary specialist, and in his translation work of the 1720s and 1730s he was concerned with making Homer and Horace 'speak good English';[6] in other words, he was engaged in precisely the mediation of classical models as were the Palladians in architecture, but evidently with far more alertness to the problems inherent in such an exercise. In short, Pope and Kent were extremely well placed to assist the advancement of each other's garden work and to exchange ideas and methods.

It is with Kent that we must begin. His work as a painter, his stage designs, his huge and amusing enthusiasm for Italy and all things Italian, and his role in Burlington's Palladian crusade were prime influences upon his garden work. This is not the place for any detailed discussion of them,[7] but two aspects need to be highlighted. First, his training and ambition (albeit disappointed) to be a history painter gave him clear preconceptions as to the centrality of subject matter in painted scenes: as I have argued elsewhere,[8] when Kent and Pope invoked the picturesque it was to direct attention at the organization of some actual or imagined picture around a central event derived from history, myth, literature or the Bible. The same was even more true of theatre work: to design settings and costumes, as we know that Kent did, was to enhance the human action at the centre of attention; scenes were arenas for actors and action. Second, in everything that Kent did his Italian predilections were decisive. His ineffective essays in history painting were done in the baroque traditions that he had studied in Rome; his architectural work emulated Palladio (clearly this was in the spirit and at the direction of such important patrons as Burlington and Leicester); his stage designs, given that he was engaged in such work during his ten years in Rome, must have been in the Italianate baroque tradition, augmented by a firsthand acquaintance with the drawings of Inigo Jones in Burlington's collections. So the questions arise, why do his garden designs have to be seen as anything different? in what ways can they be read as Italianate or Italian inspired?

---

[6] The phrase is Sir William Trumbull's, urging Pope to continue his Homer translations (see *Correspondence*, I, pp. 45–6, for the whole passage).

[7] I take them up in detail in my book, *William Kent: garden designer* (London, 1987).

[8] 'Ut pictura poesis, ut pictura hortus, and the picturesque', *Word and Image* I (1985), 97–108.

Burlington's Palladian crusade in architecture was based upon considerable firsthand knowledge of Andrea Palladio's buildings, of his *Quattro Libri*
and many surviving drawings which Burlington possessed. The villa at Chiswick is an epitome of that careful attention to the master's *oeuvre*. Palladio had
himself, as Burlington knew perfectly well, derived his own architectural
practice from an elaborate study of the architectural remains of Roman
antiquity. It was, in fact, for an edition of Palladio's drawings of classical
architecture which Burlington was undertaking that Pope wrote what became
his famous 'Epistle' (*Correspondence*, III, p. 187 and note). But Palladio –
unfortunately – left virtually no theory or practice of garden design. Therefore,
to surround the villa at Chiswick with an apt landscape constituted a major
challenge for Burlington and his coterie. That solutions were not always easy
may be deduced from several incidents in the complicated evolution of the
gardens.

Basically, Burlington was forced to extrapolate an appropriate garden style
in exactly the same way that Palladio had discovered his architectural one:
from a study of classical remains. But to complicate matters, few classical
gardens survived, so that to determine what classical gardens might have been
like required a combination of visualizing Latin literary descriptions, relying
upon Renaissance reconstructions of famous gardens in antiquity and accepting the happenstance of contemporary Rome – where recent gardens had been
established around classical ruins – as if it were an accurate image of classical
garden art. We cannot be precise about how conscious Burlington was in his
search for a suitably Palladian garden style and therefore to what extent he
relied upon any of these sources. But since from at least the beginnings of the
seventeenth century, English travellers had chosen to visualize classical gardens from that same combination of literature and the creative confusions of
actual Italian experience,[9] we may safely assume that Burlington and Kent
did the same. Indeed, Burlington's own promotion (and subsidizing of)
Robert Castell's *The villas of the ancients illustrated* implies his reliance upon one
traditional method of visualizing classical gardens. Earlier writers had tried to
extrapolate architectural plans from Pliny's letters describing two of his
villas,[10] but Castell was clearly trying to find visual equivalents for verbal
description that would chime with current English interest in the relationship
of the garden to a larger, primarily agricultural landscape[11] and thereby to
provide authority for a classically based landscape architecture. And as late as
1733 a London printing of Horace reproduced a reconstruction of a classical
garden (plate 1) that had been frequently offered in Roman guidebooks since

---

[9] This is discussed in detail in my *Garden and grove. The Italian Renaissance garden in the English
imagination 1600–1750* (London, 1986), especially Part One.

[10] See, for example, J. F. Félibien, *Les Plans et les descriptions de deux des plus belles maisons de campagne
de Pline le consul* (Paris, 1699).

[11] Specifically the writings of Stephen Switzer and Richard Bradley, for a discussion of which see
my *Garden and grove*, pp. 184–92.

the sixteenth century as specifically that of Lucullus (plate 2). Both Pope and Kent subscribed to Pine's handsome edition of *Quinti Horatii Flacci Opera*, and presumably the latter would have known the image from Roman guidebooks. What is interesting, then, is that readers of lines celebrating 'ruris amoeni Rivos' would have been encouraged by the headpiece to visualize the literary version of some classical retreat in forms actually derived, not from classical gardens, but a combination of ancient ruins and modern, Renaissance gardens. Other headpieces deployed imagery that alluded to famous Roman sights – the Vatican Ariadne, a river god, the Farnese Hercules, a map of villas along the Tiber – or to a more generalized vision of Italianate garden and grove – a statue of Mercury in a wood (as Kent would achieve in the theatre at Rousham), or pyramids, herms and temples in conjunction with some garden plot (plate 3).

The designs of William Kent that survive reveal a high incidence of *color romanus*;[12] he was clearly eager to promote Italian imagery on English estates. But as his careeer developed, he was also attentive to the alternative style and associations of Gothic; indeed, Kent was the first to use medieval subjects for history painting.[13] In the 1730s he designed a Hermitage and Merlin's Cave for Queen Caroline in Richmond Park: though the former gave special prominence to the antique by its shape of a Greek cross, by displaying sculpture (contemporaries noted this as classical) and by its Roman-looking sofas and altar, its outside of rough-hewn stones partly sunken in the ground and the missing turret gave it a much more 'British' air which was entirely in accord with the Queen's patriotic motives. Merlin's Cave, with druidical roofs and a construction of roots and branches, was even more emphatically 'British'.[14] Even at the quintessentially classical-Palladian Chiswick there were some modest introductions of Gothic/natural styles: the cascade (see plate 4) eventually acquired a rustic set of arches after the manner of the upper gardens of the Villa Aldobrandini at Frascati, but not before much more severely classical versions had been canvassed and rejected; while the exedra immediately to the north of the villa itself was laid out with statues set into shaped hedges rather than the architectural (and more unequivocally antique) construction eventually used for the Temple of British Worthies at Stowe. Elsewhere some of Kent's other early commissions allowed him (or forced him) to mix his styles: at Stowe again the Palladianesque Temple of Venus was decorated with scenes from Spenser's *The Faerie Queene*. Since this British epic–romance was one of Pope's favourite poems, we might speculate whether it was he who urged it as subject matter for Kent's decorations; one wonders, too, whether Kent would ever have worked upon his illustrations for Thomas Birch's

---

[12] For these and all subsequent Kent drawings referred to see the *catalogue raisonné* in my book on Kent.

[13] See Wilson, *William Kent*, p. 148. For Kent's *Gothick*, see John Harris, 'William Kent's Gothick', in *A Gothick symposium* (The Georgian Group, 1983).

[14] See my study of Kent for a fuller discussion of these and other, related designs.

edition of 1751 had it not been for Pope's enthusiasm for Spenser, though Kent's experience as both theatre designer and history painter, using setting to enhance the action, was crucial to those designs.[15]

Indeed, the first contacts that are recorded between Kent and Pope are precisely over illustrations. In September 1721 Pope seems to have been trying to get a portrait of Addison from Kent to decorate Tonson's four-volume edition that year; they collaborated over Pope's *Odyssey* in 1725; Pope may have promoted Kent as an illustrator for Gay's *Poems on several occasions* (1720) as he certainly did for the first volume of Gay's *Fables* seven years later; in 1728 there also seems to have been a plan for Kent to illustrate *The Dunciad variorum*, and some sketches which John Butt once suggested were the surviving traces of that project survive at Chatsworth. One result of these verbal–visual collaborations was surely that, on the one hand, Pope learned from his friend's skill at visualizing ideas, while on the other hand, Kent extended his literary knowledge and learned from Pope's essentially political attitude to literary heritage; that is, like Burlington with architecture, Pope sought to answer Shaftesbury's call for a national taste in the arts and organize modern writing *vis-à-vis* its predecessors.

Two drawings may help to demonstrate that this kind of theme was available to Kent; yet the intellectual implications of both seem much more typical of Pope's concerns. The first is a sketch for the remodelling of the hillside at Chatsworth: Kent presents the finished drawing as some kind of history painting or theatre scene, with figures watching the 'action' on the hillside. There the cascade flows first past a temple modelled upon the so-called Sibyl's Temple at Tivoli, then through arches borrowed from the Villa Aldobrandini again, to an arena flanked by two pyramided Roman temples. It is as if Italian gardening, classical and modern, is seen to arrive on Derbyshire soil.

The second and more explicit drawing (plate 5) is inscribed by Kent with some verses from Michael Drayton's *Poly-Olbion*. The Greek title means 'having many blessings', and Drayton's songs celebrated English topography together with its legends, history and natural history; one of these, from which Kent copies his inscription, featured the meeting of the Rivers Thames and Mole, near the confluence of which Kent had extended the Tudor Palace of Esher and laid out the gardens for Pelham which Pope seems to have considered his highest achievement. Kent's Drayton drawing shows Esher in the back right, with Hampton Court (another of his Gothick commissions) on the left; between them on the hillside is a fine, typically Kentian temple in the classical style. Down the Thames a triton drives his chariot. And this whole pageant representing cultural history or the progress of architecture is watched by a couple on the bank.

Such attention to how classical and Italian garden styles are translated into English and to the larger theme which incorporates that, the so-called 'prog-

[15] See Jeffrey P. Eichholz, 'William Kent's career as literary illustrator', *Bulletin of the New York Public Library* 70 (1966), 620–46.

ress' of the arts, seems far more typical of Pope than Kent. After all, the
unfinished scheme of Pope's later years, to write a blank verse epic on Brutus,
the great grandson of Aeneas and legendary founder of the British race,
declares an interest in cultural progress at once literary and political. There is
no need to exaggerate Kent's relatively poor education (to which Pope refers in
his friendly but not the less pointed gibe that Kent was 'a wild Goth . . . from a
country which has ever been held no part of Christendom' (*Correspondence*, III,
p. 417) to wonder whether Kent would have been as concerned with cultural
declensions as the Drayton illustration suggests he was without Pope's prompting. Yet Kent's contribution in both drawings is to realize such ideas in visual
forms – knowing the Italian imagery that would declare the progress of
gardening from antiquity via Renaissance Italy to contemporary England
with its parallel heritage of Gothic and Tudor styles.

In 1713 Pope, echoing Sir William Temple, had agreed that Homer's
description of the gardens of Alcinous 'contains all the justest Rules and
Provisions which can go toward composing the best Gardens'.[16] Yet with even
the best will in the world Pope's version of that passage does not yield any
material for the garden designer; a variety of plants, yes, and some items of
garden furniture; but nothing at all concerning their disposition. In 1713,
therefore, it seems that Pope had a keen sense of the absurdities of the
Dutchified taste for topiary and fiddly imagery but no positive alternatives. I
would suggest that he is likely to have derived these from Burlington and,
above all, Kent, both of whom had seen the traditions of Italian gardening at
first hand. We know that Pope owned and studied Johann Georg Graevius'
Thesaurus Antiquarium et Historiarum Italiae in six volumes; on modern Rome he
also consulted Pieter Schenk's *Romae Novae Delineatio*, and his copy in the
Beinecke Library at Yale is bound with engravings of *Veduti di giardini e fontani
de Roma e Tivoli*.[17] But for firsthand reports of Italy he must have relied upon
Burlington and Kent. That some of his earliest surviving thoughts about the
forms which gardens could take are sketched on sheets of his Homer
translations[18] may be an accident; but it is nonetheless an extraordinarily apt
one and may not be entirely a coincidence that while determining how Homer
should speak good English Pope was also fascinated by how to adapt traditional garden forms.

Pope's early acquaintance with Burlington's Chiswick (plate 5) would have
been a decisive influence upon his gardening ideas. Two aspects of the gardens
are, I think, most relevant: their theatrical organization and their studied
miniaturization. The *patte d'oie* transferred to Chiswick something strikingly
similar to the stage of Palladio's Teatro Olimpico in Vicenza. Burlington's

---

[16] *The Guardian*, 173 (29 September 1713).
[17] Spence, I, p. 235, and *TE* II, p. 237n. I am grateful to Miss Marjorie Wynne for the information
about the Beinecke copy of Pope's Schenk.
[18] Peter Martin, in *The gardening world of Alexander Pope*, first drew attention to these sketches in the
Homer manuscript.

fondness for the theatre[19] and for Palladio's work would both have urged this device. It would be echoed by two further sets of walks to the west on the other side of the river. The translation of the streets of the Teatro Olimpico into alleys of vegetation terminated with buildings and obelisks emphasized a mix of city and country that was wholly apt for Burlington's *villa urbana*. All the images we have of this garden – the vignettes in plate 5, Rigaud's drawings and Rysbrack's paintings[20] – emphasize its arrangement and use as a series of scenes, which the allusion to Palladio's theatre first suggests to the visitor as he emerges on the north front of the villa.

But the smallness of scale at Chiswick is also crucial: John Macky's *A journey through England* noted how 'Every walk terminates with some little Building'.[21] The structures of both villa and garden buildings allude to a conspectus of Italian models – something close to a memory theatre of classical and Renaissance architecture – all of which have been reduced in size to fit the site. Whether Burlington himself would have made anything of this is doubtful, though by designing the villa in 68 English feet to echo the larger 68 Vicentine *piedi* of the Villa Rotunda he thereby enforced a reduction. But Pope, concerned in the 1720s and 1730s with translating Homer and Horace into English, could hardly have failed to register such modulations. And in his own, even smaller site at Twickenham, he seems to have relished the challenge to accommodate old and modern Italy into a modest English space.

The scenes and pictures of Chiswick – both those commissioned from artists and those which the gardens themselves endorsed as an essential part of their structure – were paralleled by Pope in his own grounds. Unfortunately we have far less visual documentation for Twickenham than we do for Chiswick, but what survives does in fact endorse Pope's own invocation of pictures as an ideal garden structure, as well as the sense which he and his friends had of the Twickenham garden as a theatre. The featured 'action' of Twickenham as stage, scene or picture varied according to Pope's needs. In general, as I have argued elsewhere,[22] Twickenham's iconography – both achieved and projected – signalled Pope's location of himself in the traditions of villa life which the Italian Renaissance had revived on the basis of their knowledge of classical literature: it is a modern equivalent of Tusculum, a version by Pope of Cicero's country estate mediated by the modern villas of latter-day Frascati. And as Maynard Mack showed us in *The garden and the city*, Pope loved to play with the traditional associations of Platonic cave and Egerian grotto: that we have two surviving images by Kent of Pope in that grotto surely declares its centrality in

[19] See Cinzia M. Sicca, 'Burlington and garden design', in *Lord Burlington and his circle* (The Georgian Group, 1982).

[20] See Jacques Carré, 'Through French eyes: Rigaud's drawings of Chiswick', *Journal of Garden History* 2 (1982), 133–42, and John Harris, *The artist and the country house* (London, 1979).

[21] John Macky, *A Journey through England*, 3 vols. (1724), I, p. 87.

[22] See my 'Pope's Twickenham revisited', in *British and American gardens in the eighteenth century* (Virginia, 1984).

his gardenist philosophy. Kent's other drawing, of the Shell Temple (plate 6), incorporates not only garden imagery which locates Pope in traditions of classical gardening (temples, grottoes, Roman altars, vases designed by Kent himself,[23] busts on pedestals, tripods), but in the witty descent of some divinities down a rainbow also includes an allusion to Renaissance garden sculpture.[24]

But, unlike the Chatsworth hillside drawing, none of the figures here (Pope, Kent and the dog Bounce(?)) seem to pay any attention to that benediction. It is a fine Kentian joke, but it is also similar to Pope's constant play in the Horatian Imitations with contrasts between Horace's situation and his own. Just as Pope's Horace must be accommodated to Hanoverian England, so must his dreams of classical villa life be diminished and adjusted to the exigencies of contemporary life. This characteristically Popean perspective is surely one which Kent learned of his friend: indeed, we have evidence that Kent did not of his own accord appreciate Pope's manipulation of his garden scenes as a theatre for his carefully fashioned selves. Kent failed to respond to Richardson's portrait of Pope in his garden with the obelisk to his mother's memory in the background: 'Pope in a mourning gown', he wrote, 'with a strange view of ye garden to show ye obelisk as in memory to his mothers death, the alligory seem'd odde to me . . .'[25] Such insensitivity to a typically calculated piece of Popean imagery suggests that Pope had much to teach Kent and probably did.

Pope's grotto – and by extension his whole garden – was a 'Scene for contemplation' (*Correspondence*, IV, p. 262). This suggests a theatre or picture, for 'scene' nicely encompasses both arts, where contemplation was the action and where that activity itself asked to be contemplated. The most frequent of his themes was to use Twickenham as the locale of meditations upon the continuities and discontinuities of poetical tradition, especially in its association with country retreat.

Pope's long-standing fascination with the theatre and the theatricality of the world is well known.[26] His identification of 'th' ambitious Scene' of London[27] as a prime object of his satire required him, as *The garden and the city* showed, to establish Twickenham as the alternative scene, the stage for his own poetic persona. Pope incorporated a 'theatre' into his gardens at one point: we know

---

[23] The vases which Kent designed for Pope are engraved in John Vardy, *Some designs of Mr Inigo Jones and Mr William Kent* (1744), plate 25. For other references of work Kent did for Pope at Twickenham, none of it very precise, see *Correspondence*, IV, pp. 125, 141.

[24] In the catalogue of the Hull exhibition (see note 5), these divinities were glossed as being 'iconographically highly dependent upon a statuary group' which Kent and Pope would have been able to see in an engraving of the Villa Doria Pamphili published by G. G. De Rossi.

[25] H. Avray Tipping, 'Four unpublished letters of William Kent', *Architectural Review* 63 (1928), 209.

[26] Malcolm Goldstein, *Pope and the Augustan stage* (Stanford, California, 1958), and Max Byrd, *London transformed. Image of the city in the eighteenth century* (New Haven, Conn., 1978), chapter 2.

[27] *TE* IV, i, p. 251 (line 27).

EPISTOLA X.
AD FVSCVM ARISTIVM.

RBIS amatorem Fuſcum ſalvere jube-
mus
Ruris amatores; hac in re ſcilicet una
Multum diſſimiles, ad caetera pene
gemelli,
Fraternis animis : quidquid negat alter, et alter :
Annuimus pariter, vetuli notique columbi.   5
Tu nidum ſervas : ego laudo ruris amoeni
Rivos, et muſco circumlita ſaxa, nemuſque.
Quid quaeris? vivo, et regno, ſimul iſta reliqui,
Quae vos ad coelum fertis rumore ſecundo.
Vtque ſacerdotis fugitivus, liba recuſo,   10
Pane egeo,jam mellitis potiore placentis.
   Vivere naturae ſi convenienter oportet,
Ponendaeque domo quaerenda eſt area primum;
Noviſtine locum potiorem rure beato?

1 Pine's *Quinti Horatii Flacci Opera*, 1733

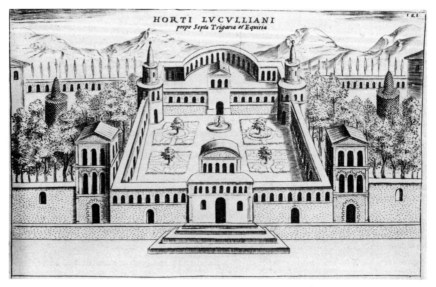

2 Engraving of Horti Luculiani from Giacomo Lauro's *Antiquae urbis splendor*, 1612

3 Pine's *Quinti Horatii Flacci Opera*, 1733

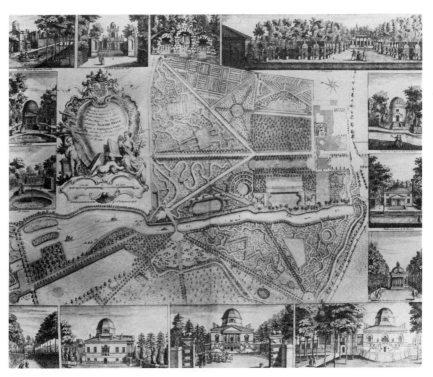

4 J. Rocque's engraved plan and views of Chiswick, 1736

5 William Kent's illustration of lines from Drayton's *Poly-Olbion*

6 William Kent's view of Shell Temple in Pope's garden

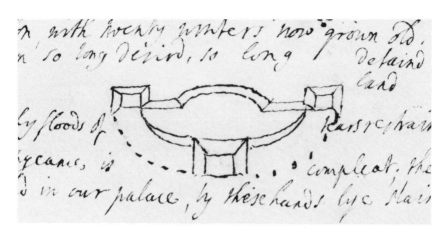

7 Pope's drawing of a garden theatre in *Odyssey* manuscript

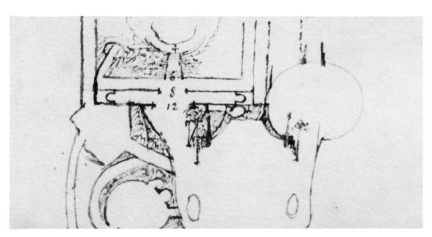

8 Pope's garden design in *Odyssey* manuscript

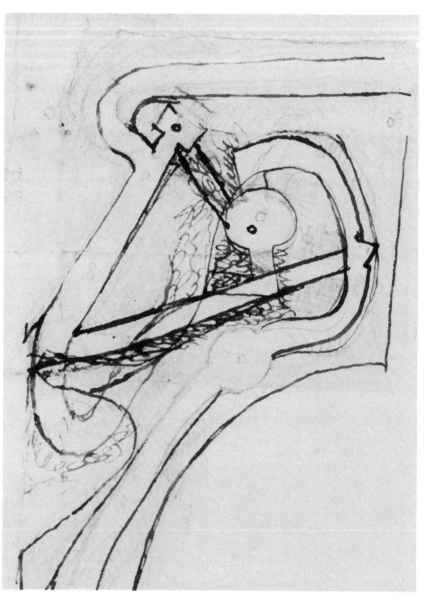

9 Pope's garden layout in *Odyssey* manuscript

that this was established by Charles Bridgeman in 1726 and Pope recorded that 'I have just turfed a little Bridgemannick Theatre' (*Correspondence*, II, p. 372). Such a feature, besides its theatrical import, had classical credentials, for Basil Kennett cited both Ovid and Juvenal as authorities for 'seats of homely turf' in theatres.[28] It was one of Bridgeman's hallmarks and such theatres can be seen on various of the plans which Peter Willis has attributed to him.[29] It is exactly such a Bridgemannick theatre that Pope draws (plate 7) in his Homer manuscript. But we also must assume that this theatre was eliminated from his gardens, since it does not appear on Serle's plan after Pope's death. I would suggest that once the whole garden was registered as a theatre then a specific structure was no longer essential: indeed it even distracted from the overall vision, especially in such a small area. Other manuscript scribbles (plates 8 and 9) look like attempts to integrate or link a theatrical structure with the far less strict geometry of garden walks: plate 8 uses a typical Bridgemannick set of rising platforms (marked perhaps with their height or intervals) and these give on to a cluster of converging walks; plate 9 tries out rectangular and circular openings in serpentine paths, a more subtle absorption of 'scenes' into an overall plan.

Kent's involvement with the theatre, his knowledge of the close relationship of gardens and theatres in Italy[30] and his willingness to retain some of Bridgeman's theatres at Claremont and Rousham, all suggest that he and Pope would have had much to share. Where Pope would have the edge was in his sense of the significance of gardens as pictures and theatres with appropriate themes represented in them. So I would like to argue for their collaboration in the development of garden styles and ideas: the 'two-way street' that Mack claims as the real mode of friendship (*Pope: a life*, p. 921) rather than Morris Brownell's emphatic subordination of Kent to Pope's picturesque taste.[31] Indeed, everything we know of Kent suggests a much more independent, inventive and energetic imagination than Brownell allows him, certainly not one to subordinate itself to either Burlington or Pope.

Two particular features of the new gardening, where an emphasis upon the collaboration of Pope and Kent as equal partners would be a more plausible adjudication, are movement through a garden's spaces and what Pope identified as calling in the countryside. Both are a crucial part of Pliny's influential *identikit* of Roman villas; both are also emphatically modern Italian features, praised and endorsed by a long line of English grand tourists (Hunt, *Garden and*

---

[28] Basil Kennett, *Romae Antiquae Notitia* (5th ed., 1713), p. 45. See Martin, *The gardening world . . .*, pp. 55–6.

[29] See the plans of Sacombe, Farley, Rousham, Stowe and Claremont in Peter Willis, *Charles Bridgeman and the English landscape garden* (London, 1977).

[30] See my *Garden and grove*, chapter 5 ('Garden and theatre'). Joseph Spence would describe Marly as like 'scenes in a Theatre' (Slava Klima (ed.), *Letters from the Grand Tour* (London, 1975), p. 199) and it was clearly a commonplace comparison; to what extent eighteenth-century gardens were used as theatres or for fêtes in England is a subject deserving of more study.

[31] Brownell, pp. 172ff.

grove, chapter 7). Kent would have registered them at first hand in his visits to many gardens in and around Rome as well as in his one recorded visit to Pratolino.[32] But equally, both these aspects of garden design were translatable: or put in the conventional discriminations of garden history, both may be implemented in formal or informal gardens. They could therefore be annexed to Pope's concern with the progress of the arts; such Italian features could be made to speak good English and yet maintain a *color romanus*. Especially with views out over agricultural land, as Kent achieved at Rousham, the continuities of classical and modern agrarianism happily and imperceptibly coincided. It is only with hindsight that such a naturalizing of Italianate forms could be read as anticipating the picturesque taste. After the deaths of Pope and Kent various commentators sought to explain English garden history as an advance towards the *belle nature* of Lancelot Brown; but the instinct to translate Italy into England which characterized all the Burlington circle had by then been forgotten or obscured and thereby allowed the endeavours of Pope and Kent to be fundamentally misrepresented.

Pope's Twickenham, by all the accounts that survive, realized two essentials of the new gardening – freedom of movement and invitations to the eye either within or sometimes beyond the physical limits of a garden. And if his garden was Kent's inspiration for the Carlton House gardens, as Walpole claimed (Brownell, p. 174), then we must also register what Kent brought to it on his own account: a skill at creating variety and invitations for movement through a largely regular site as well as the illusion of it being formed 'without either line or level'.[33] These are painterly skills, which commentators always acknowledged: Kent, said Spence, had 'the idea of mixing lighter and darker greens in a pleasing manner' (Spence, I, p. 250). But Kent also reveals at Carlton House and in some of his other major improvements (Claremont, Esher, Rousham) a talent that derives from his theatre work: creating a succession of scenes within and without the garden, an experience essential to many Italian gardens, to transformation scenes in the theatre, and to Palladio's architecture. Palladio had carefully explored Roman ruins, especially *thermae*, and was impressed by their spatial variety and its consequences for the visitor's experience of buildings. Kent borrowed such an insight for his work at Chiswick, where a thin screen of trees both hides and reveals buildings after the model of Palladio's intercolumnation at the Venetian churches of Redentore and S Giorgio Maggiore.[34]

So Kent's formal inventiveness – demonstrated throughout his other architectural and design work – was a valuable contribution to the new

---

[32] Bodleian manuscript Rawl. D. 1162, folio 3.

[33] Sir Thomas Robinson's letter of 1734 describing the 'new taste' in gardening represented by Kent's work at Carlton House is reprinted in various places: for example, Brownell, p. 175, Wilson, *William Kent*, p. 192: my *Kent*, p. 192.

[34] This point was first made, I believe, by Jacques Carré, 'Lord Burlington's garden at Chiswick', *Garden History* I (1973), 27.

gardening, even if gardening's theoretical formulations and its place in cultural history were probably Pope's. What is usually cited as Pope's praise of Kent's naturalness may in fact be acclaim of his friend's essential but subtle artistry:

> Pleas'd let me own, in Esher's peaceful Grove
> (Where Kent and Nature vye for Pelham's Love)
> The Scene, the Master, opening to my view,
> I sit and dream I see my Crags anew!
>
> (*TE* iv, p. 316, ll. 66–9)

Kent is praised for a 'scene' as fanciful as any in the theatre, an emphasis as much artificial as natural. Indeed, Pelham's attention is said to be torn between Kent and nature, nature not as partner but in creative competition with art (an interpretation which would sort better with traditional aesthetics). Other instances of what Brownell considers 'ridicule' of Kent also support Pope's shrewd appraisal of his friend's skilful mediation of art and nature and both men's lively sense of their debate.[35]

Wherever Kent worked his art called upon traditional skills and assumptions and upon a never-ending affection for Italy, which were applied to a nature which was local and English. It was this collaboration of art and nature or, as it would better be stated, a representation of English nature by an art deriving from classical and modern Italy, that constituted the fine synthesis which characterized the early landscape garden, a synthesis which is the leitmotif of Pope's lines on garden design in his epistle 'To Burlington'. That poem makes clear that it was Burlington's achievement to 'show us, Rome was glorious, not profuse, / And pompous buildings once were things of Use'. Or, as Pope put it long before he become friendly with Burlington's leading architect, his fancy, gazing upon classical landscape paintings, 'builds imaginary Rome a-new'. That was in 1715–16. Three years later Kent appeared upon the English scene, and in him Pope's imagination found an ideal collaborator to realize Roman gardening anew.

---

[35] Brownell, p. 174, citing *TE* iv, p. 225, l. 355 – more likely a swipe at Queen Caroline than Kent; *Correspondence*, iii, p. 329 – a piece written by Pope *on* Kent's behalf, and iii, pp. 417–18 – clearly a friendly gibe at Kent's hortulan fervour, notably his fondness for temples.

8

The iconography of Pope's villa: images of poetic fame[1]

MORRIS R. BROWNELL

In 1785, the year after Samuel Johnson's death, Thomas Tyers was hoping that the house in Lichfield where Johnson was born would be 'engraved for some monthly repository'. 'The print and the original dwelling,' he went on to say, 'may become as eminent as the mansion of Shakespeare at Stratford, or of Erasmus at Rotterdam; the house at Coltersworth, where Newton was born, the birthhouse of Milton, in Bread Street; Pope's villa at Twickenham, or the porch house at Chertsey, where Cowley breathed his last'.[2] It is doubtful whether the iconography of any of these famous houses, even Shakespeare's, can rival that of Pope's villa, which illustrates the surprising phenomenon that for nearly 150 years after Pope's death in 1744 – despite the destruction of his house, the erection of at least two others on the same site, and the complete transformation of the gardens and grotto – freshly drawn views of 'Pope's Villa' continued to appear in nearly every decade until the Pope bicentenary exhibition at Twickenham in 1888. The views of Pope's villa amount to a survey of English topographical art concentrated on a single subject for a century and a half.

The iconography of Pope's villa, which remains an unknown chapter in the reputation of the poet, reveals the way in which 'images reflect from art to art' in the celebration of a poet's fame.[3] The artists who depicted the house contributed to a legend about the villa that had been established during Pope's lifetime, and was perpetuated throughout the eighteenth century by a cult of verses. This essay will begin with a brief account of the myth of Pope's villa in his poetry and subsequent eighteenth-century verse; review the pictures of Pope's house as established in the catalogue for an exhibition of the views of Pope's villa at Marble Hill House in Twickenham during the summer of

---

[1] This essay is a rewriting with additions of the introduction to the exhibition catalogue, *Alexander Pope's villa* (1980). In both versions I am indebted to Jacob Simon, then assistant curator at Kenwood House, Hampstead, now assistant keeper, National Portrait Gallery, London.
[2] Thomas Tyers, 'A biographical sketch of Dr. Samuel Johnson' (1785), No. 9 in O. M. Brack, Jr., and Robert E. Kelley (eds.), *The early biographies of Samuel Johnson* (Iowa, 1974), p. 64.
[3] *Epistle to Jervas*, l. 20, *TE* VI, p. 156.

1980;[4] and conclude with an attempt to account for the iconography of what may be the most frequently portrayed private house in England.

I Twit'nam's garland: The villa's life in verse

Pope's ambitions for the fame of his gardens during his lifetime were well known to contemporaries. Philip Southcote observed that Pope 'was more fond of this sort of fame [for gardening] than any other'.[5] He opened the house and gardens to the public as early as 1736, published a famous description of the grotto in his *Letters* (1735), and made the idea of the villa central to the *Imitations of Horace*, in which, as Maynard Mack has observed, 'Pope's "creation" of Twickenham constituted an act of the mythopoeic imagination'.[6] In the Horatian myth of Twickenham, Pope ignores the sentimental meaning the villa had for him in 1720 in lines complaining about his unhappy love affair with Lady Mary Wortley Montagu ('To Mr. Gay, Who wrote him a Congratulatory Letter on the Finishing his House'):

> Ah friend, 'tis true – this truth you lovers know –
> In vain my structures rise, my gardens grow,
> In vain fair Thames reflects the double scenes
> Of hanging mountains, and of sloping greens:
> Joy lives not here; to happier seats it flies,
> And only dwells where WORTLEY casts her eyes.
>
> What are the gay parterre, the chequer'd shade,
> The morning bower, the ev'ning colonade,
> But soft recesses of uneasy minds,
> To sigh unheard in, to the passing winds?
> So the struck deer in some sequester'd part
> Lies down to die, the arrow at his heart;

---

[4] See Morris R. Brownell, *Alexander Pope's villa: views of Pope's villa, grotto and garden*, catalogue of an exhibition at Marble Hill House, Twickenham, 19 July to 28 September 1980 (London, 1980). Numbers of views in the text refer to this catalogue, hereafter cited *Alexander Pope's villa*, where documentation for descriptions can be found. Entries referred to in notes are designated 'Brownell' according to catalogue number. Plates indicated in the text, nine of them unillustrated in the catalogue, refer to illustrations for this article. Two useful bibliographies including views of Pope's villa have been published since the catalogue: Bamber Gascoigne, and Jonathan Ditchburn, *Images of Twickenham* (Richmond, Surrey, 1981); and Bernard Adams, *London illustrated 1604–1851: a survey and index of topographical books and their plates* (London, 1983).

[5] See Spence, I, No. 603. Also see Horace Walpole, *The history of the modern taste in gardening*, Isabel Wakelin Urban Chase (ed.), *Horace Walpole: gardenist* (Princeton, 1943), p. 28: 'There was a little of affected modesty in the latter [Pope] when he said, of all his works he was most proud of his garden.'

[6] In *Letters of Mr. Alexander Pope, and several of his friends* (London 1737), letter xcvi is listed in the table of contents as 'A Description of a Grotto'. See *Correspondence* II, pp. 296–7. For Pope's instruction to his servants about showing the house, see *Correspondence* IV, p. 9. On the '"creation" of Twickenham' see Maynard Mack, *The garden and the city: retirement and politics in the later poetry of Pope 1731–1743* (Toronto, 1969), p. 9.

> There, stretch'd unseen in coverts hid from day,
> Bleeds drop by drop, and pants his life away.[7]

In the *Imitations of Horace* (1733) Pope's garden and grotto are no longer 'soft recesses of uneasy minds'. The villa becomes a retreat of Roman self-sufficiency, and the grotto a sanctuary of the patriot opposition to Robert Walpole:

> To VIRTUE ONLY and HER FRIENDS, A FRIEND,
> The World beside may murmur, or commend.
> Know, all the distant Din the World can keep
> Rolls o'er my *Grotto*, and but sooths my Sleep.
> There, my Retreat the best Companions grace,
> Chiefs, out of War, and Statesmen, out of Place.
> There *St. John* mingles with my friendly Bowl,
> The Feast of Reason and the Flow of Soul:
> And He, whose Lightning pierc'd th' *Iberian* Lines,
> Now, forms my Quincunx, and now ranks my Vines.
>
> (*Satire* II, i, *TE* IV, p. 17, ll. 121–30)

In *Satire* II, ii (1734) the poet makes of his villa the modern instance of Horace's mean and sufficient estate:

> In *South-sea* days not happier, when surmis'd
> The Lord of thousands, than if now *Excis'd*;
> In Forest planted by a Father's hand,
> Than in five acres now of rented land.
> Content with little, I can piddle here
> On Broccoli and mutton, round the year;
> But ancient friends, (tho' poor, or out of play)
> That touch my Bell, I cannot turn away. (ll. 133–40)

In the same satire Pope preens himself on his indifference to proprietary ownership, and his status as a tenant of his Twickenham landlord, Thomas Vernon, from whom he leased the house throughout his life:

> Well, if the Use by mine, can it concern one
> Whether the Name belong to Pope or Vernon?
> . . .
> Let Lands and Houses have what Lords they will,
> Let Us be fix'd, and our own Masters still.
>
> (ll. 165–6; 179–80, *TE* IV, pp. 65–7, 69)

Pope's ethical and aesthetic ideal of the villa is succinctly expressed in lines imitating Horace's *Ode* IV, i (1737) disguised as a compliment to William

---

[7] *TE* VI, pp. 225–6, ll. 1–14. The lines, circulated in manuscript during Pope's lifetime, appeared anonymously throughout the century until they were finally included in Pope's *Works* (1806). See Morris R. Brownell, '"Struck" and "Stricken Deer": an image in Pope and Cowper,' *Notes and Queries* 223 (1978), 62–4.

Murray, later Earl of Mansfield, who was intending to borrow Pope's house in the 1730s:

> His House, embosom'd in the Grove,
> Sacred to social Life and social Love,
> Shall glitter o'er the pendent green,
> Where Thames reflects the visionary Scene.[8]   (ll. 21–4)

Verses written by Pope's contemporaries during his lifetime indicate how rapidly his house established itself as the seat of the Muses, and his garden as a model of landscape design. James Thomson alludes to 'Twit'nam's Bow'rs,' 'where the muses haunt,' in a passage in *Summer* (1727) praising the 'matchless vale of Thames'; and in 1736 he allows the Goddess of Liberty to extol Pope's garden design:

> 'See! sylvan scenes, where Art alone pretends
> To dress her mistress and disclose her charms –
> Such as a Pope in miniature has shown.'[9]

James Ralph's satirical lampoon, *Sawney* (1728), attacks the same bowers as spoils of Pope's literary career:

> SAWNEY, a mimick Sage of huge Renown,
> To Twick'nham Bow'rs retir'd, enjoys his Wealth,
> His Malice and his Muse: In Grottos cool,
> And cover'd Arbours dreams his Hours away.[10]

In 'Verses Written at Mr Pope's House' (1735) George Lyttelton, like Thomson, sees nature to advantage dressed in the landscape of Pope's villa on Thames's 'flowery side':

> ... where Pope has plac'd
> The Muses' green retreat
> With ev'ry smile of Nature grac'd,
> With ev'ry Art complete.

Samuel Johnson's epigram published in 1738 in *The Gentleman's Magazine*, 'To Eliza Plucking Laurel in Mr Pope's Gardens,' commemorates a visit to Pope's villa by Elizabeth Carter, and refers to 'Pope's hallow'd glades, and never tiring views' (line 3).[11]

---

[8] *TE* IV, pp. 151–3. See Morris R. Brownell, '"His House" at Twickenham and Pope's imitation of Horace, *Ode* IV, i', *Notes and Queries* 222 (June 1977), 242–3; and '"The Visionary Scene"; Pope's sensibility to landscape', *Alexander Pope and the Arts of Georgian England* (Oxford, 1978), chapter 3.

[9] James Thomson, *The Seasons: A Poem*, 'Summer' (1729), ll. 1425–8, and *Liberty: a poem in five parts* (1735–6), v, ll. 690–8, in J. Logie Robertson (ed.), *Poetical works* (London, 1908), pp. 105, 412.

[10] See James Ralph, *Sawney. An heroic poem. Occasion'd by the Dunciad* (London, 1728), p. 1, excerpted by Guerinot, no. 62, p. 126.

[11] See George Edward Ayscough (ed.), *The works of George Lord Lyttelton* (London, 1774, p. 622; and E. L. McAdam, Jr., and George Milne (eds.), *Poems, The Yale Edition of the Works of Samuel Johnson* (New Haven and London, 1964), vol. 6, p. 62.

Pope's grotto, the most notorious feature of his villa, attracted the ridicule of Lady Mary Wortley Montagu, who installs the Goddess of Dulness in the grotto in a riposte to the *Dunciad* composed in 1729:

> Here chose the Goddess her belov'd Retreat
> Which Phoebus tried in vain to penetrate,
> Adorn'd within by Shells of small expence,
> (Emblems of tinsel Rhime, and triffleing Sen∴e),
> Perpetual fogs enclose the sacred Cave,
> The neighbouring Sinks their fragrant Odours gave.[12]

But these lines were not printed until 1803, and such attacks were impotent against the myth of the grotto Pope was establishing during the 1730s in the *Imitations of Horace*. In the 1740s Pope's august 'Verses on the Grotto' (1741) were printed on three occasions in *The Gentleman's Magazine*. Later reprinted by Robert Dodsley in 1743 with translations in Latin and Greek, the poem was accompanied by a 'Sapphic Ode' on the gardens by Nicholas Hardinge, *Horti Popiani*, and Dodsley's *Cave of Pope*, which prophesies the sanctification of the grotto as a shrine:

> Grateful Posterity, from Age to Age,
> With pious Hand the Ruin shall repair:
> Some good old Man, to each enquiring Sage
> Pointing the Place, shall cry, the Bard liv'd there,
> . . .
> With aweful Veneration shall they trace
> The Steps which thou so long before hast trod;
> With reverend Wonder view the solemn Place,
> From whence thy Genius soar'd to Nature's God.[13]

Verses inspired by Pope's death in 1744 portray his villa as a monument of the didactic poet of moral virtue, situated in a sacred landscape charged with elegiac emotion. Part Two of William Thompson's lugubrious poem *Sickness* (1745) contains a 'Panegyrick on Mr Pope, on his Writings and Death', which concludes with this gloomy apotheosis of the poet in 'Twit'nam Bow'rs':

> I saw the sable Barge, along his Thames,
> In slow Solemnity beating the Tide,
> Convey his sacred Dust! – Its Swans expir'd;
> Wither'd, in Twit'nam Bow'rs, the Laurel-bough;
> Silent, the Muses broke their idle lyres;

---

[12] Robert Halsband and Isobel Grundy (eds.), *Lady Mary Wortley Montagu, essays and poems and simplicity, a comedy* (Oxford, 1977), p. 247, ll. 4–9.

[13] *Verses on the grotto at Twickenham. By Mr Pope. Attempted in Latin and Greek. To which is added Horti Popiani. Ode Sapphica. Also the cave of Pope. A prophecy* (London: R. Dodsley, 1743), pp. 15–16. See also Morris R. Brownell, 'Walter Harte, Nicholas Hardinge, and Pope's "Verses on the Grotto"' *Notes and Queries*, 222 (1977), 245–7. For a discussion of the classical allusions in Pope's 'Verses on the Grotto', see Mack, *The garden and the city*, pp. 69–72.

Th' attendant Graces, check'd the sprightly Dance,
Their arms unlock'd, and catch'd the starting tear;
And Virtue for her lost Defender mourn'd![14]

The frontispiece of William Mason's *Musaeus: A Monody on the Death of Pope* (1747) pictures Pope dying in his grotto, and Mason's elegy, 'In Imitation of Milton's "Lycidas"' laments the poet's 'widow'd grot'.[15]

Throughout the eighteenth century versifiers continued to celebrate Twickenham as the 'Muses' green retreat', seat of the Bard and garden designer. Horace Walpole's 'Parish Register' (1758) sings of

Twit'nam, the Muses' fav'rite seat,
Twit'nam, the Graces' lov'd retreat,
Where Pope in moral music spoke
To the anguish'd soul of Bolingbroke.[16]

In Book I of *The English garden* (1772) William Mason characterizes Pope as the militant champion of 'free taste' in gardening, who, after destroying the formal garden in his satire of Timon's villa in the *Epistle to Burlington* (1731), retires triumphantly to the 'wild variety' of his own garden at Twickenham:

And now, elate with fair earn'd victory,
The Bard retires, and on the Bank of Thames
Erects his flag of triumph; wild it waves
In verdant splendour, and beholds, and hails
The King of Rivers, as he rolls along.[17]

The destruction of Pope's villa in 1807 inspired lines in Thomas Love Peacock's *Genius of the Thames* (1810) which sum up the motifs of the hagiographical verses cited above, and reverence icons of house, garden, grotto and willow tree worshipped by the cult:

Now open Twit'nam's classic shores,
Where yet the moral muse deplores
Her Pope's unrivalled lay:
Unmoved by wealth, unawed by state,
He held to scorn the little great,
And taught life's better way.
Though tasteless folly's impious hand
Has wrecked the scenes his genius planned; –
Though low his fairy grot is laid,
And lost his willow's pensive shade; –
Yet shall the ever-murmuring stream,
That lapt his soul in fancy's dream,

[14] William Thompson, *Sickness: a poem. Book the second* (London, 1745), pp. 62–3. The 'Panegyrick' on Pope consists of lines 18–179 (pp. 52–63), reprinted with minor variants in John Serle, *A plan of Mr Pope's garden as it was left at his death* (London, 1745), Brownell 56.
[15] William Mason, *Musaeus* (London, 1747), p. 7.
[16] See 'The Parish Register of Twickenham. Written About 1758', in *The works of Horatio Walpole, Earl of Orford*, 5 vols. (London 1798), IV, p. 382, ll. 17–20.
[17] William Burgh (ed.) *The English garden* (York, 1783), p. 23.

Its vales with verdure cease to crown,
Ere fade one ray of his renown.[18]

It cannot be said that Pope's villa inspired memorable verses – the collection provides many examples of the art of sinking in poetry that belong in Pope's *Peri Bathous* – but Maynard Mack has observed that this 'sub-species of poetry . . . fostered something like a Pope-and-Twickenham legend'.[19] These heterogeneous and fragmentary verses – epithet, epigram and elegy, whether satirical, panegyrical or didactic – all contributed to the creation of the myth of Pope's villa as the seat of the English Bard. Conventional and derivative as they are, full of commonplaces about the union of Art and Nature, Miltonic and Spenserian tropes about the Muses departure from the Thames, together they transformed Pope's house into a monument to the poet and to English poetry. The 'visionary Scene' of his garden becomes the 'Muses' green retreat'; the grotto dedicated to the patriot opposition against Walpole becomes a shrine sacred to the poet; the villa, 'Sacred to social Life and social Love', becomes 'The House of the late Celebrated Mr. Pope', to quote the title of the most popular eighteenth-century print. The remainder of this essay will discuss some examples from the catalogue of views of Pope's villa to illustrate how artists and print-sellers contributed to the legend of Pope's villa.

II

The pictures of Pope's house belong to the same campaign celebrating the poet's fame in verse, and they amount to icons of the cult of Pope's villa. Far more numerous than the verses, at least fifty-five pictures of the villa, not including book illustrations and ceramics,[20] are extant between 1730 and

[18] Thomas Love Peacock, *The Halliford Edition of the works of Thomas Love Peacock*, H. F. B. Brett-Smith and C. E. Jones (eds.), 10 vols. (London, 1934; New York, 1967), VI, p. 147 (Part II, st. xxvii).

[19] Mack, 'The legendary poet', in *The garden and the city*, Appendix E, p. 266.

[20] Ceramics and book-illustrations were excluded from the exhibition catalogue (see *Alexander Pope's villa*, p. 21). Among ceramics, it has been conjectured that Pope's villa may have been one of the views of English landscape ornamenting Josiah Wedgwood's Imperial Russian dinner service (1774) for Catherine the Great. A view after Brownell 4 and 6 appeared on an oval meat dish in a service of Spode dinnerware dated about 1835 (plate 23). L. Schots painted 'Pope's Villa, from the Surrey Bank' on a white Minton tile dated about 1850. See George C. Williamson; *The Imperial Russian dinner service: a story of a famous work by Josiah Wedgwood* (London, 1909), p. 25; and Lynne Sussman, 'Spode/Copeland transfer printed patterns', *Canadian Historic Sites: Occasional Papers in Archaeology and History* no. 22 (Ottawa, 1979), pp. 42–3. For the Minton tile, see London Borough of Richmond upon Thames, Twickenham Reference Library (LCP 3391 Tw). Pope's villa after Turner's painting (Brownell 43) was reproduced *c.* 1810–20 on a Chamberlain's Worcester vase (plate 24), now in the Ionides Collection, Orleans House Gallery, London Borough of Richmond upon Thames. For an example of book illustration typical of vignettes and views deriving from Brownell 6 in editions of Pope's works, see G. Croly (ed.), *The works of Alexander Pope*, 4 vols. (London, 1835), I: title page (*Alexander Pope's villa*, p. 16, figure 5). For a checklist of views published since the catalogue, see Bamber Gascoigne and Jonathan Ditchburn, *Images of Twickenham with Hampton and Teddington* (Richmond, 1981), chapter 4, plates 201–42.

1888: six drawings, twelve watercolours, thirteen oil paintings, sixteen engravings, four aquatints, three lithographs and one etching. Few of these pictures have enough artistic distinction to warrant detailed iconographical analysis, but they include the work of some important English topographical artists, and a painting by J. M. W. Turner never before considered in this context.

The earliest images of the villa are to be found in a group of familial sketches, drawings, and paintings owned by the poet and his friends, which indicate that the villa was being celebrated in Pope's circle of intimates during his lifetime. These include Pope's rough sketches of plans and elevations of house and garden architecture in the Homer manuscripts; the fanciful drawings of Pope in his grotto attributed to William Kent and Lady Burlington; and the recently recovered oil portrait of Pope by Jonathan Richardson the Elder, painted in the mid-1730s for Pope's closest friend, Henry St John, Lord Bolingbroke. It shows (No. 1; plate 10) Pope in mourning dress, with the obelisk commemorating his mother in the garden in the background. The 'alligory' of this painting seemed 'odde' to Pope's friend, the painter William Kent, but the portrait confirms Maynard Mack's interpretation of the obelisk as 'the point of visual and emotional climax for the observer in the garden'.[21]

Two pictures that may once have been in Pope's own collection might have been commissioned by Pope as trophies of his pride in improvements made to his villa during the 1720s. The first is William Kent's well-known sketch of the Shell Temple in Pope's garden, probably drawn between 1725 and 1730 to commemorate the erection of this important architectural feature terminating walks in the east end of his garden.[22] The second may be one of the pictures the poet might have commissioned from artists he considered 'the two best landscape painters in England' – John Wootton (1682–1765) and Peter Tillemans (1684–1734). The 'Pope's Villa by Wootton' (No. 3), listed in a catalogue of pictures at Duncombe Park, Yorkshire, in 1812, has not been traced, but the panoramic view of the Middlesex bank of the Thames at Twickenham dated about 1730 and signed by Peter Tillemans (No. 2; plate 11), may be the picture referred to in the inventory of Pope's house taken after his death as 'a landskip by Titeman'. The picture, the only extant view of the house without the portico added by 1735 (see detail, plate 12), shows Pope's villa at left centre undistinguished from its neighbours. If Tillemans' painting was commissioned by Pope, it reveals the poet's interest in having his house depicted by the fashionable Flemish artist who late in his career in England 'was patronized by several men of quality; and drew views of their seats, huntings, races, and horses in perfection', according to Horace Walpole's estimate.[23]

[21] For Pope's marginalia in the Homer manuscript, see Brownell, *Pope and the arts*, p. 284n. For the drawings of Pope in the grotto, see Brownell, pp. 65–6, and William Kurtz Wimsatt, *The portraits of Alexander Pope* (New Haven and London, 1965), pp. 15–16, pp. 122–5. For the obelisk, see Mack, *The garden and the city*, p. 28.

[22] For Kent's Shell Temple, see Brownell 58, 'Garden architecture: i. The Shell Temple', in *Pope and the arts*, pp. 251–4; and Wimsatt, *Portraits*, p. 15, pp. 119–21.

[23] For the 'Pope's Villa by Wootton', see Brownell 3; for the 'Landskip by Titeman', see the

These personal, perhaps privately commissioned images of the villa do not contribute to its public iconography, which properly begins with an engraving dated about 1735 after a drawing by Peter Andreas Rysbrack (plate 13), subscribed with a pastiche of verses from Pope's *Imitations of Horace*, beginning with the lines 'Know, all the distant Din the World can keep / Rolls o'er my *Grotto*, and but sooths my Sleep' (*Satire* II, i, ll. 123–4, *TE* IV, p. 17). Ironically, this view identifying the villa in the subscribed verses with the Horatian myth of Twickenham was commissioned by Pope's enemy Edmund Curll. Curll visited the villa on 12 June 1735 with the artist who made the drawing to be 'engraven by the best Hands' as part of a campaign to publicize his unauthorized edition of *Mr Pope's literary correspondence* (1735).[24]

Within two years of Pope's death in 1744 his villa had been marked as a tourist's resort in a guidebook and on a map. Pope's gardener John Serle drew 'A Plan of Mr. Pope's Garden, as it was left at his Death' (1745; No. 56), which was printed by Robert Dodsley as a fold-out diagram in a guidebook to the grotto. The guide includes 'An Account of the Gems, Minerals, Spars, and Ores of Which it is Composed, and from whom and when they were sent,' and a reprint of Dodsley's encomiastic anthology of 'Verses on the Grotto' (1743), with the addition of the extract quoted earlier from William Thompson's *Sickness* (Part II, 1745). The 'Account' provides a 'who's who' of distinguished contributors and their exotic contributions to the grotto, designed like many subsequent country house guidebooks, to impress the visitor with the social status of the owner. The 'Verses on the Grotto' comprise a kind of *Festschriften* glorifying the garden and the grotto as a shrine sacred to the Bard, a legend ripe the year after Pope's death for commercial exploitation (Price 1s. 6d.).

'Mr. Popes Garden' was the only one of many important seats in the vicinity of Twickenham to be marked on Jean Rocque's *Exact Survey of the City's of London, Westminster . . . and the Country Near Ten Miles Round* (No. 57), a survey started in March 1737 and published in 1746. Rocque's proposals for a similar map, *London and its Environs* (1744), state that 'any gentleman may have his seat, and gardens as particularly inserted (in case they are not so already) upon terms which no gentleman, it is presumed, will think unreasonable', thus raising the possibility at least that Pope himself took the initiative in publicizing his villa.

Pope's villa was illustrated in magazines throughout the eighteenth century: in *The Royal Magazine* (1760; No. 8) as 'one of the most remarkable

'Inventory of Pope's Goods Taken after his Death', reprinted in Mack, *The garden and the city*, Appendix B, p. 253; and Horace Walpole, *Anecdotes of painting in England*, 4 vols. (Strawberry Hill: Thomas Kirgate, 1762–1771), IV (1771), 31; and Robert Raines, *Peter Tillemans, life and work, with a list of representative paintings*, Walpole Society, volume 47 (London, 1980), no. 58, p. 54.

[24] See Mack, *The garden and the city*, 'Notes to the Plates', no. 45, pp. 307–9; and Reginald Harvey Griffith, *Alexander Pope: a bibliography*, 2 vols. (Austin, Texas, 1922), no. 386, II, pp. 308–10. The original copperplate is preserved in The Bodleian Library, Oxford: Rawlinson copperplate b. 5.

structures . . . in and near London'; and in *The Gentleman's Magazine* (1807; No. 37) following a review of Edward Ironside's *History and antiquities of Twickenham* (1797). The engraving after Rysbrack that appeared as the frontispiece of *The Newcastle General Magazine* in January 1748 was accompanied by an interesting 'Epistolary Description of the Late Mr. Pope's House and Gardens at Twickenham' which clearly characterizes a visitor's attitude to the villa in the decade of the poet's death. The correspondent approaches the villa 'with a kind of glowing Ardour, flutt'ring at my Heart', is 'seiz'd . . . with a Gust of Enthusiasm', and enters the gardens 'with a warm offering of respect and Reverence'. Lines of Thomson and Denham 'revolve' in the visitor's mind, indicating that he regards Pope's house as a British Parnassus. He also considers it a model of taste and elegance: 'not . . . a Place that bears the high Air of State and Grandeur, and surprizes you with the vastness of Expence and Magnificence; but an elegant Retreat of a Poet strongly inspired with the Love of Nature and Retirement; and shows you, with respect to these Works, what was the Taste of the finest Genius that this or any other Age has produced'. He concludes his account with long extracts about Pope's villa from the *Imitations of Horace*.[25]

Engravings after a drawing dated 1748 by the Swiss engineer and resident of Richmond, Augustin Heckell (1690?–1770) provided the best-known image of Pope's villa in the eighteenth century, and characterize the way topographical engravings spread its fame. James Mason's engraving after Heckell (No. 6; plate 14) publicized in England and France 'the House of the Late Celebrated Mr. A. Pope . . . Now in Possession of' Sir William Stanhope (1702–1772), who purchased and enlarged the house after Pope's death. In another state (No. 10) the engraving marked the inheritance of the property in 1772 by Stanhope's son-in-law, Welbore Ellis (1713–1802). In various states (Nos. 7, 9, 11) views of Pope's house were published in numbered series of engravings of Thames seats from about 1753 until after 1776.[26] Engravings after Heckell are frequently found in extra-illustrated sets of the works of Pope and his contemporaries.[27] Prints after Heckell served as a model for copies by amateur draughtsmen (No. 12), by professionals like the architect Robert Adam

---

[25] See the reprint of the 'Epistolary Description' in Mack, *The garden and the city*, Appendix A, pp. 237–8, 241.

[26] Since the publication of *Alexander Pope's villa* Brownell 7 has appeared in a new state inscribed '3' upper right in a set of twelve 'Divers Views . . . from Gravesend to Twickenham' (*c.* 1755–70), under the imprint of C. Dicey & Co. in Aldermary Church Yard. See no. 560 in Catalogue 23 of *London maps and views* published July 1980 by Robert Douwma Prints & Maps Ltd, 93 Great Russell St, London.

[27] See, for example, Brownell 7 in the extra-illustrated set in the Pierpont Morgan Library of *The poetical works of Alexander Pope, Esq.* (Glasgow, 1785), vol. 3, Part I, p. 118; Brownell 8 in the extra-illustrated set in the Huntington Library of Samuel Johnson, *Lives of the . . . English Poets . . . with notes . . . by Peter Cunningham* (London, 1854), III, Part I, p. 44a; and Brownell 10 in the extra-illustrated set of fifty-three volumes in the library of the Earl and Countess of Waldegrave at Chewton Mendip, Somerset, of the *Works of Horatio Walpole, Earl of Orford* (London 1798), *Letters*, IV, i, p. 122.

(1728–1792; No. 13), and as the source of a *cappricio* in oil attributed to Joseph Nickolls (fl. 1713–55; No. 14).

An important group of pictures of the villa is associated with Horace Walpole, the most important apologist for and collector of views of Pope's villa in the eighteenth century. These include a number of watercolour drawings of the villa with the identification of neighbours (Nos. 15–18); an engraved view of Twickenham (No. 21, 1756), after a drawing by Walpole's protégé and factotum, Johann Heinrich Müntz (1727–1798); a drawing (No. 22) and a painting (No. 25) by Samuel Scott (1701/3–1772); and a watercolour by William Pars (1742–1782) of 'Pope's House from the Terrace of Strawberry Hill' (No. 28, 1772), which was engraved for Walpole's *Description of the villa of Mr. Horace Walpole* (1784; No. 29; plate 18). Walpole wrote to Horace Mann in 1760 that he had no objection to Stanhope's alterations to Pope's house, which he considered 'so small and bad, one could not avoid pardoning his hollowing out that fragment of the rock Parnassus [the grotto] into habitable chambers'. But he was horrified that 'he [Stanhope] has cut down the sacred Groves themselves'; and more than twenty years later he was still complaining about the desecration of Pope's gardens that 'some monuments of our predecessors ought to be sacred'. In his *History of gardening* (composed 1771, published 1785), Walpole made large claims for the importance of Pope's garden design, claims that have been largely substantiated by modern scholars.[28]

In 1764 Sawrey Gilpin (1733–1807) made a sketch (No. 27) of Pope's villa intended for illustration of his brother William Gilpin's earliest picturesque tour of the Thames, a book that was never published. In the spring of 1764 the Gilpin brothers rowed from Windsor to London, William taking notes for descriptions, and Sawrey making sketches that were to be turned into finished drawings for a volume of Thames scenery from Oxford to the sea. The Thames between Windsor and London, with its 'air of high improvement, expence, and splendor', Gilpin noted in the fragment of the tour he transcribed in the 1790s, did not conform to the ideal of the picturesque he later discovered in the unimproved scenery of the Wye, the Lakes, and the landscape of his childhood in Cumberland. Although he appreciated the 'first opening' of the village of Twickenham on the Thames, he declared somewhat equivocally that 'the richness of its villas, tho not picturesque, is amusing. Villa after villa, through a long reach, unfold themselves to the eye. Among these Mr. Pope's, with its little lawn, & two weeping willows hanging over the river, is in itself not an unpleasing object; but from the ideas it excites, will always be considered as an interesting one.' Thus Gilpin implies that Pope's fashionable Palladian villa, by this time one of the most frequently pictured seats on the Thames, is 'not picturesque'.

[28] See W. S. Lewis (ed.), *The Yale Edition of Horace Walpole's correspondence* New Haven, vol. 21 (1960): p. 417; vol. 25 (1971): p. 177. On Walpole's claims for the influence of Pope's garden, see Brownell, *Pope and the arts* (1978), pp. 146–8. For Walpole's painting of the villa by Scott, see Richard Kingzett, *A catalogue of the works of Samuel Scott*, vol. 48 (London, 1982), pp. 66–7.

Pope's villa clearly emerges in the last quarter of the eighteenth century as a Beauty of Britain in volumes of local history and illustrated scenery. The earliest of these appears to be the engraving after Heckell, 'Mr. Pope's House at Twickenham, Now in the Possession of Welbore Ellis, Esq' in the second edition of *A new display of the beauties of England* (1773; No. 10), which reached a third edition in 1776 and reappeared revised and enlarged in 1787.[29] William Watts drew and engraved a view of the villa for *The Seats of the Nobility and Gentry* (1779; No. 32). The villa, grotto, and garden are amply illustrated in Edward Ironside's *The history and antiquities of Twickenham* (1797; Nos. 35, 36, 60, 64, 68), and Ironside's view of the villa was reissued in *The Gentleman's Magazine* (1807; No. 37). The villa, drawn by Joseph Farington from a boat on 31 July 1794 (No. 39a, plate 16), was engraved in aquatint by Joseph Constantine Stadler (No. 39) for volume two (1796) of the Boydells' *History of the River Thames*, with text by William Combe praising the 'charming place . . . purchased by our great British Bard'. William Bernard Cooke's engraving of 'Pope's House' (1807; No. 41) appeared in 1816 in the Middlesex volume of *The beauties of England and Wales* (1816).

Pope's villa was demolished in 1807 by the Baroness Sophia Charlotte Howe, the 'Queen of the Goths' as she came to be called, but Pope's villa was 'still [to] live in its pictured representations' (see plate 17), as William Bernard Cooke consoled his readers in *The Thames, or graphic illustrations of seats, villas . . . on the banks of that noble river* (1811), which includes Cooke's engraving of 'Lady Howe's Villa' (No. 45), showing the surviving arch of Pope's grotto about 100 feet north of the house. In a revised edition, *Views on the Thames* (1822), Cooke entitled the plate 'Baroness Howe's Villa, and Pope's Grotto' (No. 47), and had it subscribed with the first of five maudlin stanzas on Pope's willow, each concluding with a refrain:

> Weep, verdant Willow, ever weep,
> And spread thy pendent branches round:
> Oh! may no gaudy flow'ret creep
> Along the consecrated ground!
> Thou art the Muses' fav'rite tree;
> They lov'd the bard who planted thee.[30]

The same design was executed as a lithograph in France about 1830 (No. 48). Lady Howe's house next appears as 'Pope's Villa' on an aquatint card designed to be viewed through a cut-out archway showing Pope seated at the river entrance to the grotto in an 'embellished book' called *The Natuorama* (*c.* 1825; No. 50; plate 17). An aquatint engraving after William Westall (No. 51) in Rudolph Ackermann's *Picturesque tour of the River Thames* (1828) once

---

[29] See *A new display of the beauties of England*, 2nd ed., 2 vols. (London, 1773–4), vol. 1: between pp. 20 and 21. I have not seen a copy of the first edition. The text of the second edition (p. 20) remarks that 'the improvements which he [Pope] made were so elegant, that his seat became an object of general admiration, as well as its owner'.

[30] See Mack, 'The legendary poet', in *The garden and the city*, Appendix E, p. 269.

10 Pope in mourning by Jonathan Richardson, *c.* 1738

11 *The Thames at Twickenham* by Peter Tillemans, c. 1730

12 Detail of Tilleman's *Thames at Twickenham, c.* 1730

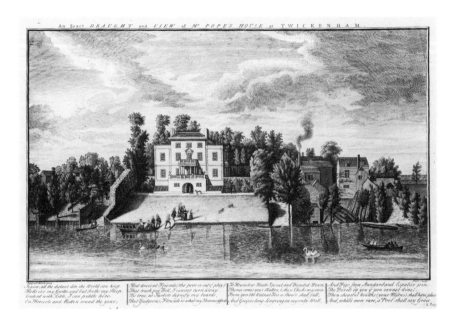

13 View of Pope's house after Rysbrack, *c.* 1735

The House of the late Celebrated Wᵐ A Pope fronting the River Thames at TWICKENHAM | Veüe de la Maison de feü le Celebre Alexandre Pope faisant face sur la Riviere de la Tamise
now in Possession of Sʳ Willᵐ Stanhope. And a View of Lady Fervers Summer House. | à TWICKENHAM Presentement Occupée par le Chevalier Guillaume Stanhope

14 Pope's villa after Augustin Heckell, 1749

View from the Terrace at Strawberryhill.

15 Pope's house from Strawberry Hill after William Pars, 1784

16 Pope's villa by Joseph Farington, 31 July 1794

17 Pope's villa from *The Natuorama, c.* 1825

The late Mr Pope's House at Twickenham.

18 Pope's house after Heckell, *post* 1776

WEEPING WILLOW.

19 Pope's willow by Louis Thomas Francia, 1813

20 *Pope's Villa at Twickenham* by J. M. W. Turner, 1808

21 Turner's sketches for Pope's villa, *c.* 1808

22 Detail of Turner's painting of Pope's villa, 1808

23 Pope's villa after Rysbrack on Spode meat dish, *c.* 1835

24 Pope's villa after Turner on Worcester vase, *c.* 1815

more illustrates as 'Pope's Villa' Lady Howe's house enlarged with a Gothic wing, showing the grotto arch on the riverbank to the north.

The 'Stanzas to Pope's Willow' composed about 1792 celebrated an icon that appears to have been the invention of artists and poets, perhaps the only example of a particular image reflecting from art to art in the cult of Pope's villa. Trees resembling willows appear in views dating from the 1750s (Nos. 20, 25, 26). William Gilpin's remarks quoted above on his brother Sawrey's view (No. 27, 1764) refer to 'two weeping willows hanging over the river'. Perhaps in emulation of Shakespeare's mulberry tree celebrated in Garrick's Jubilee (1769), willows begin to proliferate in views dating from the last quarter of the eighteenth century, during the ownership of Welbore Ellis who was reputed to be a devoted caretaker of Pope's willow (see Nos. 28, 32, 35, 39, 39a), and continue to appear as late as 1851 (No. 53). Joseph Farington made conscientious notes on 'willows' on his drawings of the villa dated 31 July 1794 for the Boydells's *Thames* (No. 39a; plate 16). Another striking sign of the acceptance of the willow among the standard features of barges, swans, and fishermen in views of the villa is the addition of a willow in an engraving after Heckell dated after 1776 (No. 11a; plate 18).

The cult of the willow flourished most vigorously in the early nineteenth century when Jacques Delille conveyed to France the legend of the 'saule fameux que ses mains [Pope's] ont planté'.[31] After Pope's house was torn down in 1807, the willow became an appropriate symbol for the destruction and desecration of Pope's villa. William Bernard Cooke quoted the verses on Pope's 'sacred willow' in *The Thames* (1811), and in the second edition he subscribed the stanza already quoted on a plate of 'Baroness Howe's Villa, and Pope's Grotto' (No. 47). The text of *The picturesque tour of the River Thames* (1828), illustrated with a similar view (No. 51), laments the fate of Pope's 'far-famed weeping willow . . . worked up by an eminent jeweller into trinkets of various kinds, which wealth, rank, and beauty were proud to wear'. After the cutting of the willow tree referred to in a letter to the editor of *The Gentleman's Magazine* (71 [July 1901], 624), Louis Thomas Francia (1772–1839) engraved in 1813 an aquatint of the 'Weeping Willow at Pope's Villa' (No. 71, plate 19), which amounts to a memorial plate. By 1837 the legend of the willow had been written into horticultural history by J. C. Loudon, who records the story that Pope had introduced the willow tree into England by planting some sticks of withy used to wrap a present from Turkey to his neighbour, Henrietta Howard, Countess of Suffolk, at Marble Hill House.[32]

Loudon's story about the willow is probably apocryphal; artists are as likely as anecdotes to have inspired the unknown poet who composed the sentimental 'Stanzas to Pope's Weeping Willow' about 1792. The painter J. M. W. Turner wrote a line on the willow in verses composed in his *Greenwich*

---

[31] *Les Jardins* (Paris, 1801). See Mack, 'The legendary poet', *The garden and the city*, Appendix E, p. 270, and Brownell, *Alexander Pope's villa*, p. 13.

[32] *Arboretum et Fructecetum Britannicum*, 8 vols. (London, 1838), vol. 3: 1507.

Sketchbook (1808), which also contains what appear to be preliminary drawings for his painting of Pope's house (No. 43; plate 20) exhibited at his own gallery in 1808. Faint pencil drawings in the sketchbook (plate 21), tracing a tree-lined bank resembling the river at Pope's villa, the grotto arch, and Lady Howe's house, may record the genesis of the artist's conception of the painting. One version of Turner's lines bids the 'Seasons fair . . . guard Thomson['s] Shrine'; another version, entitled 'Invocation of Thames to the Seasons upon the Demolition of Pope's House', strongly influenced by William Collins's *Ode Occasion'd by the Death of Mr. Thomson* (1749), expresses the artist's response to the destruction of Pope's house:

> Dear Sister Isis tis thy Thames that calls
> See desolation hovers o'er those walls
> The scatter'd timbers on my margin lays
> Where glimmering Evenings ray yet lingering plays
> There British Maro [Pope] sang by Science long endear'd
> And to an admiring country once revered
> Now to destruction doom'd thy peaceful grott
> Pope's willow bending to the earth forgot.

Painted after the demolition of Pope's house, the structure with scaffolding at the centre of the composition (see detail, plate 22) probably represents Lady Howe's villa at the time of its erection; the figures in the left foreground holding the capital of a pilaster and fragments of cornice have been interpreted as workers with relics from 'their task of dilapidation' of Pope's. But Turner's verses and the extraordinary light and colour 'Where glimmering Evenings ray yet lingering plays' make clear that the painting is the artist's eloquent elegiac tribute to Pope's villa, and to Twickenham, an elysium of English poetry that Turner associated as much with Thomson as with Pope.[33]

III

Turner's view of Pope's house is the only picture in the iconography of the villa that may be called poetic, a painting in which images reflect from art to art in a genuinely imaginative way. Most of the views of the villa are as conventional and derivative as the verses. A label designating 'The House of the Late Celebrated Mr. A Pope' (No. 6) is needed to identify images of houses that bear little or no relation to Pope's villa after it was altered and demolished. But topographical accuracy or iconographical distinction are hardly required of pictures that served primarily as icons in the cult of the poet's fame. The cult of Pope's villa was as satisfied with a pastiche, like the one attributed to Joseph Nickolls (No. 14), transplanting the obelisk in Pope's back garden and David

[33] On the intimate connection between Pope's villa and 'Thomson['s] shrine' in Turner's mind, see the companion painting accompanied by verses in the same collection, 'Thomson's Aeolian Harp' (1809). See Martin Butlin and Evelyn Joll, *The paintings of J. M. W. Turner*, 2 vols. (New Haven and London, 1977), 1, pp. 55–7; 2, plate 81.

Garrick's Temple to Shakespeare at Hampton to the banks of the river at Pope's villa, as with Robert Havell's 'embellished book', *The Natuorama* (No. 50; plate 17), allowing the observer to see Thames' seats from Richmond to Oxford through Pope's eyes.

Even if the verse and sculpture do not bear an equal part in views of Pope's villa, its extraordinary iconography is nevertheless a product of the inter-relations of the sister arts, one of the supreme fictions of the century that Jean Hagstrum has taught us to understand.[34] During his lifetime Pope made of his house, garden, and grotto 'a Piece of *Ars Poetica*' that became a cynosure of taste in the arts throughout the century. Pope propagated the fame of what one contemporary referred to as his 'Poetical Villa', and made it live powerfully in his verse as a house 'Sacred to social Life and social Love'. Pope's pseudo-Palladian villa exemplifies an architectural idea that was to triumph in the contest with the idea of the greater house during the century. Poets and artists joined in making of the villa a monument to an English poet in the tradition of the cult of British Worthies, which Pope had himself helped to inaugurate in sponsoring funerary monuments in Poets' Corner of Westminster Abbey.[35]

The score of artists and draughtsmen who pictured Pope's villa undoubted-ly recognized in the scene the same qualities Pope remarked on to Joseph Spence in 1728 while looking at the view of the river from his house: 'That idea of "picturesque" – from the swan just gilded with the sun amidst the shade of a tree over the water on the Thames'.[36] Picturesque features of swans and trees embellish most of the 55 or more extant views of the 'visionary Scene' of Pope's house reflected in the Thames, painted during a period of dynamic develop-ment in English topographical art after the poet's death.[37] But poetry made Pope's villa picturesque, and the sister arts are chiefly responsible for an iconography perhaps unique in the history of English domestic architecture.

[34] *The sister arts: the tradition of literary pictorialism and English poetry from Dryden to Gray* (Chicago, 1958). For lines paraphrased from Pope, see 'To Mr. Addison, Occasioned by his Dialogues on Medals', ll. 51–2 (*TE* VI, p. 204): 'The verse and sculpture bore an equal part, / And Art reflected images to Art.'

[35] Swift referred to Pope's grotto as 'a Piece of *Ars Poetica*', in a letter to Pope (see *Correspondence*, II, p. 326). Pope, in a letter to Allen Bathurst (*Correspondence*, III, p. 295), speaks of 'propagating the fame' of Bathurst's Cirencester park in Gloucestershire. The reference to Pope's 'Poetical Villa' appears in an attack on Pope, *Gulliver Decypher'd* (1727?), Guerinot no. 53, pp. 100–2. For the architecture of Pope's villa, see John Summerson, 'The classical country house in 18th-century England', *Journal of the Royal Society of Arts*, 107 (July 1959), 552. For Pope and the cult of British Worthies, see Brownell, *Pope and the arts*, chapter 13.

[36] Spence, I, p. 254, no. 613.

[37] See John Harris, *The artist and the country house* (London, 1979).

PART FIVE
Pope and Translation and Criticism

9

Moving cities: Pope as translator and transposer

A. D. NUTTALL

The criticism of Pope has never been the same – or ought never to have been the same – since Empson declared that he would enter 'the very sanctuary of rationality' and applaud the poets of the eighteenth century 'for qualities in their writings which they would have been horrified to discover'.[1] Empson had critical designs on Popean zeugma which, he saw clearly, worked through a tension between apparent or formal symmetry and a latent asymmetry. The result is wit (not rationality), a contained wildness of the mind. My own design in this essay is to follow Empson's lead, to pursue further the idea of instability in stability, the dynamic imagination within the static.

It might be thought that the very last place in which we should look for such tensions is eighteenth-century translations of classical authors: to look, as Empson looked, for the fluid within the fixed is surely to seek the anti-Augustan within the Augustan; what is hinted at in such an enterprise is the possible presence of proto-Romantic elements in an otherwise firmly classical body of work; that part of the work which is actually derived by direct translation from classical antiquity will scarcely exhibit the required character. 'Classic' and 'Romantic' are terms which criticism can neither define nor do without. I will content myself here with a single observation and make no further use of them in this essay. It is impossible absolutely to confine either term to a given historical period. Broad areas of literature may seem to fall under one flag or the other, but then a narrower scrutiny of a single area will cause us to make the same distinction again, and then again. Thus it might be argued that the eighteenth century is classic while the nineteenth is Romantic, but then that, within the eighteenth century, the Graeco-Roman materials are alone truly classic. Or, to cast one's net differently, one might urge that the whole of European literature from the Middle Ages constitutes a Romantic antithesis to the authentic classicism of Homer and Virgil; but move back into the ancient period and Virgil with his celebrated 'subjective style', his dream-like fluidity, his sense of landscape becomes Romantic to Homer's classic; move back once more and the magical *Odyssey* is Romantic when set not with but against the austere *Iliad*. We shall do better if we drop these terms

[1] *Seven types of ambiguity* (London, 3rd edn., 1963), pp. 68ff.

altogether and confine ourselves to the contrast between stability and flux, and in particular the literary extension of flux to that which is itself properly stable, as a means of expressing movement in the subject.

Let us begin, not with a Greek but a Roman. A strange poem called the *Dirae* (either 'Curses' or 'Furies') has been handed down to us as one of the works of Virgil. It appears in many good early manuscripts of Virgil and is listed as Virgil's by both Servius and Donatus. The Renaissance scholar Scaliger (who thought this poem was the work of Virgil's friend Varius) classed it separately, with certain other minor poems, as part of what he called the *Appendix Vergiliana*. Most modern scholars regard much of the *Appendix* as non-Virgilian. Although the *Dirae* is almost certainly not by Virgil himself, it is concerned with the special Virgilian experience of dispossession. Virgil, unlike Shakespeare, say, but like Dante, perceived a significant shape in his own life and projected it on the whole of human history in his major work.[2] Like Aeneas he was first expelled from his own land and then brought home. Virgil never forgot the traumatic loss of his farm, requisitioned for veterans returning after the Battle of Philippi. 'Traumatic' is not too strong a word. The picture of Virgil which has come down to us is of one gauche in all things but poetry, at once rustic and over-educated, almost neurotically attached to a certain landscape. In Virgil's *Aeneid* the hero is unparadised from Troy and finds his way, through varying images of ruined pastoral and spectral cities to a home more anciently his than Troy had ever been. In the *Dirae* (as in certain of the *Eclogues*) we have the personal story. Grief and imprecation are strangely mixed. The poet does not curse those who threw him off his land. Instead in a sort of hysteria he curses the land itself, as certain suicides seek to involve their own loved ones in their self-destruction. The rough usurping soldiers are barely glimpsed, in a single, Marvellian line (I accept the conjecture *succidet* in place of the impossible *succedet*):

> Militis impia cum succidet dextera ferro . . .   (l. 31)
> When with his iron the soldier's impious hand shall fell . . .

The lines which follow accelerate the impending destruction of the sweet especial rural scene and then, abruptly, seek to retard the process of change:

> Tardius a miserae descendite monte capellae   (l. 91)
> Ah, slowly, slowly now, my goats, come down from the hill.

The most remarkable lines of all (and the more Latin poetry one reads the more startling they become) are those in which the poet describes his own departure from the place:

---

[2] Many scholars now doubt the biographical reference of the first Eclogue. See the copiously documented discussion by I. M. le M. du Quesnay, 'Virgil's First *Eclogue*', in Francis Cairns (ed.), *Papers of the Liverpool Latin Seminar* 3 (1981), 29–182, esp. pp. 30–5.

Hinc ego de tumulo mea rura novissima visam,
hinc ibo in silvas: obstabunt iam mihi colles,
obstabunt montes, campos audire licebit:
'dulcia rura valete, et Lydia dulcior illis,
et casti fontes et, felix nomen, agelli'.   (ll. 86–90)

From this mound I shall look for the last time at my lands and then go into the woods,
now hills will block, now mountains, but the levels will still be able to hear, 'Goodbye,
sweet country places and Lydia sweeter still, goodbye, chaste springs and you little
fields of happy name'.

These lines stand out from the relatively coarse, sub-Virgilian versification of
the *Dirae*. Eduard Fraenkel went so far as to say that whoever wrote these lines,
it could not be the poet of the *Dirae*, and to stress a connection, indirect but
nevertheless intimate, with the authentically Virgilian fifth Eclogue.[3] The
passage is remarkable for its subtle hypallage from subject to object, not all of
which can be conveyed straightforwardly in an English version. For example,
the Latin does not actually say, 'I shall look for the last time at my lands'; it
says, 'I shall look at my newest (latest) lands'; the character of the looking
(looking for the last time) is ascribed to the thing looked at. This is not a mere
trick or metrical convenience. It is *used* poetically.

   Partly, the effect is of an extreme subjectivism: where the *pathos* of the viewer
is as strong as this it can, so to speak, appropriate the object in act of wilful
perceptual tyranny, but at the same time this is a poem about expropriation
and we are aware that this small, defiant movement of the imagination is futile.
The notion of a last embrace, hackneyed in English, but poetically powerful in
the *Aeneid*, may lie behind the thought here. Thus, together with the rhetorical
appropriation we sense the opposite of appropriation: that the subject is
drained, that a richness of identity properly his has passed into the landscape.
There is even a faint paradox within the single word *novissima*, where, because
this is a time poem, we hear for an instant the basic sense, 'newest', before it is
contested and defeated by the dominant sense 'last'. But then we have a firmly
personal assertion: *ibo in silvas*, 'I shall go into the woods', followed at once by
obstabunt iam mihi colles. I translated these words, with all the inelegance of a
studied neutrality, as 'now hills will block'. In ordinary Latin *obstabunt* following *ibo* must mean 'will bar my path'. But the context of intense subjective
perception, of looking and listening (or being heard) ensures that we do not
take it so. It is as if the poet is walking with head turned, so that *obstabunt* can
mean (as the Loeb translator takes it) 'will block *my view*'. The agency is
mysteriously transferred, once more, from the subject moving through the
landscape, to the landscape itself. We cannot quite say that the poet makes the
hills move (these hills are not like the striding mountain in the first book of
Wordsworth's *The Prelude* (1850, I, l. 412). Yet the repetition of the verb and the

---

[3] 'The Dirae', *Journal of Roman Studies* 56 (1966), 142–55; p. 152.

changing scale of its subject (first hills then mountains) suggest as it were a covert action on the part of the landscape, as if the ground moves to interpose its masses when the poet is not looking. In these lines we have, then, a certain linguistic and logical oddity, deployed to a subtle literary effect. These hints are then allowed to flower in the full-blown poetical figure of the levels still hearing the poet's melancholy valediction, a version of the quintessentially Virgilian trope of the pathetic fallacy, since we infer sympathy in the listening fields.

If these lines are not by Virgil they are by someone who, as they used to say in the sixteenth century, was deeply inward with his work – though the *Dirae* never lost its place in the Virgilian *corpus*, it seems to have been little taught in the Roman schools and to have escaped the kind of learned commentary which accreted round his *Eclogues*, *Georgics* and *Aeneid*. These lines especially are thoroughly Virgilian in their subtle manipulation of subject and object and in their heart-tearing sense of place. Virgil is rightly famous as the poet of *idem in alio*, who reworked the war and the wanderings of Homeric epic until they became instinct with futurity, with the divine history of a single city, Rome. At the same time, as I have suggested, Virgil was aware of a correlative personal history, of his own eviction, wandering and home-coming. This is picked up and accented in the *Dirae*, together (it must be confessed) with a quantity of sub-standard writing of quite another order.

I have explored this passage in some detail because it is a peculiarly rich example of something rare in Latin literature: a kind of poetry in which the moving subject implicitly imputes his own movement to the landscape, producing a strange effect of exacerbated, disorienting subjectivity. It is an effect which without further apology we may agree to call Virgilian, not least because it is given audacious expression in the *Aeneid*, where Italy *flies* before a pursuing Aeneas through a world of evanescent visions and ghost cities which rise and fall before our eyes. I chose the *Dirae* as my main specimen in preference to the more opulent tropes of the *Aeneid* because of the very smallness of the scale and the sharpness of the visual/spatial effect which go with such intimacy. I chose it because it is more Popean. Yet we cannot be quite certain that Pope ever read it. The *Dirae* is excluded from Daniel Heinsius's edition of the *Works of Virgil* (Leyden, 1636) which Pope is known to have possessed.[4] It is included in Michael Maittaire's *Opera et Fragmenta Veterum Poetarum Latinorum*, a book Pope is again known to have owned (p. 459). But the *Opera et Fragmenta* did not appear until 1713, ascribes the *Dirae* not to Virgil but to the more readily negligible Valerius Cato and, most infuriatingly of all, prints *nec adire* in place of *audire* at line 88.[5] This changes the sense from 'the levels will be able to hear' to 'it will not be possible to reach the levels', which in

---

[4] See *Collected in Himself*, p. 424.
[5] Michael Maittaire (ed.), *Opera et Fragmenta Veterum Poetarum Latinorum*, 2 vols. (London, 1713), II, [pp. 1588–9]. The sequence of pages 1525–1612 occur twice in this volume, the earlier run being distinguished by square brackets.

its turn reduces *obstabunt*, 'will block (my vision)' to the commonplace 'will bar my path'. It would really be more to the point to ask whether the *Dirae* was known to Sir William Trumbull, the friend and mentor (especially in matters classical) of Pope's youth. Pope refers on a number of occasions to the *Appendix Vergiliana* but always to the *Culex* (never the *Dirae*).[6] One particular early reference, in a letter of 11 November 1710, suggests (though we may remind ourselves that Pope liked to wear his learning heavily) a serious engagement with Virgilian *dubia*; he points out that a borrowing from the conclusion of the *Culex* occurs in the *Prolusiones Academicae* (1622) of Famianus of Strada (*Correspondence* I, p. 103). The question remains uncertain. I therefore offer the lines from the *Dirae* not as a source for Pope but as a remote, early parallel – another example of the fertilizing effect of Virgil's poetry. Of Pope's awareness of the grander, epic versions there can be no doubt, for these had been imperiously transposed and integrated in English literary culture through Dryden's translation.

> ... arva ... Ausoniae semper cedentia retro   (*Aeneid* III, l. 496)

appears in Dryden as:

> 'Fields of flying *Italy* to chase'   (*Virgil's Aeneis* III, l. 643)[7]

and:

> Italiam sequimur fugientem et volvimur undis   (*Aeneid* v, l. 629)

appears as:

> 'Through stormy sea
> We search in vain for flying Italy'
>   (*Virgil's Aeneis* v, l. 819)[8]

The ancient poet who is *not* like this at all is, of course, Homer.

When Pope was about nineteen he worked up a free translation of a number of neighbouring passages in the thirteenth book of Homer's *Odyssey*. This we now know as 'The Arrival of Ulysses in Ithaca'. By the second couplet we can see Pope Virgilianizing his author:

> At once they bend, and strike their equal oars,
> And leave the sinking Hills, and lessening Shores.   (ll. 4–5)

The first line is Homerically objective, the second is like a Virgilian antiphony, at once mirroring and modifying the first, with its insinuation of a projected subjectivity. There is nothing in the Greek about sinking hills or lessening

---

[6] See, for example, Pope's *Essay on Homer*, *TE*, VII, p. 52, and his letter to Jervas of 29 November 1716, in *Correspondence*, I, p. 376.
[7] In Dryden, *Poems*, III, p. 1136.
[8] Dryden, *Poems*, III, p. 1193.

shores, nor is there in the English versions of Hobbes, Ogilby or Chapman.[9] In a similar manner at lines 21–4 one couplet conveys the objective splendour of Homer (weakened only marginally by the faint personification of 'promis'd') while the next counters with a Virgilian moving landscape – not a *diminuendo* this time, but a *crescendo*:

> But when the morning Star with early Ray
> Flam'd in the Front of Heav'n, and promis'd Day
> Like distant Clouds the Mariner descries
> Fair Ithaca's emerging Hills arise.

There is, again, no warrant in Homer for the second of these couplets but, as Audra and Williams observe,[10] Pope may actually have had Dryden's Virgil in mind at this moment:

> When we from far, like bluish Mists, descry
> The Hills, and then the Plains, of Italy.
>
> (*Virgil's Aeneis* III, ll. 684–5)[11]

Because feelings are freer than facts, a certain easy extremism of language enters with the subjective style; hyperbole, in a manner, becomes merely natural. One result of this is that, while it is clear in the Greek that the vessel which conveys Odysseus is a *magic* ship, moving with preternatural speed, we are unsurprised when Pope tells us that the ship flew faster than an eagle (13–14); any ship may *seem* to do that. Here what is perhaps the finest image of the *Odyssey*, the sleeping hero whirled across the sea, is unforgivably reduced.

In Pope's version the Phaeacians set Odysseus/Ulysses ashore, as they do in Homer, and he hides his treasure so that no one can steal it. Here Pope does not elaborate but instead curtails his author. Homer is much more interested than Pope in the practical business of concealing the treasure, telling us, as Pope does not, that it was in a place aside from the road, where no wayfaring man would come upon it (*Odyssey* XIII, 123).

At line 55 we have the minor but still significantly un-Homeric hypallage, 'solitary shore', for strictly speaking it is the hero who is alone, not the shore, and then, with almost no warrant from the original, five lines of studied art, in which grief is expertly mingled with visual perception:

> Pensive and slow, with sudden Grief opprest,
> The King arose, and beat his careful Breast,
> Cast a long look o'er all the Coast and Main,
> And sought around his Native Realm in vain;
> Then with erected Eyes, stood fix'd in woe.   (ll. 68–72)

---

[9] Thomas Hobbes, *The Iliads and Odysses of Homer*, 2 vols. in one (London, 1677); John Ogilby, *Homer his Odysses* (London, 1665); George Chapman's translation (complete version 1616, but preceded by earlier versions) is best consulted in *Chapman's Homer, the Iliad, the Odyssey and the lesser Homerica*, A. Nicoll (ed.) 2 vols. (London, 1957).

[10] *TE* I, p. 466.

[11] In Dryden, *Poems*, III, p. 1137.

Homer says simply that Odysseus 'looked upon his native land' (XIII, 197). Otherwise, of these lines only the second can be said to occur in Homer at XIII, 198 (though there the hero smites not his breast but his thigh). At line 224 Pope again adds a note of Virgilian visual pathos with the words, 'Now lift thy longing Eyes'. The intruded line 133,

> Where Troy's Majestic Ruins strow the Ground

is, once more, Virgilian in tone, though here it is a different strand in Virgil which is being drawn upon.

But not all Pope's departures from Homer are Virgilian. The adjectives at lines 106–7:

> Her decent Hand a shining Javelin bore,
> and painted Sandals on her Feet she wore

are not in Homer but are, so to speak, Augustan–Homeric: 'painted' is influenced by Homer's ποικίλος which happens not to be used here but easily could have been. 'Decent' is indeed a Latinism, but the influence here is Horace rather than Virgil (say, *decentes malas*, Horace, *Odes* III, xxvii, ll. 53–4, transmitted through Milton, *Il Penseroso*, l. 36, 'decent shoulders'). Elsewhere Pope's changes are in the direction of gentility, as when he introduces the 'Peasant' at line 124. Here the result is that the interest in farming on Ithaca, which for Homer is immediate, is distanced as the proper province of subordinate persons. Or else he is sententious, as at lines 86–7 where he offers the reader an elevated reflection on the rarity of virtue in the Great. He omits entirely the conversation of Zeus and Poseidon together with the turning to stone of the Phaeacian ship (XIII, ll. 125–87). The full list of omissions and additions is a long one but it is the Virgilian changes which most crucially affect the atmosphere of the whole and colour the poetry. Homer's ancient, magic world is humanized, refined, imbued with sensibility.

All the while Pope, the craftsman, is learning from this crossing of cultures. Every translator knows occasions when he is tempted to convey not only the sense but the linguistic character of the original, to drop the game of equivalences and instead to transpose, by a kind of bodily violence, vocabulary, idiom or syntax from the source language to the receiving language.[12] Where a language is relatively poor, as was Middle English, say, when the Latin for 'remorse of conscience' had to be rendered by 'again-bite of in-wit', the receiving language is actually enriched and extended by such forcible incursions from the major culture. Later phases of transposition have subtler effects. The aureate diction of Sir Thomas Browne played the transposed polysyllables of Latin and Greek against Saxon simplicities to suggest a running ambivalence or balancing of equivalents in the world and in the mind. Milton's despotic transpositions of alien syntax and idiom created for all the poets

---

[12] See C. A. Martindale's admirable discussion in his 'Unlocking the word-hoard. In praise of Metaphrase', *Comparative Criticism*, 6 (1984), 47–72.

who followed a strange secondary music in the given medium of literary English.

English–Augustan classicism is an altogether less radical, more urbane affair than Milton's. Its typical effect is a certain finesse, a precision which may look for a moment, but a moment only, like imprecision. Thus in calling his poem *The Rape of the Lock* Pope knew that the grosser, ordinary meaning of *rape* (which, by the way, the reader is never allowed quite to forget), inappropriate as it is to a lock of hair, must be swiftly replaced by the Latin sense, 'seizure' (now perfectly appropriate and free, after all, from any offence).

If all translators from the Latin and Greek had followed the implicit code of, say, the Penguin Classics, in which those quirks of linguistic and conceptual organization which may be deemed to be embedded in the ancient language as such are suppressed, the varying streams of more or less classicized diction would never have entered the language, to be poetically exploited in due course by such as Pope. Of course, as long as there were people about who knew the ancient languages, abrupt trans-linguistic allusions like Milton's 'happy-making sight' at line 18 of *On Time* were always possible (here the seemingly artless phrase is ponderously *faux-naif*; a Saxonised version of *beatifica visio* and so a small prize for the learned reader). But Pope, whose learning in ancient tongues was not profound, had nevertheless an ear sharply attuned to the literary effects of transposition, whether from Greek, Latin or from contemporary high-polish Romance cultures such as French. The writer of a radically classical style gives the reader a sense of an utterly hard infra-structure of meanings which are both alien to us and clear. Milton does so systematically and Pope does not. Jane Austen inherited certain verbal habits of precision from the classicizing eighteenth century but employed them without any sense of the original infra-structure. She is therefore classical in the comic form of her novels but not in their intimate verbal texture. In our own century Evelyn Waugh is found repellent by some not only because of his politics, but also because of the hard, alienating gloss of a radically, but not ostentatiously, classical style. Something must have gone into his head at Lancing College.

The distinction between translation and transposition is, it will be noticed, a rough and ready one, with further sub-distinctions lurking within it. The translator, unlike the transposer, selects from the receiving language equivalents *which shall be wholly natural to the receiving language*. Where the Latin poet says (indeed with no religious intention) that bulls 'breathe Vulcan from their nostrils' (Ovid, *Metamorphoses* vii, l. 104) the modern translator will say they 'breathe fire' (since that is what *we* would say). But at this point a certain sort of reader, curious as to how ancient poetry was actually pieced together, will resent the modification while another sort of reader will be gratefully acquiescent. It may be that this example artificially biases the argument in favour of the literalist transposer, for it is certainly true that an exaggerated fidelity to form and idiom can result in an utterly faithless and distorted rendering of meaning (now the notion of *equivalence*, the watchword of the translator, begins to look strong again). Yet – the argument oscillates more and more rapidly – this too can beget difficulties which arise from the fact that even fictional ancient literature is engaged at certain points with historical actuality. There will be times when *praetor* may be rendered 'magistrate' and times when the translator must write, even in English, 'praetor'. In eighteenth-century England there was a perfectly clear cultural equivalent for Rome, namely London, yet to *translate* Juvenal's *Roma*, 'London', is to stretch translation so far as to turn it into what Dryden called 'imitation' (as opposed to 'paraphrase' or the still tighter 'metaphrase').[13]

The eighteenth century knew how to enjoy such ultra-translation just as it appreciated the opposite pleasure of linguistic transposition. If Johnson's *London* (a version of Juvenal's third Satire) may stand at one end of our continuum, the calque may stand as its polar opposite. A calque is a transference of a special, subordinate use of a given word in language 'A' to the corresponding word in language 'B' where that special use had not existed previously. 'Foot' in the sense of 'metrical foot' is a calque from Latin *pes*, which carried just such a subordinate technical sense. A calque is quite distinct from what is called *borrowing*, where the *form* of a word in language 'A' is simply replicated, with the minimum necessary adjustments, in language 'B'. 'Admonition' is a borrowing from Latin 'admonitio' and preserves the form of the original almost exactly. Calques became less and less common as the English language developed and borrowings were felt to be more cultivated. They are most common in the Anglo-Saxon period.[14] A learned freedom at the 'imitation' end of the spectrum (where the receiving culture is lavishly enfranchised) is answered at the other end by a tiny localized usurpation of the natural rights of the receiving language – not by the mere importation of the polysyllabic alien *form* of the word but by a more fundamental invasion of the *seme*, or meaning–structure. To refer to 'the third foot' of a line of verse is, even today, not quite natural English. Dickens makes a free and very coarse use of calques to convey the Frenchness of France in *A Tale of Two Cities* and at the beginning of *Little Dorrit*. Charlotte Brontë does the same thing, though less exuberantly, in *Villette*. Pope's touch is far too light for such gross effects.

Let us take, from nowhere, a Latin sentence: *Et blaesa voce numeris locutus sum.* This can be translated, 'I lisped in verse-time.' A bad case of form-transposition might give 'I balbutiated metrically' (where the borrowings are from other Latin words). Transposition of the subordinate sense gives, 'I lisped in numbers' and this, of course, is Pope. As soon as we read 'in numbers' we sense Augustanism and, if we enjoy it, what we are enjoying is a subtle counterpointing of semic systems. 'Numbers' is a calque, for here the English

---

[13] See his Preface to *Ovid's Epistles, Translated by several hands* (1680), in John Dryden, *Of dramatic poesy and other critical essays*, ed. George Watson, 2 vols. (London, 1962), I, 262–73.
[14] See Barbara M. H. Strang, *A history of English* (London, 1970), esp. p. 316.

word is used in a way which is, still perceptibly, unnatural. It is used as *numerus* is used in Latin. For some learned readers the intuition of Latinity in 'numbers' would be strengthened by the fact that at this point in the *Epistle to Dr Arbuthnot* Pope happens to be echoing a particular passage of Ovid (*Tristia* IV, x, ll. 21–6). Of course calques may be gradually naturalized by frequent use in the receiving language until they are no longer felt as calques – for example certain uses of *chair* influenced by Latin *cathedra*; or *left* in the political sense, influenced by French *gauche*. It is characteristic of Pope that he should use a partly naturalized calque with a surviving stylistic sense of its linguistic nature. It is not for him but for hardier spirits to introduce wholly new calques.

When the young Pope essayed the translation of Homer he brought to the task not the self-abnegating, objectivist zeal of the scholar but a civil art of interwoven tones and nuances. Was he not soon to be the foremost social poet of the age? He knew perfectly well that his job was to temper style with style, to gain point and dynamism by modulating from austerity to urbanity. But as soon as he began to write he found that such modulation did not work through a simple encounter of the (severe) ancient and the (polished) modern; ancient literature itself prescribed a startlingly rich variety of tone. The matter is further complicated – almost beyond analysis – by the varying mediations of existing translations, but for all that we continue to find an intelligible music of styles rather than a mere chaos. Certainly the *Odyssey*, as we hinted earlier, is deeply different from the *Iliad*. The later poem is spatially indistinct, magical, humorous, and to bring this out Pope found himself drawing on Virgil, who is different again. The result is not a faithful rendering of Homer (a thing worth chasing but impossible to hit) but a shimmering of styles and languages. To the eighteenth century (and still, to some extent, to us) the ancient world was marble: Vitruvian, regular, arched, pillared, founded in reason and nature. Where the modern world presents an obscure flux, the ancient presents a sunlit stability. Such is the 'mental set', the elementary binary codification of material from which we must begin. Pope's way with English poetry was always subtly to thwart or undermine seemingly stable structures, restoring harmony only at the last (and not always then). But when he engaged directly with ancient literature he found his way to what is perhaps the most imaginatively original element in Virgil: the rendering fluid of that which is normally the very paradigm of the stable, the earth under our feet, the buildings through which we move.

To be sure in the England of Pope's day the baroque was very much a living force. In the great *sotto in su* paintings of the period heroes, saints and demigods fly up on clouds above our heads and the architecture from which they rise, columns and pediments seen in an aggressively perspectival manner from below, seems to be on the point of following the figures up, wildly, into the firmament. Giovan Battisti Gaulli had painted his *Adoration of the Name of Jesus* on the ceiling of the Gesù in Rome before Pope was born, but Sir James Thornhill's Painted Hall at Greenwich was not finished until 1727. Borromini, the great architect of the baroque, took the rectilinear classical façade and caused it to undulate in serpentine curves. Strictly speaking, a curving wall is as stable and unmoving as a straight one but imaginatively, perhaps because in general we expect straightness, undulation immediately suggests movement. But the architects and architectural painters were not placed quite as Pope was placed. There was no real analogue within ancient literature for the spectacular subversions of stability they sought to introduce. Nevertheless Pope found, primarily in Virgil, a non-baroque precedent for his own less grandiose, more intimate subversions. I began with the *Dirae* as something separate and unique, neglected in the commentaries and yet exhibiting in a curiously poignant manner the imaginative trope of *movement imputed to the landscape*. Latin is, after all, capable of such things. Pope, from his side, infuses his translation of Homer with an imaginative fluidity which is recognizably akin to what we find, first, in the *Dirae* and then more largely in the *Aeneid*.

As early as the Pastorals, written in 1704, the verbs, always revealing in Pope, show this distinctive quality. Often they are inchoative, either in form or in sense:

> Here where the Mountains, less'ning as they rise
> Lose the low Vales, and steal into the Skies.
>
> (*Autumn*, ll. 59–60)

The first part of *Windsor Forest*, that 'which relates to the country', was written at about the same time as the Pastorals. Here too we find the same note struck. The phrasing of line 24, 'blueish hills ascend', may seem unremarkable but the sense that even here the Virgilian influence may be at work is strengthened by the odd and beautiful word 'blueish' used, as we have already seen, of hills in Dryden's Virgil. A couple of lines earlier we have an intuition of a landscape which seems to shift and redispose itself as we move through it in the words 'interspersed in Lawns and opening Glades', where the important word is 'opening'. At line 213 we have the marvellously judged classicism of 'pendant' in:

> The watry Landskip of the pendant Woods.

First there is the latent *linguistic* precision of 'pendant', a precision not quite natural in English. Then, behind that, we have the *imaginative* precision-within-a-seeming-inappositeness of woods seen as hanging. In Virgil's first Eclogue the shepherd apostrophizes his goats:

> Non ego vos posthac viridi proiectus in antro
> dumosa pendere procul de rupe videbo.   (ll. 75–6)

No more, stretched out in some green cave, shall I watch you in the distance, hanging from a bushy crag.

Wordsworth's comment on *pendere* is famous. He observes doggedly that goats do not in fact hang as parrots hang, that rather the word presents 'to the mind

something of such an appearance, the mind in its activity, for its own gratifica-
tion contemplates them as hanging'.[15] Wordsworth is right on the essential
point: that the character proper to the act of seeing is imputed to the thing
seen, so that the passage contrives to be both about goats and about seeing at
the same time. But of course there is more to it than that. Things threatened
can seem more precious than things secure: that which hangs can fall. At the
same time there is a contrary sense of a diminished reality, of a black-cloth
suspended before the eye (for a visual presentation of a goat, however intense, is
somehow less than the goat itself). Virgil more than any other poet taught this
art to the ages which followed and Pope was not the least apt of his pupils.
Thus Pope's pendant woods may owe something to the landscape description
at *Aeneid* I, l. 164. The famous phrase, *silvis scaena coruscis*, translated by R. G.
Austin as 'a backdrop of quivering woods',[16] where the sense of a painted
curtain becomes explicit, is followed by *horrentique atrum nemus imminet umbra* (l.
165), 'The grove hangs dark over it with its bristling shade' (*imminet* is parallel
in Latin to *impendet* and *pendentibus* itself appears in the very next line, applied to
the hanging rocks of the cave).

There is a lesson in all this for us. The twentieth-century reader of Pope
needs in a manner to have his ear educated by Virgil if he is to read the English
poet with full understanding. *Sappho to Phaon* belongs to the same year (1707)
as *The Arrival of Ulysses in Ithaea*. Here the dominant influence is Ovid, but
Virgil is not wholly absent. The *silvis scaena coruscis* passage is perhaps the most
influential piece of natural description in all ancient literature and its fainter
echoes persist even where direct influence is unprovable. Let us try to catch the
more fleeting Virgilian affinities in the following lines:

> As if once more forsaken, I complain
> And close my Eyes, to dream of you again.
> Then frantick rise, and like some Fury rove
> Thro' lonely Plains, and thro' the silent Grove,
> As if the silent Grove and lonely Plains
> That knew my Pleasures, cou'd relieve my Pains.
> I view the *Grotto*, once the Scene of Love,
> The Rocks around, the hanging Roofs above . . .   (ll. 157–64)

Here we do not have the trope of imputed movement, but the subject's
progress through plains and conscious (in the old sense) woods is reminiscent
of the *Dirae*, while the word 'Fury' evokes the stricken and sleepless Dido,
roving maddened through the night at the beginning of *Aeneid* IV (*uritur infelix
Dido totaque vagatur / urbe furens*, 'Unhappy Dido burns and wanders fury-like
through the whole city'). Meanwhile the 'Grotto', the 'scene' of love and the
'hanging' rocks take us back to *silvis scaena coruscis*, felt through Ovid, *Heroides*

---

[15] Preface to *Poems* (1815) in *William Wordsworth*, Stephen Gill (ed.), The Oxford Authors
(Oxford, 1984), p. 631.
[16] *P. Vergili Maronis Aeneidos, Liber Primus*, with a commentary by R. G. Austin (Oxford, 1971), p.
73.

xv, ll. 135ff. We must concede, I think, that Pope's 'scene' is a degree or two less assertive of the theatrical metaphor than Virgil's *scaena*; one can watch the word weakening in successive English imitations of Virgil before Pope. Milton at *Paradise Lost* IV, l. 137, writes 'sylvan scene' and then goes out of his way to make sure that the image is kept alive by 'woody theatre' immediately afterwards. Dryden, translating *Aeneid* I, l. 164, writes 'a Sylvan Scene' / Appears above'[17] and we sense that the word is paler than it was. But in both Dryden and Pope the word *scene* certainly retains the theatrical image more strongly than it does today. Virgil's poetry was then still feeding the word.

The case is similar with the (for us) unremarkable '*Alps* on *Alps* arise' which occurs in the *Essay on Criticism*, l. 232, in a sharply visual context ('tire our wandring Eyes' ends the preceding line). The line about the Alps can be linked with *Eloisa to Abelard*, l. 290: 'Rise *Alps* between us! and whole oceans roll', where we are discernibly in the world of the *Dirae* (*obstabunt montes*, the mountains which interpose themselves between the subject and the loved object).

Sometimes indeed the effect is more full-blown and closer to the baroque. Take the ascending, swelling, bending architectural splendours of *Windsor Forest*, ll. 375–80:

> Behold! th'ascending Villa's on my Side
> Project long Shadows o'er the Chrystal Tyde.
> Behold! Augusta's glitt'ring Spires increase,
> And Temples rise, the beauteous Works of Peace.
> I see, I see where two fair Cities bend
> Their ample Bow, a new *White-Hall* ascend!

It may be said that this is at best an impure specimen of the trope since the buildings to which Pope referred were actually rising. The point is less important than it appears. Even when a building is being raised the eye does not *see* it rising in the accelerated manner of these lines. When we come to the two fair bending cities, the reader is not sure whether the sense is that building works are joining them (as in fact they were) or whether they simply appear thus. It is characteristic of such poetry that questions of this sort do not trouble us but are instead merely suspended. Some may have been reminded of Aeneas at the site where Rome is later to rise, *Aeneid*, VIII, ll. 355–6, especially as in the Latin the word *oppida*, 'towns' is mildly surprising, occurring when, metre apart, we might rather have expected some such word as *arces*, 'citadels':

> Haec duo praeterea disiectis oppida muris
> reliquias veterumque vides monumenta virorum.

In Dryden:

---

17 *Virgil's Aeneis*, I, ll. 233–4, in Dryden, *Poems*, III, p. 1070.

> Then saw two heaps of Ruins; once they stood
> Two stately Towns, on either side the Flood.
>
> (*Virgil's Aeneis* VIII, ll. 467–8)[18]

The same, more grandiose, manner appears but this time with a downward motion in:

> . . . Tow'rs and Temples sink in Floods of Fire
>
> (*The Temple of Fame*, l. 478)

Years later Pope could not resist a Virgilian expansion when he translated the lament of Andromache for Hector (*Iliad* XXIV, l. 725–45). Homer makes her say that, before her child will grow up, πόλις ἥδε κατ ἄκρης / πέρσεται (ll. 728–9), literally 'This city will be destroyed from the top down.' The phrase which I have rendered, 'from the top down' is however less vivid in the Greek than in the English and Lang, Leaf and Myers have some justification in translating it simply as 'utterly'.[19] But Virgil, contrariwise, blew on the spark and made it blaze, not once but twice:

> Ruit alto a culmine Troia.   (*Aeneid* II, l. 290)
>
> Down from her high pinnacle Troy is falling.
>
> . . . divum inclementia, divum
> . . . sternitque a culmine Troiam.   (II, l. 603)

The gods, the merciless gods scatter and lay low Troy from her pinnacle down.

Translating the original Greek phrase, Pope writes, surely with a sense of the Latin *ruit* in his 'Ruin':

> For *Ilium* now (her great Defender slain)
> Shall sink, a smoaking ruin on the plain.
>
> (Pope's *Iliad* XXIV, ll. 916–17)

Compare with this Pope's *Odyssey* III, ll. 614–18 (the third book of the *Odyssey* is one of the books which Pope undertook to translate himself, without waiting for a prior version by Fenton or Broome):

> Beneath the bounding yoke alike they held
> Their equal pace, and smoak'd along the field.
> The tow'rs of *Pylos* sink, its views decay,
> Fields after fields fly back, till close of day:
> Then sunk the Sun, and darken'd all the way.[21]

The Greek here is rendered, almost word for word, by Butcher and Lang as follows:

> Nothing loth the pair flew toward the plain and left
> the steep citadel of Pylos. So all day long they swayed

[18] Dryden, *Poems*, III, p. 1274.
[19] *The Iliad of Homer*, trans. A. Lang, W. Leaf and E. Myers (London, 1914), p. 500.
[20] *TE* VIII, p. 574.

the yoke they bore upon their necks.
Now the sun sank and all the ways were darkened.[22]

In Pope's version the bounding yoke and the darkened way are both reasonably Homeric. The words 'alike' and 'equal' may look like a sheer importation
of Augustan order and balance into the headlong motion of the original but in
fact Pope may here be responding to the dual form of the verb and ἀμφίς (=
'both' or 'the pair'). The rest is a compound of Virgil and Pope's own,
unsubduable gift. This passage is linked to the one previously cited by
'smoak'd', but its chief interest is that it returns us to the trope of imputed
motion. The towers sink as Telemachus and Pisistratus leave them behind.
Virgil's fields of flying Italy are somewhere in the penumbra of the poetry but
meanwhile the startling phrase, 'views decay' is very much Pope's own.
Thomas Hobbes in his *Leviathan*, with no lyric intent, called imagination itself
'decaying sense'.[23] Pope's use of the word is full of lyric sensitivity but is at the
same time in a manner neutral (there is no sinister suggestion). He may be
writing in a classicizing mode, with an awareness of the word's remoter
derivation from Latin *decidere*, 'to fall'. What he writes is certainly poetry.
Later the word is to appear again in the terrific conclusion of *The Dunciad*, in
which creation itself runs backwards to a hell of un-being:

> *Fancy's* gilded clouds decay,
> And all its varying Rain-bows die away.
>
> (1742, IV, ll. 631–2)

This time the implication of corruption and malaise is admitted by the poetry.
Within five lines we have the finest, and the most disquieting line Pope ever
wrote:

> The sick'ning stars fade off th'ethereal plain.   (l. 636)

In *The Dunciad* Pope is no longer teaching himself by cross-breeding his
predecessors but is writing at the height of his powers. The auditory relativity
of Virgil is thoroughly transformed, appearing now in the fully Popean evocation of London, the sounding city, flooded and overwhelmed by a rising
tumult:

> But far o'er all, sonorous Blackmore's strain;
> Walls, steeples, skies, bray back to him again.
> In Tot'nam fields, the brethren, with amaze,
> Prick all their ears up, and forget to graze;
> Long Chanc'ry Lane retentive rolls the sound
> And courts to courts return it round and round;
> Thame wafts it thence to Rufus' roaring hall,
> And Hungerford re-echoes bawl for bawl.
>
> (1742, II, ll. 259–66)

---

[22] *The Odyssey of Homer*, trans. S. H. Butcher and A. Lang (London, 1903), p. 46.
[23] *Leviathan*, Part I, chapter ii, A. R. Woller (ed.) (Cambridge, 1904), p. 3. Pope is known to have
owned a copy of the Leviathan; see *Collected in Himself*, p. 414.

Pope can be seen in training for this passage in his early version of Statius (1703), with its echoing cities and remurmuring riverbanks (ll. 164, 166) followed by the baroque exhilaration of the 'guilty Dome' and the bright pavilions invaded by obscuring clouds (ll. 172–3). That Statius should himself sound like Virgil is, of course, scarcely surprising. Now, however, the language is thoroughly naturalized, not least as a result of the London place-names. It will be said that they are there for bathetic effect and are intended to contrast, according to the ordinary rule of mock-heroic, with an implied array of Roman names. Yet the sheerly heroic energy of the lines is too strong. If ever Pope were, against all the odds, to be comparable with Blake, it would be here.

In *The Dunciad* the verbs are as important as ever:

> Thro' Lud's fam'd gates, along the well-known Fleet
> Rolls the black troop, and overshades the street,
> 'Till show'rs of Sermons, Characters, Essays,
> In circling fleeces whiten all the ways:
> So clouds replenish'd from some bog below,
> Mount in dark volumes, and descend in snow.
>
> (1742, II, ll. 359–64)

The simple forward motion of 'rolls' is overtaken by the inchoative 'whiten'. 'Whiten' is used many times in the translation of Homer, mostly in descriptions of the sea, and 'blacken' is commoner still (twenty-four instances), usually with reference to storm and clouds. In the early (1707) translation of 'the Episode of Sarpedon' from the *Iliad*, an army of warriors, likened to a storm, is seen as 'black'ning in the field' (l. 58). In the *Dunciad* passage, the recurrent Homeric formula, 'All the ways were darkened' is working somewhere in the back of Pope's mind. 'Blacken' is used most powerfully in *The Elegy to the Memory of an Unfortunate Lady* (1717):

> While the long fun'rals blacken all the way.   (l. 40)

In *The Dunciad* blackening and whitening are combined and the combination is at once brilliantly mirrored in the ascending darkness of the clouds followed by the falling pallor of the snow.

Both the passages I have cited from *The Dunciad* will stand as spectacular examples of dynamic townscape, but in neither of them do we find the radical figure of imputed movement. There is perhaps a kind of vertigo in the image (from the second passage) of flying manuscripts filling the streets, which links it to certain baroque conjurings of flying buildings, but in both passages London itself remains rooted, while the human chaos swirls through it. In the vision of the Fall of Rome in Book III the movement of the buildings is not imaginatively imputed but is actual, a real fall brought about by barbarian hands:

> See, the Cirque falls, th' unpillar'd Temple nods,
> Streets pav'd with Heroes, Tyber choak'd with Gods.
>
> (1742, III, ll. 107–8)

Yet, even though all this actually happened, it is given a dreamlike quality, an air of licentious imagination by the surrealism of the second line.

Some thirty lines further on the poetry gathers to a head in the ancient figure, known as the *adynata* or *impossibilia*[24] (fishes in the trees, suns in the sea) in which nature herself runs lunatic. This special, cosmic version of imputed movement has its own literary history and I have done my best to keep it out of this essay. But six lines must be quoted:

> Thence a new world to Nature's laws unknown,
> Breaks out refulgent, with a heav'n its own:
> Another Cynthia her new journey runs,
> And other planets circle other suns.
> The forests dance, the rivers upward rise,
> Whales sport in woods, and dolphins in the skies.
>
> (1742, III, ll. 241–6)

Here the landscape moves mightily, as it does in the *Epistle to Burlington* where the golden corn flows over and buries Timon's vanity (ll. 173–6). The splendour of the lines quoted is quite untouched by the distinctive colouring of subjective visual perception we found earlier. They are as much Greek as Roman (look at Herodotus v, 92a); they are as Horatian (look at *Odes* I, ii, ll. 5–10) or as Ovidian (*Metamorphoses* I, ll. 293–303) as they are Virgilian.

To rediscover the subjective inflection we must leave the major sonorities of *The Dunciad* and go back in time. In *Eloisa to Abelard* the shrines tremble (l. 112) with Eloisa's trembling consciousness and when Abelard's image rises in her mind,

> Priests, Tapers, Temples, swim before my sight.   (l. 274)

Otherwise, we may turn to that almost perfect minor poem, the *Epistle to Miss Blount, on her leaving the Town, after the Coronation*, written in 1714. The poet, in a reverie, standing in a London street, imagines Miss Blount in her tedious country exile, imagining (in her turn) the metropolitan splendours of the court. The poem is thus an intricate Chinese box of imaginings within imaginings. Then, to represent the evanescence of an image as it is replaced by common perception, Pope uses the image of a suddenly moved fan, imputing the visual occlusion and revelation occasioned thereby, as movement, to the objects, imagined or perceived. So much for the hard, marble clarity of Augustan verse.

> In some fair evening, on your elbow laid,
> You dream of triumphs in the rural shade;
> In pensive thought recall the fancy'd scene,
> See coronations rise on ev'ry green;
> Before you pass th' imaginary sights

[24] See Ernst Robert Curtius, *European literature and the Latin Middle Ages*, trans. Willard R. Trask (London, 1979), pp. 95ff. and A. D. Nuttall, 'Fishes in the trees', *Essays in Criticism* 24 (1974), 20–38.

> Of Lords, and Earls, and Dukes, and garter'd Knights;
> While the spread fan o'ershades your closing eyes;
> Then give one flirt, and all the vision flies.
> Thus vanish sceptres, coronets, and balls,
> And leave you in lone woods, or empty walls.   (ll. 31–40)

I have argued that 'scene' in Pope carries a stronger theatrical connotation than is always perceived by modern readers. In these lines (perhaps because of their historical relation to the Coronation) Pope seems to be thinking partly of a pageant or masque and masques were of course remarkable for their transformation scenes. Stage scenery, unlike mental imagery, is part of the physical fabric of the public world, but that does not mean that the whole tenor of this passage is merely objectified, as when the falling towers really fall, toppled by the barbarian hordes. Because scenery consists of picturings, more or less flimsy and impermanent, it is naturally analogous to mental imagery. Several scholars have sensed an allusion to masque in the most famous of all the moving-architecture passages of English poetry, the rising to music of Pandemonium in *Paradise Lost* (I, ll. 710–17).[25] In Miss Blount's reverie it is not 'Doric pillars overlaid / With golden architrave' that whirl from her but 'sceptres, coronets and balls', things which are in any case mobile in themselves. When, however, we are returned to the consciousness of Pope himself, the very streets assail him and clamorously usurp his dream:

> *Gay* pats my shoulder, and you vanish quite;
> Streets, chairs and coxcombs rush upon my sight.   (ll. 47–8)

I have at times in this essay written of these effects as if they were heroic or sublime. But where they are unequivocally placed as free-floating imaginings they are of course immediately diminished. Pope – jealous to preserve, especially in a potentially sexual context, his own lightness of manner – is often anxious to secure this very diminution. Gay's hand on Pope's shoulder enables him to show Miss Blount that he is not, after all, her abject slave but an urbane man with friends and interests of his own. Pope skilfully curtails the flirtation (remember that this word has to do, as the poem itself shows us, with the use of the *fan*) and contains his own, briefly vagrant imagination. But the rushing streets are not a dream or an illusion: they are reality itself, importunate and loud. Thus Pope resists the easy baroque sublimity which by his day was virtually inherent in the trope of imputed movement. It is common, everyday London, not heroes and palaces, which is here behaving so uncommonly. One searches in vain for a just analogue in painting: something like Thornhill's ceiling if it had been painted instead by Hogarth. Gillray was later to draw mock-baroque tableaux with caricatured political personages and I am sure that Pope would have been delighted by Cruikshank's picture of London spreading into the surrounding countryside, squirting smoke and bricks in

[25] See Fowler's note *ad loc.* in *The poems of John Milton*, Carey and Alastair Fowler (eds.) (London, 1968), p. 502.

fountains. But both these examples (quite apart from the fact that they post-date Pope) are far too coarse in their technique.

I have tried to show how, when Pope entered the altered landscape of another culture, he chose not only to translate classical meanings into English meanings but also to transpose certain alien habits of speech and thought. He did this because, like all great poets, he cared about language and form, and knew that the language of English poetry itself would be strengthened and enriched by the minor violations to which he was willing to subject it. He also found that the ancient world itself was far from being a uniform field. I have written about Pope's Virgilianizing of Homer as if it were a matter of strenuously artificial interference. In fact it would have required a most artificial vigilance on Pope's part to keep Virgil *out*. Pope, who never published a set translation of Virgil, had Virgil in his bones and accepted the consequence. This was a dynamic, ever moving modulation of tone. The whole can be seen, thus far, as a marvellously managed interplay of cultural perspectives. But then we notice that the Virgilian passages are all actually *about* individual, perspectival seeing and perceptual relativities. Pope found, in the ordinary practice of translation, that a Virgilian subjectivity could quicken his page. He had to make the landscape of the past live and move and, lo, there within that very landscape was a poet who made the natural landscape live and move. Meanwhile there is a certain analogy with the situation in English poetry. Johnson said that Dryden found English literature brick and left it marble.[26] Not, of course, that Dryden is uniformly marmoreal. Johnson himself observes, earlier in the same *Life*, 'Sometimes the marble relents, and trickles in a joke.'[27] Elsewhere, one might add (a little more warmly) Dryden is full of life and energy. Nevertheless, Pope following Dryden may well have sensed that, stylistically, English poetry had been fixed in a classic mould. He knew that he must both defer to this and oppose it with his own more delicate genius, and the Virgilian infiltration of the objective epic showed him one way in which this might be done. There is, all the same, a certain irony in the fact that Virgil reached Pope partly through Dryden's version.

Pope was not the only poet to employ the trope of imputed movement any more than Virgil was the only Latin poet to do so. But there is a sense in which the fluid, subjective mode remains Virgil's property. If it is found in the *Appendix Vergiliana* it is because whoever wrote those passages loved and wished to be like Virgil. If it is in Ovid it is because he learned not only from the Hellenistic poets but also from Virgil. As for Statius, his debt to Virgil is immense. When Pope writes

> Then Marble soften'd into life grew warm
> And yielding metal flow'd to human form.

(*The First Epistle of the Second Book of Horace, Imitated*, i.e. 'The Epistle to Augustus', ll. 147–8)

[26] *Lives of the English poets*, G. B. Hill (ed.), 3 vols. (Oxford, 1905), I, p. 469.
[27] *Lives of the English poets*, I, p. 438.

he owes nothing to Horace, a little to Virgil (*Aeneid* VI, ll. 847–8) but most of all to Ovid (for example, *Metamorphoses* x, ll. 283ff.). Pope utterly lacks Virgil's love of his own soil, his religious intensity, his special pathos. Yet, in an age of mannered aggression and social vigilance Pope found a way to keep poetry alive, and Virgil helped.

Appendix

I am indebted for criticisms and suggestions to C. A. Martindale. All references, unless otherwise specified, are to John Butt (ed.), *The poems of Alexander Pope*, a one-volume edition of the text of the Twickenham Edition (London, 1968). References to Homer are to D. B. Monro and J. W. Allen (eds.), *Homeri Opera* (Oxford, 1917–19), those on Virgil are to R. A. B. Majors (ed.), *P. Vergili Maronis Opera* (Oxford, the corrected 1972 reprint of the 1969 edn.). References to the *Dirae* are, except for one specified case, to the edition by E. J. Kenney in the *Appendix Vergiliana*, W. F. Clausen, F. R. D. Goodyear, E. J. Kenney and J. A. Richmond (eds.) (Oxford, 1966).

10

The genius of Pope's genius: criticism and the text(s)

WALLACE JACKSON

I begin with a thesis founded on a paradox. My assumption is that the familiar claim – and I here choose A. E. Housman as spokesman for it – that eighteenth-century poetry, even at its best, 'differed in quality from the poetry of all those ages, whether modern or ancient, English or foreign, which are acknowledged as the great ages of poetry'[1] is the basis for the modern revaluation of Alexander Pope's poetry. What Housman proposed as a substantial deficiency, twentieth-century scholarship has refined into a virtue, and it has been the special task of this criticism to explore and sustain a conception of Pope based on what David Morris has recently called the 'genius of sense,'[2] a definition rooted in Wartonian diction and the dubious accolade offered by him: 'Surely it is no narrow and niggardly encomium, to say he is the great Poet of Reason, the *First* of *Ethical* authors in verse.'[3]

The history of Pope's clouded priority begins here and initiates a perplexed criticism of ambiguously accorded praise or blame. From time to time, and always depending upon the criteria of the speaker, Pope was without passion, unEnglish, and unnatural. The terms of approbation seemed chosen to be especially chilling: good sense and judgment, prudence, ethical and didactic intention, skilful execution or technique, and, of course, the drawing room virtue of wit. Qualities such as these were allowed and promoted by Warton and Bowles; the greater detractors in our century, such as Housman and Oliver Elton, admitted only that Pope succeeds in 'the secondary forms of burlesque, satire, and epistle; in epic or tragedy his thoughts would show small and shrunken'.[4]

I propose that it became necessary to Pope's admirers to fortify a diminished position, to build it upon the solid foundation of a poetry of allusion, and to hold strenuously the middle ground of high poetic competence. This, I take it, has been the principal strategy of Pope's most capable scholar, Professor Maynard Mack. To Elton's judgments and Housman's observation that 'Satire, controversy, and burlesque . . . are forms of art in which high poetry is

---

[1] A. E. Housman, *Name and nature of poetry* (Cambridge, 1933), p. 18.
[2] David Morris, *Alexander Pope: the genius of sense* (Cambridge, Massachusetts, 1984).
[3] Joseph Warton, *An essay on the genius and writings of Pope* (London, 1806), II, p. 403.
[4] Oliver Elton, *The Augustan ages* (London, 1899), p. 308.

not at home' (Housman, pp. 19–20), Mack has responded that Pope is 'in no sense a poet of supreme moments, whether of tragic agonies *de profundis* or of soaring exaltations'.[5] The basis of argument was in fact readied for polarized positions on which Pope's reputation depended. 'Tragedy and satire,' said Mack, 'are two ends of a literary spectrum. Tragedy tends to exhibit the inadequacy of norms, to dissolve systematized values, to precipitate a meaning containing – but not necessarily contained by – recognizable ethical codes. Satire, on the contrary, asserts the validity and necessity of norms, systematic values, and meanings that *are* contained by recognizable codes.' If tragedy, therefore, 'fortifies the sense of irrationality,' satire offers 'standards of judgment [that] are indubitable'.[6]

Yet even here the lines are not drawn as neatly and cleanly as one might expect, for a sort of lurking ambivalence has always hung around the edges of Pope criticism, perhaps finding its inception in Johnson's incomplete arbitration between the moments of exaltation in Pope's poetry and the prudence he purports to find everywhere.[7] If Pope is for Mack 'predominantly a social poet,' whose 'poetry neither laments the limits of the human situation nor seeks to transcend or challenge them,' but 'simply accepts them wryly, with a smile,' he is equally

Like his predecessors, Spenser, Shakespeare, and Milton . . . haunted throughout his life . . . by a vision of England as the ideal commonwealth to be realized on earth – a Prospero's island, House of Temperance, Garden of Alcinous, and demi-Eden, all rolled in one . . . It is for this reason that he dares invoke beside Cibber in his laureate's chair – emblem of a court's corrupted taste – the great shadow of Milton's Satan on his throne in hell; or beside the dapper Sporus – emblem of a court's corrupted morals – the shadow of the original Tempter, 'at the ear of Eve, familiar toad'.

(Collected in Himself, pp. 70, 75, 74)

To Mack's list may be added the vivid figures of Dulness, Eloisa's Black Melancholy and jealous God, Belinda's Spleen, *The Temple of Fame*'s Rumour, and the assembly of midnight hags who inhabit the second *Moral Essay*. This vein has not gone unnoticed by others. S. L. Goldberg speaks of 'an attraction in Pope towards chaos, disorder, and eccentricity, quite as powerful as that towards order, form, and moral rationality'.[8] Dustin Griffin has observed 'a visionary impulse (still inadequately recognized by critics) prompting him to prophecy and fantasy'.[9] John Sitter has spoken of Pope's 'strong attraction for

---

[5] *Collected in Himself*, p. 74.

[6] Maynard Mack, 'The muse of satire', in *Yale Review* 51 (Autumn, 1951), 85.

[7] Pope's mind was 'in its widest searches still longing to go forward, in its highest flights still wishing to be higher; always imagining something greater than it knows, always endeavouring more than it can do'. Yet, 'he excelled every other writer in *poetical prudence*; he wrote in such a manner as might expose him to few hazards'. G. Birkbeck Hill (ed.), *Lives of the English poets* (Oxford, 1905), III, pp. 217, 219.

[8] S. L. Goldberg, 'Integrity and life in Pope's poetry', in R. F. Brissenden and J. C. Eade (eds.), *Studies in the eighteenth century* (Toronto, 1976), p. 192.

[9] Dustin Griffin, *Alexander Pope: the poet in the poems* (Princeton, 1978), pp. 36–7.

a shadowy, otherworldly kind of poetry' in the earlier years of his career,[10] and Thomas Edwards has divided Pope's career between the 'Augustan' and the 'grotesque'.[11]

Such distinct, opposed and unreconciled aspects of Pope's career may be traceable further to the Pope portraits. In 1800 Hayley commissioned Blake to execute in tempera twenty heads of the poets. Some of the inclusions are curious. The sixteenth-century Spanish poet Ercilla is represented as are Otway and Blair, and, most surprisingly of all, Hayley himself. 'All these Heads were painted on separate canvases; and all, with the exception of those of Ariosto and Ercilla (which have disappeared) are now preserved in the Art Gallery at Manchester.'[12] The portrait of Pope is in the mode of one of two characteristic eighteenth-century paintings of him. Commonly, Pope was portrayed as a man of sense, as in the Charles Jervas portrait that Pope chose as the frontispiece for his collected *Works* of 1717. The second mode arises a little later in his career and in it he is frequently represented in a manner well described by David Morris: 'The secular fiction of an unseen muse or the rapt transport of genius are sufficient to explain the upward-gazing eyes and to associate Pope with a tradition of inspired writing.' Pope appears in this fashion in a later painting by Jervas, but is also so painted by Jonathan Richardson, Jean Baptiste Van Loo, Michael Dahl and others. Morris notes that 'the challenge . . . Pope accepted in his lifework [was] to reconcile the antithetical or contrary languages of genius and of sense' (p. 313), and concludes his provocative inquiry by stating that it is 'not [his] purpose to decide whether Pope succeeded in the difficult compounding of sense and genius that, as he knew, would have to be achieved in his character as poet' (pp. 313–16).

The portrait of Pope completed by Blake shows him in the pose of the visionary poet, head tilted upward, eyes more or less looking inward, hand on the side of the head, and hair swept backward as though by a divinely caressing wind. On one side of the portrait Eloisa may be seen praying; on the other is a figure that the Blake Society tells us is 'not easy to identify'. In any event, Blake was most likely familiar with the two major styles of the Pope portraits, and in choosing that of the visionary, and illustrating it with an episode from *Eloisa to Abelard* (and with another or the same moonlight female on the other side), he elected to paint Pope in the particular character that most appealed to him, though inconsistent with his other judgments of the poet.

How does one come to terms then with the *other* aspect of Pope's imagination? We can once again find our start in Mack, in an essay now over thirty-five years old. In the 'Muse of Satire,' he defends Pope against those older scholars

---

[10] John Sitter, *The poetry of Pope's Dunciad* (Minneapolis, 1971), p. 117.
[11] Thomas Edwards, *This dark estate: a reading of Pope* (California, 1963), pp. vii–viii.
[12] William Blake, *The heads of the poets*, introduction by Thomas Wright (Olney, 1925), p. 3 (unnumbered).

who find satire both inferior and offensive. He cites 'Macaulay, Elwin, Leslie Stephen – all of whom seem, at one time or another, to have regarded it as a kind of dark night of the soul (dank with poisonous dews) across which squibs of envy, malice, hate, and spite luridly explode'. To counter their objections Mack draws on the notion that all 'good satire . . . exhibits an appreciable degree of fictionality'. His argument is both formal and thematic, formal in that he locates 'a thesis layer attacking vice and folly . . . and, much briefer, an antithesis layer, illustrating or implying a philosophy of rational control'. The thematic situation 'is the warfare of good and evil . . . carried on in a context that asserts the primacy of moral decision, as tragedy asserts the primacy of moral understanding'.[13]

When Ronald Paulson takes up the subject of satiric fictions he notices that 'Dryden's particular fiction was that of a succession,' whereas for Pope the 'enveloping fiction of provocation and response informs many of the satires that intervene between the 1729 and 1743 *Dunciads*'.[14] Elsewhere Paulson remarks that the

satire of Dryden, Swift, and Pope follows a tradition beginning in Christian humanism and skipping the aberration of English Elizabethan satire; its subject is almost always religious, and when, as in Swift's *Tale of a Tub* or Pope's *Dunciad*, it is ostensibly about literary vices, it is actually about moral and religious issues . . . The Augustan view of evil is Christian, or, to be more precise, Augustinian . . . The bad will, Augustine explains, is the 'will to power' when 'the soul, loving its own power, relapses from the desire for common and universal good to one which is individual and private'.[15]

The description is applicable to *The Rape of the Lock*. Belinda's mirror is, as Wasserman calls it, a 'topos for the rites of pride,'[16] but mirror is also, in *The First Satire*, a revelatory medium, like satire itself, and thus an 'impartial Glass' in which the self is to be seen by oneself and by others: 'In me what Spots (for Spots I have) appear.' That Belinda 'bends' to her glass suggests her sovereign is the power she has assumed or arrogated. Pope's glass in the Horatian Imitation is impartial; that is, the appropriation of satire's powers carries with it the correspondent risk of self-revelation: 'In me what Spots . . .'

The single trope of glass brings *The Rape* and the *First Satire* into proximity, offering alternative commentary on the relation between illusion and revelation, as each actor, Belinda *and* Pope, is alternately served by the medium in which each appears. The topos for pride is equally the topos for self-knowledge and the text in which the reader reads history is also the text in which he reads the poet, as well as, I might add, reading himself. In much the same way the temple of fame coexists with the temple of infamy, and both poems 'occupy

---

[13] 'The muse of satire', pp. 82, 84, 85.

[14] Ronald Paulson, 'Satire, and poetry, and Pope', in *English satire: papers read at a Clark Library seminar* (California, 1972), pp. 76, 80.

[15] Ronald Paulson, *The fictions of satire* (Baltimore, Maryland, 1967), pp. 113–14.

[16] Earl Wasserman, 'The limits of allusion in *The Rape of the Lock*', *Journal of English and Germanic Philology* 65 (1966), 433.

that particular province in which a poet seeks to organize certain historical facts by means of a single allegorical principle'. (Sitter, *Pope's Dunciad*, p. 68). Mirror, for example, is a trace sign of fictions scattered throughout the Popean text. The poet's return to such signs suggests that the fiction is being reconstituted in a way that bears relation or comparison to the earlier fiction, even as (to choose one such fiction) the abiding action of predator and prey is variously reimagined throughout the body of Pope's work.

There is a kind of 'intertraffic' between and among Pope's poems long ago identified by Mack. Using that term he referred to the concourse 'between the *Iliad* translation and the *Elegy to the Memory of an Unfortunate Lady* [as] particularly intricate'.[17] A decade ago Ralph Cohen observed that it 'is not surprising that *An Essay on Criticism*, *Windsor Forest*, and *The Rape of the Lock* should have such mixtures of subject matter and that they should resemble one another in the interrelations of their parts'.[18] Learning to read Pope's poetry backward and forward or, to use a modern term, intertextually, and refusing to accept the division of his career into the two convenient phases separating the first half from the second, leads to recognitions consistent with the language of allegory. Isabel MacCaffrey has spoken of the 'ontological system where different grades of reality are continuous and congruent at different points on the scale'.[19] 'Mirror' functions in just this way to connect different grades, but many topoi within Pope's fictions behave similarly. In the tale of Sir Balaam, Pope fuses the Jupiter-daemon who descends upon Danae with the Satan-daemon who destroys Job's children: ' 'Till all the Daemon makes his full descent, / In one abundant show'r of Cent. per Cent., / Sinks deep within him, and possesses whole.' Satan as Prince of Air visiting storms upon Job's children corresponds also to the passion-tormented Atossa, whose 'Hate' and 'Gratitude' are equally a 'storm' (*To a Lady*, l. 132). Storm is the literal and metaphorical manifestation of diabolism, and it seems advisable to read the portrait of Atossa through the allusion to Satan's action, also through the correlative allusion to Jupiter, who descends upon Danae in a rain (storm) of gold. The fiction is that of possession, and 'storm' ('show'r') links widely divergent portraits and brings them under the scrutiny of a single focus composed of multiple nuances of moral light and shade.

Something of my meaning here was suggested by Reuben Brower who called Atossa 'a symbolic figure inhabiting a poetic world, not a citizen of the actual world in which Pope lived'.[20] Such a world is constituted of various actors and events both different from and correlative to each other. Thalestris and Atossa are continuous and congruent within two fictions of sexual divisiveness, *The Rape of the Lock* and *To a Lady*. The two poems are paratactically

[17] *TE*, VII, p. ccxxxviii.
[18] Ralph Cohen, 'Pope's meanings and the strategies of interrelation', in Maximillian Novak (ed.), *English literature in the age of disguise* (California, 1977).
[19] Isabel MacCaffrey, *Spenser's allegory* (Princeton, 1976), p. 29.
[20] Reuben Brower, *Alexander Pope: the poetry of allusion* (Oxford, 1959), p. 274.

related; the midnight hags haunting the later work are socially defunct versions of Belinda and her glittering crowd, though neither Pope nor the poems quite say so. At issue here is a 'grid of unspecified allusion' bridging the gaps (MacCaffrey, *Spenser's Allegory*, p. 49). *To a Lady* is in the canon at some remove from the *Rape*, yet is continuous and congruent with it. On the other hand, character can be situated in a variously graded reality that obliges us to move up the scale instead of horizontally along it. Paul Korshin defines Sir Balaam as

> a satiric reversal of Job, one of the century's most canonical types of Christ. The Balaam of Scripture is a false prophet, a hireling, a lying teacher, and a man bereft of revelation . . . The theme of Sir Balaam's temptation and fall is not quite analogous to the triumph of Dulness, but it is worth noting that Sir Balaam, 'Rouz'd by the Prince of Air' (353), rapidly expands his wealth and influence, moves from the City to the Court (directly paralleling the central theme of *The Dunciad*), overreaches himself, and comes to a bad end.[21]

For Korshin this is typological satire. For David Morris, Pope's 'most thorough analysis of new-monied corruption occurs in the tale of Sir Balaam, where we witness character in the process of self-destruction,' and, 'far from recounting a dramatic surrender to evil,' the tale of Sir Balaam 'describes the career of an entrepreneur' (pp. 186, 187). Within the canon we are always being recalled to fictive situations variously organized in relation to other fictions (*To Bathurst* and *The Dunciad*, for example), or to different grades of reality within the same text (the typological and economic interpretations offered by Korshin and Morris).

Mack remarks of Pope's Homeric translations that 'What is clear, at any rate, is that Hera's cestus, as Pope interprets it, belongs to the same world of discourse as Belinda, her Cross, and her Lock; and that either Homer's erotic set-piece has affected Pope's image of Belinda, or the image of Belinda has affected his Homer, or both' (*TE*, VII, p. ccxlv). Pope's poetry seems always attached to deeper structures, and to accommodate them within texts of a different order.

Yet there is something incomplete about Pope's lifework, particularly in light of the intentionality that pervades his own comments. The projected *opus magnum* was never finished. Some time ago Torchiana noted that if Pope 'works the Miltonic pattern of "glory, ruine, and restoration" in the *Essay on Man*, we may come to see that poem as celebrating man's precarious glory, *The Dunciad* as mocking his precipitous ruin, and *Brutus* as pointing the means for his redemption or restoration'.[22] This is a story Pope never completes, but his desire to do so suggests an elusive and unstable coherence within the canon. In another context, MacCaffrey refers to an 'unarticulated hidden sense, a sense that never reveals itself explicitly as a whole, though explicit statements about

---

[21] Paul Korshin, *Typologies in England* (Princeton, 1982), p. 315.

[22] Donald Torchiana, 'Brutus: Pope's last hero', in M. Mack (ed.), *Essential articles for the study of Alexander Pope* (Connecticut, 1968), p. 705.

aspects of it form part of the verbal fabric' (p. 51). I am reminded by this comment of the various critical observations resembling it that lie scattered over the landscape of Popean scholarship.

Ralph Cohen observes that since 'a poem is a series of parts, it is necessary to recognize that all the poems must also be considered as parts. Thus the understanding of any one part requires not merely a study of its connection in a single poem, but its connection with similar parts in other poems' (p. 120). One recent student of Pope's *oeuvre* posits nothing less than a 'continuously reciprocal reading of language and idea, a critique of ideology in which literary form is a constitutive category'.[23]

The elaborate fictionality of Pope's canon requires from us a special sort of attentiveness whereby those traces to which I referred earlier alert us to recurrent contexts that play off against one another. In *The Rape of the Lock*, Belinda's morning dream includes a glittering youth who 'Seem'd to her Ear his winning lips to lay, / And thus in Whispers said, or seem'd to say.' At the close of *The Temple of Fame*, Pope says, 'One came, methought, and whisper'd in my Ear.' And in *The First Epistle of the First Book of Horace*, 'A Voice there is, that whispers in my ear.' 'Whispering' recapitulates the Miltonic context, summoning the fiction of tempter and tempted while playing upon it within a modulated pattern. Much as Dryden's characteristic fiction includes a 'dupe for the tempter to act upon, an Adam or an Eve, or (in the case of Absalom) a pseudo-Christ,' Pope's commonly incorporates the action of predator and prey or of divisiveness introduced by a desire for power or a temptation scene which is corollary to such other fictions. At the centre is that which Paulson associates with Dryden: 'the classical-Christian conception of the nature of evil. A deception is clearly crucial: there must be a fool as well as a knave.'[24] Belinda, Cibber, Pope himself (in the *Imitations*), the adversary of the *Essay on Man*, and those of the *Horatian Imitations*, are common identities assumed by the dupe, and such tropes as 'whispering', 'mirror', 'storm' signify the recreation of interdependent fictions, parts of an apprehensible totality that is neither determined nor limited by genre.

'I am proposing,' says Paulson, 'that the large action of Pope's satires takes two general forms. One is the emblematic, allegorical, allusive anti-Pollio vision of chaos and disorder. The second action concludes with the Horatian *sermo* in which "Pope" converses with somebody; but it begins with the pastoral Alexis, whose tone is never quite lost, supporting the strong tendency toward apologia, in which the satirist defends himself and at the same time produces satire' (Paulson, 'Satire, poetry, and Pope', p. 63). The first 'action' includes not only *The Dunciad*, but the divisiveness leading to warfare between the sexes in the *Rape* and is echoed in the sustained hostility between the sexes in *To a Lady*. It is evident as well in the seduction, subversions and temptations practised or attempted in *The Temple of Fame* and *The First Epistle*. The second

[23] Laura Brown, *Alexander Pope* (Oxford, 1985), p. 5.
[24] Paulson, *The Fictions of Satire*, pp. 120, 121.

'action' is a feature not only of the *Horatian Imitations*, but of the *Essay on Man*, in which conflict between 'you' and 'I' is a central feature of the poem.

Cohen offers the topos of the flower born to blush unseen and provides examples from 'a love song by Waller, a mock-heroic epic by Pope, a fable by Ambrose Philips, a satire by Young, a georgic by Thomson, an elegy by Gray, and a didactic poem by Dyer'. Over a protracted period of time the image suggests a degree of conceptual stability, 'an example of God's fruitfulness at the same time that it suggests the unavailability of this variety to men . . .; its maneuverability rests on the potentiality of forms to accommodate perceptual responses to nature as a norm'.[25] Harold Bloom has noticed that a 'particular transumptive series in Milton to Coleridge to Emerson to Stevens involves the trope of blankness,' adding how 'curious have been the uses of Milton's universal blank, and so diverse have been the strengths of post-Miltonic transumption'. Bloom speaks of the 'retropings of earlier tropes . . . [as] transumptive or metaleptic echoings, instances of the interpretive and re-visionary power of a poetry perpetually battling its own belatedness'.[26] He cites Coleridge's *Dejection*: 'And still I gaze – and with how blank an eye!' The infrastructure of eighteenth-century poetry has commonly been predicated on a decorum of formal relationships, the ordering principles inherent in wit, judgment, nature, or in genre. 'Pope's main statement about rhetoric will turn out to be a prescription for some kind of improving conjunction or complementary interaction between the "wit" of rhetoric and the "nature" it deals with.'[27]

Complementary interaction may be equally a function of different diachronic figurations that transumption or metalepsis provides. For example, Coleridge's blankness signifies a peculiar authenticity, 'the void of decreation' (Bloom, p. 84). The series initiated by the flower born to blush unseen leads to Blake's 'The Sick Rose' of *Experience*, a subversion by way of satire of the conceptual authority of the topos and its previous employment. An earlier nature could not be sick; Blake knew how and why it could be. The normative topos of one age can become the grounds of satire in another. The main topoi in Pope's canon are, to use John Hollander's helpful term, 'figure[s] of interpretive allusion' (Bloom, p. 74); that is, an internal allusiveness defines the space within which asymmetrical fictions observe an 'improving conjunction or complementary interaction'.

This remains true even if a trope is employed for contrary fictions. Laura Brown proposes that the 'image of the spreading ripple on the tranquil lake is the central one for *The Dunciad*, but it spreads throughout Pope's poetic corpus as well' and is crucial to the creation of benevolence that presides over the close

[25] Ralph Cohen, 'On the interrelations of eighteenth-century literary forms', in Phillip Harth (ed.), *New approaches to eighteenth-century literature* (New York, 1974), pp. 53, 55.
[26] Harold Bloom, *The breaking of the vessels* (Chicago, 1982), pp. 80, 74.
[27] William K. Wimsatt, Jr. and Cleanth Brooks, *Literary criticism: a short history* (New York, 1959), p. 237.

of the *Essay on Man*. The image 'gives us a bridge from one apocalypse to the other: *The Dunciad* condemns capitalist expansion through the same ambivalent evocation of tranquillity that serves in the *Essay on Man* as the summary image of Pope's problematic moral rationale for a capitalist system' (pp. 149, 151). The ambivalent meaning of the figure here implicates two contrary fictions, the opposed progresses of good and evil, imperial triumph and the extended kingdom of Dulness. The nature of Rumour's influence within her domain is presented in the same figure in *The Temple of Fame*. Such re-visionary strategies are synchronic rather than diachronic, arguing the presence of discontinuous or paratactic narrative. In so far as Pope's ongoing discourse returns upon itself to regenerate itself it seeks a variation of Sitter's 'single allegorical principle,' the temples of fame and infamy, another trope for imperial powers.

When Empson speaks of 'the fundamental device of the Augustan style,' he chooses as his example the lines from *To Burlington*: 'To rest, the Cushion and soft Dean invite, / Who never mentions Hell to ears polite' (*TE* iii, ii, pp. 151–2, ll. 149–50). He remarks: 'This use of a word with several extended meanings so as to contract several sentences into one, is the fundamental device of the Augustan style.'[28] The multiple meaning of the complex word correlates to the multiple application of the trope and to those recurrent fictions it invokes. Cohen notes that 'Pope converts the topos of *concordia discors* into a movable relation that has both shifting boundaries and changing relations within the boundaries. The limits remain for Pope undiscovered though there is no doubt that they exist. Within the bounds, relations can be complementary, contradictory, or subtly conjoined.'[29]

Pope's story-telling tends often to suffer narrative suspension so that narrative outline is obscured. In the *Epistle to Bathurst* the presence of Satan is introduced and then suspended, only to re-emerge at the close for the ensnarement of Sir Balaam. Fredric Bogel states that the tale of Sir Balaam, 'as readers have often noticed, is something of a self-contained pendant to the poem, and when the poem itself ends with the tale we are made even more aware of its conspicuous irrelevance. For the narrative of Balaam does not overtly acknowledge its connections with the larger context of which it is a part.'[30] Yet Satan is slyly present at the beginning as 'the shining mischief' that is 'Deep hid . . . under ground,' and later 'Flam'd forth this rival to, its Sire, the Sun'. Never quite out of the poem, he is reinvoked as 'Corruption' supplied with 'lighter wings to fly!' Satan's progress in *To Bathurst* reflects, however distantly, Belinda's at the opening of Canto ii, and though less fierce she is no less of a 'shining mischief'. Moreover, Eloisa's 'rebel nature' implicates Belinda's self-deification, and both women are figures within an allegory of love variously figured and obviously discontinuous within the canon. In *Eloisa to Abelard*

---

[28] William Empson, *Seven types of ambiguity* (New York, 1949), p. 70.
[29] Cohen, 'Pope's meanings and the strategies of interrelation', p. 115.
[30] Fredric Bogel, *Acts of knowledge* (Lewisburg, Pennsylvania, 1981), p. 76.

the problem of the poem is focused on the relation between spiritual and physical love. Later, in *An Essay on Man*, the subject becomes self-love and social love. When we approach Pope in these terms we get the right sense of an extended subject, which, in *The Dunciad*, is metamorphosed into numerous corruptions of sexuality, including the lingering and abiding Oedipal fantasy that grips the relation between Cibber and his 'mighty Mother'. In *To a Lady* the 'veterans' who as 'the Ghosts of Beauty glide, / And haunt the places where their honour dy'd' are the now worn-out coquettes of Belinda's social whirl. Such crossings and re-crossings suggest the way in which distributed and diffused presences play within the body of his poetry.

We thus derive from our reading the interplay between economy and spiritual economy (*Windsor Forest* and the *Essay on Man*), between love that is of self and social, of the earth and divine, all of which implicates history (the past and the topical) and myth (the fictionality to which the event is referable). The aggressive elements constituted by predator and prey in *Windsor Forest* (Pan and Lodona, England and France) are envisaged again in *The Rape of the Lock* (Baron and Belinda), and brought forth once more in *Eloisa to Abelard* (the 'jealous God' and Eloisa). The economy of love is variously contextualized as the primitive, the nationalistic or imperial, the social. It is thereby distributed, dispersed, across a spectrum in which play many controlling fictions. Against the economy of love are set the situational realities generated in the *Rape* by the contingent values of 'honour,' 'knowledge,' 'power,' by Belinda's desire to rise (the temptation) which affiliates with other comparable seductions or attempted seductions within the canon (the close of *The Temple of Fame*, for example), presented as misapprehensions of the nature of self-love or as aberrations of social purpose and identity.

Every new poem transports us to a resumption of fictions from a different place on the scale. *To a Lady* resumes the warring antagonism between men and women that the end of *The Rape of the Lock* suspends. Belinda's rage for power, followed in *To a Lady* by the feared loss of pleasure and the disjunction between 'Nature' and 'Experience,' reveals the familiar discontinuity between states that are harmonious by design, yet subject to violations of one kind or another. Pope keeps opening spaces between the units: '*Wit* and *Judgment* often are at strife, / Tho' meant each other's Aid, like *Man* and *Wife*'; between Self-love and Reason in the *Essay on Man* or between the 'you' and 'I' of that poem. Conversely, as in *The Temple of Fame*, a malformation imposes a duplicitous and malevolent union upon the world: 'Inseparable now, the Truth and Lye; / The strict Companions are for ever join'd.'

Fictions resituated along the scale may coexist with or function within a shaping fiction (paradigm) that generates something like plot or design or, in eighteenth-century terms, the 'idea'. Thornbury observed of Dryden that he 'defended the theory of allegorical fable . . . not so much because of the allegory in itself as because the unity of idea in the allegory gives the writer his artistic pattern'.[31] The familial centre of the *Essay on Man* requires that we understand

[31] E. M. Thornbury, *Henry Fielding's theory of the comic prose epic* (Wisconsin, 1931), no. 30, p. 91.

its design in relation to *Paradise Lost*. Self-love and Reason (the 'weak queen') preside over the master passion, the divine datum given into their keeping as confirmation of God's abiding love for man. At any moment, however, Pride may seduce Reason and the master passion be subverted to Pride's purposes. The latent power of daemonization within the self creates the Selfhood, and the function of this agency is to establish the false gods of its own worship. The centre that should open, then, from man into the world, like those other expanding circles from a motivated centre, closes, with the result that man is locked within himself, a victim of the usurpation that has occurred. Reason corrupted by Pride's possession of her, and of the child that is the master passion, falls into the service of the daemon now internalized in Pope's redaction of Milton's Satan. The *Essay* recapitulates the fictions of possession that characterize the 'plots' of *The Rape* and *Eloisa to Abelard*, as well as the respective crises of each heroine. The *Essay* demands recourse to the epic pattern it invokes, and though as everyone has noticed the poem is without much action, it allusively incorporates the greater action of temptation and fall as the ground of its own progress.

'The allegorist,' says MacCaffrey, 'incorporates within his fiction the two limits of art: an upward limit where fiction merges with transcendent reality in vision; and a downward or inward limit where fiction touches clumsy life at her stupid work' (p. 80). Pope's figuralism defines that upward limit even as the many topical references, historically particular allusions, touch life immediately and directly. If we look to the changes Pope made in the 1743 text of *The Dunciad* we notice that most of them intensify the poem's theodicy. Cibber's prayer in Book I concludes with a fatherly benediction upon his own works:

> O! pass more innocent, in infant state,
> To the mild Limbo of our Father Tate:
> Or peaceably forgot, at once be blest
> In Shadwell's bosom with eternal Rest!
> Soon to that mass of Nonsense to return,
> Where things destroy'd are swept to things unborn.
>
> (*TE* v, pp. 287–8, ll. 237–42)

Cibber's limbo is the figural reality of the Cave of Poverty and Poetry, its 'spiritual womb and tomb' (Sitter, *Pope's DUNCIAD*, p. 20). In the A version of the text, Theobald's works were conceived in an alehouse and will end there; they are merely 'Unstall'd, unsold' (A, 198). Cibber's works are 'born in sin'; their 'smutty sisters walk the streets' (B, 230). Thus Pope's pun; they will be sold in the streets and end in hell, whereas those works 'purify'd by flames' (l. 227) will return quietly to that non-existence that is their fate. The tear that steals from Cibber upon conclusion of his prayer is a 'portentous sign of Grace!' (243). Pope nods in the direction of *Eloisa*: 'Devotion's self shall steal a thought from heav'n, / One human tear shall drop, and be forgiv'n' (*Eloisa to Abelard*, ll. 357–8). But Cibber is not devotion's self and he shall not be forgiven. The additions of sin, prostitution, and limbo imply a developed perspective that looks beyond the comedy of bad writing to the latent figural reality, thereby explaining the judgments passed on bad writing and those guilty of it:

The world beyond . . . is God's design in active fulfillment. In relation to it, earthly phenomena are on the whole merely figural, potential, and requiring fulfillment. This also applies to the individual souls of the dead: it is only here, in the beyond, that they attain fulfillment and the true reality of their being. Their career on earth was only the figure of this fulfillment. In the fulfillment of their being they find punishment, penance, or reward.[32]

The reality of Cibber's works in time is that of *fallen* children of a sinful father. Their misspent lives will be judged in relation to God's design, and for this reason they will be returned to that 'Chaos dark and deep, / Where nameless Somethings in their causes sleep' (55–6), or consigned to that limbo 'Where things destroy'd are swept to things unborn'. Cibber's perversion of self-love is a violation of grace, and Pope drives home his tear as a calculated irony. Occurring at his 'altar' to Dulness, it gathers into itself the references to devotion in the earlier poems. In place of the *genius loci*, who in *To Burlington* is the 'Genius of the Place,' in *Windsor Forest* is Father Thames, and in *The Temple of Fame* is Fame herself, is substituted the obscure mother whose mystery-temple is the 'sacred Dome' to which Dulness conducts Cibber. The dunce Cibber within time is the dunce Cibber beyond time, not fossilized in amber but fixed like a Dantean soul in agony in God's unchanging design. At the upper limit of Pope's satire in *The Dunciad* the satirist's fiction is indistinguishable from the allegorist's; the reality specified by each is 'God's design in active fulfillment'.

Of *The Faerie Queene*'s 'penumbra of meaning,' MacCaffrey says that all 'such layers of significance stand in complementary rather than iterative relation to the visible events, or images, of the narrative. They are mutually cooperative elements in a total *significatio*, and should not be confused with the "level of ideas," even when they take the form of discursively framed propositions' (MacCaffrey, p. 51). Paulson remarks that 'More than anyone else Milton offered a sanction for a satiric form concerned with problems of religion and extended the meaning of epic almost to encompass the satire written by Dryden and Pope' (*The Fictions of Satire*, p. 119). Anne Ferry has argued that in *Absalom and Achitophel*, 'Dryden established comparisons between his satire and *Paradise Lost* as elaborate, articulated, and pointed as the relationship between any two poems in English literature.'[33] Cohen reminds us that 'Eighteenth-century critics, like Trapp, saw the forms as hierarchical, comprehensively embodied or capable of being harmoniously embodied in the drama or epic.'[34] Under the various pressures that made for the disappearance of

---

[32] Eric Auerbach, *Mimesis: the representation of reality in western literature* (Princeton, 1953), p. 196.
[33] Anne Ferry, *Milton and the Miltonic Dryden* (Cambridge, Massachusetts, 1959), p. 12.
[34] Cohen, 'On the interrelations of eighteenth-century literary forms', p. 51.

allegory several factors worked to preserve something very like the simulacrum of it: (1) the fictive element already identified; (2) the assimilation of epic into satire; (3) an allusiveness that sustained the play of complementarity among texts of different genres; (4) the persistence of typology in satiric contexts.[35]

Significatio is consistent with anagogy, 'the final impact of the work of art itself, which includes not only the superficial meaning but all the subordinate meanings which can be deduced from it'.[36] Both conceptions are inconsistent with an idea of satire predicated largely or wholly on its immediate punitive and persuasive functions. 'In no art form,' says Alvin Kernan, 'is the complexity of human existence so obviously scanted as in satire.'[37] 'Satire,' observes Edwin Honig, 'dispenses with the gods and their standards and entirely demolishes man's image of himself.'[38] Recently, Michael Murrin has pointed and endorsed Honig's reductive conclusion: 'The neoclassical poet . . . worked within the assumptions of his audience, did not conceive of himself as inspired with profound truth, and so had no need for veiled fictions.'[39]

These remarks are limited by generic or cultural expectations (historically derived). An intertextual methodology at least allows for the designation of certain devices, structures, tropes, within the extended text to be charted and evaluated as aspects of an unfolding design. Vincent Carretta says of *To Bathurst*: Pope's 'use of medieval allegorical types, the pattern of rising and falling on Fortune's wheel, the importance of Christian values, the appearance of devils and wizards, and the final emblematic tale of Sir Balaam all strike us as somewhat old-fashioned'.[40] Pope's canon is deeply informed at every point with similar uses and patterns; they enforce satire by adjusting its determinedly topical interests to those allusively enlarged contexts in which action always occurs and to which it is always and inevitably referable. What has already been actualized in literature is summoned as a juridical standard, locating both victim and reader within a network of structures that are complementary and overlapping, forms that keep forcing the perception of one context opening alongside or into another.

It is worth recalling here that present critical orthodoxy was built upon two positions, one acceptable and the other not: that the ages of Pope and the English Romantics were poetically antithetical, and that the literature written in the years immediately following Pope's death served a teleological entity called *preromanticism*. Utter difference was, in sum, succeeded by increasing

---

[35] Korshin, *Typologies in England*: 'Swift's techniques in the digressive and narrative portions of *A Tale of a Tub* . . . are a particularly effective form of typological satire. Typology could be used for satiric purposes in both theological and secular contexts' (p. 271).

[36] Northrop Frye, *Fearful symmetry* (Princeton, 1947), p. 10.

[37] Alvin Kernan, 'A theory of satire', in Ronald Paulson (ed.), *Satire: modern essays in criticism* (New Jersey, 1971), p. 265.

[38] Edwin Honig, *Dark conceit* (Evanston, Illinois, 1959), p. 163.

[39] Michael Murrin, *The allegorical epic* (Chicago, 1980), p. 173.

[40] Vincent Carretta, *The snarling muse* (Pennsylvania, 1983), p. 79.

likeness, and where there had been previously no imaginative correspondence there was later evident a yearning towards the fulfillment of a vision dimly initiated by mid-century poets. The space between Augustan and Romantic has been exhaustingly defined. Frye's observation will do to signify the familiar opposition: 'The proper study of mankind is the natural man, which in practice means that the most fertile themes of the creative imagination will be gossip, slander and domestic trivia.' Blake, we are told, 'hated . . . Dryden and Pope' (pp. 162, 161). The tendency to polarize Augustan and Romantic has been a common strategy of twentieth-century criticism, not without tactical value to literary theorists. The antithesis has also served the interests of students of the eighteenth century intent upon preserving the literary and cultural integrity of the period. Yet the defence of Pope, as I indicated earlier, was grounded on an almost Ovidian metamorphosis of values, the pejorative transmuted into the approbative, and what was, in the vocabulary of Warton and his successors, a diminished achievement became, in the energetic and brilliant revaluation of Pope conducted by Brower and Mack and their followers, a special grace to be protected against critical dilution. Pope had become a half-century reclamation project; he was perforce the centrepiece of whatever claim could be made for the enduring values of eighteenth-century British and Tory civilization, and any effort to open a previously unexplored stratum of his poetry was inevitably suspect because the results of such deep mining were likely to be adventitious and incidental, therefore in one way or another erroneous or insignificant.

Despite the ambivalence now and then sounded within the critical chorus, a note of emergent or discordant dubiety about the adequacy of our ruling definition, we have been for some time more or less committed to a familiar pattern of analysis. At issue is the defense of a traditional text and the ways in which it is (or may be) illuminated by a vision that is (or seems) inconsistent with the canon as we know it. Our sense of Pope's genius coexists uneasily with our recognition of Pope as genius of sense, yet the groundwork for a greater textual coherence has been prepared and it is the place on which we might build for the future. I have offered some notations with that architecture in mind.

PART SIX
Pope and Posterity

11

'Wholesome country air': Pope, Pushkin and others

PAT ROGERS

A poem by Pope which has risen lately in critical esteem and in general visibility is the *Epistle to Miss Blount, on her leaving the Town after the Coronation*. Written presumably in 1714, and first published in the *Works* of 1717, this was a comparatively neglected item in the canon until a generation ago. Recent commentators have remedied that situation, and now it ranks as one of the most exemplary cases among the shorter poems. There seems to have been no recognition, however, that the epistle stands at the head of a notable series of literary essays on the theme of the bored young person (generally a lady), condemned to rustication and frustration. On one level this is simply an inversion of traditional retirement poems, celebrating the virtues of plain country living; the metropolis, commonly imaged as a scene of dissipation, here becomes an exciting alternative to the tedious routine of some provincial back-water. Here I shall attempt to set Pope's epistle in the context provided by a handful of later instances of what may be called the rustication topos. Brief parallels are provided by Johnson and (a real-life, rather than fictional, case) Mary Wollstonecraft. A much deeper mode of convergence can be seen in a poem by Pushkin, *Zima* (winter), written in 1829. Despite the gap of a century, and the different national and cultural background of the two writers, an astonishing degree of similarity in theme, tone and poetic treatment will, I hope, become apparent.[1]

I

Pope's epistle is now sufficiently well known for an elaborate description to be unnecessary. In what follows, I shall draw attention directly to features of the poem which represent its mode of operation as a treatment of the rustication theme. But this does not mean that questions of artistic merit are entirely supplanted: for the characteristic slant which Pope gives the material is

---

[1] I am grateful to Dr A. D. P. Briggs for his advice not only on Pushkin, but also on the convergences with, and divergences from, Pope's epistle. We had at one stage planned a joint article on the subject, and I hope that Dr Briggs' own discussion will appear in a separate form.

naturally defined by those qualities of tone, diction and metrics which figure so largely in his poetic workmanship.[2]

One of the most significant aspects of the epistle is its construction by means of five verse paragraphs, fairly even in length and almost stanza-like in form. As is his manner, Pope traverses large tracts of emotional space in these five sections, modulating from whimsy to tenderness, from bluff humour to meditative introspection. Usually the rustication topos includes some element of humour, but Pope is driven to portray the girl at the centre of the poem with some sympathy, and his delicate shift from satire to inward self-communion mirrors a process clearly visible in *The Rape of the Lock*, whose five-canto version is nearly contemporaneous. In the opening paragraph we are not far from the world of Restoration comedy, and though the heroine is designated 'Zephalinda' (a word obviously suggestive of high romance on the seventeenth-century model), the initial impression we are given is closer to that of a Congreve *ingénue*, perhaps some town-girl reversing Miss Prue's journey to London. The very first couplet suggests the dependence and obligations bound up in her situation:

> As some fond virgin, whom her mother's care
> Drags from the town, to wholsom country air . . .   (ll. 1–2)

A leading strategy of the poem is to subvert the Augustan manuals of health-care, and jokingly to associate their positives (avoidance of stress, spartan diet, regular hours, and so on) with all that is most tedious to a lively young girl. For Zephalinda, the art of preserving health means banishment to a rural backwater, with a total absence of worthwhile social contact – and above all sexual contact. Zephalinda's newly learnt attributes of 'roll[ing] a melting eye' and attracting a 'spark' will go to waste in the all too 'wholsom' atmosphere of the country retreat. The play on 'wholsom' makes this point without delay; the young lady is dispatched to the country for reasons that are putatively medical, but the real effect is to consign her to a safer environment where the dangers of an amorous contagion are removed.

The contrast between the tedium of the countryside and the exciting urban world she has lost is drawn most explicitly in the second paragraph. Instead of opera, assembly, playhouse and park, Zephalinda finds herself confined to an insipid round of predictable activities:

> She went, to plain-work, and to purling brooks,
> Old-fashion'd halls, dull aunts, and croaking rooks . . .
>
>   (ll. 11–12)

The epithets in the second line here are more or less interchangeable. A middle-aged, probably spinsterly routine is imposed by tiresome relatives – one can imagine the fine young lady of Swift's *Polite conversation* mouthing clichés to point up the futility of such an existence. The new regime is one of

---

[2] The text followed is that supplied in *TE* VI, pp. 124–7.

walks, prayers, reading, and tea-drinking (expressed in a characteristic zeugma in line 15). Zephalinda is reduced to unstimulating beverages like tea and
coffee; not surprisingly, as Pope expresses it in a wonderfully drawn out and
tongue-twisting line, she is brought in her disappointment and distraction to a
trance-like state – 'Or o'er cold coffee trifle with a spoon' (17). She watches the
interminable progress of the clock hand as it arrives at the biggest event of the
day so far, dinner at twelve noon precisely. Then the long afternoon, until final
release in the evening – 'Up to her godly garret after sev'n' (21), where
godliness is next to incarceration.

In the third paragraph a more robust note is introduced with the entry of the
rumbustious squire, a pathetic substitute for the sophisticated men about
town who have 'squired' her in more interesting ways. This bumpkin 'visits
with a gun', and thinks the most endearing gesture he can perform for a young
lady is to present her with dead birds which he has shot. His coarseness is
reflected in his habit of bringing his hounds into the drawing room (they are
easier for him to view with affection than a girl, perhaps), as well as his clumsy
love-making with 'nods, and knees beneath a table'. In hs archetypal English
way, he thinks that fine words are too fancy for a sturdy young fellow like
himself, not suspecting that pretty speeches are exactly what poor Zephalinda
would most like. Horsey, insensitive, smelling of the field, he represents in his
own person many of the unattractive features of country living which she has
come to dread. His very lack of sexual danger is part of his unacceptability.
Boorish manners of this kind are simply an expression of the loss of civility
which Zephalinda must endure on her translation from urban society. Pope
himself obviously did not locate virtue in metropolitan surroundings in so
callow a fashion, but at some level he certainly understood the sense of
deprivation which total immersion in plain-living country society could bring
to a sophisticated young lady from the world of the court and the city.

The fourth paragraph takes us away from the rural scene, at least in the
imagination of the heroine (now addressed directly in the second person, but
still recognizably the same figure at Zephalinda). Picturing in her mind
'Coronations . . . on ev'ry green', she transforms her hated surroundings into a
backcloth for courtly doings, with a variety of grandees (all, once more, male)
passing before her eyes as in some splendid ceremony. But the vision is soon
dispelled: the coronets and sceptres vanish, and 'leave you in lone woods, or
empty walls' (40). Again the epithets could be transferred without loss of
meaning. It requires no advanced semiological exercise to discover that the life
of the town signifies sexuality and fulfilment, as well as just pleasure; the
language applied to the rural world is drawn from the discourse of duty,
self-abnegation, moral improvement and (comically viewed, but as in the case
of Belinda seen by Pope as a truly fraught concept) chastity.

Another favourite strategy is employed in the last paragraph, where Pope
shifts to a more personal mode. Back in the town, he acts in a directly contrary
fashion to Zephalinda, musing on his mistress in the country, with her

'sprightly eyes', whilst surrounded by the bric-à-brac of city life – 'Streets, chairs, and coxcombs rush upon my sight.' In one way this mirror-image effect works to support Zephalinda's dreams, confirming the potency of the imagination and the irrelevance of one's surroundings. Yet, in a different way, the contrast also serves to point up the absurdity of her visions, since it inescapably suggests that her fine ideas of town-life are all ultimately based on illusion. London is not just coronations; there is noise and bustle, and the attractive 'sparks' are perhaps really unappealing coxcombs after all. Even in the midst of all the ceaseless activity of the urban streets, the poet finds himself abstracted and uneasy – to this extent, Zephalinda's vision of high urban living is falsified by the closing lines of the epistle. The poem simultaneously underwrites her fantasies and controverts their validity. For Pope, the fears of all too blameless country existence are understandable, and yet equally they are preposterous or risible.

It has seldom been disputed that Pope had a great sensitivity towards the interests of women (though the depth of his insight is highly controversial), and that remark is not much qualified if we add that this tendency was most noticeable in the case of young and attractive women. A number of letters reflect his characteristic concerns in this area, most obviously those written in the early years of the Hanoverian regime, when Pope along with the Blount sisters moved in a circle of bright young people in and around the court. A letter which he wrote to the sisters in September 1717 comically reduces George I's court to the level of 'a lone House in Wales', and it is indicative that the passage deals with boredom, social deprivation and isolation, all viewed from the perspective of a young woman.

We all agreed that the life of a Maid of Honor was of all things the most miserable; & wished that every Woman who envy'd it had a Specimen of it. To eat Westphalia Ham in a morning, ride over Hedges & ditches on borrowed Hacks, come home in the heat of the day with a Feavor, & what is worse a hundred times, a red Mark in the forehead with a Beaver hatt; all this may qualify them to make excellent Wives for Fox-hunters, and bear abundance of ruddy-complexion'd Children. As soon as they can wipe off the Sweat of the day, they must simper an hour, & catch cold, in the Princesses apartment; from thence *To Dinner, with what appetite they may* – And after that, till midnight, walk, work, or think, which they please? I can easily believe, no lone House in Wales, with a Mountain and a Rookery, is more contemplative than this Court; and as a proof of it I need only tell you Mrs Lepell walk'd all alone with me three or four hours, by moonlight; and we mett no Creature of any quality, but the King, who gave audience all alone to the Vice-chamberlen, under the Garden-wall.

In short, I heard of no Ball, Assembly, Basset-Table, or any place where two or three were gather'd together, except Mad. Kilmanzech's, to which I had the honour to be invited, and the grace to stay away.[3]

Mingled here are feelings of affection, pity and perhaps envy; but there are also the comic reversals or correlatives of such feelings. As with the epistle, we find Pope bantering on a subject which yet calls out some of his deepest sym-

---

[3] *Correspondence* i, p. 427.

pathies. It is hardly a proof of social ostracism to meet with only one person on an evening walk, if that person happens to be the sovereign of the realm, giving audience to a high official at court. Nevertheless, Pope's capacity to imagine is what is at issue here; and to be able to take on the *imaginary* sufferings of the spoilt and under-employed maid of honour is itself a clue to his own psychological make-up. The ennui of physically healthy and active people is tantalizing to a crippled invalid; just as the equivocal 'maiden' status of these young ladies could not fail to preoccupy a man who was debarred from normal sexual expression. In the situation of women, as in those of Belinda or Zephalinda, Pope evidently found much that reflected on his own condition.

II

One of the bright young ladies whom Pope came to know best as he approached thirty was Lady Mary Wortley Montagu. She herself revised an older poem on the very subject under consideration here. 'The Bride in the Country' deals with a girl dispatched to a secluded rural home with a bumpkin for a husband. Lady Mary had known isolation in her youth at Thoresby, and had experienced marriage to a tedious and limited husband. But autobiography is not particularly relevant: the rustication motif had developed its own impetus, and poems with titles like 'On Miss ———'s Retirement into the Country' often appear in the magazines. Charlotte Lennox's quixotic heroine ponders the restrictions that are (but maybe should not be) imposed by secluded living: 'The perfect Retirement she lived in, afforded indeed no Opportunities of making the Conquests she desired; but she could not comprehend, how any Solitude could be obscure enough to conceal a Beauty like hers.' Arabella is a descendant of Zephalinda, and differs chiefly in that her addiction to books has caused her to pine for the knights errant of romance, rather than the gartered earls of court pageantry.[4]

Another notable woman of letters, Elizabeth Montagu, provides different evidence. Her father was in the habit of breaking out in exclamations against the country, and declared that living there was tantamount to sleeping with one's eyes open. Elizabeth herself encountered a real-life version of Zephalinda's 'old-fashion'd halls'. As an eligible young woman she spent some time in Kent, where she found the available suitors to be no better than dull and boorish clods. As her biographer comments, 'their scarlet waistcoats did not impress her like Mr Lyttelton's birthday suit' (i.e. court dress). She was not to be won by some foxhunting clown. In fact, she married a man who was many years her senior, and who led a sedentary life, his prime addiction being the study of mathematics. A person who was in time to cross swords with Mrs Montagu, that is James Boswell, devoted three numbers of his periodical *The Hypochondriack* (September to November 1780) to the limited pleasures, as he

---

4 Jonathan Curling, *Edward Wortley Montague 1713–1776* (London, 1954), p. 15; Charlotte Lennox, *The female Quixote*, Margaret Dalziel (ed.) (London, 1970), p. 7.

saw it, afforded by country life, though Boswell is thinking about the lack of
stimulation he himself experienced, rather than the deprivations peculiar to a
young lady.[5]

The case is different with Boswell's own lodestar, Samuel Johnson. Three
Rambler papers from the late summer of 1750 are directly relevant to our theme
here. Two letters from Euphelia and one from Cornelia variously approach the
rustication motif. The fullest presentation of the issues comes in the earliest of
the three, that is *Rambler* no. 42, whilst Euphelia continues her narrative in
Rambler no. 46 ('While I am thus employed, some tedious hours will slip away,
and when I return to watch the clock, I shall find that I have disburdened
myself of part of the day'). Finally, in *Rambler* no. 51 Cornelia gives a slightly
different view of the retired life.[6]

In the first of these papers, Johnson writes in the person of a young lady
'bred . . . in a perpetual tumult of pleasure', and accustomed to a round of
visits, play-houses, balls, masquerades and the like. She is well educated in
fashionable dress and in the decorum of the card table. Finally, at the age of
twenty-two, she is sent off to pass the summer with 'a rich aunt in a remote
country' (aunts, in this tradition, are synonomous with a backwater existence). Euphelia's hopes are initially high, since she has imbibed unrealistic
ideas from literature – but disillusion is soon to overcome these expectations:

> I will confess to you, without restraint, that I had suffered my head to be filled with
> expectations of some nameless pleasure in a rural life, and that I hoped for the happy
> hour that should set me free from noise, and flutter, and ceremony, dismiss me to the
> peaceful shade, and lull me in content and tranquillity. To solace myself under the
> misery of delay, I sometimes heard a studious lady of my acquaintance read pastorals, I
> was delighted with scarce any talk but of leaving the town, and never went to bed
> without dreaming of groves, and meadows, and frisking lambs.
>
> At length I had all my cloaths in a trunk, and saw the coach at the door; I sprung in
> with ecstasy, quarrelled with my maid for being too long in taking leave of the other
> servants, and rejoiced as the ground grew less which lay between me and the comple-
> tion of my wishes. A few days brought me to a large old house, encompassed on three
> sides with woody hills, and looking from the front on a gentle river, the sight of which
> renewed all my expectations of pleasure, and gave me some regret for having lived so
> long without the enjoyment which these delightful scenes were now to afford me. My
> aunt came out to receive me, but in a dress so far removed from the present fashion, that
> I could scarcely look upon her without laughter, which would have been no kind
> requital for the trouble which she had take to make herself fine against my arrival. The
> night and the next morning were driven along with enquiries about our family; my aunt
> then explained our pedigree, and told me stories of my great grandfather's bravery in
> the civil wars, nor was it less than three days before I could persuade her to leave me to
> myself.
>
> At last oeconomy prevailed, she went in the usual manner about her own affairs, and

---

[5] Dr [John] Doran, *A lady of the last century* (London, 1873), p. 15; James Boswell, *The Hypochondriack*, Margery Bailey (ed.) (Stanford, Cal., 1928), II, pp. 15–28.

[6] Samuel Johnson, *The Rambler*, W. J. Bate and A. B. Strauss (eds.), in *The Yale Edition of the Works
of Samuel Johnson* (New Haven, 1969), III, pp. 229–31, 247–52, 273–9.

I was at liberty to range in the wilderness, and sit by the cascade. The novelty of the objects about me pleased me for a while, but after a few days they were new no longer, and I soon began to perceive that the country was not my element; that shades, and flowers, and lawns, and waters, had very soon exhausted all their power of pleasing, and that I had not in myself any fund of satisfaction with which I could supply the loss of my customary amusements.

I unhappily told my aunt, in the first warmth of our embraces, that I had leave to stay with her ten weeks. Six only are yet gone, and how shall I live through the remaining four? I go out and return; I pluck a flower, and throw it away; I catch an insect, and when I have examined its colours, set it at liberty; I fling a pebble into the water, and see one circle spread after another. When it chances to rain, I walk in the great hall, and watch the minute-hand upon the dial, or play with a litter of kittens, which the cat happens to have brought in a lucky time.

My aunt is afraid I shall grow melancholy, and therefore encourages the neighbouring gentry to visit us. They came at first with great eagerness to see the fine lady from London, but when we met, we had no common topick on which we could converse; they had no curiosity after plays, operas, or musick: and I find as little satisfaction from their accounts of the quarrels, or alliances of families, whose names, when once I can escape, I shall never hear. The women have now seen me, know how my gown is made, and are satisfied; the men are generally afraid of me and say little because they think themselves not at liberty to talk rudely.

Thus am I condemned to solitude; the day moves slowly forward, and I see the dawn with uneasiness, because I consider that night is at a great distance. I have tried to sleep by a brook, but find its murmurs ineffectual; so that I am forced to be awake at least twelve hours, without visits, without cards, without laughter, and without flattery. I walk because I am disgusted with sitting still, and sit down because I am weary with walking. I have no motive to action, nor any object of love, or hate, or fear, or inclination. I cannot dress with spirit, for I have neither rival nor admirer. I cannot dance without a partner, nor be kind, or cruel, without a lover.

'Such is the life of Euphelia', we are told, and the letter ends with a plea for sympathy and guidance:

I shall therefore think you a benefactor to our sex, if you will teach me the art of living alone; for I am confident that a thousand and a thousand and a thousand ladies, who affect to talk with ecstacies of the pleasures of the country, are in reality, like me, longing for the winter, and wishing to be delivered from themselves by company and diversion.

Euphelia is cousin to Arabella in *The female Quixote*, and of course we are reminded of the 'glimpse of pastoral life' in chapter 19 of *Rasselas*, where the false expectations induced by literary pastoralism are exposed to merciless gaze. However, the closest analogue is with Zephalinda, and in this instance we may reasonably suspect a line of direct influence. Johnson would certainly have known the epistle, and his *Rambler* paper may be seen as an extended paraphrase of the earlier work, with terse Popean phrases such as 'dull aunts' or 'purling brooks' subjected to comic amplification. It is one of the most brilliant literary renditions of the topos, even though its tone is more distant than that of Pope – Johnson assuredly shared in some of Euphelia's distaste for

a vacant life, but he does not allow his own feelings to enter the text as Pope's
do in the epistle.

A final English example takes us back to real life, rather than fictional
expressions of the theme. The passage in question occurs in a letter from Mary
Wollstonecraft in November 1786, written when she was serving unhappily as
a governess in deepest County Cork. She reported gloomily to her sister
Everina on her nervous irritability, caused by the uncongenial way of life in a
remote district, where her employer Lady Kingsborough oppressed her with
pet-dogs and empty talk. But the real Mary secretly rebels as she pretends to
comply:

I am almost tormented to death by dogs – But you will perceive I am not under the
influence of my darling passion pity; it is not always so, I make allowances and *adapt*
myself – talk of getting husbands for the *Ladies* – and the *dogs* – and am wonderfully
entertaining and then I retire to my room, form figures in the fire, listen to the wind or
view the Galties a fine range of mountains near us – and so does time *waste* away in
apathy or misery – I would not write thus to Eliza – she cannot discriminate; but to you
I *cannot* be reserved – and I hope the dreadful contagion will not infect you – I am
thought to have an angelic temper.

This is the first fully serious passage on the theme which we have encountered,
and we might feel some embarrassment about permitting its inclusion in the
tradition at all. But the phrasing approaches Pope's so closely when Mary
speaks of 'form[ing] figures in the fire' that one is led to observe the parallels
with the literary topos, however they may be transmuted by Mary's anguish.
Taken as a whole, her letter provides a nonfictional control by which we may
gauge the development of the rustication motif in fictional contexts. The
'boisterous spirits and unmeaning laughter' of Mary's companions represent
what was possibly a more actual threat than the hallooing and nudging of a
clumsy squire. The comparative refinement of Lady Kingsborough's family
embodies a shift in social history; the new boors, at the end of the eighteenth
century, are as likely to have read a few books as to have learned plain-work,
even though their chief topics of conversation remain 'matrimony and dress'.[7]

III

Pushkin's poem dates from November 1829, when he paid a visit to friends in
the country. It is not among his best-known works, either in Russia or in this
country, but recently A. D. P. Briggs has made an excellent case for seeing the
work as a highly representative item in the canon:

If the formal characteristics of this poem may be taken as typical of Pushkin's method,
it is no less true that the content reflects a number of familiar Pushkinian preoccupations and attitudes. The naturalistic, detailed description of country life, thoughts
about the distractions available for bored people, the consolation provided by litera-

[7] Ralph M. Wardle (ed.), *Collected letters of Mary Wollstonecraft* (New York, 1979), pp. 126–7.

ture, the processes of poetic inspiration, the transcendent excitement of erotic adventures, the deep integration of the poem into actual events of the poet's life and its lightly
mocking general tone – all of these salient characteristics of 'Zima . . .', here presented
in encapsulated form, are to be found widely dispersed and embellished throughout the
whole body of Pushkin's lyric and other poetry. It may safely be said, in fact, that . . .
few other poems encompass such a broad range of the poet's main ideas.[8]

It is astonishing how much of this applies directly to Pope's epistle. We do not
find much in the way of detailed or naturalistic description in Pope; literary
consolations are only very obliquely contemplated, whilst any reference to
Pope's own life at the close of the epistle is playful and teasing. Nevertheless, as
Briggs's close analysis of *Zima* brings out, the central concern of Pushkin's
composition is very nearly allied, the tone is instantly recognizable, and the
local strategies again and again are reminiscent of Pope. The most obvious
distinction lies in the narrative stance, for Pushkin writes in the first person,
and experiences boredom rather than observing it. In practice this is not so
important a difference as we might expect.

Pushkin begins with a one-word sentence, followed by a mock-petulant
question – 'Winter. What is there for us to do in the country?' The narrator is
brought an early-morning cup of tea by a servant, and bombards him with
questions. Is it worth getting up to ride, or would it be better to pass the time
until lunch dragging one's way through old magazines left by a neighbour? (As
with Zephalinda, mealtimes are an oasis in the desert of tedium.) The members of the house-party decide to go hunting, but without success. There
follows a cacophonous, spluttering line, 'Kuda kak veselo! Vot vecher: v'yuga
voyet' (What fun! Now it is evening; the blizzard howls). As Briggs puts it, the
line 'possesses an abecedarian clumsiness that seems unbelievable in such an
accomplished versifier'. This 'over-emphatic alliteration' is used, the critic
argues, to bring out 'the deadening dullness of empty country life [which] is
about to descend once more'. Such techniques are the more attainable because
of Pushkin's choice of the dignified iambic hexameter as his verse-form: the
potential tedium of the long line is apt to his purposes. Other verses (lines 15,
22, 29) exploit this potential. The second of these actually expresses an idea
very close to Pope's 'needless Alexandrine' (a point Briggs does not overlook):
'The verse crawls lamely along, foggy and frigid'. 'It is another distinguishing
feature of Pushkin's work', remarks Briggs, 'that he is attracted to the depic-
tion of different moods in quick succession and has a particular facility for easy
modulation from one to the next', as at line 13 (pp. 35–6). It needs no
emphasis that such transitions in mood are central to Pope's purposes in his
epistle.

The narrator tries to read in order to allay his boredom, but he is unable to
concentrate; he closes the book, seeks to write with no more success, and goes
into the adjoining room. There he finds a conversation in progress on banal

[8] A. D. P. Briggs, 'An approach to Pushkin through one poem' in *Alexander Pushkin: a critical study*
(London, 1983), pp. 27–43; quotation from p. 37.

local topics. His hostess is knitting away with sour attention, or turns to the cards for a little fortune-telling (not much more promising than the squire's 'Whisk'). The poet's feelings burst forth at line 29: 'Toska! Tak den' za dnem idet v uyedinenii' (What sheer pain! So it goes day after day, out in this total isolation). The Russian word *uyedinenii*, literally solitude or seclusion, can have a more favourable overtone of 'retirement': but that is of course an irony inherent in Pope's epistle too, for to withdraw as Zephalinda does from the bustle of the city was the gesture of many an Horatian versifier in the eighteenth century. Both poets achieve part of their effect by silent refutation of conventional wisdom concerning the benefits of retirement.

There is a major shift in *Zima* at this point. Indicatively the new scene is incorporated in an 'if' clause, much as Pope wraps up his message within a putative simile: 'But if in the sad village as evening comes on and I sit in a corner over the draughts board, a coach or a sleigh should unexpectedly arrive with a family from far off . . .' Then a new burst of social activity will begin, all the more vivid by contrast – again the dialectic is parallel with the court/country opposition of Pope's epistle. Above all, there is a promise of sexual intrigue: at first lingering but oblique glances, then a few hesitant words, developing into freer conversation, laughter and songs; ultimately lively waltzes, a whisper at the table, languorous gazes, light-hearted badinage, a chance to prolong encounters on the narrow staircase. This is the kind of social and sexual round which Zephalinda dreams of when she is deprived of city life; put otherwise, it is the sort of courtship which the squire's behaviour crudely parodies. Pushkin has this world of amenity brought into his rural retreat at the climax of his poem; a reversal, as Pope's ending had been, but executed in a different direction. *Zima* ends in a mysterious way, its last line unrhymed as the couplet is left suspended halfway through its course; where Pope brings us a tantalizing hint of sexual desire, apparently unfulfilled, in his concluding paragraph, Pushkin suggests consummation without any explicit reference: 'How cool and crisp is the Russian girl, dusted with the snows [of her country].'

There is much in Briggs' thoughtful reading of the poem which helps to explain Pushkin's, as it were unconscious, absorption of an English topos. He sees Pushkin's treatment of the 'patrician' form of the alexandrine as exemplifying the writer's 'attitude to inherited literary canons, an attitude nicely summed up by [A. Tertz (Sinyavsky)] as follows: "Pushkin did not develop and extend tradition, he teased it, lapsing at every end and turn into parody' (p. 31). Literary parody generally involves playful treatment of conventional postures, more widely defined, and the congruities between two poets at either end of Europe, a century apart, reflect their similar response towards conventionality in behaviour and in poetic idiom. The most immediately striking resemblances concern small details of observation, closely allied minutiae of country life: the obligatory teacup, the somnolent pose, the silent lovemaking, the waiting for an appointed mealtime. However, a deeper level of imaginative convergence is apparent in the way that each writer exploits poetic form (locally, rhythm and syntax, deliberate cacophony; more broadly, verse-paragraphs which are typographically visible in Pope but not in Pushkin). Briggs speaks of the Russian poet's 'unique capacity in versification for the exact attunement of ends and means' (p. 33). Perhaps 'unique' is too strong, even if we grant Pushkin greater eminence overall: for the epistle shows Pope in his most virtuosic manner, notably in the second paragraph. His elision of strong active verbs in lines 15–22, with its emphasis on directionless and almost somnambulistic infinitives, until even these disappear and are replaced by prepositions as the only agent of motion – this is all in the vein of Pushkin. Both poets use clear and almost conversational language, interspersed with recollections of higher literary pretension: romance, epic, noble Horatian acts of renunciation. Both dramatize contrasts through stylistic means; both convey the *frisson* of sexual excitement through hints and gestures rather than explicit narrative. Above all, each poem conveys a sense of expectancy amid the boredom, and manages to make the subject of dullness an object of intense imaginative vitality.

The topos which we traced first in Pope finds echoes and transpositions in Johnson and Mary Wollstonecraft among others; but its more richly suggestive implications lie dormant until we reach Pushkin, an even greater poet but one who could not have read Pope's original. Finally it is the most surprising testimony to the enduring centrality of Pope in European literature that his little drama of rustication should have been replayed, with so many nuances still precisely in place, at such another time, in such another place by such another author.

12

Pope and the tradition in modern humanistic education: '. . . in the pale of Words till death'

G. S. ROUSSEAU

Humanism is a logocentrism that precipitates a binary logic . . .'
(William Spanos, 'The Apollonian investment of modern humanist education', 1985)[1]

Pope and outrage

Since Pope's death in 1744 biographers and critics have commented prolifically about his seemingly unquenchable thirst for admiration, but Pope also had the need to rile his readers with calculated expressions of outrage and contempt. Less has been written about these voices of outrage: their psychic origins – perhaps embedded in dark psychosexual caverns; the unassailable fact that Pope was a member of at least four minorities (Catholic, cripple, bachelor, poet); and the narrative techniques and complex poetic images he assumes will display this contempt. This discrepancy between the overflowing admiration Pope sought and the remarkable critical silence about outrage, is not surprising in view of the epistemology of the latter. Like desire and hypocrisy, outrage remains a fundamentally elusive state of mind. It is, more primitively, a localized emotion about which little has been written, and the hurdles involved in comprehending precisely what outrage is discourage the student of poetry from grasping it. Admiration, on the other hand, surrenders itself to discussion, especially to annotation of the poet's wit and craft, his perfection of techniques within particular genres, and – of course – the purple passages he, like all poets, labours so hard to achieve. Outrage is a less secure emotion, and is therefore more cumbersome and problematic for the critic, ultimately necessitating a special relationship between the agent – or agency – of provocation and the provoked; it remains a state of mind incapable of adequate interpretation apart from its cultural dimensions. It is historically, politically and rhetorically accountable to its cultural determinants. What pleases the aborigine in the jungle revolts the gentleman at Hampton Court or Windsor Palace, as Pope, no relativist in our modern sense, would have been the first to concede. In our time we have practically witnessed the demise, and

[1] See William V. Spanos, 'The Apollonian investment of modern humanist education: the examples of Matthew Arnold, Irving Babbitt and I. A. Richards', in *Cultural Critique*, 1–2 (1985–6), 7–72, 105–34.

perhaps even the death, of outrage, as our collective psyche refuses to be shocked by almost anything we encounter, see, or hear. In the process, we have become anaesthetized to the anger and pain (devaluing them both) that precipitates the outrage in the first place; but unlike Pope and his contemporaries, we in the late twentieth century harbour an almost universal city-hall mentality that causes us to feel inconsequential when in the face of political bureaucracy, corruption, fraud, and inefficiency. No equivalent of these emotions of inconsequentiality can be found in the early or mid-eighteenth century, when England was still a relatively small and tightly-knit country where an individual voice could count for much.

Pope's poetic voice focused the attention of his contemporaries more resonantly than most others; his pugnacious temperament and prickingly negative attitudes (hence his labelling by some of his enemies as 'the wicked wasp of Twickenham'), energizing much of his best satire, with its auricular and visual richness and such musical variety that no sensitive reader of poetry can fail to appreciate it. In this essay I attempt to show that Pope's pugnacity and outrage is nowhere more combative in his mature poetry than in the satire on education in Book IV of *The Dunciad*, maintaining, moreover, that he composed it well aware it would stun a segment of his readership who were persuaded that there was nothing inherently wrong with the national education system. It is also my view that at least two expressions of outrage are evident in Pope's mature poetry: *personal outrage*, as when some action or individual has precipitated a personal insult (the sometimes friendly but often hostile interlocutor of the *Epilogue to the Satires* who inquires, 'for God's-sake, where's th' Affront to you?'), and *poetic outrage* of the sort found when the poet dramatizes himself and concludes that his public image (rather than his *personal* character) has been tarnished or assaulted. In brief, some of Pope's most powerful poetry arises – in *The Dunciad, An Epistle to Dr. Arbuthnot*, and the *Epilogues to the Satires* – when the two versions converge, as they do in the satire on education in *The New Dunciad*.

A thorough study of Pope's techniques of outrage would occupy an entire book and necessarily survey a large body of his poetry, including the reasons why he evoked uncommon hostility among his contemporaries (as Pope himself dramatized the recoil, '*Fr*. This filthy Simile, this beastly Line, / Quite turns my Stomach' (*TE* IV, p. 323, ll. 181–2), as well as in posterity (here Byron stands out in unparalleled opposition, and as his marginalia to Owen Ruffhead's *Life of Alexander Pope*, published in 1769, make clear, Byron was the most sympathetic and protective reader Pope had throughout the entire nineteenth century). Such a much-needed study would explore the psychology of a poet who consciously set out (and there can no longer be any doubt that it *was* conscious) to accomplish what no poet in the English language had ever attempted before: to equate himself with the ancients; and who, despite his being a deformed Catholic bachelor in possession of a crazy carcass that was both hunch-backed and crippled, managed to succeed remarkably well in these conscious aims. Literate England must have been amazed in the second quarter of the eighteenth century as it watched Pope's translation of Homer actually replace the real Homer ('And when I die, be sure you let me know / Great *Homer* dy'd three thousand years ago' (*TE* IV, p. 115, ll. 123–4) is the response of Pope's narrator to a bevy of imaginary sycophants in the confessional verse-epistle he wrote to his friend Dr Arbuthnot), and Grub Street and Fleet Street, construed loosely, galled at the very least – especially those who also fancied themselves great authors and who were immensely jealous of Pope – as they watched him replace Homer and transform his personal liabilities into unprecedented strengths. Such a study obviously cannot even be outlined here, let alone properly undertaken.

But by examining the biographical evolution, critical reception and cultural determinants of a particular passage within a work, I believe we can at least begin to understand a hitherto unexplored dimension of Pope's originality. My selection of a text is not arbitrary. *The Dunciad*, especially *The New Dunciad*, has been the poem by Pope that has moved me most, as a consequence, perhaps, of my keen interest in the so-called (after C. P. Snow and F. R. Leavis) 'two-cultures controversy' of our era, and the treatment Pope gives the arts and sciences in Book 4. But I have been equally intrigued by the survival of all types of 'dunciads' in our own age, especially in such parodic forms as A. D. Hope's *New Dunciad*, as well as in the modern university where 'new dunciads' surface almost daily. Among these productions are a proliferating array of programmes causing the humanities to surrender actively (not passively lose) their cultural vitality, partly as the result of a widespread cultural relativism, partly because post-structuralist methods have compelled them to. One reason, moreover, that we can sympathize today with the criticism of *all* systems of education based on memory and rote (not merely those seeking to inculcate the wisdom of the humanities), is that our versions have become equally mechanical: on the one hand too specialized, on the other too pluralized and supposedly objective for the development of individual talent – indeed, so self-professedly objective and dehumanized that we often proceed, it seems, like Pope's pedant, 'examining bit by bit,' 'seeing hairs and pores,' mechanically observing 'how parts relate to parts, or they to whole,' only to terminate tragically, like Pope's three pedants (Kuster, Burmann, Wasse – men who would command a good deal of so-called academic respect if they were alive today), in the total loss of significance, 'When Man's whole frame,' as Pope says, 'is obvious to a flea'. At a time when many of our best contemporary social commentators assure us that 'higher education has failed democracy and impoverished the souls of today's students,'[2] Pope's great satire takes on magisterial and timely significance indeed.

The philosophical Pope has been associated with *An Essay on Man* since the

---

[2] The subtitle of Allan Bloom's *The closing of the American mind: how higher education has failed democracy and impoverished the souls of today's students* (New York, 1987). Bloom would have written a better book if he had performed a modicum of research on the history of his subject: caricatures of education, or mis-education; he would have realized that his is not the first lampoon, that Pope, and others, anticipated him long ago.

eighteenth century, when it was obvious, at least to some readers, that he was a philosopher of cosmology. But Pope is equally a philosopher of education, and in some senses his ideas on education are original, deriving neither from Bolingbroke (to whom Pope is of course indebted), nor from the ambitious Warburton who reshaped so many of Pope's ideas, but from his own life's experience and very random but nevertheless wide reading. The Pope who was disturbed by the seeming disappearance of the hierarchies and the possible breaking of the Great Chain of Being in *An Essay on Man*, was in some ways a different mentality from the man and poet we find here. By the time he composed this section of *The New Dunciad*, his imagination had altered, and nothing less than utter contempt and outrage will explain his brilliant lampoon on those masters who teach by rote and keep the imagination in check, 'hang[ing] one jingling padlock', Pope contends, 'on the mind'. In short, this is the outrage Pope – a wordsmith all his life – must have felt at those who abused words in this entirely mechanical way, which kept students and adults alike, 'in the pale of Words till death'.

The reception

The satire on education has received rather little attention when compared to other parts of *The Dunciad*, especially the sections on metaphysics and the New Science that succeed it.[3] Occasionally acknowledged from the time of publication on 20 March 1742 as containing some of Pope's greatest poetry, the section on education has been discussed, but its targets that extend beyond individuals (Richard Bentley, Robert Freind, the schoolmen) have never been identified with any precision. Furthermore, Pope's silences in this passage have been equally overlooked: all the things about education he does *not* say. Pope's earliest commentators (Ruffhead, Samuel Johnson, Warton) were confident of their complete understanding of Pope's intentions, but named so many different targets (for example, the schools, education, humanism, government, politics) that one wonders – two centuries later – if Pope actually had all these in mind, and, if so, precisely what he meant to do by attacking them.

Ruffhead, Pope's first biographer who relied on Warburton for much of his information about Pope, set the stage for the ensuing discussion in 1769: 'the keenest satire on the preposterous plan of scholastic education'; 'a fine ridicule on the preposterous method of forcing all boys to make verses, whether they have a poetical turn or not'; 'turning men's attentions from the study of things, to that of words and sounds'; 'to expose the defects of fashionable education, in the character of a youth just returned from his travels, attended by his governor and a courtezan'.[4] These were the topics that continued to be

---

[3] For example, Arthur Friedman, 'Pope and deism (*The Dunciad* IV, 459–92)', in J. L. Clifford and L. A. Landa (eds.), *Pope and his contemporaries: essays presented to George Sherburn* (Oxford, 1949), pp. 89–95.

[4] Owen Ruffhead, *The life of Alexander Pope* (1769), pp. 50, 51, 53 respectively. For reasons of space, I intentionally avoid discussion in this essay of travel and the Grand Tour, as well as concepts of

discussed as the object of Pope's scathing satire, as commentators as diverse as the highly critical William Cowper and the disciplinarian Samuel Johnson, who assured the young Boswell in 1763 that 'a man' – presumably a boy as well – 'ought to read just as inclination leads him', noted.[5]

Thirteen years later, in 1782, Joseph Warton, who was himself a product of Winchester and Oriel College, Oxford, and ultimately no friend of Pope's poetry, was less sympathetic to Pope's objectives. Intent on demonstrating 'the malignity' of *The Dunciad*, he recoiled from the attack on education, as he would fifteen years later in his 1797 edition of Pope's works, where he indicted Pope for having read Locke's *Thoughts Concerning Education* too seriously. 'This false opinion' of English education, Warton charged in his notes to *The Dunciad* passage, derived 'from that idle book on education, which Locke disgraced himself by writing.'[6] It is a curious allegation in view of the lack of evidence: Pope must have known Locke's book and possibly read it, but he was hardly known as an avowed or radical Lockian. In his *Essay* of 1782 (volume one had appeared in 1756), Warton was even more critical of this explicitly Lockian view: 'Pope', he wrote, 'was ill-informed of what was taught and expected in our great schools; namely . . . reading, interpreting, and translating the best poets, orators, and historians, of the best ages [the Ancients]. . . .'[7] Warton buttressed his charges with a three-page defence of English education in the eighteenth century, commenting on the schoolmasters' right to blend 'memory and judgment,' their preference for Quintilian over Locke, Ancients over Moderns, and on Bentley (despised by Pope because he had dissuaded the University of Cambridge from subscribing to his translations of Homer and who became the original of Pope's Scriblerian 'Aristarchus') as the archetype of the pedantic scholar.[8] One of Warton's intentions in the *Essay* was 'a strong confutation of this [Pope's] opprobrious opinion' (II, p. 381) of English education of his time. Warton's conclusion in both the *Essay* and his edition of Pope's works was strident and alleged that English education had done nothing, as Pope falsely claimed, to deserve epitomes of the egregious sort found in *The New Dunciad*: we 'hang one jingling padlock on the [student's] mind'. On the contrary, Warton petulantly maintained, thinking in part of his own labours, 'since the total decay of learning and genius was foretold in *The Dunciad*, how many very excellent pieces of *Criticism, Poetry, History, Philosophy*, and *Divinity*,

---

the gentleman in relation to education; these are large subjects that cannot adequately be discussed in the space of a few pages. Pope clearly had foreign travel, especially the Grand Tour, in mind when ridiculing the 'Whore, Pupil, and lac'd Governor from France' (*TE* v, p. 370, l. 272), but it would take another essay of equal length to explain how Pope, who himself never took the Grand Tour or crossed the Alps, came to adopt this view.

---

[5] G. B. Hill (ed.), *Boswell's Life of Johnson*, 6 vols (Oxford, 1934; rev. ed.), I, p. 428, 14 July 1763.

[6] J. Warton (ed.), *The Works of A. Pope*, 10 vols. (1806; rep. 1797), v, p. 282.

[7] J. Warton, *An essay on the genius and writings of Pope. In two volumes* (1782; vol. I, 1756), II, p. 381; the passages cited here are found on pp. 381–3.

[8] For Pope and Bentley, see *Pope: a life*, pp. 481–4 and pp. 225–6, below.

have appeared in this country, and to what a degree of perfection has almost every art, either useful or elegant, been carried!'

Warton's negative estimate of the satire on education reigned unchallenged in the early nineteenth century, in part because many Romantic critics (William Lisle Bowles, Leigh Hunt, Byron, Coleridge, et al.) were preoccupied by more pressing controversies about Mr Pope: whether he was a poet at all! Yet the Victorians and Edwardians altered all this. In view of their all-consuming interest in English education, as many social historians of the nineteenth century have now demonstrated, one would have thought they would have grasped at Pope's satire for purely didactic purposes, or, at least, for copious historical commentary. But they could not be bothered; they were, with a few exceptions at the end of the period – Housman, the Bloomsbury group, Virginia Woolf's nephew Adrian Bell, who died on the battlefields of Spain during the civil war still hoping to write an appreciative long essay about Pope – no ardent admirers of Pope or his *Dunciad*. The Victorian and Edwardian schoolmasters and university dons (some of whom are discussed in Donald Greene's essay in this volume), could find in Book IV only further examples of Pope's malignant spite, without comprehending what was at stake in his eclectic approach to education or to the targets he (and Warburton) identified for satire. Indeed, the nineteenth-century reception of Book IV demonstrates that virtually nothing was written about the satire on education, except for Courthope's long introduction of 1882 where Pope's specific targets are discussed; though Courthope, like his nineteenth-century predecessors, remains predictably silent about Pope's schoolmen, focusing instead on the *virtuosi* because – Courthope commented in a characteristic elision – Pope's 'party spirit again scarcely disguises itself'.[9] Elwin and Courthope, like other nineteenth-century editors, attributed the substance of virtually *all* Pope's targets – here and in other poems – to his anti-Whig, anti-Walpolian sentiment. Their urgent concern was comparison of the scientific curricula of the 1880s (in their perception strong and growing stronger) with the 'literary tradition' of the early eighteenth century. 'To an age like our own', Courthope lamented using Pope as a convenient synecdoche for previous, non-scientific eras, 'moved by an absorbing passion for the solution of scientific problems, such an attitude of mind [i.e. as Pope's derogatory representation of the *virtuosi* in Book IV] is not easily understood; yet it was almost a part of the literary tradition of England in the first half of the eighteenth century' (p. 35). It may

[9] E-C, IV, p. 35. For Pope's nineteenth-century critics see F. W. Bateson *et al.*, *Alexander Pope: a critical anthology* (London, 1971), pp. 169–230, and D. J. Greene, 'The study of eighteenth-century literature: past, present, and future', in P. Harth (ed.), *New approaches to eighteenth-century literature: English Institute essays* (New York, 1974), pp. 5–7. William John Courthope had learned to distrust Pope's 'correctness' and 'artificiality' while still a student at Oxford, perhaps disagreeing with Pope's unfriendly interlocutor at the opening of the first dialogue to the *Epilogue to the Satires*: 'You grow *correct* that once with Rapture writ' (*TE* IV, p. 297, l. 3); after the Reverend Whitwell Elwin threw up his hands in disgust, Courthope finished his edition of Pope's works.

be so, but this says nothing specific about Pope's attack on education; and that Pope was attacking only the *excesses* of the virtuosi, not science *qua* science, meant nothing to them. Education in their time inevitably yielded, according to Elwin and Courthope, to the sway of *science*, and was anything but 'arbitrary', as in the Goddess Dulness' 'Arbitrary Sway' of line 182. But Courthope knew little about the science of the Restoration and early eighteenth century, let alone had he familiarized himself with its historiographical traditions in anything resembling the depth we have today: the New Science versus the traditions of rhetoric and language, Royal Society versus Wits, Croll versus Jones, Newton versus Locke, reason and the imagination, and so forth. Tersely put, Courthope's commentary on Book IV is a disaster because his cultural map of Pope's England was so defective.

In our century the response to Pope's satire on education has been much more thorough, if no more objective. James Sutherland, the Twickenham editor of the poem, identified Pope's targets – general and specific – in his very first annotation. Recognizing that 'different aspects of contemporary [i.e., eighteenth-century] education' are involved, Sutherland glances at Warton's defence of eighteenth-century education (cited above) and comments that 'much of Pope's criticism of the classical education of the day is shrewd enough' (*TE* v, p. 356). That Pope's target (or targets) includes the 'classical' portion of the curriculum is beyond doubt: the ghost of Dr Busby, the famous headmaster of Westminster School and 'Spectre' of one of the most stinging mock-epic speeches in the satire, reveals why:

> . . . Since Man from beast by Words is known,
> Words are Man's province, Words we teach alone.
> When Reason doubtful, like the Samian letter,
> Points him two ways, the narrower is the better.
> Plac'd at the door of Learning, youth to guide,
> We never suffer it to stand too wide.
> To ask, to guess, to know, as they commence,
> As Fancy opens the quick springs of Sense,
> We ply the Memory, we load the brain,
> Bind rebel Wit, and double chain on chain,
> Confine the thought, to exercise the breath;
> And keep them in the pale of Words till death.'
>
> (*TE* v, p. 356, ll. 149–60)

'Spectre-Busby', about whom more will be said, did hang 'padlocks on the minds' of his boys by compelling them endlessly to recite 'Words' they did not understand; in this sense, Pope's target, as Sutherland notes, is indeed 'classical', particularly to the degree that rhetoric and oratory, especially Cicero's and Quintilian's versions, were required school subjects in Pope's time. But 'classical' is an empty label unless made explicit, and an attack on it in any of its protean forms is meaningless – especially when Pope is the original source – unless the stakes it involves are sharply delineated. Aubrey Williams has

provided some of the reasons, if not the solutions, in the illuminating fifth
chapter ('Of Wisdom – and Dullness') of his own now classic study of *The
Dunciad*.[10] Prudently guiding his reader by five signposts – humanism, wisdom, rhetoric, eloquence, oratory – Williams aims to capture the essence of
Pope's mindset when conceptualizing this part of the poem:

> To pin the label of 'rhetor' on Pope would be of course a vast over-simplification of the
> actual facts, but what we can do to advantage is to regard him as a writer living within
> the humanist milieu of attitudes, a milieu which received its clearest expression in the
> Ciceronian ideal of the Renaissance, and which even in his own time was kept fresh by a
> constant influx from the same traditional well-spring. It was only natural that the
> supreme philosophy for Pope, as for his predecessors, should be moral philosophy, that
> he, like them, should favor 'humane wisdom' in opposition to what appeared to many
> as a 'proud scientism.'
> (p. 108)

Here, then, is a link to Courthope's concern for the incremental scientism of
his own day: that is, Pope's preference for 'humane wisdom' over a 'scientific
education' that could guarantee results but which might be morally empty or
even morally corrupt. An opposition between humanism and scientism is
therefore to be expected, as is the critic's sedulous temptation, as Williams
notes, to locate Pope in what may crudely be called the rhetorical way of life.
But what constituted 'humanistic' or 'humane' wisdom for one thinker – in the
Renaissance as well as Pope's time – was not necessarily true, or even relevant,
for another. Less cumbersomely put, one would have to specify to precisely
which 'moral philosophy' Pope adhered, if one hoped to understand the
humane wisdom to which Williams refers. This Williams did not do, but his
discussion, entirely new in 1955, was nevertheless illuminating even if we want
more than this today. Furthermore, Williams' treatment dictated the categories for all subsequent discussions of this part of Pope's last major poem (see
note 10), just as his signposts, mentioned above, led him to the very heart of the
matter that preoccupied Pope. In Williams' words: 'the decline of rhetoric into
mere verbalism', the existence of a 'rhetorical ideal' to which Pope must have
adhered, and, perhaps more consequentially, 'the separation of words and
ideas that Cicero, Ascham, [Thomas] Sheridan – and Pope – found so
baneful'.[11]

In all these judgments was the residue of the New Criticism of the 1950s,

[10] A. L. Williams, *Pope's Dunciad: a study of its meaning* (Baton Rouge, 1955), pp. 104–30. I omit
discussion of the contributions of later scholars because they have not, in my view, significantly
altered Williams' position; but see J. E. Sitter, *The poetry of Pope's Dunciad* (Minneapolis, 1971)
and H. H. Erskine-Hill, 'The 'new world' of Pope's *Dunciad*', *Renaissance and Modern Studies* 6
(1962), 49–67; C. R. Kropf, 'Education and the Neoplatonic idea of wisdom in Pope's *Dunciad*',
Texas Studies in Language and Literature 14 (1973), 593–604. Among earlier scholars, the education of the duncés is nowhere discussed by Austin Warren in *Alexander Pope as critic and humanist*
(Princeton, 1929).

[11] Williams, pp. 112–15 for these phrases. Thomas Sheridan, the author of an important work on
English education, is discussed in note 15 below. For the 'rhetorical ideal' and its history, see
R. A. Lanham, *The motives of eloquence: literary rhetoric in the Renaissance* (New Haven, 1976). I. A.
Richards' *Philosophy of rhetoric* (New York, 1936) is discussed below.

especially the proleptic notion that 'the rhetorical ideal' could be a way of life for serious twentieth-century humanists beleaguered by socio-political problems. Williams himself had been a product of academic New Criticism at both Yale and Louisiana State University, whose university press published *Pope's Dunciad*. If Williams' estimate of Book IV, especially the point about 'the separation of words and ideas,' appears to be something of a cliché thirty years later to a generation of readers bred on Foucault's binary opposition of *les mots* and *les choses*, it did not seem so in 1955 when *The Dunciad* was a much less well understood work than it is today. At that time, the separation of words and things (Williams' 'words and ideas' amounts to the same opposition) and the implications of the division, constituted one of the most original aspects of Williams' discussion, not because the opposition was new (classicists and Renaissancists had been referring to it for centuries), but because Williams had applied it to Pope's poem for the first time and seen what was disturbing Pope.[12] Williams' notion that 'in its overall structure Book IV expounds, in poetic terms, the humanist position that the segregation of words and things is fatal' (p. 123), appeared to be genuinely novel in 1955. The notion was indeed new, as the reviews of Williams' book demonstrated.

Novel as it was, it did not answer questions about Pope's reasons for the attack on education, or identify what his 'humanist position' might be. Excellent as Williams' discussion was, it was both eclectic and incomplete. Selective in holding up Pope as the exemplar of 'humane positions' and 'rhetorical ideals' without describing the biographical and historical evidence for doing so, and without adumbrating how Pope came to adopt these ideals (convenient as it was in 1955 for a then young 'New Critic' to purport that the greatest poets of the past had also privileged the 'rhetorical ideal' and sobbed when it was threatened); it was also incomplete by virtue of Williams' remaining silent about the ideological consequences of these humanistic and rhetorical views. Indeed, not a word is to be found on the *politics* of humanism or the *politics* of rhetoric in Pope's time, or about the ideologies of those who favoured the separation of words and things (that is, scientists, projectors, *virtuosi*, as well as

---

[12] See J. E. Sandys, *A history of classical scholarship* (New York, 1967; rev. ed.), Rudolph Pfeiffer, *History of classical scholarship from 1300 to 1850* (Oxford, 1976), and A. Grafton and L. Jardine, *From humanism to the humanities* (Cambridge, Mass., 1986). The footnotes to chapter five of Williams' book demonstrate the resources he had to build on: Volume V of the *TE*, a few books about Renaissance education, Sheridan and Turnbull (see below note 15), Croll and Jones; and, for the background of the gulf between words and things, A. C. Howell's 'Res et verba: words and things', *ELH* 13 (1946), 131–42. Williams seems to have overlooked R. Quintana's important article, 'Notes on English educational opinion during the seventeenth century', *Studies in English Literature* 27 (1930), 265–87, which discusses the opposition in terms of Renaissance humanism and Baconian naturalism; and which is particularly illuminating on Sir Henry Wotton's *Surveigh of education* (1654) with its appended *Aphorisms of education*. More recently, words and things (*res/verba*) are discussed in Paul Fussell, *The rhetorical world of Augustan humanism* (Oxford, 1965); Murray Cohen, *Linguistic practice in England 1640–1785* (Baltimore, 1977), and R. L. King, '*Res et verba*: The reform of language in Dryden's *All for Love*', *ELH* 54 (1987), 45–62.

the hacks and dunces with whom they then seem to have been allied so far as their philosophies of language and humanism were concerned), as distinct from those moralists and statesmen for whom – in Williams' words – separation 'is so baneful'. Williams is thoroughly persuasive about the reasons *why* eighteenth-century projectors (whose subjects were things: objects, materials, matter) favoured the split, and why a segment of Pope's contemporaries, especially the dunces in Grub Street, encouraged the decline of this rhetorical ideal into mere verbalism. Pope himself had described the psychological process brilliantly:

> We only furnish what he [the student] cannot use,
> Or wed to what he must divorce, a Muse:
> Full in the midst of Euclid dip at once,
> And petrify a Genius to a Dunce.

(*TE* v, pp. 369–70, ll. 261–4)

But Pope provided no explanations to gloss the very category – duncery – he himself had elevated to a cultural norm in his long poem. And Williams' discussion is embedded within a context and conceptual framework in which politics and ideology play no part – indeed, a context in which they seem not to exist at all.

Humanism and historiography

Williams, in fairness, could not profit from the vast library of secondary works on education in the Restoration and eighteenth century compiled in the last three decades,[13] or from Rivers' 1976 doctoral dissertation on the intellectual backgrounds of Pope's satire.[14] Rivers' study, somewhat inspired by Williams'

---

[13] For example (arranged chronologically): E. C. Mack, *Public schools and British opinion 1780–1860* (New York, 1939); N. Hans, *New trends in education in the 18th century* (London, 1951); (for the dissenting academies) G. F. Nuttall (ed.), *Philip Doddridge 1702–51* (London, 1951) and J. W. A. Smith, *The birth of modern education: The contribution of the dissenting academies, 1660–1800* (London, 1954); G. C. Brauer, Jr., *The education of a gentleman: theories of gentlemanly education in England 1660–1775* (New York, 1959); A. C. F. Beales, *Education under penalty: English Catholic education from the Reformation to the fall of James II, 1547–1689* (London, 1963); J. D. Carleton, *Westminster School: a history* (London, 1965); T. W. Bamford, *The rise of the public schools* (London, 1967); W. A. L. Vincent, *The grammar schools: their continuing tradition 1660–1714* (London, 1969); J. Lawson and H. Silver, *A social history of education in England* (London, 1973); Lawrence Stone (ed.), *Schooling and society: studies in the history of education* (Baltimore, 1976); S. Rothblatt, *Tradition and change in English liberal education* (Routledge, 1976); James Bowen, *A history of western education. Volume III* (New York, 1977); D. Leinster-Mackay, *The rise of the English prep school* (London, 1984). For French education during Pope's lifetime, which developed along different lines from British, see Roger Chartier, *L'Education en France du XVIe au XVIIIe siècle* (Paris, 1976). No eighteenth-century equivalent of John Chandos' *Boys together: English public schools 1800–1864* (New Haven, 1984) exists. Ellen Pollak includes a section on 'Educational theorists' in *The poetics of sexual myth: gender and ideology in the verse of Swift and Pope* (Chicago, 1985) but, oddly, does not discuss Pope.

[14] William E. Rivers, 'Backgrounds to Pope's satire of education' (University of North Carolina, PhD Diss., 1976), a work of 409 pages with a copious bibliography of primary and secondary books.

discussion, aimed to reconstruct the humanist tradition in English education from the sixteenth century onward. Yet despite the erudition of Rivers' chronological history of humanism, it too ignores the political–ideological milieu, construing didactic authors at face value for the words written on their pages without linking these positions to their socio-political filiations. Locke and the contemporary schoolmen are present in Rivers, as they had not been in Williams; but the New Science, together with the methods of scientific education adopted in schools and universities, is omitted, as are ideological matters of party and faction. Pope's contemporaries who wrote on education – for example, J. T. Philipps, John Clarke, George Turnbull, Thomas Sheridan (respectively tutor, schoolmaster, social commentator, actor/acting teacher)[15] – are discussed as if having lived in an ideological vacuum; as if it is now sufficient for the literary historian to decipher the words they wrote without consulting the larger contexts in which these ideas were generated. 'My final chapter', Rivers writes, 'is an attempt to show Pope's awareness of and debt to the humanist tradition, where Pope found early expressions of his philosophy of education, including antecedents for the basic criticisms he levelled at the educational institutions of his day – particularly for his objection to the study of words merely as forms apart from their meanings in literature' (Rivers, p. i). But *which* 'humanist tradition' (there were competing ones) and *what* 'philoso-

---

[15] J. T. Philipps (d. 1755), a private tutor entrusted with the children of George II, was the author of many books on grammar and wrote *A compendious way of teaching ancient and modern languages* (1727) for the use of his students. John Clarke (1687–1734) was a schoolmaster and author of various treatises, including *An essay upon the education of youth in grammar schools* (1720; 2nd ed. 1730) and *An essay on study* (1731), all intended to reform the whole system of rote learning in education. George Turnbull (fl. 1740) called attention to himself in 1740–1 as Pope was beginning to compose *The New Dunciad*, publishing several books dealing with literature, painting, and morality, and a long treatise called *Observations upon liberal education, in all its branches: containing the substance of what hath been said upon that important subject by the best writers ancient and modern; with many new remarks interspersed* (1742). Here he claimed that 'the best things may be perverted; but surely the securest barrier against bad taste or corruption of any kind, is to form early, by proper education in young minds, a just sense of the excellency of virtue, and a thorough good taste of all the arts that may be rendered subservient to it or from which men of easy fortunes may fetch amusements to themselves, without making one step towards vice; and an aversion from every abuse of them' (p. 460). Twelve years after Pope's death in 1744, Thomas Sheridan (1719–88), the actor/author who must not be confused with his father, Swift's friend, or with his son the famous playwright, Richard Brinsley, believed he had discovered the superlative source of England's decline at the start of the Seven Years' War in the corrupt system of national education. A graduate of Westminster, he elaborated this theory in *British education: or, the source of the disorders of Great Britain* (1756), claiming, in his opening, that 'such symptoms in a state [i.e. England on the brink of ruin] are sure prognosticks of approaching ruin; and its end cannot be far off, unless prevented by adequate remedies' (p. 4). All three commentators on English education shared an aversion to the use of Lily's grammar (declared the national one to be used in all schools by Henry VIII); objected to the mere rehearsal of words during the most formative period of the boy's life; and recoiled from the separation of words and things (*res/verba*) in the manner promoted by Lily. They are therefore accurately described as aligning themselves, to different degrees, with the tradition of education advocated by Milton and Locke (see below section IV) rather than the one promoted by the schoolmasters and grammarians denounced by Pope in *The New Dunciad*.

phy of education?' (Did Pope actually *have* one?) These labels entail slippery
terms and catch-alls whose ideological underpinnings need to be ferreted out.
Rivers, despite his wealth of detail, has fallen into the very same trap, it would
appear, described acerbically by Pope's narrator in *The New Dunciad*:

> The body's harmony, the beaming soul,
> Are things which Kuster, Burman, Wasse shall see,
> When Man's whole frame is obvious to a *Flea*.
>
> (*TE* v, p. 366, ll. 236–8)

In Rivers' learned study the part is gleaned, though the 'whole frame' is lost
by the lack of a meaningful context; and the social milieu and ideological
underpinnings of this humanist tradition are either spurned or ignored.
Though this work is erudite and expansive, Rivers has surveyed Williams'
tradition of humanism as it pertains to school and university education within
a dyadic mindset that embraces merely the oppositions of binary sets (that is,
humanism and non-humanism, rhetoric and anti-rhetoric, oratory and false
oratory, etc.). Writing according to the laws of conventional academic pro-
tocol, Rivers has either suppressed his own perspective, or has overlooked all
that has transpired since 1744. The omission is not insignificant in view of the
high stakes to be won or lost when discussing a subject as controversial as
education, all the more so in view of the decline of the rhetorical ideal into mere
verbalism *sans* referentiality with which our own culture today appears to be so
obsessed.

Neither Williams nor Rivers steps *outside* the so-called humanist tradition
(writing as if there had been one triumphant humanism inherited from the
Renaissance by the eighteenth century), and neither introduces into the
discussion party politics or – equally important in my view – the disparate
ideologies of humanism. The politics of eighteenth-century humanism are
omitted, as are the politics of our versions of humanism today. More recently,
Vincent Carretta has provided a corrective, or at least revisionist view, entitled 'The Politics of Education in *The Dunciad*'.[16] Carretta shifts the discussion from Williams' 'humanism', a term Carretta never uses, to 'politics',
claiming 'it would be inaccurate to say that *The Dunciad* IV is alone either a
satire on education or a satire on politics. The satire on education has a
political purpose' (pp. 159–60). For Carretta, this 'purpose' includes the
defence of liberty and monarchy in a well-ordered state, as well as the representation of their antitheses, and the referent or target of Pope's satire is made
chronologically explicit:

. . . if Walpole is the primary referent, the lines [at the conclusion of Book 4] are
anticlimactic because he had already fallen from power when the poem first appeared . . . Certainly the Opposition had long charged that he was the effective ruler of

---

[16] Vincent Carretta, *The snarling muse: verbal and visual poetical satire from Pope to Churchill* (Philadelphia, 1983), chapter 5.

England, but in keeping with the general tone of *The Dunciad* 4, Pope is more likely
inveighing here against the allegedly tyrannical system developed by Walpole.

(p. 157)

Carretta's amalgam of the first half of Book IV with the second – the
transformation of England into 'One Mighty Dunciad of the Land' – is
significant for the light it sheds on his revisionist context and sense of the
boundaries, or limits, within this context. Among the printed books he specifically includes Thomson's *Liberty* (1735–6), because it is, like *The Dunciad*, a
'dissident Whig panegyric' (p. 141), Bolingbroke's *Remarks on the History of
England* (1730–1), which contains an implicit philosophy of education, and *The
Craftsman*, the important Opposition paper to which both Bolingbroke and
Pope, of course, as well as others of the patriots, contributed: all tied together
in Carretta's treatment by the rope, so to speak, of 'political miseducation' and
'political tyranny', which function as critical concepts to describe the poet's
radical aims. Carretta, like Miriam Leranbaum in *Alexander Pope's opus magnum
1729–44*,[17] also relates the satire on education in *The Dunciad* to the plan of *An
Essay on Man,* and gives some weight to Pope's various claims made to Spence
and others about his own education and his (Pope's) continuing desire to write
an 'Epistle on Education'. Finally, Carretta cites Pope's letter of 25 March
1736 to Swift, describing the new project in 'four Epistles', and epitomizing the
last epistle as discussing 'merely the use of *Learning*, of the *science of the World,*
and of *Wit*', which 'will conclude', according to Pope, 'with a Satire against the
Misapplication of all these, exemplified by pictures, characters, and
examples'.[18] Carretta's goal in constructing this explicitly political context is
to heighten appreciation of the whole *Dunciad*, not merely this section of Book
IV: 'Viewing the *New Dunciad* from a political perspective', he affirms, 'will
enable us to recognize that Pope sees contemporary education as serving the
political ends of Dulness' (p. 141).

The link is vital; cast in this way, Carretta's discussion sheds new light on
Book IV, particularly its relation to the engraved political caricatures of the
time. But his discussion of 'contemporary education' is too brief for completed
revisionism, and does not address Pope's explicit references: particular schools
and schoolmasters, methods, strategies. Throughout his argument Carretta
continues to refer to 'contemporary miseducation' and the 'metaphor of
miseducation in Pope' – metaphors presumably germane to all Pope's mature
poetry – but unless we happen to be social historians, or historians of education in possession of the various schemes of education then, we could not
possibly know what Pope believed had specifically gone wrong. From Pope's

[17] See Miriam Leranbaum, *Alexander Pope's 'opus magnum' 1729–1744* (Oxford, 1977), pp. 133–7;
150–3.
[18] See Carretta, p. 160. Both Locke and Pope stress the importance of 'pictures' in education (see
pp. 216–20 below); it would be interesting to learn if Pope derived this idea from Locke's
Thoughts.

harsh accusations – rote learning, too much memorization and recitation, not
enough understanding, an emphasis on words rather than things, an obsession
with the classics – we might surmise the strategies of schoolmasters in their
classes; but conjecture in historical scholarship is often a perfidious enterprise,
as the whole history of the identification of specific Popean targets shows.
Carretta mentions Dr Busby once as the 'Spectre' who possesses an 'index
hand' (p. 151), but there is no consideration of Busby as schoolmaster or
politician, perhaps because Carretta thought Sutherland had exhausted the
obvious facts in his Twickenham Edition. Yet the educated reader today
cannot know which specific sins Busby committed to deserve this opprobrious
Popean verdict. Carretta's only detailed comment comes in a footnote: 'Pope's
comprehensive indictment of contemporary education . . . anticipates Catharine Macaulay's very similar attack in the "Introduction" to her *History of
England* (London, 1763). Macaulay (who is discussed later) also sees the
educational system that embraces grammar school, the universities, and the
grand tour as inculcating the principles of tyranny and absolutism' (p. 270).
Indeed she did, as we will see below, but Carretta does not explore this
'educational system' or tell us what these malignant principles were, any more
than he treats the Lockian revolution in education, or the public spokesmen
(the Turnbulls and Sheridans), mentioned by Williams and Rivers.

I do not measure these boundaries and anatomize these contexts to criticize
Carretta. His revisionism, intended to correct the earlier contexts (Williams
and Sutherland) he found lacking, is entirely illuminating, and has succeeded
in shifting the ground from a rather amorphous 'humanistic rhetoric' (Williams) to a more concretely 'political' one. Yet questions about the educational
system and the specific principles on which it was founded, as well as Pope's
specific targets and niche in our own continuing debate about education
remain unanswered. First among these is Pope's own education. One need not
be a Freudian or psychoanalytic critic of any type to recognize that a man who
in his maturity lambasts contemporary education may have suffered intensely
– in a profound psychological sense – during his own schooling. Much has
already been written about Pope's early education: his never having attended
university, his prolific remarks uttered to Spence, his gleanings on education
in his letters, and – most recently – the cogent synthesis offered by Maynard
Mack in his new biography (*Pope: a life*, p. 52). Suffice it to say that Mack is no
doubt right to attach just the right amount of emphasis to its Catholic origins,
without losing sight of the general, or philosophical, issues at hand. 'Essentially,' Mack writes, 'it was not the books that were at fault, but the method of
instruction', and then explains what the method entailed:

This called for constant parsing of Latin sentences, construing of inflections, memorizing of rhetorical figures, and composing of Latin verses. Rote-minded, heavily insistent
on the forms of language for their own sake, everywhere emphasizing fragments over
wholes and means instead of ends, the system could not prevent a bright student from
getting an education, for no system can; but it could make the process intellectually
wasteful and physically a torture.

A large chunk of early eighteenth-century manuscript material, especially letters between friends recollected in tranquillity, documents this ongoing torment. Furthermore, the printed literature adumbrating the curricula at just the time Pope himself was at school (*c.* 1700) demonstrates to what radical degree emphasis was placed on the recitation and memorization of these 'sentences'. In and of itself there was nothing particularly 'Catholic' about this daily routine except for its religious regimen; had Pope not been educated by priests and Catholic schoolmasters, he probably would have responded in the same, extraordinarily negative way. As Mack comments, laying great store in Pope's psychology as a youth rather than in a particular regimen of study to which the Catholic schoolmasters may have subjected him: 'Still, the curriculum of studies in a late seventeenth-century school was not well calculated for the meridian of a lively imagination' (*Pope: a life*, p. 51). It is an observation superlatively pertinent to Book IV, where, as Carretta has suggested, the link between 'contemporary miseducation' and 'political tyranny' is vital. Mack does not demonstrate whether the curriculum of these Catholic schools differed from that of their Anglican counterparts, though he cites a 'typical specimen' of Anglican pedagogy entitled *Notes on the method of education of youth in Merchant Taylors' school in the year 1671* from which he generalizes about Pope's education and presumably much education then.[19] Our interest today in Jacobite (as distinct from Anglican) life in England from 1688 onwards, may eventually lead to a clearer picture of this daily curriculum that will, in turn, prompt us to view Pope's rebellion in a different light. But it won't alter the specificity of Pope's attack in Book IV, or change the way this form of education essentially placed 'padlocks on the mind' of all students. We already know enough about the processes of education then to make such fine distinctions the stuff of historical scholarship. We gain a firmer grasp of these 'padlocks' by ascertaining whether the daily routines of Pope's early Catholic schoolmasters at Twyford (Messrs Wait, Grove and Barlow), and, later on, the Catholic convert schoolmaster Thomas Deane at the Marylebone School, involved any unusually tedious procedures capable of inflaming an already (as Mack aptly calls it) 'lively imagination' – and, we may add, especially lively *reading* imagination. Research that could produce evidence about Pope's schoolmasters' techniques – disciplinary (flogging) or instructional (religious and secular studies) – would fortify an increasingly clear picture of the methods of the time.[20]

The psychological torture of these methods of instruction is more significant than the curricula for understanding Pope's degree of rebellion. What counted to Pope's lively imagination was not merely *what* was taught, or whether taught by Papist or Anglican, but what was *not* taught; and – perhaps as

[19] *Pope: a life*, p. 830, quoting from an anonymous *Merchant Taylors' school: its origin and present surroundings* (Oxford, 1929), pp. 50–1.

[20] The most complete description of the daily routine in this period I have found appears in W. A. L. Vincent, *The grammar schools: their continuing tradition 1660–1714* (London, 1969), chapter IV, 'The daily round'.

consequentially – what was forbidden: not merely the religious works considered sacrilegious to his priests, and the Locke who (he assures us in Book IV)
they banned, but the romances, novels, plays, he might have consumed with
gusto if he could have obtained these books. Leisure of any sort was outlawed,
as the manuals for teachers demonstrate.[21] The routine for both teachers and
students was gruelling: they awoke about 5 a.m. (according to contemporary
reports) and were occupied in study – under the threat of the rod – until the
boys were delivered to their dormitory beds early in the evening. Furthermore,
teachers were paid much less around 1700 than they had been during the
Tudor or Commonwealth eras, one of several signs that primary education
had declined in importance during the Restoration.[22] Those who extem-
porized about its decay – the Obadiah Walkers (1673) and John Gailhards
(1678) – wrote on the premise, later discredited by Locke and others, that
children were young adults in whom discipline needed to be inculcated.[23]
They uttered every type of platitude about the relation of the contemplative
life to the active, and about the value of learning, but little of their hollow
liberalism (Walker actually called it 'verbal liberalism') was ever put into
practice judging by the memories of most students of the time.[24] No wonder
that Christopher Wase, a schoolmaster and beadle of civil law at Oxford,
called for a national inquiry into the state of English primary education twenty
years before Pope went to Twyford. And in the decade (the 1690s) when Pope
himself was in school, Locke began to formulate his own theories of education
based on the reforms of Wase, Comenius, Hartlib and Leibniz.[25]

'Spectre' Busby, the venerable headmaster of Westminster from 1638 to
1695, who ruled there for fifty-seven years, represented the extremely tyrannical 'Genius of the Place'. Small wonder that Pope conjures him here as the
humbler of all human flesh, 'Dropping with Infant's Blood, and Mother's
Tears', a ruthless Walpole translated to the schools. Yet Busby was not singled
out because Pope had any inside knowledge about the school or its master.
Westminster and its headmaster were selected because both were so famous
(Pope probably knew about individual English schools only by what he

[21] For some of these, see Vincent, *The grammar schools*, pp. 58–62 and 194–208. Valuable
information about the authors of these and similar works is found in Brauer (n. 13).

[22] For documentation of the point, see Vincent, chapter 7, 'The salaries of schoolmasters', pp.
153–71.

[23] O. Walker, *Of education, especially of young gentlemen* (Oxford, 1673; 7th ed. 1699); J. Gailhard, *The
compleat gentleman: or, directions for the education of youth as to their breeding at home and travelling abroad*
(1678). For children as young adults, see also Francis Brokesby, *Of education with respect to
grammar schools and the universities* (1701; rep. with additions in 1751 as *A letter of advice to a young
gentleman at the university*). These and many other similar works were addressed 'to gentlemen'
who wished to better themselves, the consistent advice being that gentlemen ought to free
themselves from pedantry, learn sound religion, perpetuate the teachings of the Established
Church, and prepare themselves for government office or a useful trade.

[24] See the examples cited by Rivers, pp. 10ff.

[25] For Wase see Vincent, *The grammar schools*, chapter 2, 'The Wase inquiry', pp. 23–39; for the
tradition of reform in the schools, T. H. Rae, *John Dury reformer of education* (Marburg, 1970), pp.
339–41.

learned through their common mythology), and, secondly, because West-minster School was geographically located so close to the politicians – a crucial detail that strengthens Carretta's idea of 'political miseducation'. Nothing else can explain the selection of Westminster over (for example) Eton, Harrow, Rugby, etc. in an era when all these schools were guilty of the methods of rote.[26] But if England's schools were as debased as Pope intimates, then her leaders – her politicians and statesmen – would eventually become as malig-nant. In short, by the turn of the century – 1700 – England's primary schools, public and private, large and small, rich and poor, were institutions of unre-lenting drudgery that had failed to teach their students to use their minds and bodies, as they had failed to encourage any but the most minimal forms of recreation. This decline cut across all the social classes, high and low, and was not limited to those poor members of society who harboured no hope of ever becoming gentlemen. The cry of Thomas Sheridan and others, to the effect that these primary schools, like the universities, were actually producing men of corruption rather than virtue, was to come later, in the mid eighteenth century. At the turn of the eighteenth century, when Pope was in school, only Locke (about whom more will shortly be said) seems to have understood what magisterial reforms were needed if public and private primary education were to survive. The main charge then was that *all* the schools had sunk into disarray – the whole institution of education, as Gibbon and Cowper would later explain, had fallen on hard times. But unfortunately, the reforms needed in Pope's time were not undertaken for another hundred years, until the beginning of the nineteenth century.

More fatally for someone as curious about books as the young Pope, there was no opportunity at school to browse through books and feed the channels of his reading imagination. At Twyford and Marylebone – poor schools by any standard – there weren't even the books in which to browse! 'Let your imagination loose', Walker unrealistically instructed young scholars in 1673, 'both before and when you read; discourse, doubt, argue upon and against; and draw consequence from your author; who is many times but a ladder to your own inquisitiveness.'[27] But the Pope who in his satire conjures a sado-

[26] Nowhere in the satire on education does Pope mention Thomas Knipe, Busby's successor at Westminster who ruled from 1695 to 1711. J. Sargeaunt characterizes Knipe's mastership as follows (*Annals of Westminster School*, 1898, p. 136): 'The sixteen years of Knipe's mastership... witnessed another step in a movement which had begun under Busby. Westminster, always a School of poets and divines, became under Knipe also a nursery of statesmen. The statesmen were of many parties, and had not learned, as [Robert] Freind's boys did, to make their school acquaintance the basis of a party.' Freind, like his brother John (now dead), was a Christ Church man who had been educated at Westminster and who joined in the attack on Bentley in the Ancients–Moderns controversy, 'Let Freind affect to speak as Terence spoke' (*TE* v, p. 364, l. 223), Pope complimented him in the satire on education but not without an ironical job. The reason for Westminster's prominence in Pope's satire is thus strengthened by its historical development during this period, a fact contributing much to the mere geographical proximity of the school and the government.

[27] O. Walker, *Of education* (1699), p. 121.

masochistic scenario hewn out of Blakean fetters ('We ply the Memory, we load the brain, / Bind rebel Wit, and double chain on chain', *TE* v, p. 357, ll. 157–8), had discovered anything but the opportunity to 'let loose the imagination'. How he would have welcomed Johnson's precept – if it could be applied to schoolboys – that 'a man ought to read just as inclination leads him; for what he reads as a task will do him little good'.[28] The blessed isles of browsing leisure were to come later in life for Pope: after he had abandoned his priests and tutors and moved to London where books could be found in abundance. In public schools the reading imagination was effectively stifled, even crippled; Pope was the rare exception who managed to escape the chains of domination. How he achieved this freedom may remain forever unknown, but his satire in Book iv attests to the indelible memories these early experiences left on him. The pronouncement of a recent historian of Westminster School that Westminster would have been 'a disaster' for Pope, is intuitively sound.[29] Pope would have deplored school life there as much as, and perhaps even more than, the confining atmosphere he encountered at Twyford and Marylebone.

Locke and the revolution in education

Locke annotated the decline of the schools in his *Thoughts concerning education* (1693) when discussing a child's need to browse in books that offer pictures and pleasure – *dulce* rather than *utilita*:

. . . some easy pleasant Book suited to his Capacity, should be put into his hands, wherein the entertainment, that he finds, might draw him on, and reward his Pains in Reading, and yet not such as should fill his Head with perfectly useless trumpery, or lay the principles of Vice and Folly . . . If [the book] *has Pictures* in it, it will entertain him

---

[28] G. B. Hill (ed.), *Boswell's Life of Johnson*, 6 vols. (Oxford, 1934, rev. ed.), iii, p. 385. Boswell's *Life* contains many variations on this theme, with Johnson always emphasizing that the boy should be permitted to read anything he pleases and never forced to study by rote, as in the famous comment he made in 1763, quoted by Boswell, that 'a man ought to read just as inclination leads him' (n. 5 above). Nevertheless, Johnson, a former schoolmaster himself, remained a traditionalist so far as the rod and corporal punishment were concerned, as in his disquisition on education recited to Boswell on 25 May 1778, when he explained why Milton and Locke had hurt modern education more than any other two men (for Johnson contra Locke's *Thoughts on education* see *Rambler* no. 85). Johnson also rebelled against new schemes to reform education; see the entry under education in Hill's index in the *Life*, vi, p. 114. But however thoroughgoing a traditionalist and however wedded to discipline, he continued to insist that a boy's reading imagination must have the liberty to roam wherever it wished, and he advised Strahan (the printer) while still a student at Oxford not to 'omit to mingle some lighter books with those of more importance; that which is read *remisso animo* is often of great use, and takes great hold of the remembrance'; see R. W. Chapman (ed.), *The letters of Samuel Johnson*, 3 vols. (Oxford, 1952), i, p. 173.

[29] See J. D. Carlton, *Westminster School* (Rupert Hart-Davis, 1965), p. 26. For Busby's curriculum and daily routine, see J. Sargeaunt, *Annals of Westminster School* (Methuen, 1898), chapter vi, 'Busby's curriculum', pp. 79–112, still the most reliable account of the school in this period despite a growing body of secondary literature that plunders from it, such as J. L. Tanner, *Westminster School* (London, 1934).

much the better, and encourage him to read, when it carries the increase of Knowledge with it. For such visible Objects Children hear talked of in vain, and without any satisfaction, whilst they have no Ideas of them; those Ideas being not to be had from Sounds; but from the Things themselves, or their Pictures.[30]

Here then, amplified in detail, is a philosophy of education not very remote from Pope's in Book IV. No wonder Warton believed Pope copied it from Locke. Its psychology is self-evident: picture books and the leisure to browse and read in them; stimulation of the child's reading imagination; a growing desire in the student to read and learn more. The process was painless, Locke thought, yet produced results. Locke's *Thoughts*, as James Axtell has demonstrated, offered an alternative for reform of the declining schools as well as theoretical reasons why they should revise their curricula. In brief, Locke proposed an altogether different manner of schooling opposed to Busby's servile methods and dead set against his corporal punishment. Persuaded that children loved liberty and freedom most, and that they learned best when nurtured in these specific environments, Locke offered a veritable antidote to conventional English education. The rod and the whip he considered altogether pernicious; and he was certain that the common practice of flogging – which seems to have peaked at just at this time[31] – ought 'very rarely to be applied, and that only in great Occasions, and Cases of Extremity' (no. 52). Locke was also opposed to learning by rote, particularly by memorization. 'Pray remember,' he cautioned parents, 'Children are *not* to be taught by Rules' (no. 158), and, later, in the context of the teaching of Latin grammar, he inserted a small dissertation against what Pope more vividly called 'plying the memory' and 'loading the brain':

. . . learning Languages . . . 1. in my Opinion, should be made as easie and pleasant as may be; and that which was painful in it, as much as possible quite removed. That which I mean, and hear complain of, is, their being forced to learn by Heart, great Parcels of the Authors which are taught them; wherein I can discover no Advantage at

---

[30] J. L. Axtell (ed.), *The educational writings of John Locke* (Cambridge, 1968), p. 259. The introduction and apparatus of Axtell's edition offer a brilliant survey of the state of education then. Not even by the end of the nineteenth century could Victorian schoolmasters like Sargeaunt (n. 29) forgive Locke for writing contra Busby, an attitude demonstrating how much was at stake in a national system of public education that taught by rote and the rod during Pope's time, and further affirming the cultural bases of Pope's satire. 'Nowadays it needs some courage,' Sargeaunt exclaimed, 'to suggest that, in so far as they conflict with Busby's principles, there is on the whole a retrogressive and unworthy spirit in Locke's *Thoughts concerning education*. Locke's fault is not so much that too little place, as Johnson said [see note 28 above] is given to literature: it is rather that too much is thought of mere worldly success' (*Annals of Westminster School*, p. 125).

[31] Locke believed that flogging had reached its peak during the Restoration and viewed it as one of the period's worst social institutions; see Axtell, pp. 148–51, for Locke against flogging and the rod. Locke also opposed learning by rote and memorization (Axtell, pp. 157, 287, 355); he viewed pleasure as the only genuine end of learning, above all other utilitarian reasons (pp. 222–3); and most importantly, he endorsed a method of education that taught through the recognition of things rather than of words (pp. 259–60), this last theory being the one that would have most pleased Pope if the poet could have (or indeed if he had) encountered it.

all, especially to the Business they are upon. Languages are to be learn'd only by
Reading, and Talking, and not by Scraps of Authors got by Heart; which when a Man's
Head is stuffed with, he has got the just Furniture of a Pedant.   (no. 285)

The ring is Popean and smacks of dunciads, but Locke (perhaps again
resembling Pope more than we have been accustomed to think) was no less
vigorously opposed to 'their making verses of any sort,' unless the student
'have a poetic vein'.[32] Locke's philosophy of education may not have been
congruent with Pope's, and given that the poet never composed his projected
'epistle on education' we are unable to make easy comparisons of their ideas.
However, in the poet's concern for pedants and blockheads ('Forever reading,
never to be read'), Book IV shares some of the ideas found in Locke's *Thoughts*.
Both men see the inculcation of non-pedantic knowledge as education's priority; both denigrate foreign travel for the young. Locke's programme is the
better defined: education occurs in an atmosphere of liberty and pleasure,
where 'None of the Things they [children] are to learn should ever be made a
Burthen to them' (no. 73). Educated at Oxford in medicine and afterwards a
practising physician, Locke has much to say about the healthful aspects of
these reforms *vis-à-vis* the body, and although it is frivolous to conjecture about
the unknown, it would be interesting to know what he would have recommended for the young Pope, who was shrinking rather than growing, if he
could have examined him in his consultating rooms.

At this point it may seem that Pope's satire on education is a poetic
correlative of Locke's prose philosophy, but this position presents insurmount-
able hurdles. For one thing, Pope nowhere explains to us what he thinks of
Locke's *Thoughts*, and, as I have already suggested, there is no evidence that he
ever read it, though it is inconceivable that he would not have heard about its
contents, just as it is unimaginable in our century that well-read poets like
Joyce and Lawrence should not have heard about Freud's *Civilization and its
discontents*. Locke appears, of course, in *The Dunciad*, just as he had in *An Essay on
Man*, although the interpretation that should be given to these appearances
remains unclear. Though *both* Locke and Pope refer to Franco Burgersdijk, the
Dutch philosopher who had written Latin textbooks on Aristotelian logic of
precisely the type Locke objected to in the *Thoughts* and Pope derided in Book
IV ('Each fierce Logician, still expelling Locke, / Came whip and spur, and
dash'd thro' thin and thick / On German Crousaz, and Dutch Burgersdyck',
TE v, p. 361), no one should claim that Locke's *Thoughts* was Pope's source for
this passage. Locke had already appeared in Book III in the company of other
geniuses: Bacon, Milton, and Newton. Now, in our satire on miseducation, he
reappears in the assembly at Oxford, where 'Each fierce Logician, still expelling Locke' responds to the Goddess' call to establish a reign of dulness at the

---

[32] Axtell, p. 355; Locke's opinion of poetry and wit, like Plato's, coloured his view against
'children's making Latin themes at school'; see Axtell, p. 355 and Locke's *Letters to Edward
Clarke on education, 1684–91*, in Axtell, pp. 341–91.

British universities. To annotate this line, Pope or Warburton (or perhaps both in collaboration) wrote: 'In the year 1703 there was a meeting of the heads of the University of Oxford to censure Mr. Locke's *Essay on Human Understanding*, and to forbid the reading it.' But Warton, who had intermittently been at Oxford between 1703 and 1742 and who may have remembered the trials, later lamented: 'Whatever might have been the case in the year 1703, certain I am that Locke's *Essay* has [*sic*] been universally read and recommended at Oxford for above fifty years past.'[33]

Whether read or not does not solve our dilemma about Pope and Locke. Moreover, the point of this discussion does not rest on Locke's *Essay* but on his *Thoughts on education*, and Pope's attitude to the magisterial reforms it offered remains unclear.[34] It is certainly possible, after all, that Pope's notions of reform derived from his own experience of frustration at school and were therefore the product of his own invention: the results of an extreme outrage that increased as he grew older. Likewise, he may have read Locke's *Thoughts* without attributing these ideas of reform to him, or merely heard about them. If it can more or less be assumed, as Mack contends in his biography, that Pope's lively reading imagination was thwarted at school, this historical fact in itself does not automatically align him with Locke, or make of him a disciple, tempting as it is to think he was. On balance there simply is not enough evidence to justify the contention, not even any biographical evidence, that Pope knew which ideas of reform were specifically Locke's and which were only tangentially associated with him. Ultimately, then, it is impossible for us to know if Pope was influenced by Locke or adopted a pro-Lockian position by merely reading Pope's satire. But if one temporarily abandons empirical scholarship and speculates about the meeting of these two minds, so to speak, it is hard to overlook the similarities. Pope's view of education (Warburton's view is another matter, as we shall see) was probably identical with that of the outraged narrator of Book IV. It resembles Locke's in so far as both men considered morphic wisdom – the wisdom of the memory – to be the anatomical brain's dull child, the pedant's tool. Despite the tendency of contemporary scholars to view Pope and Locke – like wit and judgment – as antithetical thinkers, and while admitting that no direct influence is known, Pope nevertheless aligns himself with Locke in Book IV in the matter of educational reform. It is probably going too far to suggest that Pope also allied himself – for personal reasons – with the underdog: not with the biographical Locke who was, of course, no outsider, but with the image of Locke as iconoclast during

[33] See J. Warton, *The works of Alexander Pope*, 10 vols. (London, 1806), v, p. 282. If Warton is correct in his 'above fifty years', the date would be *c.* 1747, perhaps too late for Pope to have used this information in his and Warburton's notes.

[34] Axtell does not treat the responses to Locke's *Thoughts* after 1700, but some sense of the antipathy to these radical views is gained in R. Ashcraft, *John Locke* (Princeton, 1986) and F. Rudolph (ed.), *Essays on education in the early republic* (Cambridge, Mass., 1965). For Locke among Pope's books, see M. Mack, 'Pope's reading', in M. E. Novak (ed.), *Literature in the age of disguise* (Berkeley and Los Angeles, 1972), pp. 215, 219.

Pope's adulthood. So far as Pope's collaborator Warburton was concerned, Locke may as well have remained an outsider, religious traitor that he still appeared to be as late as the 1730s, but a strong case would have to be mounted to demonstrate that Locke (dead since 1704) continued to symbolize an alien vision then. Even so, biographical similarities within obvious difference could not have eluded the perspicacious Pope who noticed details like these, no matter how little he actually knew about Locke's *Thoughts*. England did not recognize either man until late in life – indeed both were exiles of a type: Locke the radical exile who literally had to flee his country to become a philosopher, Pope the Catholic cripple–poet who, no matter how close he came to England's intellectual and social nerve-centres, never felt he belonged. In this sense both men shared symbolic ground with Bolingbroke, Pope's former mentor (former to Pope's publication of Book iv) and the philosopher behind *An Essay on Man*, as it were, who fled to France shortly before Pope composed his diatribe against English education.

Bolingbroke contra Warburton

Bolingbroke's view of education fundamentally differed from Locke's.[35] He could agree with Locke about the pedantry of the schools and the futility of teaching words without things, but he continued to see history and the past as the most important subject to teach *sine qua non*. This place of privilege endures in all his works: from his *Remarks on the history of England* published in *The Craftsman* in 1730–1, to his *Letters on the study and use of history* which he composed in 1735 and gave to Pope in manuscript. A similar view extolling history is found in *The idea of a patriot king*, which Pope almost certainly read before publishing Book iv in March 1742. Despite similarities with Locke's views (for example, endorsement of the Lockian notion that the study of geometry enables students to carry through 'long trains of ideas' and develop the ability to penetrate through sophisms),[36] Bolingbroke's epistemology and psychology of education was fundamentally different. An advocate of discipline, he did not construe education or the knowledge it produced as the offspring of pleasure and liberty. Like Pope, he had spent the first ten years of his life in the company of women who nurtured and educated him, thereby sparing him the tortures of an English public school. One wonders if the two friends ruminated

---

[35] Here my discussion owes much to: B. S. Hammond, *Pope and Bolingbroke: a study of friendship and influence* (Columbia, Missouri, 1984); I have also made use of B. Goldgar, *Walpole and the wits: the relation of politics to literature, 1722–1742* (Lincoln, 1976); S. Varey, 'The craftsman 1726–1752: a historical and critical account' (1976 Cambridge Ph.D. thesis) and his *Henry St. John, Viscount Bolingbroke* (Boston, 1984); H. T. Dickinson *Bolingbroke* (London, 1970); J. P. Hart, *Viscount Bolingbroke: Tory humanist* (Toronto, 1965). The facts of Bolingbroke's education remain dubious, as virtually all his modern biographers have observed, without any authoritative evidence that he attended Eton or Christ Church. For the role of history in education c. 1700–50 more generally, see John Vance, *Johnson and history* (Athens, Georgia 1984).

[36] H. Bolingbroke, *Letters on the study and use of history*, 2 vols (London, 1752), I, p. 66.

about these similarities of their childhood in the heyday of their intimacy, especially during the long periods early in the 1730s which Pope spent at Dawley, Bolingbroke's farm in the country. Whether or not they did, by the time Pope wrote the original *Dunciad* in 1728, not to mention Book IV almost fifteen years later, he could predict Bolingbroke's response to a crucial subject like education. In summary, Bolingbroke, like Locke, saw the need for the reform of the schools, but was too much of an ancient to tamper with their books and curricula, which formed the heart and nerves of this educational system.

Yet by 1740 his influence on Pope had diminished, and the question we must ask in relation to Book IV and Pope's view of education is what replaced it. Carretta has assembled a number of quotations explicating how Bolingbroke construed 'political miseducation' (Carretta, pp. 159–61). This elaboration amounts to a pastiche of ideas about the past and present culled from Bolingbroke's works, starting as early as the columns on history published in *The Craftsman*, and continuing through the period of opposition to Walpole at the end of the decade. No reason exists to reiterate Carretta's findings here, or to doubt that Bolingbroke, like Pope, interpreted many of England's miseries under Walpole through the metaphor of 'political miseducation'. More specifically, Carretta's view is that education (words), filiation (party) and culture (a reign of wit or dulness) enmesh themselves at a rudimentary level, and that 'the miseducation of the people is the necessary precondition for the establishment of political tyranny so essential to her [Dulness'] reign' (p. 147). But Carretta localizes and even restricts Bolingbroke's criticism of education to the Opposition: 'Bolingbroke had warned in the "Introduction" to *The Idea of a Patriot King* what would happen if the crimes of kings and ministers were not checked' (p. 159).

All this is true, but remove Walpole – so Carretta's argument suggests – and the tyrannical structure Walpole had initiated evaporates. By implication Carretta views the imaginative energies behind Pope's satire on education – indeed behind the whole of Book IV – as also originating in opposition to Walpole: 'Pope is more likely inveighing here against the allegedly tyrannical system developed by Walpole' (p. 157). Carretta acknowledges that 'the fall of Walpole in 1742 brought little change in the corrupt system he had built, and most members of the Opposition simply took whatever places they could get' (p. 159). But Pope's satire was conceived *before* Walpole fell, and no matter how closely tied to the Opposition its original thrust was, it reveals aspects entirely apart from Bolingbroke and the Opposition; aspects ranging from childhood memories to a quasi-metaphysical belief (this is why Pope continued to express interest in composing a full-blown epistle on education) that political tyranny can *only* arise when a nation's educational system has gone to ruin. For Carretta, therefore, the satire possesses nothing to universalize about or extrapolate from, all of it specifically deriving from the defects of a Whig ministry rather than a social institution (education) direly in need of reform.

By enriching Carretta's revisionism with social history, I do not intend to diminish the force of his analysis: indeed, he demonstrates his points well and adumbrates them with a discussion of the allegorical iconographic and emblematic dimensions of Book IV. But he demonstrates little awareness that Pope has seen Walpole's tyranny filter down to an essential social institution: primary and secondary education; and displays no desire to lift Pope, so to speak, out of his time and view his satire as a general, universal commentary on education. Yet nothing less than Pope's reputation as a philosophical poet is at stake, and not merely a cosmic philosopher of 'Worlds on worlds without end', as he had been in *An Essay on Man*, but, like Locke, a philosopher of education prepared to grapple with the complex relation of the acquisition of knowledge and cultural attainment.

Given the biographical circumstances of composition in 1740–2, Pope's relation to Warburton is even more central, if more perplexing, than to Bolingbroke. Had Pope remained under the older man's wing during the composition of Book IV, the philosophical resonances underpinning the satire on education and fuelling the outraged narrator's voice might be traced, as scholars have followed them in *An Essay on Man*, to Pope's Lucretian-like guide. But Bolingbroke was continually in France from 1735 to 1744, except for brief visits to England at the end of the period to settle his father's estate and tend to his own affairs. Pope still read whatever he wrote, and in 1740 privately printed *The Patriot King*, but the relation of the friends had cooled down, as observers could see. The reasons for this gradual distancing are myriad, and have been ably narrated at booklength by Brean Hammond.[37] They include Pope's sense (easy for him to justify because he could so readily feel aggrieved) that in some profound way Bolingbroke had betrayed him, and that his philosophical views – including his sense of history and its implications for any theory of education – should also be abjured. Yet friendship and influence are always reciprocal interchanges, as Professor Mack emphasizes,

[37] Hammond, *Pope and Bolingbroke*, especially pp. 105–9. Maynard Mack provides a different account of Pope's relation to, and separation from, Bolingbroke in his recent biography, *Pope: a life*, pp. 746–52, and observes (p. 921) that Hammond's 'argument would be more persuasive if it took into account the fact that influence between two friends is a two-way street'. It may be, though, that the Mack who underestimated Bolingbroke's influence on Pope in his *TE* of *An Essay on Man* (1950) also underestimates the consequences of the breaking away of Pope and Bolingbroke for *The New Dunciad*. The point is not merely that by breaking away Pope opened himself up to a void he would have to fill with another adviser (Warburton), but rather that in some crucial ways, and not merely in the satire on education, Book IV represents the antidote to *An Essay on Man*. No longer interested in mediating between miracles and revealed religion, Pope turns away from the metaphysical dilemma (except in the famous passage about those who 'nobly take the high Priori Road') and confronts mundane reality – those real social places where 'Senates and Courts with Greek and Latin rule, / And turn the Council to a Grammar School!' (*TE* v, p. 359, ll. 179–80). For Pope's relation to older men generally – from Henry Cromwell and William Wycherley to Bolingbroke and Warburton – see Carol Flynn, 'A softer man', *South Atlantic Quarterly* 84 (Winter 1985), 51–62 and G. S. Rousseau, 'Threshold and explanation: the social anthropologist and the critic of eighteenth-century literature', *The Eighteenth Century* 22 (1981), 127–52.

and no one should minimize the toll this rejection by Pope took on Bolingbroke. 'Pope and Bolingbroke', Hammond astutely comments, 'certainly did
not come to open rupture in the poet's lifetime. Indeed, Bolingbroke's behaviour during his friend's last illness [in 1744] is an ennobling testament to
the strength of this intricate bond' (p. 108). It was indeed, but, as Hammond
observes, the dissolution of their intimacy nevertheless took its course:

> . . . in truth, Pope had been weaning himself away from Bolingbroke's influence over a
> period of some years, at first through the acclaim given by the Patriots to his poems and
> the subsequent status he carved out for himself with that group – a status greater than
> Bolingbroke's own . . . As far as religion and philosophy are concerned, Pope was by
> 1738 quite ready to have his beliefs replaced on the shelf of orthodoxy. The *Epistle to
> Bolingbroke* further indicates the respects in which Pope felt confused and disappointed
> by Bolingbroke's counsel.

This estimate may be psychologically astute but does not tally with Pope's
stand in the satire on education, where he hardly adopts ideas (Warburtonian
or otherwise) from 'the shelf of orthodoxy'. As we have seen, Pope's views in
the satire are anything *but* orthodox, and resemble Locke's notions rather than
Bolingbroke's, or – as we shall soon see – Bolingbroke's replacement, Warburton. For Hammond, the period immediately after the composition and publication of the *Epistle to Bolingbroke* (1737) marks a break: after 1738 Pope set
out, whether consciously or not, on a new course apart from his former friend.
Bolingbroke's jealousy – this line of reasoning continues – was that Pope had
become the more influential political figure by 1739, and Hammond notices
how Pope's associates among the Patriots, especially Pulteney and Lyttelton,
continued to warn him that Bolingbroke must not return to England lest the
Opposition be ruined by his interference.[38] Among Bolingbroke's various
disappointments during his exile in France were his diminishing influence
among the Patriots and shrinking national popularity, and it must have
pained him that the poet he had idolized could veer from him now, not only by
abjuring his deistical tendencies, but by failing to encourage him to return to
England. Betrayal – if Hammond is right to conceive of the reciprocal cooling
off as betrayal – was thus sensed by both parties for different reasons. Had
Pope rejected Bolingbroke, his response may have been less anguished: in that
case all was lost, the act irrevocable. Yet Pope's slow dissociation from his
influence (political, philosophical, religious) served as a constant reminder of
the ways they had once assimilated each other's ideas, and this rift is not at all
irrelevant for the satire on education.

The implications of this argument are subtle and have terrific impact on
Pope's last major poem. They involve a psychological process that extended
over a number of years and within a context of kinship that is not easily
reduced to neat patterns. It may be that Hammond has read too much into the

---

[38] If Pulteney and Lyttelton held attitudes to education, their writings do not reveal it; see R. J.
Phillimore, *Memoirs and correspondence of George, Lord Lyttelton* (London, 1845).

evolution of Pope's 'weaning himself away' from the father figure, the philosopher king. But neither the dynamics of the process nor the complexity of the *dramatis personae* diminishes the *effect* of Bolingbroke's lost influence. If Hammond's 'breaking away' can be explained in a number of ways, the effect itself remains unassailable. Yet however it is justified, the fact remains that by 1740–1 Warburton had replaced Bolingbroke, having cultivated Pope and quickly realizing what a boon for his career this association could be. 'Just as Pope's friendship among the Patriots,' Hammond notes, 'and the greater self-reliance he drew from them rendered him more critical of Bolingbroke's expertise, his friendship with Warburton introduced him to a system of philosophy that was far removed from Bolingbroke's' (p. 106). More orthodox in matters theological, it also leaned less towards abstract deistical inclinations. Likewise it accommodated the urgency of current affairs and turned away from purely speculative matters in a way Pope had been incapable of before his association with the Patriots of the Opposition. This veering, exclusive of its psychological implications, was consequential for the satire on education, and accounts in part for Pope's 1739 remark to Spence just before his (Pope's) death about having hoped to expand the material on education.[39] *The New Dunciad* of 1742 shows Pope with a mind and heart of his own: abjuring one man's influence (Bolingbroke), adopting another's (Warburton), while launching out on a subject (education) about which he had held the strongest views since early manhood. For all these reasons it will not do to pretend that the satire on education could have been a satire on *anything*, or that Pope is merely versifying what Warburton instructed him to. Neither Bolingbroke nor Warburton was so disturbed by the conditions of English education as the outraged narrator of Book IV. Besides, neither had the imagination to understand how English education had become the visible symbol of the fallen *logos* in a clearly postlapsarian world. 'In the pale of words unto death' indeed.

Furthermore, as Pope had grown disenchanted after 1738 with the ethical integrity of many of his political colleagues in the Opposition, so he had come to recognize that a chaotic social structure, especially a flawed system of national education, literally prepared the way for (not merely permitted) Walpole's corruption. The images of the dunces marching on paved roads and byways, pacing down cemented avenues and lanes, attest to this preparation, particularly when following their bandleader Bentley:

> Before them march'd that awful Aristarch;
> Plow'd was his front with many a deep Remark . . .
> Full in the midst of Euclid dip at once,
> And petrify a Genius to a Dunce:
> Or set on Metaphysic ground to prance,

---

[39] Spence, I, pp. 132–4, 151 and Osborn's index entry on 'education' (II, p. 880); see also I, pp. 13–14, for Pope's opposition to the teaching of words alone. For Pope to Warburton, 28 December 1742, see *Correspondence*, IV, p. 434.

> Show all his paces, not a step advance . . .
> All Classic learning lost on Classic ground;
> And last turn'd *Air*, the Echo of a Sound.
>
> (*TE*, v, pp. 362, 369–70, 374, ll. 203–4, 263–6, 321–2)

But Walpole had not caused the schools to decline: they had been decaying long before his ascent – so the satire is not to be interpreted merely in its local context. For Pope, it was not at all fortuitous that the schools (and by implication the Reign of Dulness they helped instigate) had bottomed out during Walpole's term of office, and the more that Warburton replaced Bolingbroke in Pope's sensibility, the more flawed this social institution of education appeared to be. Pope's well-known and often quoted gratitude, and the reliance on Warburton Pope developed while sequestered with him at Prior Park during the composition of Book iv, must be viewed in the light of these rearrangements:

> The Encouragement you gave me to add the fourth book, first determin me to do so: & the Approbation you seemd to give it, was what singly determind me to print it. Since that, your Notes, & your Discourse in the Name of Aristarchus, have given its Last Finishings & Ornaments.
>
> (*Correspondence* iv, p. 434, Pope to Warburton, 28 December 1742)

The hostile relation of Bolingbroke and Warburton helped nothing. They disliked each other in print, perhaps never even having met, and a decade after Pope's death Warburton was still expending time and energy compiling the case against Bolingbroke's various 'heresies': a weighty two-volume critique of *Lord Bolingbroke's philosophy; in four epistles to a friend* (Hammond, p. 108). The ins and outs of this animus need not concern us here; besides, both Mack and Hammond have documented it (*Pope: a life*, pp. 746–52; Hammond, pp. 105–9). But in the primary literature it is amplified in Pope's correspondence and Spence's anecdotes, as well as in Ruffhead's biography (which Warburton supervised), and after Pope's death in the fuss made over the surreptitious printing of *The Patriot King* and the 'Atossa' affair.[40] In all these paper scuffles and terminal acts of despair on both sides, there is a genuine sense in which Bolingbroke's actions amounted to an attack on the dead Pope, and the more Warburton defended the integrity of the deceased poet, the more vigorously the bitter and defeated sexagenarian Bolingbroke struck back.[41]

By 1741–2, when Pope was composing the *New Dunciad*, an increasingly influential Warburton supervised aspects of the project. As Pope reiterated in

---

[40] *Pope: a life*, pp. 749–52, quotes the full repertoire of secondary scholarship; Hammond, pp. 108–9, 174.

[41] A flurry of exchanges occurred in 1745–6, 1749 and 1754–5; for example, Warburton's *Apology for the late Mr Pope; on occasion of the editor's preface to . . . the spirit of patriotism* (1749) and his *Letter to the editor of the letters on the spirit of patriotism . . .* (1749); then Bolingbroke's reply *To the author of a libel . . .* (1749); Bolingbroke was dead by the time John Leland published *Reflections . . . on Bolingbroke's letters on the study and use of history* (1753) and when Warburton published his massive two-volume attack (*A view of Lord Bolingbroke's philosophy*) in 1754–5.

his letters, Warburton had 'encouraged' the scheme for the satire on education, but he neither invented nor imagined it. The germ of the idea and the
poetic correlative it would take remained entirely Pope's own creation, and
antedated his meeting with Warburton. Warburton, admittedly, provided
information for the notes and solid ammunition against the Aristarchan
professors and pedants – the Busbys and Bentleys – particularly, as Pope
indicates in his letter of 28 December 1742, for the 'Discourse in the Name of
Aristarchus'.[42] And Warburton undoubtedly seasoned the parodic, if prolix,
notes by flavouring them with the salt and pepper of exegetical scholarship,
especially the lingering Ancients–Moderns controversy, a quarrel that had
hardly terminated by the time Pope was composing the *New Dunciad* and one in
which the ambitious *parvenu* Warburton was steeped.[43] In this connection it
would be interesting to know whether Pope or Warburton, or both writing in
collaboration, penned this significant note typically signed 'P. W.' Appended
to the description of 'Silenus' ridiculing Thomas Gordon, the translator of
Tacitus, and demonstrating how he enslaved his students 'First . . . to Words,
then vassal to a Name, / Then dupe to Party; child and man the same', the note
explains the links between education and corrupt government, as well as
suggests concrete targets:

A Recapitulation of the whole Course of Modern Education describ'd in this book,
which confines Youth to the study of *Words* only in Schools, subjects them to the
authority of *Systems* in the Universities, and deludes them with the names of *Party-
distinctions* in the World. All equally concurring to narrow the Understanding, and
establish Slavery and Error in Literature, Philosophy, and Politics. The whole finished

---

[42] Warburton's contribution to the portrait of 'Aristarchus' (Bentley) in Book IV appears in the
notes signed 'W' or 'P. W.' and included information about Bentley and Trinity College, the
schools at Cambridge and Oxford, as well as the 'blind old Scholiasts' of line 232 (*TE* v, p. 365)
who had debated matters grammatical, linguistic and textual, Warton believed that Warburton inserted couplets into the passage at Pope's request, but Warton 'could not vouch for the
truth of the assertion' (*TE* v, p. 376).

[43] A. W. Evans, *Warburton and the Warburtonians* (Oxford, 1932), pp. 18–19, 88–93. Warburton and
Bentley had been enemies ever since Warburton attacked him in 1738 in *The divine legation of
Moses* for his views on the spuriousness of the *Epistles to Phalaris*, and Bentley is known to have
cast the gravest doubts on Warburton's abilities as a scholar–editor (see Evans, p. 18). But
unlike other verbal critics, Warburton had somehow spared Bentley's edition of Horace
(1711). Richard Johnson, typical of the pedantic grammarian-type despised by Pope and the
legally-insane headmaster of the Nottingham Free School from 1707 to 1721 (when he drowned
himself in a lake), pounced on Bentley's *Horace* in *Aristarchus Anti-Bentleianus: Quadranginta Sex
Bentleii Errores super Q. Horatii Flacci* (Nottingham, 1717). It would be interesting to learn if
Warburton read this attack on Bentley before composing his own 'Ricardus Aristarchus. Of the
hero of the poem', prefacing Book IV, which would have delighted him for attacking Bentley so
ferociously. But no mention of Richard Johnson or his *Aristarchus* seems to have been picked up
by Warburton or Pope in the notes to *The New Dunciad*. And Gilbert Wakefield, with whom both
Pope and Warburton corresponded, and who considered Johnson's *Aristarchus* to be 'a spear
launched against the buckler of Neoptolemus', apparently did not tell them about its existence;
see G. Wakefield, *Memoirs, written by himself* (London, 1792), p. 95. See also R. C. Jebb, *Bentley*
(London, 1882), p. 134 and R. J. White, *Dr Bentley* (London, 1965).

in modern Free-thinking; the completion of whatever is vain, wrong, and destructive to the happiness of mankind, as it establishes *Self-love* for the sole Principle of Action.

(*TE* v, p. 391)

The milieu of education and the later eighteenth century

Emrys Jones has written that '*The Dunciad* is both a work of art and something else: it is, or was, an historical event, a part of literary and social history, an episode in the life of Pope as well as in those of his enemies.'[44] It is a shrewd estimate, particularly its perception that Pope's great lampoon was something more than another poem and that it somehow measured and then turned the tide of English culture in the 1740s. The reception of the sprawling work in four books (1743) was mixed, as its critical heritage shows and as most Pope scholars know.[45] More significantly for our story, the satire on education was as responsible as any other part of the Pope–Warburtonian sprawl for the sense that something urgent had to be done to improve the state of English education. But amelioration would not come easily to a nation already sunk into such a wretched state of cultural ruin, where '*Art* after *Art* goes out, and all is Night'. In this sense, *The New Dunciad* of 1742 had served the muse of satire well by attending to her goals of improvement and reformation, and one could rephrase Jones to say that if the satire on education was a literary achievement, it was something else as well: a moment in the history of Western education. To have achieved this was no mean feat for a poet whose name was already synonymous, by 1740, with Enlightenment, as international scholars as diverse as Leibniz, Voltaire and Crousaz would have been the first to attest no matter what their view of Pope's country or its role in international politics.

Yet the English schoolmasters seem not to have heeded any of Pope's advice. By approximately 1750, just as the Bolingbroke–Warburton attacks were subsiding, the schools were not improving. Except in the dissenting academies, Locke's innovations had been overlooked or repudiated, and the universities were still sunk, as Gibbon would later claim, in the masters' 'dull and deep potations'.[46] Years later, when writing his memoirs, Gibbon presented a more balanced picture of the schools and universities, especially those of his own education, but he still had to confess that 'our seminaries of learning do not exactly correspond with the precept of a Spartan king "that the child should be instructed in the arts which will be useful to the man," since a finished scholar may emerge from the head of Westminster or Eton in total ignorance of the business and conversation of English gentlemen in the latter end of the eighteenth century'. And all the good Gibbon could remember was that they taught the Greek and Latin 'they pretended to teach'. When William

---

[44] See Emrys Jones, 'Pope and dullness', *Proceedings of the British Academy*, 54 (1968), 231.

[45] See John Barnard (ed.), *Pope: the critical heritage* (London, 1973), pp. 474–5.

[46] B. Radice (ed.), *Edward Gibbon – memoirs of my life* (London, 1971), pp. 80 and 69 for these passages.

Cowper – the poet – enrolled at Westminster in 1741, he found under John Nicoll's mastership all the drudgery and misery described by Pope as belonging to the bloodthirsty Aristarchus, and would write at length about his torture later on. Throughout this time the cry that education and politics were inextricably mixed continued. 'An unhappy Ambition reigns at present among Parents', the anonymous author of 'Modern Good Breeding destructive to Good Manners' complained in the weekly press as Walpole's government was tottering.[47] The ambition was 'to educate their Children in too much Knowledge and Politeness. Laying aside *Political* Reasons our good Breeding in England has introduced such a Corruption that it were to be heartily wish'd that we had less Manners and more Virtue.' The lament endured: for years the *Universal Spectator* – led by an Opposition group – deplored the methods of rote employed by educators under his regime, particularly the inculcation of the Classics without clear emphasis of their Christian virtues, as in its series of 'Persian Letters' in which 'Selim writes to his Friend Mirza on this Subject [Education].'[48]

The repeated charge was that students were taught to memorize and pronounce words, but had little comprehension of what they meant. In one of the 'Persian Letters,' Selim encounters a 'Clergyman' who presides over the education 'of several young Noblemen' (*The Gentleman's Magazine*, p. 250). They debate the clergyman's methods; Selim is appalled to discover that English history, government, and constitution have all been omitted. 'Well,' Selim exclaims acerbically, 'You at least instruct your Scholars in Grecian and Roman Virtue, You light up in them a Spirit of Liberty.' The tutor–cleric remains silent, but a member of the company – who presumably sees what this clergyman, and Pope's 'Kuster, Burman, and Wase' never could – explains:

The natural Vigour of their [the students'] Spirits is restrained; the natural Ingenuity of their Tempers varnished over; the natural Bent of their Genius curbed and thwarted: the whole Purpose of their Education is to acquire some *Greek* and *Latin* Words . . . if they are backward in this, they are pronounced Dunces, and often made so from Discouragement and Despair.

The charge was widespread in the realm, its brunt falling on private tutors and clergymen, as well as masters in public and private schools. Their response to *The New Dunciad*, unwritten or undiscovered, is the one we would like to have, especially a record of the shock and revulsion they must have experienced when reading the indictment Pope and his tutorlike Warburton had compiled against them. Only the dissenting academies (flourishing by the time Pope wrote Book IV), whose methods heeded Locke's quasi-hedonistic pragmatism and taught a more useful programme that emphasized science

[47] *Universal Spectator*, 8 March 1740, rep. in *The Gentleman's Magazine* 10 (March, 1740), 115.
[48] *Universal Spectator*, 6 May 1738, rep. in *The Gentleman's Magazine*, 8 (May, 1738), 250–1.

over classics, things over words, were spared the scalpel of Pope's ignominy.[49] Their methods minimized memory and recitation, and emphasized the sciences of arithmetic and geometry over Greek and Latin. Practical subjects were crucial for progress, as Priestley later noted when composing his own *Liberal education for civil and active life*.[50] It is perfidious to generalize about an institution as diverse as the dissenting academies and public schools, but one generality will probably hold up: their students, originating in less affluent circumstances than those of the public schools, appreciated their education more, and demanded more from their masters than boys at Pope's Westminster and Oxbridge. Pope, recognizing how well they had coped with the perennial *res/verba* problem, had known better than to include them in his onslaught against the schools.

After 1742, when the Pelham–Newcastle ministry filled the vacancy created by Walpole, this state of affairs *vis-à-vis* education altered rather little, as commentators from different backgrounds noted, or, at least, the perception of status quo continued. Thomas Gray and his constant correspondent Gilbert West were among the first readers of the *New Dunciad* when it appeared in March 1742. West particularly endorsed the 'justice' of the satire on education; Gray also deemed it 'as fine as anything [Pope] has written', except for 'the Metaphysicians part'[51] – which may refer to the passage about 'Metaphysic smokes involve the pole' (lines 248 ff.) or the famous section on 'the high Priori Road' (lines 471ff.). Six years later, in 1748, Gray remained inspired by Pope's poem and wrote a 'Hymn to Ignorance', which Roger Lonsdale, Gray's most recent editor, believes originated in Gray's reading of Book IV, and three years after that, he composed yet another poetic fragment on the subject called *The alliance of education and government*. The hymn – also a fragment – tries to dignify the sentiment Pope had excoriated:

> Oh! sacred Age! Oh! times for ever lost!
> (The schoolman's glory, and the churchman's boast.)
> For ever gone – yet still to Fancy new,
> Her rapid wings the transient sane pursue,
> And bring the buried ages back to view.

Then, in 1751, West, who had by now versified the gardens at Stowe, composed an imitation of Spenser lamenting that the landed rich were receiving no education at all, certainly not at university, but wasted away instead 'in

---

49 For the dissenters' methods see: I. Parker, *Dissenting academies in England* (Cambridge, 1914); H. McLachlan, *English education under the Test Acts: being the history of the non-conformist academies 1662–1820* (Manchester, 1931); J. W. A. Smith, *The birth of modern education; the contribution of the dissenting academies* (London, 1954).

50 Priestley's *Liberal education for civil and active life* (1765) demonstrates how far his views were from the traditionalists.

51 See P. Toynbee and L. Whibley (eds.), *Correspondence of Thomas Gray*, 3 vols. (Oxford, 1935), I, pp. 188–95; Thomas Gray, *An alliance of education and government. A fragment* (1748–9) and 'Hymn to Ignorance', both in R. Lonsdale (ed.), *The poems of Gray, Collins, and Goldsmith* (London, 1969), pp. 85–99, 77.

studious Shades their fruitless Hours', as West himself had observed at Christ Church under Freind, 'with fond Indulgence led / By *hireling* and in all Depths sustain'd'.[52]

A much more vituperative document, over a hundred pages long, appeared a year earlier, in 1750, from the pen of an obscure 'S. Butler, a Gentleman of Bristol'.[53] This was Samuel Butler (no relation), who opened an expensive experimental school in Bristol at mid-century and hoped that his treatise, *An essay upon education, intended to shew that the common method is defective*, would call attention to his new school. Instead it caused head-on collision with local Bristol schoolmasters, who had penned their own defences of education, and amazed many of those who read it. Three years later, in 1752–3, Butler's experimental academy failed, his curriculum reform relegated to mere paper. Here, in the essay, he relied on Locke's belief that parents must take an active role in the education of their children and Addison's in the *Spectator* that teachers must be better paid. Butler portrays a national system of education tottering on chaos. Even so, the teaching of Latin remains the genuine subject of Butler's sustained attack. 'A Fondness for Latin is now become so general', he maintains, 'that almost every Boy who is intended to manage a Farm, or follow any little mechanic Profession shall be sent to a Grammar School, let what will become of that more useful Knowledge of Pounds, Shillings, and Pence' (p. 41). To a confirmed Lockian, as Butler may have been, the sheer wastefulness of this Latin system was sufficient to form his main complaint, its rote methods of memory and recitation close rival complaints. Butler believed, again following Locke and a few English reformers (Turnbull and Sheridan) who tried to put his ideas into practice, that the teaching of English language and literature was more important. It is scandalous, he exhorted his readers, that only the Bible and translations of Latin classics are read, 'so that when a Boy leaves School, we often find he acquired no greater Accomplishments than to decline a Noun, conjugate a verb, or give the Rule when it governs a Dative, an Accusative, or any other Case' (p. 49). How familiar the charge sounds, how prudent the advice at a time when the Industrial Revolution in England was beginning to make its greatest strides, and when committed system-builders like Walter Shandy must construct *Tristrapaedias* (*Tristram Shandy*, volume 5, chapter 16) to ensure that their sons receive a decent education at

[52] See Gilbert West, Esq., *Education, a poem: in two cantos. Written in imitation of the style and manner of Spenser's Fairy Queen* (London, 1751).

[53] *An essay upon education, intended to shew that the common method is defective. With a plan of a new method more extensive and of more general use in religion, morality, our own language, history, geography. . . . and that the custom of teaching dead languages when little or no advantage can be expected from them is absurd* (London, [1750]), an octavo of 115 pages, the only copy of which I have seen is in the British Library. It was neutrally reviewed in the *London Magazine* (December, 1752), p. 580, and brought Butler into conflict with William Foot, the baptist minister who had written his own *Essay on education* (1748) and John Jones, an eloquent schoolmaster in the Bristol Academy whose conventional *Steps towards an English education* (1749) differed from Butler's experimental method. I am grateful to Dr Jonathan Barry of the University of Exeter for calling my attention to Butler's Bristol connections.

home (although Sterne's readers probably interpreted the activity as comic and satiric of a system of British education already floundering in chaos, especially as Tristram outstrips the pedagogical theory). Latin – always the rote methods of inculcating Latin – exasperated Butler most, for here he glimpsed the consequences this mechanical form of instruction was having on the nation. 'A Smattering of Latin', he concludes at the end of the *Essay upon education*, 'will only make a Man a coxcomb or a Pedant, and frequently tempt him to expose his ignorance' (p. 113). It is a maxim whose truth can be documented an hundredfold in the minor English novels of the 1750s, and – at the end of the decade – in Goldsmith's 'Of education', contributed to *The Bee* on 10 November 1759, where the inadequacy of the schoolmasters rivals the inferior education that boys received in schools; and–even later in Goldsmith's writing career–in *She Stoops to Conquer*, when Mr Hardcastle comically explains why the rigours of Latin would probably kill the already sickly Tony Lumpkin.

But the teaching of Latin in the English schools – whether by rote or not – was old by the mid eighteenth century: why object to it now? It is a question that historians of education, such as those referred to above, have not often asked themselves. Walter J. Ong, the American scholar–critic, has provided a clue in his penetrating anthropological study of the teaching of Latin during the seventeenth and eighteenth centuries:

The reasons why any particular society follows the education curriculum which it does follow are always exceedingly complex. Because, in being a preparation for the future, it is inevitably a communication of what is available from past experience, education is always primarily a traffic in this experience and only secondarily a matter of theory. The theories concerning the handling of this experience never quite compass the actuality and totality of the experience itself. They are generally rationalizations, afterthoughts, however valuable or venturesome they may be under certain of their aspects.[54]

Ong's 'traffic in experience' suggests how Pope's contemporaries were also mediating between an increasingly inaccessible Roman past (many did not even *want* to access it), and an English present that strove for new knowledge as society strained under the stress of vast demographic rearrangements. Ong's argument need not be repeated here; suffice it to say that his point about 'the traffic in education' sheds light on the contexts of Pope's satire. Covering some of the ground covered by Aubrey Williams, Ong states that while 'no one bristled with educational theory more than Renaissance man' – extending the label to about 1800 – 'yet his theories never quite came to grips with everything in the pedagogical heritage'. Even the debate over Locke's reforms, occurring during Pope's maturity, demonstrates why: these theories could never cope adequately with the territories to be preserved. Yet this Latin heritage and the values it sought to preserve and protect – discipline, rigour, parts, breeding,

[54] W. J. Ong, 'Latin language study as a Renaissance puberty rite', *Studies in Philology* 56 (1959), 103 for all these passages.

moral fibre – continued to trouble diverse commentators in the aftermath of
Pope's satire. If Ong views the 'puberty rite' of Latin language study in the
ancien regime as ultimately harmful, many of Pope's contemporaries, and
obviously Pope himself, would have agreed with him. Book IV reveals why:

> 'Tis true, on Words is still our whole debate,
> Disputes of *Me* or *Te*, of *aut* or *at*,
> To sound or sink in *cano*, O or A,
> Or give up Cicero to C or K.   (*TE* v, p. 364, ll. 219–22)

The system also had positive features, and a case can be made that English
primary education (though certainly not university education) was as good as
could be found anywhere.[55] Still, the defects outweighed the strengths so many
times that it is not surprising to discover the Butlers and Thomas Sheridans of
the day complaining. Actually, they were only a few of the voices crying out in
the wilderness: Butler in 1750; in 1751 a second edition of Brokesby (discussed
above), an anonymous but nonetheless devastating indictment entitled *Free
thoughts on education*, and Smollett's satiric novel *Peregrine Pickle*, containing the
magisterial satire mounted there on Perry's boarding school and Perry as a
reckless Wykehamist. And so on down through the 1750s and 60s. The record
of this hostile tradition awaits the diligent historical scholar who wishes to
trace it year by year, and if it is not so comically negative as Pope's couplets –
which remain poetry to the end no matter how grounded in social fact – it is
nevertheless critical of the national system that had lost its credibility. Even
the panegyric historians of England – Hume, Smollett, Catharine Sawbridge
Macaulay – could not spare the disgrace of education. Mrs Macaulay, considered by Mary Wollstonecraft 'the woman of the greatest abilities this country
has ever produced,'[56] debunked its pedantry and rote learning at the end of the
Seven Years War with a ferocity worthy of her sex, believing it to have been
responsible, in part, for the war itself:

Whilst the languages of these once illustrious nations [Greece and Rome] are the
objects of attention, the divine precepts which they taught and practiced are totally
neglected [today]. From the circle of these barren studies, the school-boy is trans-
planted into the university. Here he is supposed to be initiated in every branch of
knowledge which distinguishes the man of education from the ignorant herd; but here,
as I am told and have great reason to believe, are taught doctrines little calculated to
form patriots to support and defend the privileges of the subject in this limited
monarchy.[57]

55 Further examples are provided in E. C. Mack, *Public schools and British opinion 1780–1860* (New
    York, 1939), pp. 56–65, J. W. Adamson, *A short history of education* (Cambridge, 1922), pp.
    204–41, R. H. Quick, *Essays on educational reformers* (New York, 1904).
56 Mary Wollstonecraft, *A vindication of the rights of women* (New York, 1967), p. 167. There is no
    space to discuss the female education of such figures (for example) as Mary Astell, Lady Mary
    Chudleigh, Lady Mary Wortley Montagu and others. A survey of their writings, among other
    women, would show that they harboured their own views of male education and that their
    opinions were permeated with negative criticism.
57 Catharine Macaulay, *History of England* (London, 1763), p. xiv.

Never having attended university (women could not enter Oxbridge until the nineteenth century), she relied on external sources who were monolithically critical. Otherwise Mrs Macaulay is a kind historian, but here she sees only 'barren studies' that have sunk 'this limited monarchy' into tyranny and war, and this was twenty years *after* Walpole's and Pope's opposition.

Poets throughout the ages have rebelled against their schoolmasters. It is in the nature of poets to revolt – William Cowper was no exception. He suffered as much in school as any other poet of the eighteenth century; not at Busby's school, where he was lucky enough to lean on the poet–master Vincent Bourne (whose locks the reckless boys set on fire), but at Dr Putnam's private school in Berkhamstead.[58] Here Cowper's imagination – especially his poetic fantasy – was as thwarted as Pope's reading imagination had been at Twyford. Even in the depths of depression later on, Cowper never forgot his torture there and wrote, as Gibbon did, some of the century's severest criticism of education, especially its inhumane separation of student from parents and family. Like Pope, Cowper objected to the iron methods of discipline, and – worst of all – to the widespread rote learning. A Lockian in his approach, his *Tirocinium, or a review of schools* (1784) is Popean in its sting and Wordsworthian in its anticipation of a hedonistic theory of reading. This poem contains all the charges we have heard for over a century – actually since Obadiah Walker's inquiry in the Restoration – yet slants everything towards the corruption of morality. Worse yet, Cowper charged, teachers instilled no nourishment of the sacred Christian religion:

> But conjugated verbs and nouns declined . . .
> For such is all the mental food purvey'd
> By public hackneys in the schooling trade;
> Who feed a pupil's intellect with store
> Of syntax, truly, but with little more;
> Dismiss their cares when they dismiss their flock.[59]

If the caustic narrator of *Tirocinium* approaches Pope's in *The New Dunciad*, there is nevertheless a difference: Cowper's criticism is multi-headed while Pope's centres on the folly of pedants who 'examine bits by bit,' studying parts but never seeing the whole. No friend of pedantry, Cowper continued to attack the classics on the utilitarian ground that for whole segments of the middle classes they served virtually no useful purpose. 'With respect to the Education of Boys,' he wrote to his friend William Unwin with whom he had a sustained correspondence about English education in the autumn of 1780, 'I think they are generally made to draw in Latin & Greek Trammels [confinements] too

---

[58] For Cowper as a critic of education, see E. C. Mack, *Public schools and British opinion*, pp. 59–65, and Cowper's biographers from William Hayley and Robert Southey in the early nineteenth century to Maurice Quinlan and James King in our own time.

[59] Cowper, 'Tirocinium', in H. S. Milford (ed.), *The poetical works of William Cowper* (London, 1934), pp. 242–5.

soon.'[60] Unwin had a son of school age and turned to Cowper for advice. He got shrieks about the 'debaucheries of the public schools' and exhortations about pedantic servitude to the classics. Cowper was severest on the neglect of the 'mother tongue' and the empty praise – at schools like Westminster and Eton – of merely *mechanical proficiency* in Latin: 'Not One in 50 of those who pass through Westminster & Eton, arrive at any remarkable proficiency in the . . . Mother Tongue' (p. 396). Even worse, 'there is nothing so Pedantic as the Stile of a Schoolboy,' Cowper complains, while noting that 'the same Lad that is often commended for his Latin, frequently would deserve to be whipped for his English, if the Fault were not more his Master's than his own' (p. 397). Other contemporary critics – Chesterfield, Adam Smith, Gibbon – buttressed these charges with their own experiences, and Smith, writing in *The wealth of nations* in 1776, introduced class considerations so vigorously into the discussion of education that anyone who had not consulted it before 1776, and who read his book, must have wondered how it had ever been omitted.[61]

By the 1780s, then, economic and ideological considerations entered the debate in ways unavailable to Pope. Much public opinion resembled Cowper's poetic strain: a sentimental lament for more moral instruction, as well as the nostalgic pipe-dream that schools like Westminster and Eton could replace the 'warmth and glow' of the hearth the boy had enjoyed in his father's lap. For others of a less sentimental cast, who considered themselves the educational heirs of Milton and Locke, Defoe and Adam Smith, the matter rested on entirely utilitarian footings: the devising of a system that could produce virtuous men in a well-organized nation. For yet others at the end of the century, revolution and reform were at cross purposes: what Carretta had called 'the politics of miseducation' for the earlier era, now – in the morass of the French Revolution – became the platform for a liberal education capable of transmitting the best wisdom of the French. If we surveyed public opinion after Cowper's letters to Unwin in 1780–2, we would see, as E. C. Mack did long ago (pp. 71–90), that it reduced to one or another of these categories. Vicesimus Knox, the evangelical apologist for the English public schools, painted an idyllic picture of them, but could not restrain his finger of criticism in *Liberal Education* (1781), where he mourned their failing in the moral domain.[62] One wonders whether the indictment derived from philosophical beliefs developed in adulthood, or whether Knox remembered that – in his own words uttered later in life – 'as a fag at school I had lived under a state of oppression from my schoolfellows unknown to any slave in the plantations'. And Boswell, reading and quoting Pope while writing his columns in the *London Magazine*, and perhaps remembering how Johnson had read *The Dun-*

---

[60] J. King and C. Ryskamp (eds.), *The letters and prose writings of William Cowper* (Oxford, 1979), I, p. 389. Cowper to William Unwin, 7 September 1780.

[61] E. Cannan (ed.), *Adam Smith's Wealth of Nations*, 2 vols. (London, 1950), pp. 249–73, 'Of the expence of the institutions for the education of youth'.

[62] Vicesimus Knox, *Liberal education*, 2 vols. (London, 1781).

ciad aloud to him, anticipated the whole nineteenth-century utilitarian debate about liberal education. 'I will go further', he ventured at the close of his column for November 1781, where he argued that not everyone should be subjected to the 'pedantry' and 'learned lumber' of the masters, 'for I cannot help thinking that a great deal of the metaphysical speculation [could he have had Warburton in mind?], which hath employed the ablest heads, is not only of no service to the world, but absolutely pernicious.'[63] His logic resembled the Pope he was reading: 'A man of a weak mind may be overloaded with learning, so that his faculties which might have served him very well, if left to their natural play, are buried in what Pope well expresses by "learned lumber"; for lumber it certainly must be, when not sustained by an intellect sufficiently vigorous.' A year later, in 1782, John Bettesworth and H. Fox rebelled against the Maritime School at Chelsea, started their own naval school on the principle that sailors needed to learn 'humane subjects' in addition to mathematical ones, and that no education could be called 'liberal' without the juxtaposition of both.[64] How familiar the argument sounds today, as the Harvards and MITs slug out their 'core programs'. Down to 1800, distinguished masters like Samuel Parr and Samuel Butler (who eventually became the Bishop of Lichfield and Coventry) bravely tried to transform education while responding to the monolith of criticism that had been hurled from the days of Pope and Warburton. As the century closed, Erasmus Darwin, the physician–poet, reasoned very sweetly in his *Plan for the conduct of female education in boarding schools* (1797) that if women were granted the rights of males 'to board out' this would crush the old system of harsh discipline, as the masters would be kinder to them. But the misprision of the English schoolmasters was exploded, or at least explored, when Hazlitt's grandson, W. Carew, published *Schools, schoolbooks and school masters* in 1838. Here he pungently captures what the eighteenth-century critics – the Philippses, Turnbulls, Sheridans – had been charging all along about rule and misrule under the Busby-like clergymen–pedagogues. The fact that Lily's grammar, Carew lashed out, could endure for so many centuries, was itself living 'proof of the conservative bigotry of those who so long exercised control in schoolroom and college'.[65]

Modern humanistic education

There isn't space to continue in this vein down through the nineteenth and twentieth centuries, nor is it necessary to reconstruct the impassioned rhetorics of Matthew Arnold, Irving Babbitt and I. A. Richards – three important

[63] For both quotations see Margery Bailey (ed.), *Boswell's column, being his seventy contributions to the London Magazine . . . from 1777 to 1783* (London, 1951), no. 50, 'On learning'.

[64] J. Bettesworth, *Observations on education in general, but particularly on naval education, with a plan of a naval academy* (London, 1782).

[65] W. Carew Hazlitt, *Schools, school-books, and schoolmasters: a contribution to the history of educational development in Great Britain* (London, 1888), p. 4.

thinkers – in defence of humanistic education. But let us briefly relate Pope
and his *New Dunciad* to a very recent attack on modern education (quoted in
the epigraph of this essay) by William V. Spanos, an American professor of
English literature who has now mounted one of the most sustained campaigns
against 'The Apollonian investment of modern education' to be found in a long
time (see note 1).

Spanos returns to the very root of education as a 'leading out from' (*educare*).
His assumption is that education begins *only* when its conditions permit
students to break out of the dominant paradigms of Western Civilization. He
recoils from any notion that education *preserves* the best of the past, and would
heartily disagree with Bolingbroke, Johnson and Santayana about the immense value of history (that is, the line about history being philosophy
teaching by example), unless history is construed as a synecdoche for the
continuing dialectic of the present with the past. Certain trends, Spanos
claims, have been inimical to this true education of which humanism is
patently the most culpable. 'Humanism', in fact, 'is a logocentrism that
precipitates a binary logic – Being/time, Identity/difference, Order/chaos – in
which the first term is not simply privileged over the second, but is endowed
with the authority and power to colonize the latter or to relegate it . . . to
preterition.' In this view, humanism – interpreted according to the traditions
we have surveyed above – remains the arch foe of genuine education because it
has so much to protect and preserve: 'Humanism comes to be understood as an
intellectual legitimation of the dominant economic, social, and political power
structures, which reproduces the world in its own image, i.e. assimilates and
circumscribes the Other to the central power self of Capitalistic Man' (Spanos,
(pp. 8–9). If echoes of Nietzsche and the neo-Marxists are not-so-faintly heard
here, this is because Spanos aims to locate his *logos* and 'Apollonian investment' in a fundamentally pre-Christian and pagan world view of the cosmos.
Humanism, especially Christian humanism, must be shown – according to
Spanos – to have been the logical extension of supernatural explanations
presiding over fair-minded and open-ended empirical investigations. 'The
Humanistic Tradition', Spanos assures his readers, 'is the naturalized supplement of the supernatural Tradition of the Word of God. Thus, like positivistic
science, humanistic education, despite its appeal to the disinterested "play of
mind," assumes a preordained Norm immune to the assaults of temporal
process and becomes essentially re-formist and disciplinary' (p. 16).

This brave view transcends Pope's more local concerns of rote and memory,
but incorporates the strictures and *structures* of *The New Dunciad*, particularly
their inextricable tie between the 'binary logics' of chaos and order, etc. as well
as the 'humanistic logocentrism' (to use Spanos' phrase again) that remains
the material substance of the realm Pope has vigorously rejected in his last
great poem. Furthermore, Pope's binary opposition of order and chaos – that
very global chaos the schools had enacted through their political miseducation

– directly leads to the opposition of culture and anarchy at the end of Book IV. Here is the ultimate global chaos in an ancient order composed:

> Of *Night* Primaeval, and of *Chaos* old! . . .
> Lo! thy dread Empire, C H A O S ! is restor'd;
> Light dies before thy uncreating word:
> Thy hand, great Anarch! lets the curtain fall;
> And Universal Darkness buries All.
>
> (*TE* v, p. 409, ll. 630, 653–6)

In these verses of high poetic distinction Spanos' 'binary oppositions' are pulled tightly together by the energies of night: chaos, anarchy, the fallen word. Pope's irony, sustained over hundreds of lines, can leave no reader in doubt that he has privileged, in precisely Spanos' sense, these contrary states. The point is not that Pope has prioritized day over night, light over dark, the *logos* over chaos, or that he has anticipated Nietzsche and the Dionysian Romantics of the nineteenth century (although in a palpable sense he has), but rather that Pope has erected a cosmic nightmare out of the bricks and mortar of the schools. The reverse of this position is certainly false: that in Pope's gaze evil Dionysian forces have conspired to bring about the downfall of mankind and society, as 'Art after Art goes out'.[66] Apollo's vigilant armies of reason, light, anamnesis (memory), logic, discipline – the so-called ministers of Christian humanism – had prevailed in the schools. Even so – and as Pope himself had witnessed in his lifetime – peace and stasis yielded to the misrule of dullness and chaos. More biographically, Pope's own fields of Apollonian light had darkened when, in youth, his priests and schoolmasters presided over the Dionysian meadows of his reading imagination. More historically, no social institution in Pope's culture mandated a rage for order more brutally than the schools, as the Busbys and Freinds quashed the slightest traces of anarchy among their boys in the name of 'Christian humanism'. Westminster and the court were nothing to this fierce empire of rigid reason (*un*reason would be more accurate) that then called itself 'school'. Yet anarchy had prevailed nonetheless, just as it does in the brave new world of *The New Dunciad*. By 1742, the outraged narrator of *The New Dunciad* was persuaded that night had replaced day, darkness light, chaos order, and – less symbolically – that it was folly to think any politician (a Walpole, Pelham or Newcastle) could have been capable of accomplishing all this morass in education single-handedly.

Pope's recent criticis have not usually viewed Book IV in this context, and on the few occasions when they have, it has usually been with ulterior motives in mind. Laura Brown, for example, while attempting to mount a neo-Marxist

---

[66] Comparison of *The New Dunciad* and Nietzsche's *The birth of tragedy* may appear frivolous but the two works share several common grounds that extend beyond the obvious binary opposites and binary logics to 'the birth' of an entirely new intellectual world, in Pope's case as nature and history broke down under the sway of political and ideological discontinuity, in Nietzsche's as language and structure replaced the older paradigms of nature and history.

feminist interpretation of Pope that centres on capitalism and imperialism, discovers what is essentially Spanos' 'binary logic' (although she could not have read him) everywhere in Book iv. 'Indeed', she perceptively writes, ' "CHAOS" [in Book iv] seems to have two distinct meanings: change and stasis, energy and debility, dynamism and tranquillity.'[67] This dualism of strength accorded to 'CHAOS' resembles Spanos' 'Apollonian investment', although Brown never uses these words. The one thing it does not do is privilege the former over the latter (change over stasis, energy over debility, and so forth), despite Brown's sense that Pope displays a terrific ambivalence in moving from the one to the other. Yet Brown is apparently blind to the historical and cultural underpinnings of these oppositions. She claims for Book iv that 'despite its attacks on the commodification of literary culture, *The New Dunciad* represents one of the period's most detailed expressions in poetic form of the workings of capitalist ideology, and it enacts that ideology's deepest and most essential contradiction' (p. 152). Even if it were correlative of this contradiction (which I doubt), it also embodies the contradiction in a uniquely Popean structure that *enacts* and *dramatizes* Spanos' binary logics. What Brown cannot, or will not, acknowledge is that Pope's oppositions are not merely ambivalent *responses*: they are also vigorous challenges to the privileged humanism which mercantilist ideology had come to take for granted.

This bold challenge lies at the heart of Pope's dramatic vision in *The New Dunciad*, and is of the same strange ferocity as the one he extended to England's social order when daring to damn the Howards, the first family of the realm, in the *Essay on Man* iv, 205–16, as 'the whores of Kings'. Without taking account of life in the academies and universities that were producing England's prime ministers and political leaders, no sense of the creating *logos* that is ultimately God, or the anarchic new world that is energy in *The New Dunciad*, can be gained. This achievement does not automatically transform Pope into a great philosopher of education any more than his performance in *An Essay on Man* rendered him a metaphysician of note. But for all these caveats, and despite all of Samuel Johnson's reservations about Pope's limited philosophical ability, Pope belongs to the lineage of Erasmus: not in the religious sense,[68] but in a humanistic – or perhaps more accurately *anti*-humanistic – line that extends down to Arnold, Babbitt, I. A. Richards and all those other 'new humanists' of the nineteenth and twentieth centuries whose 'binary logics' Spanos has now taken to task.

Some academic Popeans will be startled to find the traditional pieties dislodged in this way. But ultimately Pope would not have been unsympathe-

---

[67] See L. Brown, *Alexander Pope* (Oxford, 1985), p. 148. H. Weinbrot, *Studies in English Literature*, 25 (Summer 1985), p. 692 comments that Brown's 'critical mode . . . is primarily Marxist, in which Pope is either consciously or unconsciously the vehicle of a contradictory, malicious capitalism and imperialism, which he sometimes supports and sometimes deplores'.

[68] There is also much to Brean Hammond's notion that especially in the religious domain Pope is always less than genuinely Erasmian; see Hammond, *Pope and Bolingbroke* p. 145.

tic to Spanos' diatribe against 'modern humanistic inquiry and educational theory and practice'. And Pope would have commended Spanos' argument that 'the central and inviolable tenet' of this humanism is a 'disinterestedness' that attempts 'to circumscribe, contain, and comprehend the expansive play of difference in being, language, culture, and society within its orbit'. Centuries of course separate Pope and Spanos, as they do Erasmus and Arnold, Milton and Babbitt, the Restoration reformers and Richards, Locke and the critics of our contemporary education today; but for all these philosophers of education, as Spanos suggests, 'the study of the classics assures the reproduction and perpetuation of a circumscribed, inclusive, unified, and hierarchical culture at the apex of which an elite cadre presides'. Despite his own entrenchment in the classics, Pope had as much contempt for this group (whether they were the friends of Walpole or the enemies of his newly adopted favourite Warburton), as Spanos does today, and could we revive Pope today, he might concur with Spanos that 'the Apollonian investment in education renews its vigor' (Spanos, pp. 19 and 40), just as it does in *The New Dunciad*, when coming under the gun of a binary threat.

For the dominant high culture of the early eighteenth century could more easily have been found at Westminster School, and across the green in the political Westminster, than in Pope's poetic workshop at Twickenham. It requires no effort to align Pope with all those eighteenth-century, self-professed humanists, the Aristarchuses of wit, who had viewed English culture's anti-Christ as the dispenser of pagan forms of knowledge; or, as Spanos calls it, 'the emergence of difference activated by the definitive rupture of the Tradition – the decentering of the *logos* in the modern world'. Yet the opposite may have been closer to the truth. Pope may not have given his heart entirely to the camp of Dionysius, any more than he gave it to that of anarchy, but he certainly aligned himself in *The New Dunciad* with their causes as much as he does with those of their opponents. In the last analysis then, this ambivalence may be the source of the dramatic tension he senses between the forces of order and chaos, or any of the other binary logics that lead to the much wished-for anarchy. Perhaps this ambivalence was one genuine source of Pope's outrage in *The Dunciad* (it cannot have been the key to unlock the whole mystery of his outrage), or as Allen Tate tersely put it a half century ago, the source of 'the rage between his teeth'.[69]

[69] Allen Tate, *Mr Pope and other poems* (New York, 1928), 'Mr Pope', p. 1.

13

An anatomy of Pope-bashing

DONALD GREENE

The man who cannot enjoy Pope as poetry probably understands no poetry.
(T. S. Eliot)

And curses Wit and Poetry and Pope.
(*Epistle to Arbuthnot*)

I

Those of us who grew up in the first half of the twentieth century witnessed the
rescue and rehabilitation, from Victorian detraction, of much of eighteenth
century art. I remember, when I was a junior instructor in a western Canadian
university, inviting an older academic friend, an accomplished pianist, to
listen to a long-playing record – then a novelty – of some of Bach's harpsichord
music. I expected him to be, if not delighted, at any rate interested. I was
wrong: I was told that the harpsichord sounds like someone twanging the
wires of a birdcage with a toasting-fork, and that Bach's compositions are dry,
unemotional mathematical exercises, a boring display of intellectual ingenuity
typical of the Age of Reason. Indeed, most of the Bach heard at the time was in
the form of Stokowski's lush transcriptions. Handel survived in the pieties of
Messiah, but his immense operatic output was deemed beyond resuscitation
(few who heard the lugubrious 'Handel's Largo' as a church organ voluntary
were aware that it was a travesty of the delightful comic aria that opens *Serse*).
Indeed, a late-Victorian music critic lamented that although Mozart's *Marriage of Figaro* had great musical merit, the work was so obscene that it could
never again be publicly performed. It is curious that the Victorians could
denounce the eighteenth century – definitely including Pope – as being, at the
same time, aridly restrained and decorous, and shockingly libertine.

In England, lovely eighteenth-century churches were replaced by, or converted to, Victorian pseudo-Gothic. In North America (except in New England, where historical, if not aesthetic, considerations preserved the fine old
ones that followed the design of Gibbs' St Martin-in-the-Fields, an eighteenth-
century innovation) tens of thousands of newly built churches were relentlessly pseudo-Gothic (the only truly Christian architecture, Ruskin insisted,
anathematizing the paganism of such buildings as Bernini's St Peter's). The
attitude is well illustrated by this account of Bertram Mitford, who was
secretary – permanent Civil Service head – of the Office of Works in London
from 1874 to 1886, and ennobled as Baron Redesdale for his services:

He had a particular dislike for the Georgian epoch, which, he says in his essay *A Tragedy in Stone*, 'was fatal to many of our finest antiquities throughout the country. The prevailing *dearth of taste* is shown by the ruthless way in which picturesque old manor-houses of the Tudor and even earlier times were swept away by the score to make room for Grecian temples or Italian villas.' Our italics [write his descendants, Jonathan and Catherine Guinness]. The convention now is to suppose that, far from suffering a dearth of taste, the eighteenth century was precisely the most tasteful in world history. Batsford [his country seat] was to be Bertie's revenge on the period; he tore down an eighteenth-century house which prints indicate to have been not only charming but also quite big enough, and replaced it by a cheerless essay in Victorian Tudor.[1]

Clearly a manifestation of the nationalistic spirit of the late eighteenth and nineteenth centuries discussed below (p. 272): no truck or trade with the Continent; everything must be *echt*-English. It must be said, however, that Mitford did little harm in his official capacity, being too fully occupied with the huge tasks of repairing the Tower of London and (Tudor) Hampton Court to turn his hand to demolishing or remodelling the great English monuments of eighteenth-century architecture.

As for literature, the only eighteenth-century English novel I ever heard discussed during my undergraduate years, in a course on the history of the novel, was *Pamela*, which was presented as an object of ridicule. The instructor, an elderly but not unintelligent lady, concluded her summary of the plot with 'And so at last she became a *decent married woman*,' with incomparable sarcastic emphasis on the last three words. *Clarissa* was mentioned in the textbook in passing, as another forgotten and unreadable example of 'the sentimental novel,' though I was never able to see what is sentimental about a story whose plot consists of what led up to a rape, the rape itself, and the aftermath of the rape. Nor were we encouraged to explore *Tom Jones* or *Joseph Andrews*, no doubt for moral reasons. Best to dispose of them by assuming that, like most of the rest of eighteenth-century art, they were dead and never to be read again, except as historical curiosities. Deadest of all was Alexander Pope. 'Survey' anthologies included a few snippets from the *Essay on Criticism* and *Essay on Man*, in order to demonstrate, what was continually drummed into us, that the poetry (or, more accurately, verse) of 'the age of prose and reason' had been mercifully replaced, for all time, by 'Romanticism'.

Things have changed. In their tercentenary year, 1985, Bach and Handel were heard everywhere, and given full recognition as the giants they were. Peter Shaffer's *Amadeus* was immensely popular, even winning, in its screen version, the Academy Award for the best film of the year; although it involves a good deal of factual inaccuracy, it gives a fair representation of the range and delight of Mozart's music, and (perhaps its best feature) contains something of the mixture of comic frivolity and underlying seriousness, even tragedy, found in Mozart's finest work – and Pope's. *Tom Jones* and *Joseph Andrews* also became popular films, though with a fair amount of distortion (wisely, no producer has

[1] Jonathan and Catherine Guinness, *The house of Mitford* (New York, 1985), pp. 92–3.

yet tackled *Clarissa*, though what a tremendous film it could be, if handled by a producer of genius!). Modern architecture has yet to produce a Wren, Hawksmoor or Vanbrugh, though their glories began to be recognized in the 1920s by Geoffrey Scott and Sacheverell Sitwell, among others, but some might argue that its eyesores are at least no worse than the Albert Memorial and St Pancras Station; and Blenheim Palace and Castle Howard (now familiar to millions as 'Brideshead Castle') are no longer despised. Just where does Pope stand in all this?

I don't wish here to attempt another detailed survey of the tortuous history of Pope's reputation: that has been competently done by others.[2] It is true that the twentieth century has seen splendid appreciations of Pope's poetry by such critics as Geoffrey Tillotson, Maynard Mack, Reuben Brower and Aubrey Williams, and inevitably I shall be repeating points made by them. But has his reputation recovered from Victorian detraction as those of Bach and Handel, Hawksmoor and Vanbrugh, Richardson and Fielding have done?

I think not. For those who might accuse me of beating a dead horse, I give some illustrations. In 1970 F. W. Bateson delivered a paper at the annual meeting of the Modern Language Association of America entitled 'Isn't Pope overrated now?' and vigorously argued the affirmative.[3] In 1976 there appeared James Reeves' book-length onslaught on him, which, to make my task here easier, is a splendid recapitulation of most of the earlier detraction of him.[4] On a lower intellectual plane, there were such words of wisdom addressed to teachers of literature as

There have . . . been periods in the history of poetry which evolved severe and rigid conventions of form. The heroic couplet . . . was a required device of anything claiming to be a poem in eighteenth-century England. [Clearly anyone capable of writing this had little first-hand acquaintance with eighteenth-century English poetry.] . . . A poet in the eighteenth century . . . ran the risk of censorship in form as well as content. If he said anything seamy, they could get him for content; if he didn't use the heroic couplet in saying his seamy thing, they could fault him for form.[5]

This talk about mysterious authorities 'getting' poets sounds more than a little paranoid, as versions of the Victorian myth about the eighteenth century often do. Again,

The eighteenth century requirement is very unpopular with undergraduates. Traditionally, we drag them screaming through an anthology . . . from Dryden to Johnson. . . . Most students are bored stiff. A young lady once wrote for a professor at Carnegie-Mellon University:

---

[2] In particular, G. S. Rousseau, 'On reading Pope', in Peter Dixon (ed.), *Alexander Pope* ('Writers and their backgrounds') (Athens, Ohio, 1972), pp. 1–59; John Barnard (ed.), *Pope: the critical heritage* (London and Boston, 1973) (criticism up to 1782); F. W. Bateson and N. A. Joukovsky (eds.), *Alexander Pope* (Harmondsworth, 1971) ('Penguin Critical Anthologies') – the most wide-ranging of these collections; referred to below as BJ.

[3] Parts of which he includes in BJ (see pp. 20, 287, n.2).

[4] James Reeves, *The reputation and writings of Alexander Pope* (London, 1976).

[5] Anthony C. Winkler, *Poetry as system* (Illinois, 1971), pp. 103–4.

> Nothing so true as what you [the professor presumably] once let fall:
> Most English majors don't dig Pope at all.[6]

And no doubt many undergraduates don't dig Bach or Newton or Watteau or Adam Smith when they are first exposed to them and required to extend their aesthetic and intellectual horizons somewhat beyond what they are accustomed to. But generally their instructors don't begin their introduction to those subjects by denigrating them.

Still more recently, in 1982, a distinguished senior professor of German published in *PMLA* one of those wide-ranging essays in *Geistesgeschichte* from the Renaissance to the present which impress selection juries, and it was awarded the coveted prize for the best article of the year in the official journal of the Modern Language Association of America.[7] In passing, he casually dropped a remark about 'the decline of poetry in the eighteenth century'. When I ventured to say something in defence of the poetry of that century, I was harshly rebuked for my 'bad manners' in questioning a truth so universally acknowledged. And even later (1985) we have had Laura Brown's Marxist tract demonstrating that Pope was a hireling lackey, a running dog, of capitalist imperialism.[8] Nothing unusual about that of course: similar theses could be written, and probably have, about Dante, Chaucer, Shakespeare, Johnson, Wordsworth, Tennyson, Eliot, Yeats and many others. What is astounding is the short preface by Terry Eagleton, regarded as one of the more progressive, even radical, critics of his generation. It is a mish-mash of long-exploded errors about the eighteenth century which makes one wonder what it is that British sixth-formers and undergraduates are still being taught. It deserves quoting at length:

Few periods have proved so alluring to traditional English studies as the early eighteenth century. Since 'English' itself was established in the nineteenth century as a 'civilizing' discipline . . . what more natural than that it should model itself from the outset on the age of Pope, with its good sense and fine taste, its appeal to universal Reason, its passion for symmetry and stability? The ideological reading of the early

---

[6] Barrett John Mandel, *Literature and the English department* (Chicago, 1970), p. 57.

[7] Hans Eichner, 'The rise of modern science and the genesis of Romanticism', *PMLA*, 97 (January 1982), 8–30.

[8] Laura Brown, *Alexander Pope* (Oxford, 1985) ('Rereading Literature'). There have been few more preposterous misreadings of literature than that which Ms Brown gives of the conclusion of *Windsor Forest*, celebrating the Peace of Utrecht and envisioning a future in which Europe will make reparation for its brutal aggression against the natives of the New World ('Peru another race of kings behold, / And other Mexicos be roofed in gold' – lines carefully not quoted by Ms Brown). Line 400, 'And seas but join the regions they divide', reminds one of the poem's affinity with Walt Whitman's *Passage to India*, on the opening of the Suez Canal: 'All these separations and gaps shall be taken up and hook'd and link'd together, / The whole earth, this cold, impassive, voiceless earth, shall be completely justified.' Both poems enunciate the 'one world' ideal of liberals of the 1940s. According to the *Dictionary of American biography* (Supplement 3, 1941–45), Wendell Willkie's book *One world* (New York, 1943) 'sold millions of copies in a few months. His main theme was the desire of the awakening Colonial peoples to join the West in a global partnership based on economic, political and racial justice'.

eighteenth century we know as 'Augustanism,' where the world was still a fit place for gentlemen, needed of course to edit out the less palatable social realities of the time: the squalor and exploitation, the material destitution and imperialist violence, even, from time to time, the embarrassingly vituperative excesses of its most admired authors, which hardly seemed wholly compatible with literary decorum.[9]

Eagleton is mistaken. Far from 'English studies' in the nineteenth century believing that 'it should model itself from the outset on the age of Pope', it rejected that age with a shudder. If it 'edited out' from the literature of the time 'the less palatable social realities of the time', as found, say, in Smollett and Fielding, and the 'vituperative excesses' of *The Dunciad*, it did so because they were incompatible, not with its image of the eighteenth century, but with the decorum of the nineteenth, because they would bring a blush to the cheek of the Victorian young person. The age's 'good sense' and 'appeal to universal Reason' were condescendingly dismissed by Matthew Arnold, who proclaimed it 'an age of prose and reason' and condemned Pope's and Dryden's poetry, which was 'conceived and composed in their wits', whereas 'genuine poetry', such as Arnold's presumably, 'is conceived and composed in the soul'. (A nice problem: when one sits down to pen a poem, how does one tell whether it is one's wits or one's soul which is operating?) Arnold's attitude was that of many others before and after him in the nineteenth century.

The only commentator who quickly comes to mind as supporting Eagleton's postulate of the eighteenth century's appearing as 'a consolatory golden age' is George Saintsbury, whose *Peace of the Augustans* was published in 1916, a year when almost any earlier age might have seemed golden, and when Saintsbury was old, tired and disillusioned. That 'we know' the age as 'Augustan' is probably due to Saintsbury – and to various British scholars who (like H. H. Erskine-Hill, who has written a book of many hundred pages defending the age as 'Augustan'), having absorbed the term in their school days, cannot bear to give it up. The silliness of the epithet has been challenged by many, notably Howard Weinbrot, who point out that Pope in particular, among his contemporaries, despised the actual Augustan age and the tame poets who toadied to

---

[9] Brown, pp. vi–vii. It passes understanding how those who have seen the fantastic baroque variety of Wren's, Gibbs', and Hawksmoor's churches – no two steeples are alike – and the deliberately asymmetrical landscape gardening of Bridgeman, Brown, and their fellows in the great parks at Stowe, Blenheim, Chatsworth, Stourhead, and elsewhere – which are among the glories of England and set the fashion throughout the world for 'natural' landscaping – can refuse to believe the evidence of their eyes and go on repeating the hoary falsehood that 'the age of Pope' had a 'passion for symmetry', unaware that Pope was one of the chief propagandists for asymmetry. They should at least read the *Epistle to Burlington*, with its satire of landscape in which 'Grove nods at grove, each alley has a brother, / And half the platform just reflects the other' (*TE* iii, ii, p. 149, ll. 17–18). On the history of English studies of the eighteenth century, see my 'The study of eighteenth-century literature: past, present, and future', in Phillip Harth (ed.), *New approaches to eighteenth-century literature: papers from the English Institute* (New York, 1974), pp. 1–32. On 'Augustanism' see Howard Weinbrot, *Augustus Caesar in 'Augustan' England: the decline of a classical ideal* (Princeton, 1978).

the tyrant Caesar Augustus. This aberration on Eagleton's part would be unimportant were it not for his continuation:

But it was not just a question of English studies constructing a past after its own image . . . it was also a matter of its obediently reproducing the *self-image* of a minority social group in early eighteenth-century England, one equally blinded to the determining social forces of which it was the privileged product . . . At the very centre of that charmed enclave were the silver-tongued couplets of Alexander Pope which – gracefully purged of the old splenetic paroxysms – could stand as nothing less than the embodiment of Nature and Reason . . . [After Laura Brown's book] it should be less easy to mistake the patrician values of Alexander Pope – values already to some degree archaic in his own day – for the unchanging truths of the human heart.[10]

(Arnold might have written 'soul' instead of 'heart', but that word may not be in Mr Eagleton's vocabulary.)

There seems some contradiction here. If we are now discussing an eighteenth-century 'self-image' exemplified by Pope, how did the graceful purging of his splenetic paroxysms get accomplished? Pope didn't purge them – as he grew older and *The Dunciad* got longer, his denunciations of the contemporary scene grew more and more violent. It was the nineteenth, not the eighteenth, century that ungracefully purged them. Certainly Pope belonged to a minority social group – to several, in fact, but hardly privileged ones: he was the son of a small London tradesman, a cripple, a Roman Catholic incapable of admission to a university and in law denied many of the civil rights of other Britons. He despised the older literary custom of flattering the great in hope of a gratuity for a dedication or a minor government sinecure. Such silver-tongued couplets as the following hardly endeared him to leading members of the 'patrician' establishment:

> What can ennoble sots, or slaves, or cowards?
> Alas! not all the blood of all the HOWARDS –
> (*Essay on Man, TE*, III, i, p. 147, ll. 215–16)

So much for the premier dukedom of the realm, that of Norfolk, and half a dozen other peerages as well – or his characterization of the Dukes of Buccleuch, Richmond, Grafton, and St Albans, descended from Charles II's bastards, as 'sons of sons of sons of whores'. Nor did his satiric profiles of Bufo (the Earl of Halifax?) and Atossa (the Duchess of Marlborough or perhaps Buckingham?), nor his unceasing vilification of the head of the oligarchy himself, Walpole.

> Worth makes the man, and want of it the fellow;
> The rest is all but leather or prunella
> (*Essay on Man, TE*, III, i, p. 146, ll. 203–4)

he wrote, anticipating Burns' 'The rank is but the guinea's stamp; / The man's the gold for a' that'. How Pope's values can be called 'patrician' is hard to say,

---

[10] See Terry Eagleton's preface to Brown, *Alexander Pope*, pp. vi–vii.

when so many of his contemporary patricians are condemned as lacking them. Has Eagleton never *read* the *Epilogue to the Satires* or the last book of *The Dunciad*, where the whole of the 'establishment' – king, queen, prince, prime minister, all five grades of the peerage, bishops, the legal profession, Oxbridge dignitaries, headmasters of the great public schools, wealthy dilettantes, *la jeunesse dorée* – are denounced and swept away to oblivion? It would almost seem not; and the purpose of the rest of this paper is to examine some of the reasons why Pope's poetry is not read.

II

Pope's art has sometimes been compared, by perceptive readers, to Mozart's, and I should like, in a heuristic temper, to explore an analogy which may seem simple-minded, but could conceivably have useful practical consequences. This is to suggest that poetry – good poetry – is like opera, in that it appeals, or should appeal, simultaneously to a conjunction of aesthetic and intellectual senses:

1. The aural, or musical: in poetry, the flow of sheer sound – rhythm, the accord of vowels and consonants (the 'incantatory' element, as Eliot called one variety of it);
2. The visual: imagery, the 'pictures to the mind', to use Johnson's phrase;
3. The dramatic: the interplay of action and emotion among the speakers in the poem (in 'non-dramatic' poetry, the imaginary speakers, the various personae of the implied speaker and his dialogue with his audience). This may be construed as including the use of irony, at which Pope was so adept;
4. The discursive, the best word I can think of at the moment for what used to be called 'the moral': what of importance the poem as a whole is trying to convey to the reader concerning the human situation.

The application of the first three of these to opera is obvious – the musical element (the score); the visual (the *mise en scène*, costuming, stage direction, ballet); the dramatic (the words and actions of the characters). Perhaps the fourth component, the discursive, the 'lessons' of most of the familiar operas, is rightly regarded as of less significance: the course of true love never did run smooth (*Traviata, Aida*), revenge can have unpleasant consequences (*Carmen, Rigoletto*), crime doesn't pay (*Don Giovanni*), crime sometimes does pay (*Die Dreigroschenoper*), never trust an American sailor (*Madama Butterfly*). Of course these capsulizations are oversimplifications, especially of *Don Giovanni. Le Nozze di Figaro*, where Da Ponte and Mozart add nuances to Beaumarchais's fairly straightforward sermon about class warfare, and the eternally puzzling *Zauberflöte* are greater challenges. And there is always Wagner, most moralis-

tic of all, especially if one takes seriously the recent production of the *Ring* as a
tract against capitalism.[11]

My point is the simple one that readers' difficulty with Pope – and sometimes other poetry of the highest order – is their inability to respond to one or
more of these components, an inability which they are grateful to find con-
doned by such propaganda as Reeves' and Eagleton's, comforting them with
the assurance that the fault is in Pope, not themselves. To be sure, not
everyone who goes to the performance of an opera responds fully to all four of
these kinds of stimuli. Indeed, it may well be that the great majority of
opera-goers respond to few of them, but go for quite extraneous reasons:
would-be society ladies (especially, I've noted, in the provinces) to show off
their own costumes; the upwardly mobile to demonstrate that they support
'culture' in their communities; a great many fans of Pavarotti or Domingo,
Sutherland or (once) Callas, to demonstrate their loyalty to their chosen idol,
on the same kind of ego-trip that brings out tens of thousands to confirm their
identification with the Los Angeles Dodgers, the Toronto Maple Leafs or
Manchester United. When opera first reached England, even such aesthetical-
ly responsive people as Addison and Pope himself were baffled by it (though
the definition 'an exotic and irrational entertainment' has often been attributed to Johnson it is not by him). I am surely not the only one who, as a
teenager (and sometimes later), declined a friend's invitation to join in some
activity on a Saturday afternoon because I wanted to listen to the Metropolitan Opera's broadcast, and was then harangued to the effect that no one could
really *enjoy* such stuff, and that I and others who claimed to be doing so were
merely putting on an act of snobbish affectation.

James Reeves seems to have a similar conviction that current praise of Pope
is a ramp concocted by academics, chiefly American. When he finds himself
having to quote T. S. Eliot's 'Indeed it might be said in our time that the man
who cannot enjoy Pope as poetry probably understands no poetry',[12] he feels it
necessary to point out that Eliot 'as a critic began his career in the role of a kind
of extramural professor', whatever that may mean. Reeves maintains that all
'the ordinary reader' can get out of Pope is 'copybook maxims' (though even
that, now that copybooks are no longer found in schools, might be a good
thing). The only other possible enjoyment, this for the 'sophisticated critic', is
self-congratulation on recognizing the source of Pope's literary allusions – the
'capacity for reminding him of other poems'. At the conclusion of his general
discussion of Pope, Reeves proposes, in the following section of his book,
dealing with individual poems, 'Whichever of these attitudes you prefer ... to
show you what you prefer'; if you 'enjoy Pope as poetry (in Eliot's phrase), all I
can do is to show you what you enjoy' (p. 113). It would have been fascinating

[11] Of course Bernard Shaw first promulgated this thesis in *The perfect Wagnerite*, 1898.
[12] Reeves (p. 53) cites this as from 'the preface to his 1928 selection from the poems of Pound',
which I haven't seen. But I'm happy to take it on trust from Mr Reeves.

to overhear Mr Reeves explaining to Eliot just what it was that Eliot enjoyed in Pope.

One can certainly agree with Mr Reeves' statement that 'Pope, in short, is a scholar's poet', 'the admiration of trained specialist readers'. And what, one may ask, is wrong with that? Shakespeare is eminently a scholar's dramatist, and yet his plays continue to attract large audiences of 'non-scholars'. Bach is certainly a scholar's musician, although general listeners now have the opportunity to listen to his music and get much pleasure out of it. Eliot's early poems and Joyce's *Ulysses*, because of their erudite allusions and complexities of technique, were much denounced by philistine journalistic critics as incomprehensible except to scholarly pedants, yet somehow, over the years, they have become generally known and, one supposes, enjoyed. There was a time when the paintings of Turner, Van Gogh and Picasso, the architecture of Vanbrugh and Hawksmoor, would have been dismissed by the same critics as of interest only to specialists. Yet the crowds that flock to the Tate Gallery and to Blenheim and Castle Howard seem to indicate that they have provided enjoyment for others.

Granted, many of these, if they were forced to choose what to take with them to a desert island, might still pick the great poetic best-sellers of the twentieth century, Ella Wheeler Wilcox, Edgar Guest and Rod McKuen rather than Pope, Spenser, Milton or Eliot, reproductions of Norman Rockwell's *Saturday Evening Post* covers rather than of Caravaggio or Pissarro, records of Guy Lombardo or Bruce Springsteen rather than Bach and Handel. But to divide the potential audience of Pope, or any other great artist, into, on the one hand, 'specialist scholars', and, on the other, 'the ordinary reader', is too reminiscent to be comfortable of the society of Orwell's *1984*, with, on the one hand, the élite, the rulers, and, on the other, 'the proles', to be kept in intellectual and emotional subjection by being fed with sentimental slop.

A better way of making Reeves's point is Peter Dixon's statement that Pope is 'a difficult poet – subtle and complex'.[13] Of course he is: all great poetry, Dante, Chaucer, Shakespeare, Spenser, Donne, Milton, Wordsworth's *Prelude*, Tennyson's *In Memoriam*, Eliot, Yeats, Wallace Stevens, is difficult, subtle and complex, as are Bach's music and Wren's architecture. But one doesn't have to receive formal classroom instruction from a professor to get pleasure from them. True, once one senses that they can be a source of pleasure and enlightenment, one may recognize that listening to someone who has spent much of his life studying their subtleties may be able to make one aware of subtleties which one has missed, and can add further enjoyment to one's experience of them. But that the only kinds of enjoyment possible from reading Pope are those of copybook maxims and recognition of tags from earlier literature is simply not so.

---

[13] Peter Dixon, *Alexander Pope*, 1972, p. xiv.

III

To return to my analogy. The causes of current and earlier Pope-bashing seem to me to include one or more of the following:

1. Failure to respond to the aural component of poetry

In the three centuries or so since the general spread of literacy in the English-speaking world, the fact that poetry is primarily addressed to the ears has been more and more forgotten. The student nowadays casts his eye, like an optical scanner, over printed marks on a page, and 'reads', say, *The Rape of the Lock* as though it were an historical or anthropological treatise whose 'content' he has to assimilate for examination purposes. Whether he ever 'auralizes' its words is questionable (and one can silently auralize the words on a page, just as a musician can the notes in a score). The teacher who asks him to read aloud a passage from it is often shocked by the complete insensitivity to rhythm that transpires. This state of things might be corrected by the playing of records of poetry by fine performers, such as the late Dylan Thomas. Ideally, one should encounter a poem for the first time through one's ear rather than one's eye. At the very least, schools should insist on students' reading poetry aloud from the printed page, and, even better, reciting it from memory. It is not so long ago that this practice was abandoned. For some of us, the rollicking anapests of 'The Assyrian came down like a wolf on the fold', the calm dactyls of 'This is the forest primeval; the murmuring pines and the hemlocks', the rousing 'fourteeners' of 'Lars Porsena of Clusium / By the nine gods he swore / That the great house of Tarquin / Should suffer wrong no more' still ring in our ears after decades. Nor were the aural effects of prose neglected: pupils in early nineteenth-century American schools – indeed, at Eton – were encouraged to memorize and recite the great orations of Edmund Burke and Daniel Webster. No poetry has suffered more than Pope's from this neglect.

Whatever one thinks of the laudatory biographical section of Edith Sitwell's book on Pope, its final chapter, on Pope's sound effects, in spite of its flowery language, should not be overlooked by the beginning reader of Pope.[14] Auden, whose own ear was admirable, once wrote of Tennyson, 'He had the finest ear, perhaps, of any English poet.' But up there, among the half-dozen or so competitors for that title – Shakespeare, Milton, Tennyson, Hopkins, Yeats, even (at times) Wordsworth – is certainly Pope. The sheer variety of his sound effects is staggering. Tennyson, Milton, Yeats are superbly euphonious; but can any of them compete with Pope in the poetic use of cacophony: the 'enormous' opening lines of *The Dunciad*, as Sitwell calls them, 'with the thick, muffled, dull thud of the alliterating *m*'s' so evocative of Dulness:

---

[14] *Alexander Pope*, 1930 (BJ, pp. 276–81). Auden praises her work here: 'The beauties and variety of his verse have been . . . brilliantly displayed by others, notably Miss Sitwell' (BJ, p. 539).

> The Mighty Mother, and her Son, who brings
> The Smithfield Muses to the ears of Kings
>
> (*TE* v, p. 267, ll. 1–2)

and the wonderful line describing Dulness herself, in which not only the denotation but the sound of every word counts:

> Laborious, heavy, busy, bold, and blind?
>
> (*TE* v, p. 270, l. 15)

It is hard for any lecturer on Pope to resist letting his own declamatory powers loose on this, emphasizing the explosive *b*'s; or, at the end of Book One, to reproduce the crescendo of croaking in:

> Loud thunder to its bottom shook the bog,
> And the hoarse nation croak'd, 'God save King Log!'
>
> (*TE* v, p. 294, ll. 329–30)

and the mad accelerando of:

> The monkey–mimics rush discordant in;
> 'Twas chatt'ring, grinning, mouthing, jabb'ring all,
> And Noise and Norton, Brangling and Breval,
> Dennis and dissonance, and captious Art,
> And Snip-snap short, and Interruption smart,
> And Demonstration thin and –
>
> (*TE* v, p. 307, ll. 236–41)

subito lento –

> theses thick,   (l. 241)

a tempo –

> And Major, Minor, and Conclusion quick.   (l. 242)

Anyone who thinks Pope's heroic couplets 'mechanical' or 'monotonous' should simply do a scansion of first two feet of many of them, finding such frequent variants as (from the first few dozen lines of *The Rape of the Lock*) strong–strong–weak–strong ('What dire offence'); strong–weak–weak–strong ('This ev'n Belinda'); weak–weak–strong–strong (one of his favourites) ('And in soft bosoms'; 'And the press'd watch'); strong–strong–strong–strong ('Say what strange motive'), weak–weak–weak–strong ('What tho' no credit'). There is his use, pointed out by Sitwell, of the tribrach (weak–weak–weak) and the delicate short *i* to convey a pianissimo:

> And other *Mexico's* be roof'd with Gold
>
> (*TE* i, p. 192, l. 412)

(has anyone else ever demonstrated how beautifully musical a word 'Mexico' is?), and of course the frozen beauty of the couplet which Pope said was his favourite (Johnson couldn't see why, but Johnson's ear, though good, was not quite up to this. Of course Pope's poetry needs to be recited at about one-third the speed it usually is.)

> Lo where Maeotis sleeps, and hardly flows
> The freezing Tanais thro' a waste of snows.
>
> (*TE* v, p. 324, ll. 87–8)

For lush onomatopoeic use of liquid consonants, Pope could do as well as Tennyson's 'the moan of doves in immemorial elms' in:

> Die of a rose in aromatic pain?   (*TE* iii, i, p. 70, l. 200)

and

> To isles of fragrance, lily-silver'd vales . . .
> To lands of singing or of dancing slaves,
> Love-whisp'ring woods and lute-resounding waves.

There are few lines more haunting, more aphrodisiac, if one insists, in 'Romantic' poetry than these, and the effect comes less from the Tennysonian liquidity of the first and last line than from the straightforward rhythm and syntax, as well as the visual imagery, of the second. There are the solemn organ tones of the long vowels in:

> Oh stretch thy Reign, fair Peace, from Shore to Shore
>
> (*TE* i, p. 192, l. 407)

and

> Lo! thy dread Empire, CHAOS! is restor'd;
> Light dies before thy uncreating word.
>
> (*TE* v, p. 409, ll. 653–4)

There is the brilliant effect created by Pope's very rare use of a feminine ending, almost bringing the movement of the poem to a halt, at the climax of *The Rape of the Lock*:

> The meeting Points the sacred Hair dissever
> From the fair Head, for ever and for ever!
>
> (*TE* ii, p. 179, ll. 153–4)

Edith Sitwell was a practising poet. So was John Keats. Yet one wonders whether young Keats' ear had responded to such effects when he wrote the notorious passage in *Sleep and Poetry* so often quoted in histories of English literature as the definitive diagnosis of what was wrong with eighteenth-century poetry:

> Yes, a schism
> Nurtured by foppery and barbarism
> Made great Apollo blush for this his land.
> Men were thought wise who could not understand

His glories; with a puling infant's force
They swayed about upon a rocking-horse
And thought it Pegasus. . .
                    Ye were dead
To things ye knew not of – were closely wed
To musty laws lined out with wretched rule
And compass vile; so that ye taught a school
Of dolts to smooth, inlay, and clip, and fit,
Till like the certain wands of Jacob's wit,
Their verses tallied. Easy was the task:
A thousand handicraftsmen wore the mask
Of Poesy.

                    Sleep and Poetry, ll. 181–7, 193–201, (BJ, p. 190)

The rocking-horse is presumably the 'end-stopped' iambic pentameter couplet, and, though Pope is not mentioned by name, Keats does not exclude him from the category of dolts or teachers of dolts whose only concern is to smooth and clip and fit their verses in accordance with musty laws. Gosse hailed Keats' breakthrough here in introducing enjambment into his own couplet verse – 'verses in which the sense is not concluded at the end of one line or of one couplet':

In its simplest definition, then, the formular difference between the two classes or orders of English poetry is that the romantic class is of a loose and elastic kind, full of these successive overflows, while the classical is closely confined to the use of distich, that is to say, of regular couplets, within the bounds of each of which the sense is rigidly confined.[15]

Gosse goes on to ring the changes on how, from earlier 'freedom' in versification, late seventeenth- and eighteenth-century poets went on to 'trammeling themselves by a series of pedantic and artificial rules, the function of which was to reduce to a minimum the effects possible to poetic art'. Exactly what these rules were, and who prescribed them, remains vague, though their existence was an article of faith in the nineteenth century.

No doubt mediocre eighteenth-century versifiers used the couplet in unim-

---

[15] Edmund Gosse, *From Shakespeare to Pope: an inquiry into the causes and phenomena of the rise of classical poetry in England* (Cambridge, 1885; rep. New York, 1968), p. 6. This was his notorious series of Clark Lectures at Cambridge, in which his ignorance of eighteenth-century literature was so thoroughly exposed by John Churton Collins that Gosse's latest biographer devotes a whole chapter to the incident, titled 'The scandal of the year' (Ann Thwaite, *Edmund Gosse: a literary landscape* (London, 1984)). The previous year Gosse had delivered the lectures in the United States, with an amusing variant of the subtitle, 'From Shakespeare to Pope: a history of the decline of romantic poetry' (Gosse, *America: the diary of a visit, winter 1884–1885*, Robert L. Peters and David G. Halliburton (eds.) (Indiana, 1966), p. iii). For all the current disesteem for Gosse – his cousin Evelyn Waugh wrote, 'To me he epitomised all that I found ignoble in the profession of letters' (*A little learning* (London, 1964), p. 65) – he remains an important figure in the transmission of Victorian detraction of eighteenth-century poetry. He writes (p. 11), 'There is not a text-book that fails to instruct that the guarded generalities of eighteenth-century poetry were bald and insipid', and he passes on the instruction.

aginative, mechanical ways – just as mediocre poets (always the great majority) of other centuries similarly used verse forms then fashionable: in the
nineteenth century, the interminable spate of forgettable and forgotten son-
nets, the equally forgotten long blank-verse epics and unstageable tragedies.
But do Keats' and Gosse's strictures on the 'end-stopped' couplet – strictures
one still hears repeated in lecture rooms – apply to Pope? I should like to make
four points: first, the charge that 'the sense is rigidly confined' within the
bounds of each of Pope's (or Dryden's) couplets or even, as we have seen Gosse
saying, each line of them, is easily refuted by an examination of their verse;
second, that their couplet technique is the product of certain 'rules' laid down
in the late seventeenth century or thereabouts is not so; essentially the same
technique is found in the 'untrammeled' English poets of much earlier times;
third, the 'untrammeled' enjambed iambic pentameter couplet pioneered by
Keats and so highly praised by Gosse was a failure. To establish these
assertions requires extensive quotation, which I give in an appendix below.

My fourth point is that, if it were true that eighteenth-century poets were
taught to write only in discrete 'regular couplets, within the bounds of each of
which the sense is rigidly confined', Pope, Dryden, and others did not take the
instruction very seriously. Pope gives far more than a disjointed series of
two-line epigrams, a bare collection of 'copybook maxims'. It is possible,
certainly, to think of the couplet as the primary unit, the individual building
block of the whole. But only the most obtuse reader can fail to see that these are
bound together, by the use of brilliantly controlled syntax, into larger units,
verse paragraphs carefully indicated, in the originals and good modern editions, by graphic indentation. He must be aware of the existence of at least the
most obvious of these, the 'profiles', twenty or more lines long, of Atticus, Bufo,
and Sporus in the *Epistle to Dr Arbuthnot*, the great concluding perorations of the
two parts of the *Epilogue to the Satires* and of *The Dunciad*; and, when he becomes
more perceptive, he will become aware that the rest of these poems is also
organized in verse paragraphs, from which it is impossible to segregate individual couplets without disturbing the rhythm of the whole paragraph.

Moreover, notably in the four-part *Dunciad* but also on a smaller scale in the
epistles and satires, the verse paragraphs themselves are combined in ways
comparable to the movements of a sonata or even (in *The Dunciad*) a symphony. To pursue the analogy with music: in the score of, say, Beethoven's first
symphony, we begin with short melodic statements of a few measures, often
four – couplets, as it were. Then we find these combined into longer units, of
perhaps ten to forty measures, given such editorial designations in my miniature score as 'Introduction', 'Subject', 'Exposition', 'Principal Theme, Part I',
'Principal Theme, Part II', 'Subordinate Theme, Part I', 'Subordinate Theme,
Part II', 'Codetta', and the like – musical paragraphs, so to speak. Then (like
the 'scenes' in a play or opera, themselves grouped into 'acts'), these are
combined and organized to become the symphony's four 'movements' – I.

Allegro con brio, II. Andante cantabile, III. Menuetto, IV. Allegro molto e vivace. It is perhaps not too far-fetched to say that a major poem by Pope – and many major poems by other great poets – are intended to be read (or, better, listened to) thus.

To read them, as Gosse and Keats and many later critics seem to do, as a miscellaneous jumble of autonomous 'closed couplets,' is of course to miss nearly everything. When a beginning piano student is learning to play a simple piece – say, Beethoven's familiar 'Minuet in G' – he begins of course by 'getting right' a few measures at a time (couplets). He then combines these in larger units (verse paragraphs – and here the good teacher will emphasize the importance of 'phrasing,' a tactful way of indicating both the separation and connection of these larger units). Finally, these intermediate components will be merged into the three 'movements' of this simple *da capo* piece, with appropriate colouring in the way of tempo and dynamics, to make it a fully unified work. Those who read Pope a disconnected couplet at a time are like a youngster still struggling with the notes in each measure.

2. *Failure to respond to the visual component of poetry*

The reader who is deaf to the rich and subtle sound in Pope's poetry may well be blind to its wealth of visual imagery – for the same reason, that he has been firmly indoctrinated that Pope, the incarnation of the 'abstract', 'general' eighteenth century, cannot possibly furnish such concrete sensual experience.[16] Thus visualization and 'auralization' are both inhibited when the fatal word 'Pope' is spoken.

There was a time when Samuel Johnson's poetry and prose were likewise dismissed as eighteenth-century 'abstraction'. It is somewhat encouraging that in recent serious study of Johnson this myth has begun to be laid to rest, and Johnson's concern to provide in his own writing vivid 'pictures to the mind' and to praise their provision in that of others has begun to be

---

[16] The most astonishing expression of this view is found in the long wrangle that took place in the 1950s between F. W. Bateson and F. R. Leavis. Leavis had noted an affinity between a couplet of Marvell's, 'Tortur'd, besides each other part, / In a vain head and double heart', and Pope's 'Bounded by nature, narrow'd still by art, / A trifling head and a contracted heart'. Bateson denied that there could be any such affinity, since the two expressions belong to different 'social contexts': 'as Marvell used the words *head* and *heart*, the sense-impression predominated, whereas for Pope the words were primarily conceptual', and this was an instance of 'the transition from the primarily visual Renaissance to the primarily cognitive early eighteenth century'. That is, people born before 1660 or thereabouts, encountering the words 'The cat sat on the mat', formed a mental picture of a cat sitting on a mat; those born later, such as Pope, couldn't or wouldn't. On such unproven and unprovable fantasy imposing structures of literary theory have been erected. The debate is reprinted in F. R. Leavis (ed.), *A selection from Scrutiny* (Cambridge, 1968), II, pp. 280–316 – if debate it can be called: Bateson merely reiterates his dogma, offering no evidence to support it, since no such evidence exists.

recognized.[17] Long ago, Saintsbury, not the most radical of critics, was shocked by Coleridge's and Tennyson's obtuse reading of the opening couplet of *The
Vanity of Human Wishes*,

> Let Observation with extensive view
> Survey mankind from China to Peru,

as 'bombast and tautology', as saying no more than 'Let observation with
extensive observation observe mankind extensively.' Saintsbury gave them a
lesson in how to read the English language:

Observation may be either broad and sweeping, or minute and concentrated; Johnson
specifies the former kind in the last half of the first line. Observation may be directed to
men, to things, etc.; it is to mankind that he wishes it to be directed, and he says so in the
first half of the second. Further, as this is too abstract, he gives the poetic and
imaginative touch by filling the waste atlas with 'China' and 'Peru,' with the porcelain
and the pigtails, the llamas and the gold associated with those countries.[18]

Even Saintsbury here misses much of the point. China and Peru connoted to
Johnson and his readers much more than pigtails and llamas. If, like Observation (a personification of course), we survey a map of the world on the
Mercator projection with Great Britain in the centre, we see, in the northeast
corner, China, then legendary as the home of a peaceful and enlightened
civilization far superior to that of war-torn Europe, and, in the diagonally
opposite corner, Peru, scene of the ghastly atrocities committed not long before
on the unarmed natives by the Spanish invaders. The history of Pizarro's and
Cortez's exploits in the New World still appalled humane individuals like
Johnson and Pope, Swift and Voltaire. What one is expected to visualize is not
pointless detail like llamas and pigtails, but the enlightened China of Matteo
Ricci, with benevolent mandarins supervising the complex system of government examinations that enabled bright youngsters of however poor origin to
arise to administrative posts suited to their ability (*la carrière ouverte aux talents*, a
concept that must have appealed to Johnson), and, on the other hand, the
brutal murder of the Inca Atahualpa and his subjects for the sake of their
stores of gold – in short, a survey comprehending the best and the worst
exploits of mankind. Pope does it even better in his lovely evocative lines,
prophesying, in vain, a new era of world peace when restitution shall be made:

> Peru another race of kings behold,
> And other Mexicos be roofed with gold.
>
> (*Windsor Forest, TE* i, p. 192, ll. 411–12)

---

[17] I think I may claim credit for having reversed the older doctrine, enunciated by W. K. Wimsatt
in particular, that Johnson was an 'advanced abstractionist'; see my '"Pictures to the Mind":
Johnson and imagery', in Mary Lascelles *et al.* (eds.), *Johnson, Boswell and their circle: essays
presented to Lawrence Fitzroy Powell* (Oxford, 1965). It was gratifying to see my conclusions
affirmed by Professor W. W. Robson of the University of Edinburgh, if without acknowledge-
ment, in his 'Johnson as a poet', in *Samuel Johnson, 1709–1784: a bicentenary exhibition* (London,
1984), p. 26. It seems to take around twenty years for such radical views to 'trickle down'.

[18] George Saintsbury, *A history of modern criticism* (Edinburgh, 1904), i, pp. 96–7.

The picture of the forlorn palaces of Mexico being re-roofed with the gold pillaged from them by the European invaders could hardly be more vivid, reinforced by the quiet tribrach and short *i* in 'Mexico' rightly singled out for praise by Edith Sitwell.

The fact is that few, if any, major poets have been more concerned with or better instructed in the visual arts than Pope. (There is Rossetti, of course, but one would hardly call him major.[19]) One thinks of the months he spent in Charles Jervas' house taking lessons in drawing and painting ('Smit with the love of sister-arts,' as he puts it in his fine 'Epistle' to him) and his long friendship with Jonathan Richardson, pioneer English theorist of painting. It is thus not unexpected that the great scene at the end of Epistle I of the *Epilogue to the Satires* should be a composition in words of a Renaissance allegorical painting, with the goddess Vice ascending her throne in the centre of the picture, with her victims and her admirers before and around her:

> Her Birth, her Beauty, Crowds and Courts confess,
> Chaste Matrons praise her, and grave Bishops bless:
> In golden Chains the willing World she draws,
> And hers the Gospel is, and hers the Laws:
> Mounts the Tribunal, lifts her scarlet head,
> And sees pale Virtue carted in her stead!
> Lo! at the wheels of her Triumphal Car –
>
> (*TE* IV, p. 309, ll. 145–51)

One is intended to *see*, in all detail, the chaste matrons and grave bishops on each side of the throne applauding her; her scarlet head, the golden chains, the triumphal car, and all the rest –

> Old *England*'s Genius, rough with many a Scar,
> Dragged in the dust! his Arms hang idly round,
> His Flag inverted trails along the ground!
> Our Youth, all liv'ry'd o'er with foreign Gold
> Before her dance: behind her crawl the Old.
> See thronging Millions to the Pagod run,
> And offer Country, Parent, Wife, or Son.
>
> (*Epilogue to the Satires, Dialogue I, TE* IV, p. 309, ll. 152–8)

Not only do we have such vividly detailed 'still' pictures, as the above might be called, although there is plenty of action in them: we have extended 'movies', like the whole of Books II and IV of *The Dunciad* – the ceremonial 'games' celebrating the coronation of Cibber, King of Dulness (so realistic, indeed, that in the late nineteenth century, Professor William Minto advised his students at Aberdeen, 'Most of Book Two you had better skip'), and the fantastic *Walpurgisnacht* of Book Four (one of my students, when the term was fashionable, called it 'psychedelic'): the Goddess Dulness 'mounts the throne':

---

[19] And, I suppose, Blake. But if I may utter a heresy, not everyone agrees on just how major he is, either as a poet or an artist.

> Beneath her foot-stool Science groans in chains,
> And Wit dreads exile, penalties, and pains.
> There foam'd rebellious Logic, gagg'd and bound,
> There, stript, fair Rhet'ric languish'd on the ground
> <div align="right">(<i>Dunciad</i> IV, <i>TE</i> V, p. 342, ll. 21–4)</div>

and so on. Presently there comes the long procession of miseducators, the public schoolmen, the faculties of Oxford and Cambridge, the Grand Tour bearleaders, doing homage to her in long speeches of self-congratulation, all this followed, after her apocalyptic yawn, by the wild dissolution of civilization into chaos. Few poets are as cinematogenic as Pope. An inspired producer, with an inspired cameraman following the River Thames from its source to its estuary, with a fine speaker doing a 'voice over,' could make a memorable film of *Windsor Forest* – in colour, of course, so that, during the sequence showing hunting and fishing during the four seasons of the year, we should see the pheasant's

> purple crest and scarlet-circled eyes,
> The vivid green his shining plumes unfold;
> His painted wings, and breast that flames with gold,

and

> The bright-eyed perch with fins of Tyrian dye,
> The silver eel, in shining volumes roll'd,
> The yellow carp, in scales bedropp'd with gold,
> Swift trouts, diversify'd with crimson stains.
> <div align="right">(<i>Windsor Forest</i>, <i>TE</i> I, pp. 161, 163, ll. 116–18, 142–5)</div>

In these, and most of the rest of Pope, there is so much to see that one could quote indefinitely. It will do here to mention two small instances of, first, blindness, and second, vision, by readers. The first is James Reeves' stricture on the passage

> heav'n
> Who sees with equal eye, as God of all,
> A hero perish or a sparrow fall.

Reeves finds this 'a false antithesis. . . . Why not "a sparrow perish or a hero fall"?' (p. 89 on *Essay on Man*, *TE* III, i, pp. 24–5, ll. 86–8). The answer is simple: heroes seldom fall from branches of trees, as baby sparrows do. Clearly Reeves does not believe that visualization should be applied to Pope – or, for that matter, to St Matthew and Shakespeare, from whom Pope took the image.

The second is Aldous Huxley's response to the incomparably squalid scene of Buckingham's end, paying tribute to its 'most accurate particularities':

> In the worst inn's worst room, with mat half hung,
> The floors of plaster and the walls of dung,
> On once a flock-bed, but repair'd with straw,
> With tape-ty'd curtains, never meant to draw,

> The George and Garter dangling from that bed
> Where tawdry yellow strove with dirty red,
> Great Villiers lies.
>
> (*TE* III, ii, pp. 117–18, ll. 299–305)

(Incidentally, the enjambment might be noted.) 'I remember,' Huxley wrote, 'the first time I read Pope's line, being profoundly impressed by those walls of dung. Indeed, they still disturb my imagination. They express, for me, the Essential Horror. A floor of dung would have seemed almost normal, acceptable. But *walls* – Ah, no, no!' Clearly Mr Reeves' imagination, or that of others who still believe, as Huxley puts it (wondering at 'the doctrine'), that 'The theorists of "classicism" decreed that all poetical description should be couched in generalities', is not going to be disturbed by such particularities in Pope.[20]

3. Failure to recognize and respond to the dramatic element in poetry

'Every poem is "dramatic" . . . someone is speaking to someone else,' Robert Frost once wrote.[21] And that 'someone' is not necessarily, or perhaps ever, to be identified with the biographical construct we know as the individual whose name appears at the beginning or end of the poem as its author. If we did so, Frost's poetry in particular would suffer gravely, since the sensitive, morally perceptive, socially responsible, eminently likable 'someone', the 'I' of 'Stopping by Woods on a Snowy Evening' and 'Mending Wall,' seems to have been a very different person from the unpleasantly irascible Frost of recent biography. How fortunate for the authors – and readers – of, say, the 'Pervigilium Veneris' and 'Sir Gawain and the Green Knight' that we know nothing about them! Even Shakespeare, about whom we know virtually nothing, suffered at the hands of Bernard Shaw, who denounced him for his fatalistic view of life, as promulgated through the mouth of Macbeth: 'It is a tale told by an idiot, full of sound and fury, signifying nothing.' It is not the damage to William Shakespeare's reputation, however, that might be caused by such a charge that is of concern, but the damage to the reader's and viewer's response to

---

[20] Huxley, 1932, in BJ, 306–07, quoting *Moral Essays*, Epistle III, ii ('To Bathurst'), *TE* III, pp. 117–18, ll. 299–305. Huxley's bewilderment is understandable: the line is a difficult one. A primitive shed with a floor of an impacted mixture of mud and manure is imaginable. But, as Huxley says, walls? On the other hand, who ever heard of a floor constructed of plaster, a fragile substance that would disintegrate after being walked on a few times? The closest I can come to a solution is that the floor of the room was covered with fragments of plaster fallen from the dilapidated ceiling, and that the walls were smeared with traces of human excreta. The three extant autographs of the poem, though at other places heavily revised, show no variants from the printed text of the line (*Pope's Epistle to Bathurst: a critical reading with an edition of the manuscripts*, Earl R. Wasserman (ed.) (Baltimore, 1960).

[21] Quoted by Reuben Brower, *The fields of light* (New York, 1962), p. 19. First published 1951. On the following section, see my '"Dramatic texture" in Pope,' in F. W. Hilles and Harold Bloom (eds.), *From sensibility to romanticism: essays presented to Frederick A. Pottle* (New York, 1965), pp. 31–54.

Macbeth if it were read or viewed as a polemic by Shakespeare attempting to convert us to such a fatalistic philosophy. Fortunately, audiences over the centuries have had too much sense, and are too much enthralled by the *dramatic* qualities of the piece, to do anything so nonsensical.

Some writers, apparently more or less at random, seem to have escaped the ham-handed application of the biographical fallacy. Few readers have made their way through Browning's dramatic monologues – one of the most salutary critical terms ever invented – identifying Bishop Blougram, the Duke of Ferrara, Mr Sludge the medium, and the rest with the robust Robert. Biographers may have fun speculating about odd quirks in Browning's psyche that enabled him temporarily to put himself in the shoes of these individuals, but such speculations really have no relevance to the reader's ability, thanks to Browning's powers as a creative dramatist, to do so. Likewise, few readers who have been moved by 'Gerontion' and 'Prufrock' have been much concerned by the fact that Eliot was neither a desiccated old man nor a nervous middle-aged hanger-on of Boston intellectual society when he wrote them, however much enjoyment biographers get from finding traces of Eliot's psychological make-up in them. On the other hand there are those – Swift, say, or Byron, though the list could be much extended – whose writings the critic seldom seems to be able to dissociate from what he thinks he knows about their biography. If Swift's 'Cassinus and Peter' had been published anonymously, it might be read as a hilarious satire on a silly 'romantic' young man who, though no devotee of personal cleanliness himself, is put off sex for ever and driven to the verge of suicide by his discovery that his girlfriend Celia 'sh——', and the conclusion the reader might be expected to draw is that it is ridiculous to make so much fuss over such trivial everyday bodily functions.[22] But no: since we are solemnly assured by biographers, on the basis of Swift's supposedly unsatisfactory relationships with women, that he had a physical aversion to them, even an 'excremental obsession,' the plain words of the poem cannot possibly mean that.

No one has suffered more than Pope from the biographical fallacy. We might consider the *Pastorals*, written when he was in his late teens or not much older. They have almost unanimously been written off as clever exercises in classical conventions and practice in versification – 'Rococo vignettes in a gilt scrollwork,' Maynard Mack quotes one critic. Reeves sums up the consensus:

Pope was engaged in an elaborate word-game, primarily as the amusement of an invalid, and then as a means of gaining reputation. As personal experience he could have had no interest in the subject-matter of the *Pastorals*.[23]

---

[22] See my 'On Swift's "scatological" poetry', *Sewanee Review*, 75 (1967), 672–89.

[23] Reeves, p. 118. Reeves ignores modern study of the pastoral genre, as in William Empson, *Some versions of pastoral* (London, 1935). Its conclusions are admirably summarized by James Smith: *A selection from Scrutiny*, F. R. Leavis (ed.) (see note 16), II, p. 187:

[Pastoral] is not an attempt to portray a shepherd's life: but in its purity . . . to portray a life in which physical misery is reduced to a minimum or has disappeared. Traditionally such a life is

That seems to dispose of the *Pastorals* for the modern reader. But why, for heaven's sake, should Pope not have had an interest in their subject-matter? Their central subject-matter, as in Virgil's and other classical pastoral poetry, is sex – quite down-to-earth sex (to venture a pun), in a setting of the archetypal circuit of the natural year – a real toad in an imaginary garden. Spring sees the young shepherd's love tenderly burgeoning; in summer it rises to heat; autumn sees it withering away; with winter it has become frustration and bitterness, culminating in suicide.

> I know thee, Love! on foreign mountains bred,
> Wolves gave thee suck, and savage tigers fed.
> Thou wert from Ætna's burning entrails torn,
> Got by fierce whirlwinds, and in thunder born
>
> (*Autumn, TE* i, pp. 86–7, ll. 89–92)

is Pope's version of the famous lines in Virgil's eighth Eclogue, perhaps more effectively translated by Dryden. If by 'personal experience' Reeves means that because of Pope's physical condition, he was unable to consummate his sexual desires, this may be true (though one remembers Cibber's unsavoury tale of the experience in the brothel). But failure to consummate does not diminish one's 'interest in the subject matter' – just the reverse. The 'love story' in the poem is precisely one of unconsummated desire. Indeed, in the work of few English poets is the theme of physical attraction to women more frequent and convincing than in Pope's, and it doesn't require the tabulations of a Kinsey to be aware that a male's sexual urge is at its height at the age when the *Pastorals* were conceived and written. But the history of Pope's libido is really of no more relevance to the reader's response to this universal and eternal theme than Virgil's youthful crushes (about which, fortunately, we know nothing) are to the story of Damon and his unfaithful loved one in the eighth Eclogue (or of Corydon in the second), or of Keats' sex life, or lack of it, to one's response to 'La Belle Dame Sans Merci'. The reader can identify himself with the palely loitering Knight-at-Arms, and be moved by the poem, as very many have, without ever having heard of Fanny Brawne.

---

called a shepherd's: in which, therefore, man is held to enjoy every happiness if only his desires will let him. But, as becomes clear with the progress of the pastoral, his desires will not. Removed from the danger of physical pain those of the intellect and the imagination become acuter; in particular, the passion of love, with neither social pressure nor economic necessity inclining it in any direction, becomes incalculable in its vagaries. It remains an ever open source of calamity. A tragic note or undertone is thus inseparable from pastoral, and if subdued is only the more insistent. It is in permanent contrast with the composure or gaiety of the rest of the score.

That Pope fully understood this is evident, as well as in the *Pastorals* themselves, in his controversy with Ambrose Philips, who, as Reeves says approvingly (p. 125), 'reflected the interest in the native English tradition which looked back to Spenser' – another manifestation of the growing 'patriotic' nationalism of eighteenth-century English literature. Pope looks back farther, to Theocritus and Virgil.

No more powerful and fundamental principle of literary criticism has ever
been formulated than the opening paragraph of Johnson's *Rambler* no. 60:

> All joy or sorrow for the happiness or calamities of others is produced by an act of the
> imagination that realizes [makes real] the event however fictitious, or approximates it
> [brings it closer] however remote, by placing us, for a time, in the condition of him
> whose fortune we contemplate; so that we feel, while the deception lasts [while 'the
> willing suspension of disbelief for the moment,' as Coleridge was later to put it,
> endures], whatever motions [emotions] would be excited by the same good or evil
> happening to ourselves.
>   (D. J. Greene (ed.), *Samuel Johnson: The Oxford Authors* (Oxford, 1984), p. 204)

Empathy, we now call it (Johnson and his contemporaries said merely 'sympathy'). For all Johnson's generally high praise of *Paradise Lost*, he complains,
with justice,

> it has this inconvenience, that it comprises neither human actions nor human man-
> ners . . . The reader finds no transaction in which he can be engaged, beholds no
> condition in which he can by any effort of imagination place himself; he has, therefore,
> little natural curiosity or sympathy.   ('Life of Milton' in Greene, pp. 709–10)

It is worth noticing Johnson's emphasis on 'imagination', to which he is often
said to have been hostile, as an essential element in the literary experience, and
his pioneering practice of what is now called 'reader-response criticism'.

What are the possibilities in Pope's poetry of the reader's imaginative
identification and empathy with the passions, pains and joys of others? For
those unfamiliar with it, the pastoral convention needs some getting used to for
full response to the emotions of the love-lorn lads in Pope's *Pastorals*. But it is
not surprising that *Eloisa to Abelard* and the *Elegy to the Memory of an Unfortunate
Lady* are the poems of Pope most appealing to young college students (those
whose instructors have given them permission to 'dig' them). It is not difficult
for the reader to 'empathize' with their protagonists and share their relatively
straightforward emotions – though those of Eloisa are perhaps not all that
simple, and there has been much controversy (a healthy sign) about just what,
deep down, her feelings and motives really are: the kind of puzzle one so often
encounters in a Henry James novel.

As Pope himself (and his reader) matures, however, things become more
complex. It would be pleasant to report that, on encountering *The Rape of the
Lock*, attractive young women who have recently been their high school's
'homecoming queen' (I am speaking of American undergraduates) and have
been 'dated' by the stars of the high school football team and other prestigious
young males, at the same time scoring points with their female contemporaries
by not allowing them to 'go all the way' ('By keeping men off, you keep them
on', as Mrs Peachum shrewdly put it) identify themselves with Belinda, and
that these same lads, who boast to one another about how often they have
'made out' with them, recognize themselves in the Baron. But to do so would

require a greater wrench of their sexist conditioning than they are at present capable of. Or indeed later: even among fairly mature graduate students I have never been able to work up much enthusiasm, seldom more than a grudging intellectual assent, for Clarissa's wise and realistic view of the war between the sexes.

It is in Pope's latest, most mature poems, the epistles and the satires, that the dramatic element becomes most crucial. 'He Do the Police in Different Voices' was Eliot's original title for *The Waste Land*, the point being that young Sloppy the orphan could delight his protector Mrs Higden, when reading the police court reports in the newspapers, by 'acting out' the words of the various individuals involved.[24] And certainly a chief source of the popularity of Eliot's poem, after the denunciations of it by the critical establishment had died away, has been its variety of speakers: Marie, cousin of the Archduke; the prophet Ezekiel; the hyacinth girl; Madame Sosostris, the wisest woman in Europe; the City wage-slave, friend of Stetson, watching the crowds flow over London Bridge; the unhappy chess players; Lil, recently aborted, wife of Albert, just demobbed; Tiresias; the secretary who raised her knees supine on the floor of a narrow canoe and can connect nothing with nothing.

Pope's *Epistle to Dr Arbuthnot* might be called 'He Do the Misunderstood Artist in Different Voices'.[25] First, we have the busy, successful, usually urbane man of letters, conscious of his own importance and irritated by the crowd of 'admirers' looking for favours from him—

> Shut, shut the door, good *John*! fatigu'd, I said,
> 'Tye up the knocker, say I'm sick, I'm dead . . .
>
> (*TE* IV, p. 96, ll. 1–2)

There is a spell of half-humorous self-pity:

> All fly to *Twit'nam*, and in humble strain
> Apply to me, to keep them mad or vain.
>
> (*TE* IV, p. 97, ll. 21–2)

Then the mask of the busy public man is dropped, and the speaker becomes the simple, lonely, wistful, modest poet, appealing to his one faithful confidant, Arbuthnot:

> Friend to my Life, (which did not you not prolong,
> The World had wanted many an idle song).
>
> (*TE* IV, p. 98, ll. 27–8)

Sometimes the self-pity is consciously exaggerated, and 'Pope' – it is well to put quotation marks around the name of this protean persona – dons another of his favourite roles, that of the hurt little boy (we are expected to smile at it):

[24] William Empson (*Using biography* (Cambridge, Mass., 1984), p. 189) calls the draft of the work 'a growing rag-bag of character-sketches'. No doubt; but it must be kept in mind that the sketching is done dramatically, by the characters' own words and actions.

[25] I give a fuller analysis of the poem in my essay '"Dramatic texture"' (note 21 above).

Seiz'd and ty'd down to judge, how wretched I!
Who can't be silent, and who will not lye. . . .
I sit with sad Civility, I read
With honest anguish, and an aking head.

(*TE* IV, p. 98, ll. 37–8)

And so it goes, with interventions from a prudent, appeasing friend, advising
'Pope' to cool it, not to rock the boat – like other such late poems of Pope's, this
is not a dramatic monologue but a dialogue; interventions which have the
effect, successively, of raising 'Pope's' temper, in gradually intensified stages,
to a white heat of indignant denunciation of the socially and politically
approved philistinism that fears and would repress the truth-telling function of
the artist.

It perhaps needs to be pointed out that the tradition of the dramatic
monologue (or duologue), with the supposed speaker expressing his views and
feelings on a subject (or subjects) in an informal, conversational manner (often
rising, by stages, to an emotional climax), giving free rein to changes of mood,
of *persona* (a 'stream of consciousness' – why not?), goes back to the satires
('sermones', conversations) of Horace and Juvenal. But its continuing appeal
does not consist (as James Reeves would have it) in an occasional scholar's
recognition, 'Ah, yes, this is the kind of thing Juvenal used to do,' but in the
perceptive reader's ability to 'empathize', to 'identify' with the fictive speaker
as he passes from one mood or *persona* to the next, whether in Horace's,
Donne's and Pope's *Satires* or Milton's *Lycidas* or Gray's *Elegy in a Country
Churchyard* or Wordsworth's *Prelude*, down to Eliot's 'Prufrock' and Pound's
Mauberley or – again, why not? – Mollie Bloom's dramatic monologue in
Ulysses? To repeat Frost, all poetry – and some prose – is dramatic, and to read
it merely as a footnote to what may be a very inadequate supposed biography
of its author is not to read it at all.

*4. Failure to grasp the full significance of the commentary on the human condition of
thoughtful and sensitive poetry*

This is not something unique to Pope, of course. There are still those who
believe that the subject of *The Vanity of Human Wishes* is 'the vanity of human
life', that the moral of *The Ancient Mariner* is 'Be kind to animals,' and that
Hamlet (to quote the marvellously fatuous opening statement of the old Laur-
ence Olivier movie) is 'the story of a man who could not make up his mind'.

It may not be necessary at this point to spend much time persuading the
reader that there is more than meets the eye – some eyes, at least – in Pope's
major poems. Perhaps enough has been said above to suggest to him that the
Pastorals are more than a juvenile exercise in versification, but have to do with a
universal and eternal subject; that *The Rape of the Lock*, far from being merely a
piece of 'dainty filigree', as it has been called, or a good-humoured little

occasional composition intended to persuade Arabella Fermor to renew the engagement to Lord Petre that she had broken off, is a profoundly searching analysis of what was and continues to be wrong in the relation between the sexes in modern society (it says something for Arabella's greater perceptiveness than that of many later critics that she was outraged by the piece and would have nothing more to do with Petre or Pope); that *The Dunciad* is more than a petulant discharge of spleen at a number of hack writers who had annoyed Pope personally. It is instead a devastating analysis of the causes of the social and political ills that plagued Pope's world, and still plague ours, concluding with a most brilliant description of the kind of miseducation that resulted – and still results – in products who are

> First slave to Words, then vassal to a Name,
> Then dupe to Party; child and man the same;
> Bounded by Nature, narrow'd still by Art,
> A trifling head, and a contracted heart.
>
> (*TE* v, pp. 391–2, ll. 501–4)

It of course saves us mental energy, and helps to preserve our complacency about things as they are, to turn our eyes aside from these things and insist that poor old Pope, of whatever minor 'historical' interest he may be, is no longer 'relevant'. But he is: very much so.

One does not become able to respond fully to Pope overnight – nor indeed to Virgil, Dante, Shakespeare, Milton, Wordsworth or Eliot. Let me return to my analogy with opera, concentrating on the minuet which ends the first of the two acts of *Don Giovanni*. It begins with a delightfully simple melody, which many a six- or seven-year-old has learned to play on the piano, under the supervision of his or her teacher:

– one-and, two-and, three-and, one-and-a, two-and, three-and, with the instruction if needed added that the succession of stresses is strong–weak–weak. Eventually, after a bit of bass is added, it may be pointed out that the triple rhythm is more interesting if the third beat in the measure is accented a bit more strongly, strong–weak–medium, and an attempt is made to get the pupil to respond to and reproduce in his playing the classic minuet–waltz–bolero rhythm, so frequent in Haydn, Mozart, and Beethoven, and apotheosized in Chopin and Ravel. Then perhaps a bit of harmony, maybe just a simple alto line, a third or sixth below the treble: thus,

The Minuet

W. A. Mozart

p

1. When dames wore hoops and powdered hair, And ve - ry strict was
2. O - ver his la - dy's outstretch'd hand Each gal-lant bends right

et - i - quette, When men were brave and ladies fair, They danc'd the min - u - et.
grace - ful - ly; Gra - cious of mien, with manner grand, She sweeps a cour - te - sy.

mf

Slip - pers, high-heeled with poin - ted toe, Trod state - ly measures to and fro.
Our whirl - ing steps of mod - ern days Those lords and la - dies would a - maze,

cresc.   *f*

Quite de-mure, sedate, and bow - ing low They danced the min - u - et.
Yet the min - u - et we still must praise For grace and dig - ni - ty.

When the pupil becomes responsive to harmony, he might listen to the simple yet charming harmonic additions Mozart introduces in the orchestral part of the *Don Giovanni* score. So much for the relatively simple aural component of the work. With similar extended and progressive experience with metrical verse, a reader might begin to respond to the subtleties of Pope's versification.

The fatuous words attached to the score above – designed for pupils of elementary schools in western Canada in the 1920s – are not entirely irrelevant. They do quite a competent job of representing the visual component – what the stage director of *Don Giovanni* should do in producing the scene before the eyes of the audience. He should certainly have a group of decorously clad ladies and gentlemen of the *corps de ballet* doing such a charmingly demure and sedate minuet. There was a time when elementary school teachers, during 'art' periods, used to assign pupils the job of illustrating some scene from their reading of poetry or prose. Whatever the results as art, the practice did encourage more vivid response to literature. Who, even now, can think of *Alice in Wonderland* and keep the Tenniel illustrations out of his mind? Some experience of this kind would certainly help in making it possible to read Pope as he deserves to be read.

But then comes the dramatic and ironic part, the part that the Victorians and the author of the words in the score above would have hated. The words and actions to which Mozart set this graceful, innocent tune completely contradict its demureness and dignity. At the beginning of the scene, three ominous masked characters enter – Elvira, Anna, Ottavio – all intent on avenging themselves, by murder if necessary, for the wrongs Giovanni has inflicted on them. To the sweet notes of the minuet, they discuss among themselves their hostile motives and intentions. Giovanni's intentions are quite different: to rape, if necessary, the perhaps not so innocent Zerlina, whom he has little difficulty enticing off stage. Meanwhile, on stage, the grace of the minuet is burlesqued when Leporello, to keep him from interfering, seizes the suspicious Masetto, Zerlina's fiancé, and forces the lumbering peasant to dance the minuet with him. In the midst of all this confusion, a discordant shriek – Zerlina's – bursts in upon the innocent music of the minuet, and the scene dissolves into chaos. I cannot help thinking that Pope would have loved both the comedy and the seriousness of it. Pope, like Mozart, wrote for adults not pre-adolescents. Cleanth Brooks has pointed out in effect that the literal significance of the word 'rape' in the title of Pope's most popular poem, dainty filigree though it may be, is not to be lightly dismissed.[26]

Finally, what I have called the discursive element – the reflections that may occur to one on the way home from a performance of *Don Giovanni*. What is the reason for the universal fascination, since the Renaissance at least, of the Don Giovanni/Faust legend (they *are* the same, aren't they?) Is it possible, since the time of such Giovanni/Faustian (and Nietzschean) figures as Napoleon and Hitler to retain a shred of admiration for them, or are we to take seriously the dragging-down-to-hell business and the triumphantly self-righteous moralizations over him at the end by the 'good guys', Elvira, Anna and Ottavio? What are we to make of Giovanni's attraction for Elvira – and perhaps Anna, and certainly Leporello? Such puzzles are perhaps not too different from those that occur to us after we finish reading *The Rape of the Lock*, *Eloisa to Abelard*, the *Epistle to Dr Arbuthnot*, and *The Dunciad*: how do these situations come about, anyway, and what is the explanation of them? Pope had a better mind and was better educated than Lorenzo da Ponte; his talent for dramatization was at least as good; in his own medium of English verse, his musical expertise was not unworthy of being compared with Mozart's. But certainly no one is going to arrive at full enjoyment of what there is to enjoy in either Mozart or Pope without considerable preliminary exposure to the elements of the arts they practised.

The capacity to respond to poetry, as to music, is something that should begin to be developed long before college age. But I have had some success in getting undergraduates to see what is enjoyable in Pope by introducing them to his shorter (incorrectly called 'minor') poems and getting them to recognize there, on a smaller scale, the techniques of sound, vision, and drama they will

---

[26] Brooks, 'The case of Miss Arabella Fermor', in his *The well-wrought urn*, 1947 (excerpted in BJ, pp. 360–77).

encounter, at greater length and in greater complexity, in his more ambitious ones.[27]

IV

What follows is a miscellany of reasons for avoiding Pope. Most of them have no real relationship to the essential matter discussed above, the ability to read poetry. Rather, they are like the 'stock responses', socially conditioned irrelevancies in I. A. Richards' *Practical criticism* cited by undergraduates for their liking or disliking various specimens of verse. But a brief consideration of them may be of some use here.

Immorality (I. Personal). Sir Leslie Stephen concluded his book on Pope with It is . . . difficult to say what will be the final element in our feeling about the man. Let us hope that it may be the pity which, after a certain lapse of years, we may be excused for conceding to the victim of moral as well as physical disease.[28]

It is true that Pope, in his personal relationships, could be devious and not altogether truthful. But if one takes the line that anything written by so immoral a person must be flawed and should be rejected, it is interesting to look at the records of some of Pope's critics (not to mention the personal relationships of many other great writers, both before and after his time). His most influential early critic, Joseph Warton, has recently been charged, along with his brother Thomas, Professor of Poetry at Oxford, with printing poems of their own as their father's, so as to push back the inception of 'Romanticism' a good many years.[29] Pope's most outspoken Victorian enemy, Edmund Gosse, is still under suspicion of having connived in T. J. Wise's even more blatant forgeries (Thwaite, p. 389). The Reverend Whitwell Elwin, who was so appalled by Pope that he could not bear to go on editing his foul mouthings,

---

[27] Auden, in one of the finest short appreciations of Pope ever written (BJ, pp. 328–42; first published 1937) wrote, 'As he confined himself to the couplet, the couplet is labelled as the medium of Augustan poetry' (p. 338). Of course, he didn't so confine himself: a hasty count has netted me 86 of his poems not in iambic pentameter couplets, but in a host of other forms. But, being short, they have been collected in one volume of the Twickenham Edition and stigmatized as 'Minor Poems'. If one were to do this to Milton or Wordsworth or Tennyson – to segregate their shorter poems from their longer ones and label them 'minor' – we should have a very different picture of their achievement from what we have now. The one-volume edition by John Butt (London, 1963) is more satisfactory in that it gives a roughly chronological ordering; though a *strictly* chronological order would give an even better idea of the variety and richness of Pope's poetic technique. See a paedagogical piece of mine, 'Alexander Pope and the Constant Muse', *Forum: A Journal of the Humanities and Fine Arts* 17, 1 (Winter 1979), 21–8.

[28] Stephen, *Alexander Pope* (New York, n.d. [*c.* 1880?]) ('English men of letters'), p. 209. The copy I am using – probably the first American edition or a reissue of it – has an exquisite Freudian slip: instead of 'excused for', it reads 'excused from'. To save Sir Leslie's reputation for humanitarianism, I have made the emendation shown.

[29] See David Fairer, 'The poems of Thomas Warton the Elder?', *Review of English Studies* 26 (1975), 287–300, 395–406, and n.s. 29 (1978), 61–5, and John A. Vance, *Joseph Warton and Thomas Warton* (Boston, 1983), pp. 81–2.

had, like his contemporary, the Reverend Charles Dodgson (Lewis Carroll), a penchant for young girls which in pre-*Lolita* times was generally deemed innocent, though Mrs Elwin and Alice Liddell's mother were not so sure.[30] And Leslie Stephen himself, as described by his daughter and recent biographers and editors, is not without some claim to pity.

Immorality (2. Authorial). In his poetry, Pope was realistic and anything but mealy-mouthed about the relations between the sexes – a shocking attitude, which the Victorians readily attributed to his own reprehensible morals and those of his time. When he 'exhorts a female friend not to "quit the free innocence of life / For the dull glory of a virtuous wife,"' Professor Henry Reed of the University of Pennsylvania ejaculated in 1855, 'What a line for a poet to utter! And what a contrast to those bright images of womanly heroism and beauty which the older poets delighted to picture in marriage!'[31] Such, no doubt, as Shakespeare in Goneril, Regan and Lady Macbeth, and Milton in Dalila. Indeed, Pope's exhortation today might have a good deal of serious appeal to a theorist of feminism.

One is not too surprised to encounter this attitude among the Victorians. It *is* somewhat surprising to encounter something not too dissimilar in 1986 by a senior professor of the University of California at Los Angeles, a locality not reputed for inhibition in sexual matters, discussing Pope's *Sober Advice from Horace*:

This 'sermon' . . . directs young men to lay their hands on any cheap and available piece of womanflesh they can catch. It discusses the promiscuity of Pope's enemies but also of his friends; it calls attention to its own obscenities of language . . . it concludes with 'moral' advice which questions the value of moral standards as such. . . How does this piece fit with the general tenor of his other moral teachings?[32]

As in Victorian times, 'moral standards' and 'moral teaching' here seem to refer primarily, or exclusively, to sexual activity. In fact, Dr Adams misses the moral point of the 'sermon': it is a homily not in recommendation of *luxuria* but in reprobation of *superbia*. With numerous allusions to recent scandals in English high-life, males are cautioned, if they must seek a sexual partner, not to gratify their pride by demanding a woman of high rank. This is likely only to cause trouble – damaging publicity, expensive divorces, beatings-up by angry husbands. Lay off duchesses: a pleasant 'wench' of lower social status will

[30] Lady Emily Lutyens (*née* Lytton), *A blessed girl: memoirs of a Victorian girlhood chronicled in an exchange of letters* (New York, 1954). The intimacy between Lady Emily (aged thirteen) and Elwin (aged seventy-one) seems not to have extended beyond cuddling together in an armchair and going for long walks hand in hand. But much of the later part of her fascinating book recounts the determined if unsuccessful assaults on her virtue by Wilfrid Scawen Blunt, a younger (late forties) and more experienced man (including an attempt to force his way into her bedroom at night). She narrates these in detailed letters to 'the Rev', who displays great interest and replies with much sage advice.

[31] Henry Reed, *Lectures in English literature* (Philadelphia, 1855), p. 234.

[32] Robert M. Adams, *New York Review of Books*, 13 March 1986 (a review of Maynard Mack, *Alexander Pope: a life*), p. 30.

serve the immediate purpose just as well. Down to earth, of course – and comic, except for those whom Victorian high moral standards prevent from seeing how comic the vicissitudes of the male sexual urge often are. It is refreshing to find Samuel Johnson, not often accused of preaching immorality, giving the same realistic advice: 'Were it not for imagination, a man would be as happy in the arms of a chambermaid as a duchess.'[33]

Standards of 'obscenity of language' vary from age to age, of course, and Pope's mildly amusing use, in his parodic notes to the poem, of *cunnus* and *futuo* (in 'the decent obscurity of a learned language') is hardly in the same league as the huge repertoire of Eric Partridge's *Shakespeare's bawdy*. Does anyone (except Dr Adams) really worry about such things at a time when William Burroughs and Allen Ginsberg have practically become Grand Old Men of Letters, and the 'four-letter words' are commonplace in imaginative literature and 'high-brow' as well as 'lowbrow' conversation?

'Wit,' irony, humour, incongruity. One of the most memorable comments on Victorian attitudes is a cartoon by Max Beerbohm, showing an immensely tall and gaunt Matthew Arnold with a faint ghost of a smile on his face (apparently on rare occasions he could actually smile at a decorous joke). Reaching up to his knee and plucking at his trouser leg is a tiny Mary Augusta Arnold, perhaps six years old (later the formidable Mrs Humphry Ward), who is reproaching him, 'Why, O why, Uncle Matthew, will not you be always *wholly serious?*'

The author of the touchstone of 'high seriousness' probably deserved this gibe, the point of course being that solemnity is not necessarily seriousness, and the lack of it not necessarily evidence of the lack of seriousness. Irony and wit ('a kind of *discordia concors*; a combination of dissimilar images, or discovery of occult resemblances in things apparently unlike': Johnson[34]) are enemies of solemnity, and the nineteenth century generally seems to have been suspicious of them. No doubt Arnold and others felt it beneath the dignity of a poet to have fun, as Pope did, with syllepsis, trifling with sacred moral matters, as in 'Stain her honour, or her new brocade' (and had Dr Adams discovered the not very occult connection between the staining of her new brocade and that of her honour, he might have had a further charge of obscenity against Pope)[35] or with anticlimax, 'Not louder shrieks to pitying Heav'n are cast / When husbands or when lap-dogs breathe their last.' They were the same voices that in the 1920s denounced Eliot for his juxtaposition of the 'sublime' and the 'trivial' or everyday ('Let us go then, you and I, / When the evening is spread out against the sky / Like a patient etherised upon a table'; 'I grow old . . . I

---

[33] James Boswell, *Life of Johnson*, Hill-Powell (ed.) (Oxford, 1934–64), III, p. 341.

[34] G. B. Hill (ed.), *Lives of the English poets* (Oxford, 1905), I, p. 20 ('Cowley').

[35] As early as 1714 Charles Gildon had called disapproving attention to the 'bawdy' in *The Rape of the Lock*, as in 'Oh! hadst thou, Cruel! been content to seize / Hairs less in sight, or any hairs but these!' and 'Sought no more than on his foe to die' (*Pope: the critical heritage*, pp. 94–6).

grow old ... I shall wear the bottom of my trousers rolled'); the voices too of the critics who, when Shaffer's *Amadeus* was first performed, were shocked at the sight of Wolfgang rolling about on the floor in amorous pursuit of Constanze (yet Mozart's high seriousness remains as high and serious as ever); the voice of a scholar of the 1920s who explained Johnson's disqualification as a critic of poetry in terms that shed much light on nineteenth- and early twentieth-century criticism of Pope: 'The conception of poetry as a chariot whirling us heavenward in glory above the commonplaces of daily life was not his' – high seriousness indeed.[36] But it must be confessed that neither was it the conception of many great poets, or indeed artists of any kind, throughout the centuries.

'Correctness.' This term has probably done more harm to Pope's reputation over the years than any other (it seems paradoxical that the Victorians should censure him both for the excessive correctness of his poetry and the excessive incorrectness of its morality). But what does it mean? F. W. Bateson writes, 'Pope's interpretation of "correctness" was primarily metrical.'[37] No doubt he was concerned that his lines would scan, with the right number of syllables and stresses, unlike Donne, who, Ben Jonson said, deserved hanging for not keeping the accents. But Donne's way of writing verse had long been abandoned, and the iambic pentameters of Pope's predecessors, Waller, Denham, and Dryden seem just as metrically 'correct' in this sense as Pope's.

What is puzzling is line 3 of the first Dialogue of the *Epilogue to the Satires*, where the hostile interlocutor is scolding 'Pope' for his new practice of writing harsh satires on contemporary politicians and other offenders:

> You grow *correct* that once with Rapture writ.
>
> (*TE* IV, p. 297, l. 3)

I give the typography as it appears in John Butt's Twickenham Edition. Butt does not annotate the word here, nor has anyone else done so, so far as I know.

[36] Joseph Epes Brown, *The critical opinions of Samuel Johnson* (Princeton, 1928), p. xxxi. Reeves (p. 72), summarizing James R. Sutherland's *Preface to eighteenth-century poetry* (1948), quotes Dryden's gibe at Elkanah Settle, who believes 'he has a light within him, and writes by inspiration'. 'Almost a century later', Reeves writes, 'Johnson, *who by that time should have known better* [my italics], was sneering at Gray for a similar "fantastic foppery". The poet wrote not by supernatural inspiration nor by the light within himself; he wrote by the light of public favour and at the dictates of the *beau monde*.' Evidently the theory that the poet writes by supernatural inspiration still had its adherents in 1976.

[37] BJ, p. 487. In his index (p. 499) Bateson gives a different definition: '"Correctness" (the neo-classical ideal, to be reached by following the "rules").' One of the references there is to an essay by W. K. Wimsatt which sets out the 'rules' concerning the use of figures of speech of such rule-makers as Bysshe, Puttenham, Blount, and the like. But as far as I can make out from Wimsatt's rather opaque prose, Pope paid little attention to such 'rules', learning his use of those devices (as Reuben Brower points out) from earlier poets, Virgil, Spenser, Milton, and so on. Wimsatt concludes his essay, 'There is a marked correlation not between poems and contemporary poetics but actually between poems and anti-poetics', a statement which seems to contradict Bateson's definition.

What can it mean to say that Pope's earlier poetry – e.g. the smooth, melodious lines of the *Pastorals* – is written with rapture, but presumably *not* with correctness, whereas the rugged, staccato versification found in the late satires *is* correct (or at least becoming so)? Since the interlocutor stands for everything that 'Pope' in the poem is against, blame by him of such 'correctness' must mean that 'Pope' applauds the growth of this new quality. The only explanation I can think of at the moment, though I am not at all sure of it, is that Pope means that he is now writing in authentic contemporary language, without archaic and artificial 'poetic' ornament.

At any rate, if the modern student shudders at the thought of reading anything stigmatized as correct, it may reassure him to learn that at least one Victorian critic lashes out angrily at Pope, calling him 'eminently incorrect'. This is De Quincey:

Correctness in what? In developing the thought? In connecting it, or effecting the transitions? In the use of words? In the grammar? In the metre? Under every one of these limitations of the idea, we maintain that Pope is *not* distinguished by correctness.

He goes on to tear the *Essay on Criticism* to pieces: 'It is a collection of independent maxims, tied together into a fasciculus by the printer, but having no natural order or logical dependency . . . Many of the rules are violated by no man so often as by Pope.'[38] De Quincey, it seems to me, has a point: that far from being hidebound by musty rules and precedents, Pope, like all great artists, is a bold innovator and experimenter, possessing, as Johnson says, 'a mind active, ambitious, and adventurous, always investigating, always aspiring; in its widest searches still longing to go forward, in its highest flights still wishing to be higher, always imagining something greater than it knows, always endeavouring more than it can do' (*Life of Pope* in *Lives . . .*, III, p. 217).

Nationalism and its consequences.   Keats' tirade against eighteenth-century poets in *Sleep and Poetry* reaches its climax with

> they went about
> Holding a poor, decrepit standard out
> Mark'd with most flimsy mottos, and in large
> The name of one Boileau!   (ll. 203–6)

Again and again Boileau is depicted as the villain of eighteenth-century English poetry, the standard-bearer of French influence to which, after 1660, English poets were supposed to have succumbed. Much was made of the fact

---

[38] BJ, p. 222 (published 1842). When I argued in my '"Logical structure" in eighteenth-century poetry' (*Philological Quarterly* 21 [1952], 315–36), that Pope's *Essay* is 'illogical', unaware that De Quincey had earlier reached the same conclusion, my thesis was received with some astonishment – everyone *knows* that the poetry of 'the age of reason' must be 'logical'. Unlike De Quincey, however, I did not regard this as a fault. Like good poetry of other centuries, that of Pope does not make its effect by trying to imitate a scholarly treatise: the *Essay*'s structure is dramatic, not logical.

that Charles II, before his restoration, spent a good deal of time in France,[39] and somehow this was supposed to have caused English writers to become slavish imitators of French models. 'It was thoroughly consistent with this desire for smoothness and gentility,' wrote Gosse, 'that the English writers of the new school should look to France and to French literature, where sentiment and elegance had been so long made the subjects of deliberate study' (p. 223) – though it might be questioned whether smoothness and gentility are really the best words to characterize the fierceness of Racine's *Phèdre*. 'It is,' Warton explodes, 'perpetually the nauseous cant of the French critics, and of their advocates and pupils, that the English writers are generally incorrect' and '[Pope's] turn of mind led him to admire French models; he studied Boileau attentively, formed himself on him. . . .' (BJ, pp. 108, 117). Certainly Pope studied Boileau, a fine critic well worth studying, as he studied many other earlier writers, but in what way he formed himself – that is, formed his poetry – on him remains vague.

Warton wrote the first of these comments in 1756, the year of the declaration of the Seven Years War, the third of the wars between England and France with which almost the whole of the eighteenth century was to be filled, and wrote the second just before the end of the fourth and the beginning of the fifth (Keats wrote his comment at the conclusion of the last of them). It was the century of Britain's successful struggle to break the hold of France (and its ally Spain) on overseas commerce, and to set up her own imperial power throughout the world. Along with it went the efforts of many popular writers to establish a recognized British literary 'identity' (as United States writers were to do in the nineteenth century and Canadians and Australians in the twentieth). It was the century of Thomson's 'Rule, Britannia, rule the waves!' The heroes of the nationalist and imperialist myth were Edward III and Henry V, who showed the French their place, and Elizabeth I, who showed the Spanish theirs. The Stuarts, with their Continental connections – many of them Roman Catholics too! – came off badly. And Dryden and Pope, both Catholics, both sympathetic to the Stuarts, both with a vision of literature that transcended that of their tight little island, shared in their disfavour.[40]

---

[39] In fact, he spent less than a third of his time in exile in France, where he lived in poverty and was not on the best of terms with the French court. He later spent much more time in the Low Countries, from which he sailed to England at the time of his restoration.

[40] The foreign threat now seems to be the other side of the Atlantic. In support of his 'conviction that his [Pope's] poems have been over-valued in the present century', Reeves cites (Preface, unpaged), 'the great American take-over', which 'has injected into the industry new capital in the form of research and critical enthusiasm' – undesirable activities, clearly – 'evident in the many exhaustive studies by American academics', and he has other gibes at 'the later American criticism' (e.g. p. 95). Bateson too was convinced that Pope is overrated, 'especially, for reasons I don't fully understand, in the United States' (BJ, p. 20) – though Bateson did pay the late George Sherburn what one supposes was meant as a compliment: a 'professor successively at Chicago and Harvard, whose elegant English prose style might nevertheless have emanated from Oxford or Cambridge' (BJ, p. 284). 'Nevertheless'!

It might be easier to understand the reasons for the persistence of the Victorian stereotype of

The epitaph his friend Mason composed for Thomas Gray's monument in
Westminster Abbey deserves pondering:

> No more the Grecian muse unrivall'd reigns;
>   To Britain let the nations homage pay;
> She felt a Homer's fire in Milton's strains,
>   A Pindar's rapture in the lyre of Gray.

In a brilliant study of Gray's family, financial, and political background,
James Steele sums it up: 'Gray's world vision, then, was consistently that of a
whiggish, imperialistic bourgeois, later a Pittite' (Gray's family's fortune, like
Pitt's, derived from the East India trade).[41] The great PR man for Gray's
poetry was of course Horace Walpole, whose family background and political
associations need no description, who was Joseph Warton's patron, and who
rejected the Grecian muse of architecture in order to 'revive', as he thought,
the English Gothic style, which was to dominate the following century.

The most damaging rejection of 'French influence' came from Gray, who
wrote:

The language of the age is never the language of poetry; except among the French,
whose verse, where the thought or image does not support it, differs in nothing from
prose. Our poetry has a language peculiar to itself. . . . Our language not being a settled
thing (like the French) has an undoubted right to words an hundred years old, provided
antiquity have not rendered them unintelligible.[42]

So began a century and a half in which English poets, unlike those of France,

the eighteenth century in Britain, where the college tutorial system of instruction fostered by
Jowett in the nineteenth century still prevails. It was bitterly attacked by his Oxford colleague
Mark Pattison, who described it as 'the complex system of cram, which grinds down all specific
tendencies into one uniform mediocrity. . . Our young men are not trained; they are only filled
with propositions, of which they have never learned the inductive basis. . . . The youth is put in
possession of ready-made opinions on every conceivable subject'. At the same place in Jan
Morris (ed.), *The Oxford book of Oxford* (Oxford, 1978), pp. 282–3, Arthur Waugh quotes his
tutor as having condemned an essay of his which began with a statement of Cicero's date and
place of birth: '"No, never", cried my tutor, "begin an essay like that. . . [Begin with] What did
Cicero stand for? Was he a genuine politician? Was he a trimmer? Did he do good for the state
or evil?"' Waugh comments approvingly, 'The whole of Oxford teaching was in that condemnation – ideas not facts. . .' American graduate schools have their faults – much current
American academic condemnation of Pope is quoted in this essay – but in some odd corners,
perhaps because of the Continental ancestry of American postgraduate education, there
remains a feeling that facts (such as the actual text of Pope and the actual artefacts of his time)
should precede ideas (such as the inability of those living in the eighteenth century to visualize
and their passion for symmetry), and that ideas not based on facts are not worth considering.
   Perhaps I may say this without being charged with chauvinism, as a Canadian who holds
degrees from Canadian, American and British universities (two from the last), and who has
had some direct experience of the British tutorial system.

---

[41] Steele, 'The season for triumph', in *Fearful joy: papers from the Thomas Gray bicentenary conference at
Carleton University* (Montreal and London, 1974), p. 235.
[42] Paget Toynbee and Leonard Whibley (eds.), *The correspondence of Thomas Gray* (rev. ed.; Oxford,
1971), I, 192–3.

Germany, and Italy, felt a compulsion *not* to write in the language of their contemporaries, but in a language peculiar to English verse, assiduously cultivating archaism – Shelley's 'Thou wast not born for death, immortal bird', Arnold's 'Who prop, thou askst, in these bad days, my mind?', T. E. Brown's much anthologized 'A garden is a lovesome thing, God wot.' If these compositions had purported to be laid in earlier times, the device might be understandable. But they are supposed to be the words of young or middle-aged nineteenth-century men, speaking to their contemporaries about contemporary matters, and, unless one has been brought up on the convention (as, of course, a great many twentieth-century readers were), the effect is somewhat ludicrous. Dryden and Pope made relatively little use of archaism (though a statistical study would be helpful), and generally spoke to their contemporaries in contemporary language. Perhaps when Arnold accused them of writing prose (or for an age of prose – much the same thing), he meant only that they did not include a sufficient quantity of *'ti*ses, *'twa*ses, *ywi*ses, and the like, so that what they wrote could not be classified as poetry.[43]

The Gray–Arnold doctrine was overthrown in the early twentieth century when Eliot, in his magisterial essay on Johnson's poetry, directly confronted it with the assertion that 'to have the virtues of good prose is the first and minimum requirement of good poetry,' and praised Dryden for 'cleans[ing] the language of verse and once more bring[ing] it back to the prose order. For this reason he is a great poet.'[44] And he and his fellow American Pound wrote poetry which eschewed archaism and, to the distress of critics, made reference to operating tables and turned-up trouser cuffs. The convention of poetic archaism vanished almost overnight: whatever one's opinion of the English poetry being written in the later twentieth century, one will look long before finding a *'tis* or *thou askst* in it. Moreover, Eliot and Pound were concerned to break through provincialism and bring English poetry back into the context of classical and world literature – nor did the prospect of thus having to expand their intellectual horizons much appeal to those who, like poor Sir Francis Hinsley in Evelyn Waugh's *The Loved One*, had made their critical name contributing engaging little essays to *The London Mercury* on 'Flecker's Debt to Henley'. Eliot apparently did succeed in rescuing Dryden from Arnoldian and Gossean detraction: it is hard to imagine anyone now presenting a full-dress,

---

[43] Reeves's patriotic indignation reaches its height with Reuben Brower's suggestion that part of the greatness of Pope comes from his familiarity with poetry in other languages than English – 'the European heresy', Reeves calls it. 'The evolution of poetry', he writes (p. 99), 'is bound up with that of a nation's language, a national possession. By the time of Shakespeare and the King James Bible, if not before, England had achieved a poetry second to none in Continental Europe or anywhere else. This is partly because the English language is the most poetic instrument ever evolved in the minds of men'. If so, there is of course no point in English poets acquainting themselves with Homer, Virgil, Dante, Goethe, Baudelaire, Li Po, etc.

[44] Introduction to *Johnson's 'London' and 'The Vanity of Human Wishes'*, London: Haslewood Books, 1930, rep. in Phyllis M. Jones (ed.), *English critical essays: twentieth century* (Oxford, 1933) ('The World's Classics'), pp. 305–6.

book-length challenge, like Reeves', to Eliot's *Homage to John Dryden*. It is a pity that Eliot did not publish a similarly extensive work on Pope, who, as we have seen, still bears the brunt of the remains of nineteenth-century animus against the clarity of Pope's language and his cosmopolitan view of poetry.

There are other matters that might be considered here. There is the charge against Pope of using 'poetic diction', something made much of by Words-worth in his Preface, 1800, to *Lyrical Ballads*, though he does not specifically accuse Pope of perpetrating it: indeed, he later (1815) compliments Pope by excepting him, along with Lady Winchilsea, from his dictum that eighteenth-century poetry 'does not contain a single new image of external nature'. But later critics were not so sparing. Stopford Brooke wrote,

He [Pope] talked of Nature, it is true, but one hears in the set, soulless artificial phrases of description that not a single true impulse came from her to him. The terms used, and the things concerning which they are used, are in no living relation one to another. The same terms are used again and again. A dictionary of them might be made. When the poet wanted an adjective for a tree, a stream, a mountain, he dipped into a box, where half a dozen descriptive adjectives were kept in separate compartments, one for trees, one for hills, etc., and used the first in the compartment that came to hand, it mattered not which.[45]

And he goes on to complain of 'sylvan scenes', 'verdant alders', 'soft retreat', 'gentle breeze', 'sweet echo', and the like, expressions generally found only in Pope's early poetry, such as the *Pastorals*. In an unfortunately neglected study, Ann Winslow gleefully tabulated the occurrence of such stereotyped epithets in the poetry of the Romantics, and found that they used them far more often than Pope did:

In the last two stanzas of Keats' *To Autumn*, a poem of 33 lines, the word 'soft' is used three times: 'soft-lifted', 'soft-dying', 'treble soft'. In his poem beginning 'I stood tip-toe', and in *Calidore* and *Sleep and Poetry*, we find 'luxuries soft', 'soft wind', 'softer than the ring-dove's cooings', 'soft rustle of a maiden's gown', 'softest rustle through the trees', 'soft breezes', 'soft numbers', 'soft shades', 'soft luxury', 'soft humming', 'soft closer of our eyes', 'soft floatings', 'fingers soft'. In Shelley's *Queen Mab*, *Alastor*, and *Adonais* appear 'softer than the west wind's sigh', 'sensation's softest tie', 'soft orbs', 'soft mossy lawns', 'soft enamoured breath', 'softer light', 'soft Form', 'soft sky', 'softer voice'. In Wordsworth's *The Prelude* there are 'soft alarm', 'soft couch', 'soft breeze', 'soft starry nights', 'soft airs', 'moon's soft pace', 'soft green turf', 'ye breezes and soft airs', 'soft forgetfulness', 'soft west wind', 'softest influence'.

In her statistical appendix Miss Winslow lists 42 'sweets' ('sweet life', 'sweet

---

[45] Quoted from Stopford A. Brooke, *Naturalism in English poetry* (New York, 1920), p. 21, in Ann Winslow, 'Re-evaluation of Pope's treatment of nature', *University of Wyoming Publications*, IV, 2 (1938), pp. 21–43, from which the following quotations are taken. Defending Pope's witty imagery in 'While China's earth receives the smoking tide', Auden (BJ, p. 341) points out that Wordsworth might instead have written, 'While boiling water on the tea was poured', but doubts that this would have been an improvement.

lips', 'sweet spot', etc.) and 28 'gentles' ('gentle soul', 'gentle wave', 'gentle moon', etc.) in *Endymion*, and 22 'sweets', 20 'silents', and 16 'pleasants' in *The Prelude*. 'Lovely', 'beauteous', 'glorious', and 'wondrous' were also very popular. In spite of Romantic and Victorian complaints about eighteenth-century 'abstractness', how very abstract, as well as monotonous, these adjectives are!

Then there is the complaint that Pope is so very hard to understand that he can't be read without much elaborate and erudite annotation, and therefore no one can be blamed for not trying to do so (it sounds a little like what used to be said about Bach). Here is Dr Adams again:

> Pope is difficult today because he was in good part a social poet, deeply involved in the life of his time. As with Dryden, his satiric verse comments in intimate detail on political events and personalities about whom few modern readers either know or care. The rights and wrongs of the Popish Plot [which took place ten years before Pope was born, and plays very little part in his poetry], the deeds and misdeeds of Lord John Hervey [*sic*], are only to be approached nowadays through a cheval-de-frise of footnotes; and who is to say the unprofessional reader is wrong when he decides simply not to bother?

Or, one might continue, not to bother about Dante's account of the misdeeds of Pope Boniface VIII and his contemporaries (Dante having been deeply involved in the life of his time), or Shakespeare's numerous Yorkist and Lancastrian heroes and villains (someone recently coined the phrase 'as irrelevant as the Wars of the Roses'), or the participants in a probably mythical ten-year siege of a small town in Asia Minor some three millennia ago? If Dr Adams confines his dealings with literature to what unprofessional readers – say, UCLA freshmen – know and care about, his repertoire will be severely limited. Out would go, for instance, writers requiring so much footnoting as Eliot, Pound and Joyce.

In fact, Pope does not need all that much footnoting to be understood and enjoyed: Sporus, Atticus and Bufo are created in the poem itself; to know the biography of their supposed originals may add some appreciation of nuances in their portraits; yet it is no more essential than a knowledge that Mr Micawber has some traits of Dickens' father is essential to appreciating and enjoying that creation.

But a full discussion and documentation of the matters alluded to in this last section would require an essay even longer than this already overlong one.

Appendix: Enjambment in Pope and others

1. Gosse asserts that 'classical' English poetry (e.g. Pope and Dryden) is characterized by 'regular couplets, within the bounds of each of which the sense is rigidly confined', whereas 'romantic' poetry, both before and after the eighteenth century, introduces 'verses in which the sense is not concluded at

the end of one line or one couplet'.[46] By way of contrast to 'romantic' technique, illustrated by the excerpt from Keats' *Sleep and Poetry* above, he gives, as an example of 'classical' technique, the opening of Dryden's *Mac Flecknoe*:

> All human things are subject to decay,
> And when Fate summons, monarchs must obey.
> This Flecknoe found, who, like Augustus, young
> Was called to empire, and had governed long,
> In prose and verse was owned, without dispute,
> Through all the realms of Nonsense absolute.
> This aged prince, now flourishing in peace,
> And blessed with issue of a large increase,
> Worn out with business, did at length debate
> To settle the succession of the state,
> And, pond'ring which of all his sons was fit
> To reign and wage immortal war with wit,
> Cried, "'Tis resolv'd, for Nature pleads that he
> Should only rule who most resembles me.'

Gosse's 'sense', which is 'not concluded at the end of one line or one couplet', could do with more precise definition. It seems to mean syntactical constructions normally written close together – in the Keats, a verb and its subject or object, a word and its modifying prepositional phrase – which are placed on separate lines: 'schism . . . made', 'understand . . . glories', 'dead / To things', 'school / Of dolts'). As far as line-to-line enjambment goes, it can easily be seen that Dryden is as free with it as Keats. In five of the seven couplets given above, the first line 'enjambs' syntactically with its successor: 'who . . . young / Was called', 'was owned . . . absolute', 'debate / To settle', 'was fit / To reign', 'he / Should only rule'. Likewise, it requires little inspection of Pope's poetry to find that such line-to-line enjambment, verses 'in which the sense is not concluded at the end of the line', is very frequent also. If one takes the odd-numbered lines at the beginning of the *Epistle to Augustus*, one gets

While You, great Patron of Mankind sustain
Your Country, chief, in Arms abroad defend [not an independent imperative clause,
    but part of the relative clause beginning 'While You']
How shall the Muse, from such a Monarch, steal
Edward and Henry, now the Boast of Fame
After a Life of gen'rous Toils endur'd

(TE IV, p. 195, ll. 1–6)

Hardly rigid confinement of the 'sense' by the end of a line.

So much for the novelty, the breakthrough into poetic liberation of line-to-line enjambment. To be sure, enjambment ('overflow' as Gosse calls it,

---

[46] Gosse, pp. 6–7. Is the pleasure derived by Gosse and others from contemplating metrical 'freedom from confinement', 'liberation', 'untrammeling', somehow connected with nineteenth-century praise of British political 'freedom', as contrasted with French governmental *dirigisme*?

following Austin Dobson) from couplet to couplet is a different matter. Pope, like others before him, uses it sparingly and cautiously, as he does the triplet and the alexandrine, for it has a powerful braking effect on the rhythm of the verse, like a sudden *fermata*. But he does use it when he thinks he needs it: not only in formulaic epic or Georgic openings:

> What dire Offence from Am'rous Causes springs,
> What mighty Contests rise from trivial Things,
> I sing.   (*TE* II, p. 144, ll. 1–3)

> Fraternal Rage, the guilty *Thebes* Alarms,
> Th' Alternate Reign destroyed by Impious Arms
> Demand our Song.   (*TE* I, p. 409, ll. 1–3)

> Thy forests, *Windsor*! and thy green Retreats,
> At once the Monarch's and the Muse's Seats
> Invite my Lays.   (*TE* I, p. 148, ll. 1–3)

but elsewhere, for special effects:

> But wave whate'er to *Cadmus* may belong,
> And fix, O Muse! the barrier of thy Song
> At *Oedipus*.   (*TE* I, p. 410, ll. 19–21)

> Ye shady Beeches, and ye cooling Streams,
> Defence from *Phoebus*', not from *Cupid*'s beams,
> To you I mourn.   (*TE* I, p. 72, ll. 13–15)

> The Mossie Fountains and the Sylvan Shades,
> The Dreams of *Pindus* and th' *Aonian* Maids,
> Delight no more.   (*TE* I, p. 112, ll. 3–5)

> This Nymph, to the Destruction of Mankind,
> Nourished two Locks, which graceful hung behind
> In equal Curls.   (*TE* II, p. 160, ll. 19–21)

A final instance of both line-to-line and couplet-to-couplet enjambment:

> High on a gorgeous seat, that far out-shone
> Henley's gilt tub, or Fleckno's Irish throne,
> Or that where on her Curls the Public pours
> All-bounteous, fragrant Grains and Golden show'rs,
> Great Cibber sate. The proud Parnassian sneer,
> The conscious simper, and the jealous leer,
> Mix on his look.   (*TE* V, p. 296, ll. 1–7)

Not once here is the 'sense . . . concluded' at the end of the line or the couplet.

What is overlooked in this line of criticism – and it still persists – is the unifying and connecting force of syntax – and 'sense' means syntax.[47] The fourteen lines in the Dryden passage above comprise three sentences, one of two lines, one of four, and one of eight. To attempt to read this last sentence as

---

[47] Analysis of versification can never be divorced from the study of syntax. See Donald Davie, *Articulate energy: an enquiry into the syntax of English poetry* (London, 1955).

an aggregation of four 'closed couplets' is not to read it at all. Pope's verse sentences can be at least as long and complex, sometimes as complex as Milton's, and they deserve the same sentence-by-sentence (not to mention verse paragraph by verse paragraph) reading as Milton's.

2. One gathers from Gosse, Keats, and the standard nineteenth-century (and later) manuals of English literary history that the (mostly) end-stopped iambic pentameter couplet was an invention of Dryden, Pope, and the 'neo-classicists' of the Restoration and eighteenth century. Much is usually said of the influence of Boileau and the French (though, to anyone with an ear, the French dodecasyllabic couplet with its four faint stresses and anapestic rhythm is a far different thing from the English iambic pentameter). The fact seems to be that the pentameter couplet was of purely English origin, long predating Boileau. Something like 12,000 lines of *The Canterbury Tales* are in that form; both Dryden and Pope were serious students of Chaucer, and the couplets in Dryden's version of the Nun's Priest's tale are no more 'closed' than in its original. In the first 100 lines of the General Prologue, I can find only six unmistakable couplet-to-couplet enjambments: lines 6–7, 'inspired hath in every holt and heeth / The tendre croppes'; 24–5, 'a compaigny / Of sondry folk'; 38–9, 'the condicioun / Of ech of hem'; 44–5, 'the tyme that he first began / To riden out'; 62–3, 'foughten for oure feith at Tramyssene / In listes thrice'; 70–1, 'never yet no vileyne ne sayde / In al his lyfe'. The last twenty lines of the hundred, the portrait of the Squire, are as rigorously end-stopped as anything in Pope. When Shakespeare uses the iambic penta-meter couplet, as in *Love's Labour's Lost*, it is almost invariably end-stopped. In the first 100 lines of Donne's *The First Anniversary*, there are only eight or nine couplet-to-couplet enjambments. What Boileau and the alleged eighteenth-century passion for 'correctness', restraint, slavish compliance with rules could have had to do with the early traditional English preference for closed couplets is hard to say.

3. What Keats does with the iambic pentameter couplet is of course entirely different. Of the seven couplets from *Sleep and Poetry* quoted above, six are enjambed. In the first fifty couplets of *Endymion* I count thirty couplet-to-couplet enjambments. But in the first fifty couplets of *Lamia*, written two years later, I find only eleven. The fact seems to be that the run-on iambic penta-meter couplet, for all that Gosse hails it as a great advance in the liberation of English poetry from the 'trammels' of eighteenth-century versification, was not a success, with Keats himself growing tired of it. The second rhyming word in a couplet does naturally bring the rhythm to a pause, if only a slight one; to override it syntactically needs to be done cautiously, as Pope does, for some special effect. To do it routinely, as in 'could not understand / His glories' and 'taught a school / Of dolts' produces a rhythmically very awkward effect. Such running-on is much more at home in blank verse, and after *Lamia*, in which enjambment begins to dwindle to the proportions found in Chaucer and Pope, it is not surprising that Keats turned, perhaps with relief, to blank verse in *The*

Fall of Hyperion. If as has been said with some justice of Johnson's *Irene*, it is blank verse struggling to become couplets, it could also be said of *Endymion* that it is couplets struggling to become blank verse. Has any serious poet since Keats ever done anything worth remembering in the run-on iambic pentameter couplet? It seems to have been a failed experiment, a gimmick that didn't work.

Index

Adams, Robert M., 269–70, 277
Addison, Joseph (1672–1719), 6, 45, 48, 105, 248
Alexander the Great (356–323 BC), 38, 48
Amazons, 10, 36–40, 67
Ancients and Moderns, 23
Apollonian and Dionysiac, 52–4, 56, 58, 60–2
Arbuthnot, John (1667–1735), 201
Aristippus (*fl. c.* 400 BC), 99, 101
Aristotle (384–322 BC), 23–4, 81, 91, 107
Arnold, Matthew (1822–88), 235, 238–9, 245–6, 270, 275
Astell, Mary (1688–1731), 7, 10, 12, 19
d'Aubignac, François, abbé (1604–76), 25–6, 43
Augustanism, 65, 138–9, 165, 167, 245
Augustus Caesar (65 BC–14 AD), 246

Babbitt, Irving (1865–1933), 235, 238–9
Bach, Johann Sebastian (1685–1750), 241–2, 244, 249
Bacon, Francis (1561–1626), 91, 218
Beethoven, Ludwig van (1770–1827), 254–5, 265
Bentley, Richard (1672–1742), 202–3, 226
Blake, William (1757–1827), 173, 178, 184
Blenheim Palace, 243, 249
Blount family, 20, 75
Blount, Martha (1690–1763), 74, 190
Blount, Teresa (1688–1759), 74, 167–8, 190
Boileau Despreaux, Nicolas (1636–1711), 41, 272–3, 280
Bolingbroke, Henry St John Viscount (1678–1751), 83, 87–8, 91–2, 99, 140, 202, 211, 220–5, 227, 236
Bona, Giovanni, Cardinal (1609–74), 13, 15
Boswell, James (1740–95), 112–13, 191, 203, 234–5
Boutauld, Michel (1604–89), 13, 17
Bowles, William Lisle (1762–1850), 204
Briggs, A. D. P., 194–7

Brower, Reuben, A. (1908–75), 96, 175, 184, 243
Brown, Laura, 130, 237–8, 244, 246
Brownell, Morris R., 129–31
Burlesque, 26–33.
Busby, Richard (1606–95), 205, 212, 214, 217, 226, 233, 237
Butler, Samuel (*fl.* 1750), 230–2
Butt, John (1906–65), 125, 170, 271
Byron, George Gordon, Baron (1788–1824), 200, 204, 260

Caretta, Vincent, 183, 210–13, 215, 221–2, 234
Carter, Elizabeth (1717–1806), 64, 136
Caryll family, 13–15
Caryll, John (1667–1736), 15, 105
Castle Howard, 243, 249
Catholicism, *see* Pope, Alexander
Charles II, King of England (1630–85), 22
Chaucer, Geoffrey (*c.* 1345–1400), 4, 86, 244, 249, 280
Chesterfield, Philip Stanhope, Earl of (1694–1773), 37, 97, 101, 234
Chatsworth, 125, 129
Chiswick, 123–4, 126–7, 130, plate 4
Chudleigh, Lady Mary (1656–1710), 8, 19
Cicero, Marcus Tullius (106–43 BC), 84, 88, 91–2, 99, 127, 205–6
Claremont, 129–30
Cleveland, John (1613–58), 9–10
Cohen, Ralph, 41, 175, 177–9, 182
Coleridge, Samuel Taylor (1772–1834), 178, 204, 256, 262, 264
contractual theory, 80–2, 85
Cornwall, Charles, 26, 29
The Count of Gabalis, see Gabalis
Courthope, W. J. (1842–1917), 204–6
Cowper, William (1731–1800), 203, 215, 228, 233
Cromwell, Henry (1659–1728), 16, 52, 54
Crousaz, Jean-Pierre de (1663–1750), 218, 227
Crowther, Arthur (1588–1666), 13–17